Jesus Son of Man

JESUS SON OF MAN
by Rudolf Augstein

Translated by Hugh Young

Preface by Gore Vidal
Afterword by David Noel Freedman

Urizen Books   New York

Originally published in Germany in 1972 as *Jesus Menschensohn* by
C. Bertelsmann Verlag

© 1972 Verlagsgruppe Bertelsmann GmbH/
  C. Bertelsmann Verlag Munchen, Gutersloh, Wien

© This translation Urizen Books, Inc. 1977

© Preface Gore Vidal 1977

© Afterword David Noel Freedman 1977

Scriptural quotations from the Revised Standard Version of the Bible, © 1946,
1952, © 1971, 1973, by the Division of Christian Education of the National
Council of Churches of Christ of the U.S.A., and used by permission.

First American edition published by:
Urizen Books
66 West Broadway
New York, New York 10007

Library of Congress Cataloging in Publication Data

Augstein, Rudolf, 1923–
    Jesus Son of Man.
    Translation of Jesus Menschensohn.
    Bibliography: p. 347
    1. Jesus Christ—Person and offices. I. Title.
(BT202.A8413)   232   76-57698
ISBN 0-916354-63-6

Contents

Preface

by Gore Vidal

Whether or not Jesus actually resembles the mysterious and contradictory figure described in the Gospels (Greek for "good news") is unknowable and unimportant. In fact, it is quite possible that Jesus never existed in history. On the other hand, there is no doubt that the life of the West for nearly two millennia has been dominated by Christianity, that protean yet always somber creed which has not only served beautifully the princes of this world but also afforded occasional solace to those made wretched by their anointed lords.

·The genius of Christianity has been its unfailing ability to adapt to new necessities. When the vices and absurdities of the 16th century church became too obvious, there was the Reformation and a reprieve for Christianity until the 19th century when human misery became so great that Christianity acquiesced to a fun-house mirror of itself, to what Archbishop Temple of Canterbury termed "that Christian heresy" communism.

It seems to me that Augstein has written a much needed history of a truly marvelous (charismatic?) phenomenon of which Diderot remarked, "Never has any other religion been so fecund in crime as Christianity; from the murder of Abel to the agony of Cales, there is not a line of its history that has not been bloody . . . the abominable cross has caused blood to flow on every side." In JESUS SON OF MAN, much of the bad news that resulted from the good news out of Galilee is reported with a dry elegance that would have earned for its author a bonfire in the Campo dei Fiori three cen-

7

turies ago. As it is, in the bleak dominion where the heresy is still militant, he would no doubt be enjoying a season in a psychiatric rehabilitation center for questioning the absolute truth of Marx/ history (a.k.a. God/Jesus) and its priests, the commissars. JESUS SON OF MAN is a highly useful and informative record of continuing human folly.

Foreword

How does it affect us?

No one believes anything without first asking himself whether it has to be believed.
—St. Augustine[1]

There is hardly any conclusion put forth in this book which has not been quite well known for perhaps a hundred and twenty, perhaps even two hundred years. No new theory about Jesus is added to those that already exist. I am now probing how the Christian church dares appeal to a Jesus who never existed, to a mandate he never issued, and to a claim that he was God's son, which he never presumed for himself.

It is true that theologians—especially of late the Catholics—have thoroughly examined almost all the problems of their religion. But it is no less true that the churches still draw no conclusions from the discoveries of their theologians, who themselves prefer to keep their gods in the storehouse instead of distributing them among the people. The true meaning is often found in the footnotes, set out in fine print as on the back of an insurance policy; a false certainty is suggested by the use of foreign words ("prolepsis," "kerygma," "paraenesis"), and the theologians always freely assert more than they actually know. It is still true, as the Quaker theologian and Harvard professor Henry Joel Cadbury believed he had discovered, that "today as at all times theology tends to obscure the approach to the historical face of Jesus."[2] There is a rope ladder between dogma and fact, but it is always hauled up in case of need.

9

Why should this concern us? It must, so long as the churches attempt to influence our social conditions by imposing standards for which they claim a superhuman authority. On such questions as abortion, divorce, the pill and sterilization, artificial birth, pollution of the plant and animal kingdoms, capital punishment, euthanasia, nuclear warfare—on all these there must be varying views based on ethical, moral or traditional grounds. There cannot be a single, absolute, divine view entrusted by a divine master to the churches.

This is how Knopf, Lietzmann and Weinel see it in their introduction to the New Testament for Protestants (1960): "The New Testament is the word of God. This sentence is our given starting point, admitting no furtherdiscussion: anyone who rejects it need not bother any more with the problems considered here."[3] And there is the subtle catch. Anyone who denies that the Christian ethic — or at any rate, that sanctioned by the churches — possesses an absolute quality not found in other persuasions is bound to concern himself with the problems of the New Testament. "Form your own judgment on what I say," writes Paul in his first Letter to the members of the communion in Corinth.

We understand only too well Pope Paul's claim: "God entrusted the holy scriptures not to scholars for private study, but to his church."[4] The church as an institution can only maintain itself if it insists on its right to discipline people, and how can it do that unless it has a right directly granted it from above? The Pope must insist on the divine origin of the Roman church as distinct from any other church, on the church as a divine institution. Where his church is hemmed in, as it is in East Germany, it takes a moderate and reasonable attitude towards ethical questions. But where, as in West Germany, it has more influence than authority, it intervenes in elections, supporting as always the party of those who do not wish to give anything up.

So long as the church wants to decide elections, no choice is left to us. The official church ought not to give us any political recommendations. "It is possible, indeed probable," writes the Jesuit priest F.J. Trost, "that in his political choice the Catholic sets quite different priorities from those of the established church."[5] Quite different: not those decreed by an established church which also judges matters in its own interests, still less those of the people who find their faith a useful social lubricant, thus treating it with more contempt than the most unthinking

10

mocker.

Even the Protestant churches maintain that God manifested himself once for all in Jesus, that he confirmed him through the resurrection and so "endorsed his teaching" (as the theologian Heinz Zahrnt wrote in 1969 in his book *It Began with Jesus of Nazareth*).[6] It is thus advisable to examine what the scholars have to say of this teaching and to carry out studies of one's own. It is hard to find anything more interesting in the history of ideas than the rise of the Christian religion. "It is the will of the Holy Spirit," writes Ernst Fuchs, the New Testament scholar from Marburg, "that we should interest ourselves very closely in the text of the word of God."[7]

Whether Jesus really was the son of God, whether he was bodily resurrected — non-Christians looking at the matter from outside may think these questions of no great account. But it is because of their exclusive claim that Jesus was the son of God and rose from the dead that the church — and not only the Roman church — exercises its power. We shall do well to go to work ourselves, not leaving the conduct of the retreat to the theologians. Religion is too important for that.

When Cardinal König maintains against the Catholic teacher Adolf Holl that Jesus was the son of God with the words: "by this the whole of Christendom stands or falls,"[8] that is his conclusion. Against him, we echo the objection of the Jews of old, if the Gospels report them correctly: "Neither are we base-born."

The scriptures included in the canon of the Roman church, works of man like any others, must still, as we are taught in Michael Schmaus' *Catholic Dogmatics,* be regarded as holy and canonical, "because, being written under the inspiration of the Holy Spirit, they have God as their original author and as such were given to the church"[9]—together, presumably, with authority to define and correct, year by year, the errors in these holy and canonical works.

"Faith does not mean dismantling the apparatus of reason," the famous preacher Thielicke[10] has encouraged us, and he is expert in both fields. The Mainz professor of practical theology, Gert Otto, dares to hope: "He who wishes to believe today must be taught to follow the path of reason."[11] But some millions have been suspected and punished — or let us just say liquidated — because they let their reason stray where it did not belong. For some time now, the forms have been more civilized. Yet we still cannot see

11

how the cnurches can bring themselves to allow freedom of thought.

Today, it is considered opportune to bring thought and faith together at the conference table; this is lifemanship. But no thinking person can still believe that a personal God, in order to redeem mankind, sent his personal son to be incarnate, and to be executed, on this earth, and then made him rise from the dead. We have to listen to the voice of reason about that kind of myth and symbolism. "To be able to believe with certainty without thereby becoming intellectually dishonest," as the theologian Heinz Zahrnt[12] recommends: it is not, or it is no longer, possible to do just that.

It is a characteristic of institutions that they want to survive. But can even so old an institution as the Roman church survive, if what the Dominican Olivier Rabut[13] says about the Gospel of Jesus becomes generally accepted: that it has one basic idea, to which he, Rabut, clings, but that "this suggests more than it defines"? What sort of a basic idea is that? Perhaps this will help: "To accept responsibility, to live, not to weaken, to fulfill the all-embracing mission of mankind," "to grasp the initiative demanded by the situation."

For if this is the meaning that lies hidden even in the Gospels, then there are scriptures in which it is revealed more clearly. The impact of the Gospels lies not in their practical appeal but in the breaking through of the darkness, the incomprehension, the archaic formalities of the basic human condition by a puzzling, youthful figure. It is not the active example that the Gospels illumine, but the non-example, the suffering and death for a cause not to be defined and not to be understood by anyone.

The Gospels are a self-service store. Everyone can find in them what he thinks he needs: Thomas Münzer and Charles V, Che Guevara and Generalissimo Franco. Not what a man called Jesus thought or wished or did, but what has been thought, wished and done with him since his death — that is what the Christian religion has established, and with it the history of the so-called "Christian West." Whatever Jesus was, he was not a man of the West.

The Christian community — theology reached this point long ago — has "put words into the mouth of Jesus which he never spoke and attributed actions to him which he never performed," writes Heinz Zahrnt.[14] But the truth is different again. Jesus spoke scarcely any of the words put into his mouth and did hardly any of the deeds ascribed to him. The risen Christ is the invention of the community. It can be said of the history of Jesus what Montaigne said about the laws: it is dangerous to trace them back to their origins. "They are like our rivers, which grow strong and powerful as they flow down to us; but if you follow them upstream to their source, this is a poor little trickle of water that you can hardly see and that only becomes so proud when it has grown much older."[15]

It is hard to see how the churches can survive if they admit what they must not admit, that they are based on ancient fictions, on the confused dreams of men of earlier times. But neither can we see how we are to defend ourselves against the demands, especially of the Roman church, without damaging what we should wish to leave to them, and to all others, unhurt: the unconsciously invented Jesus of the primitive Christian community.

Those who have listened to the Gospels from their childhood believe they can recognize, amid all the cuts and emendations, an unchanging tone which one has only to follow to reach the man Jesus. But the deeper you penetrate, the more indistinguishable this voice becomes in the chorus of other noises. What once was clear breaks down into fugitive colors. *There* is the objection to all scientific theology, and indeed even to this book.

1. Traces of the historical Jesus

The church lives in practice on the fact that the conclusions of scientific research into the life of Jesus are not made public.[1]
—Hans Conzelmann

Of the man called in the Greek language, Ἰησοῦς; in Latin, Iesus; and in our Bible, Jesus, there is virtually no evidence at all outside the writings that make up the New Testament.[2] His Semitic name may have been Jeshua, derived from Jehoshua, like that of the successor to Moses, also Jehoshua, whom we call Joshua; it means "Yahweh helps." The name of the Joshua who followed Moses is written Ἰησοῦς[3] in the Greek translation of the Old Testament.

Before the year 50 of the present era — the first Letter of Paul to the Thessalonians, said to have been written in Corinth, is dated at the earliest in that year — no document relating to Jesus has been passed down to us. Paul wrote then of his belief "that Jesus died and rose again," and assured the Thessalonians that "we who are left alive until the Lord comes shall not forestall those who have died." Moreover, "we who are left alive shall join them, caught up in the clouds to meet the Lord in the air. Thus we shall always be with the Lord." (1 Thessalonians 4:14−17.)

Not later than the year 56, Paul must have written his first letter from Ephesus to the Corinthians, in which (15:5−8) he declares that the risen Christ "appeared to Cephas, and afterwards to the twelve. Then he appeared to over five hundred of the brothers at once, most of whom are still alive, though some have died. Then

14

he appeared to James (the Lord's brother) and afterwards to all the apostles. Last of all, as to one untimely born, he appeared also to me."[4]

Paul deals suprisingly little with the historical Jesus, whose disciples he followed though he had never seen him. Paul (according to the Heidelberg New Testament expert Günther Bornkamm) "knew remarkable little of the details" of what is known to us through the Gospels.[5] His theme is the risen Christ, Christ glorified, Christ sanctified, who appeared to him "as to one untimely born." Paul emphasized that the gospel he preached was no human invention. "For I did not receive from man, nor was I taught it, but it came through a revelation of Jesus Christ." (Galatians, 1:11−12.)

In the year 70, at the time of the destruction of Jerusalem, some forty years after the death of Jesus, the executed man is still attested to by historical research.[6] The earliest trace of him outside the writings that make up the New Testament is to be found in the book *Antiquitates Iudaicae* (in English, *Jewish Antiquities*), written in Greek, which the Jewish historian Flavius Josephus completed in Rome, by his own account, in the years 93−94.

Thus, not a word survives from any contemporary non-Christian writer to record the work and death of Jesus, although, judging by the miracles reported in the Gospels, the impression made on the people of Jerusalem at the time must have been lasting and profound. The account of the crucifixion in the Gospels says that:

° the veil of the temple was torn in two from top to bottom;
° an untimely darkness fell from the sixth to the ninth hour (noon to 3:00 P.M.);
° the earth quaked;
° many of the dead rose from their graves and appeared to many living persons.

Even the murder, attributed to King Herod, of the children "at Bethlehem and in the whole region," all little children "who were more than two years old or less," did not make sufficient impression on the memory of the people of the time for Flavius Josephus to have observed this extraordinary event, although he describes the reign of Herod the Great (37−4 B.C.E.) with all his misdeeds, in close detail.

From the works of this historical writer, born about 37 C.E., it is quite clear that the execution of a man was not in itself an event worth recording. What he records about the execution of John the Baptist, a nobleman who stirred up unrest among the people, shows the way he could have written about the death of Jesus, though he did not necessarily have to. Incidentally, according to Josephus, it was not on account of the stepdaughter Salome that the Baptist lost his life. He died rather for just the reason that can also be regarded as a possible reason for the death of Jesus: that in consequence of his "extraordinary powers of attraction," a huge crowd of people flocked to John." The Tetrarch Herod Antipas, a son of King Herod, "feared the man's reputation: his advice always seemed to be taken and he might drive the people to revolt, and so it would be better to get him out of the way at once."[7] It is this Herod Antipas, ruler under the Romans not over Jerusalem and Judea, but over Galilee and Peraea, who in the Gospel accounts always had designs on the life of Jesus, yet in the end lost all interest in the prosecution of the arrested man, though he certainly had jurisdiction over him ("having heard about him, he had long been wanting to see him," Luke 23:8); who in the year 39 C.E., as an old man, was banished by the Romans to what is now the city of Lyons in Gaul.

He must have had the Baptist executed in 29 or 30 C.E., though it could have been even later. We read only that the death of the Baptist, according to Josephus, took place before the war of Herod Antipas in 36 against his former father-in-law, the Arab prince Aretas. Later, the followers of the Baptist expected him to return, and the Baptist's disciples attacked the dead Jesus as a false prophet.[8] All four Gospels record that Jesus was baptized by John. That does not necessarily mean that it is true. The sermon of the Baptist is thought to have been reported by the Evangelists in a garbled form. They had to have an example of Christian baptism: Jesus, who had not himself baptized, must at least have been baptized. Says the theologian Hölscher: "Jesus too is traditionally, and perhaps rightly, included among those baptized by John."[9] The fact that he is not recorded as having baptized, although the community baptized in his name, could be evidence of his historical existence.[10]

In the career of the Baptist we can look for one of the rare possibilities of fixing a date. The Bible states that John protested to Herod Antipas because he had married his brother Philip's wife; but the Bible has got it wrong. In 27 C.E., Herod Antipas divorced the daughter of Aretas and married Herodias, the wife of his still living half-brother Herod. The marriage of Herod Antipas offended not so much against good morals as against the law of Moses, by which marriage to the wife of a brother was forbidden. Herodias was not only the sister-in-law of her new husband, she was also his niece, and the Essenes,[11] to whom the Baptist stood close, were passionately opposed to marriage with a niece.

Flavius Josephus deals mostly with armed risings and other acts of violence, so that the peaceful appearance in Jerusalem of an unarmed, and later executed, prophet claiming to be the Messiah would not necessarily have attracted his attention as a historian, assuming, that is, that it was a peaceful appearance and not the appearance of an agitator, and that it was an appearance at all, and that it did take place in Jerusalem at the feast of the Passover.

Easter, the feast of "unleavened" or "sweet" bread, the festival of the Passover that commemorated the flight of Israel from Egypt, was observed from 14−21 Nisan (the first month in the Israelitic festival calendar, from mid-March to mid-April). It was a favorite time for riotous assemblies, because thousands of Jews (some generous versions say millions) felt it a duty to pay their visit to the temple at that time.[12] But did Jesus really die at the Passover?

Miracles of the kind that Jesus is said by his followers to have worked might well not have appealed to Josephus, who regarded Messiahs and miracle workers as responsible for the decline of his country. In any case, it is a fact that in his book, *History of the Jewish Wars*, completed about 77, he does not devote a single line to the activities of the followers of the dead Jesus then living in Jerusalem, although he describes minutely, with exact details of time, the events leading up to the war of the Romans against the Jews.

Since there is no discernible reason why he should have deliberately ignored the followers of Jesus, it appears that during the forty or so years between the death of Jesus and the destruction of Jerusalem, they played no role which would have drawn the attention of Flavius Josephus to them. "We perceive from this," Günther Bornkamm, professor of theology at Heidelberg, sums up, "that the contemporary historical records did not regard the appearance of Jesus, insofar as they knew about it at all, as in any way an epoch-making event."[13] The implication is that they did not know about it at all.

Josephus, who took the surname "Flavius" because he was entitled to it as a freedman of Vespasian, a Flavian, wrote the *Jewish Wars* in Rome six or seven years after the destruction of Jerusalem. A Pharisaic priest and son of a priest, he was introduced at the age of 26 to Nero's wife, Poppaea, who is said to have been Jewish,[14] during a visit to Rome. At 30, he commanded Jewish forces during the uprising, fell into the hands of the Romans in the year 67, and called on his countrymen to surrender from the towers of Jerusalem. He wrote the *Antiquities* in his mid-fifties, and in them our Jesus appears, along with eight other men of the same name, once incidentally in a doubtful passage and again, more prominently, in a passage which is now generally agreed to be spurious.[15]

The earliest manuscript of the *Antiquities* that we have comes from the eleventh century,[16] but Eusebius, one of the fathers of the church and court theologian to the Emperor Constantine (whom he glorified as a god), mentions in his *History of the Church*, dated about 320, a passage in Josephus about Jesus which very closely resembles that found in the mediaeval texts. As translated by Eusebius, it reads: "Now there lived about this time Jesus, a wise man, if indeed one may call him a man. For he was a doer of marvellous works, a teacher of such men as receive what is true with pleasure; and many of the Jews, and many also of the Greeks, he won over to himself. This was the Christ; and after that Pilate had condemned him to the cross on the indictment of the chief men among us, they who had loved him at the first did not cease (to do so). For he appeared on the third day to them, living again, the divine prophets having stated these and countless other marvels concerning him. And even now the tribe of the Christians, named after him, has not become extinct."[17]

Even a casual reading of the context in which this passage, called the *Testimonium Flavianum*, appears, leads to the suspicion that the passage as it stands cannot be genuine. The reformed jurist Hubert van Giffen doubted its genuineness as early as 1559, as a young man barely 25 years old.[18] The disputed extract follows the lines of the preaching of the evangelist Luke; thus the theologian Conzelmann holds that it has been inserted as a complete addition.[19]

Josephus records altogether four or five Jewish nationalist uprisings that he condemned as ruinous. In his third chapter, he describes two of them, one after another. Then comes the passage

18

about Jesus. It contains nothing about disturbances; its characterization of Jesus is not unfavorable but entirely positive. Josephus then goes on: "Also at this time, another misfortune befell the Jews ... "; an impossible continuation. Indeed, Josephus, the Pharisee, who was opposed to all Messianic movements, which he held responsible for the fall of Israel, could not have expressed such approving views of a man specifically described as the Messiah, the Anointed, the Christ. The Lutheran theologian Osiander wrote as early as 1565: "If Josephus had been of this opinion ... he must have been a Christian."[20]

Two texts of the patristic writer Origen (died 254) make it clear that this passage in Josephus must have read quite differently. He writes of Josephus as one "of those who do not believe in (the) Christ" and reproaches him "that he has not received (the belief) that our Jesus is (the) Christ."[21] If Origen had read the Josephus text as we have it, these utterances would have been inexplicable. Josephus mentions Jesus once more in the *Antiquities*, actually after the disputed passage. He makes a passing reference to "the brother of Jesus, who is called Christ, by name James," when he describes James's being stoned, which is said to have occurred in 62.* The expression "who is called Christ" is quite neutral; the same phrase is found in Matthew's Gospel (1:16) where he speaks of Mary "who gave birth to Jesus called Messiah," ὁ λεγόμενος χριστός

---

*This is the complete passage about James: "The Jewish Ananias, whose nomination as High Priest I have just mentioned, was of strong and bold character and belonged to the sect of the Sadducees, who, as already noted, are harder and more ruthless in judgment than all the other Jews. Now that Festus (the Governor) was dead and Albinus (his successor) had not yet arrived, Ananias believed he had found a favorable opportunity to gratify this hard-heartedness of his. He called the high council together to the court of justice and set before them the brother of Jesus who was called Christ, by name James, together with several others, whom he accused of breaches of the law and sent out to be stoned. But this infuriated even those who observed the law most strictly, and they secretly sent messengers to the king (Herod Agrippa II, great-grandson of Herod the Great) with a plea that he should write to Ananias demanding that he should not in future approve a similar action, since he was even now fallen deeply into injustice. Some of them even went to meet Albinus, who was coming from Alexandria, and put it o him that Ananias ought never to have been appointed to the court without the nomination of the high council. Albinus agreed with these recommendations and in the greatest anger wrote a letter to Ananias in which he imposed the appropriate punishment. But (King) Agrippa deposed him in consequence of this event after he had only been in office for three months and nominated Jesus the son of Damnaeus to be High Priest." (Flavius Josephus, *Jewish Antiquities*, XX, 9.

Knowing just this one not very significant passage in Josephus, Origen can hardly declare that Josephus was an unbeliever, that he did not believe in Jesus as the Christ. But all references to Jesus in Josephus could be Christian interpolations.[22] In fact, Origen had seen yet another alleged passage in Josephus, which is not to be found in any of the editions of Josephus we now have. In it, Josephus is said to have written that Jerusalem had fallen and the temple had been destroyed "in atonement for James the Just," because the Jews had killed so just a man (the brother of Jesus):[23] apparently a duplication of the report written by Josephus in which the fall of Herod Antipas was attributed to punishment by God for the execution of John the Baptist.

Quite recently, in 1971, a tenth-century Arabic edition of the *Testimonium Flavianum* was discovered, which may even come from Eusebius's *History of the Church*, though quite likely it is from an earlier version. This text runs literally: "At this time there was a wise man called 'Aisu (Jesus). He led a good life. And he was known to be virtuous. And many Jews and members of other peoples were his disciples. Pilate condemned him to death on the cross. But his disciples did not abandon his teaching. They declared that he appeared to them three days after being taken down from the cross, and that he was alive. Perhaps he is the Messiah about whom the prophets foretold wonderful things."[24]

Professor Schlomo Pinès of the Hebrew University in Jerusalem sees here "perhaps the earliest written evidence on the part of a non-Christian concerning Jesus."[25] Actually, this may appear to be so only if we look at the passage by itself and not at the context in which it appears in Josephus. It is more plausible to assume that Eusebius had first included a forgery — his own? someone else's? — in an earlier edition of his *History of the Churches* and that this was later confirmed in a later edition — by him? by someone else? Even this newly discovered version will not do, although it presents fewer problems with regard to Josephus's own convictions. But this version too, if it was not simply interpolated, must have read quite differently in Josephus.

Be that as it may, Josephus possibly writes of James as a brother of "Jesus, called the Christ"; if he did, this brother James must have existed, and it appears hardly credible that the first Christians in Jerusalem could have invented James first and then added Jesus as James's brother. Certainly the passages in Paul's letters which refer to his meetings with Peter and James and his disagreements with both of them do not sound as if the two of them did not exist or as if they or their followers had invented Jesus. (Only the Pope disputes that the four brothers of Jesus mentioned by name in the Gospels were in fact brothers and suggests that they must have been some other relations. Michael Schmaus postulates two Marys as of 70 C.E., one the mother of Jesus, the other of his brothers.)[26]

Certainly there is a contradiction. In the book called the *Acts of the Apostles*, written at least thirty years after Paul's death, it seems that a Christian called Barnabas took Paul in immediately after his conversion and introduced him to the apostles in Jerusalem. Paul apparently stayed with them, moving about freely in Jerusalem (9:27—29). Paul, on the other hand, in his letter to the Galatians (1:17—19), declares that he first met the apostles very much later, when he had a meeting with Cephas (Peter) and James:

1:17 . . . nor did I go up to Jerusalem to those who were apostles before me, but I went away into Arabia; and again I returned to Damascus.

18 Then after three years I went up to Jerusalem to visit Cephas, and remained with him fifteen days.

19 But I saw none of the other apostles except James the Lord's brother.

If that is how it happened it must have been in 36—38, for the conversion of Paul at Damascus happened between 33 and 35. James — called "the Just" in the Gospel according to Thomas (discovered 1946) and also by the not particularly reliable writer Hegesipp about 180, as well as in the quotation from Josephus reproduced by Origen[27]—was leader of the congregation in Jerusalem and brother of the Lord. He must have died before Paul, for whose execution (in the year 64?) there is little evidence.*

---

*In the so-called *Acts of Paul*, written some time between 180 and 200 in the present era, Paul is said to have fallen a victim of the hate of the emperor Nero. At his execution with the sword, milk flowed instead of blood. Shortly afterwards, he appeared to Nero and said: "Emperor, here am I, Paul, the champion of God; I am not dead, but live with my God." Further, one Clement of Rome, between 95 and 140 of this era — these time spans are based on those of the theologian Hans-Werner Bartsch in his book *Charge: Arson* — reported to the Christian congregation in Corinth that Paul had received "the true glory of his faith," "the greatest example of endurance."[28]

This particular brother of Jesus, who plays a considerable role in the *Acts of the Apostles*, figures in the four Gospels no more often than his other brothers, who, if we are to believe the Gospel according to Mark, thought Jesus was mad. John's Gospel says quite plainly about Jesus: "Even his brothers were not believers in him."

That Paul mentions James as being the brother of Jesus shows that he himself believed him to be that. It cannot have been welcome to him in his disputes with the Jewish Christians in Jerusalem to find their authority strengthened by an actual relationship. They denied him the title of apostle, and in 2 Corinthians 11:5, he refers ironically to his opponents as "superlative apostles." James, to whom the uncanonical Gospel according to the Hebrews ascribes the first appearance of the risen Christ,[29] seems to have shouldered Peter aside in the congregation of Jerusalem, even though Peter had followed Jesus during his lifetime and James had not. Unlike Peter, who was nothing less than that "rock," the subject of Matthew's pun (Πέτρος and πέτρα, 16:18), James seems to have been a man with great powers of persuasion and perseverance.

The most important document of the continual quarrel between Paul and the Jewish Christians of Jerusalem is the Letter to the Galatians, who may have lived in the region of present-day Ankara. Paul had founded Christian congregations there and enjoined them not to listen to the precepts of the Jews. Indeed, he makes it a point of honor, and considers every Gentile to be disobedient if he submits to the Jewish law. Later, representatives of the Jewish Christians came openly and demanded, with some success, that the members of the congregation submit themselves to the precepts of the law such as circumcision, dietary laws, and the Sabbath observance.

In his letter, Paul really lets loose regarding the hypocritical behavior of Peter, who had settled with the Gentiles in Antioch "until certain persons came from James." He condemns Peter's duplicity, curses all those who preach a Gospel different from his, and advises them to have themselves castrated (Galatians 5:12) — which Luther, coy and boorish, translates with the words: "Would God they were rooted out."[30] The church festival of "Peter and Paul" is a notably odd creation of the primitive church.

We must give a little more time to Paul's attitude to the Jewish law. For the moment, let us merely bear in mind that he speaks of

James, whom he must have seen as the strongest of his opponents, all the more credibly as "the Lord's brother."

Only two authors are known to have written about Jesus by name and in person during the first century after Christ: Paul and possibly Josephus. Neither of them knew him. Both, coming from Pharisaic circles, are closely involved with the fate of the Jewish people, though perhaps in different ways. Josephus, if he mentions Jesus at all, only passes on what he learned from the Christian community. Only the far more forceful assertions of Paul are fit to be regarded as evidence, though where Paul's Christology is concerned, it is always possible that he might have considered the living, "corporal" existence of Jesus to be fortuitous and insignificant, not worth further investigation. The theologian Wilhelm Wrede wrote in 1904: "Paul already believed in such a Heavenly Being, in a divine Christ, before he believed in Jesus."[31] Central to Paul's argumentation stands the Christ sanctified and justified by his resurrection. But since no one can rise from the dead unless he has previously lived, we can take it as certain that Paul at least included the existence of Jesus in his scheme — that he "believed" in it.

For the witness Josephus, the fact remains that he records the execution of a man who, unlike Jesus, had baptized. Any description by Josephus of stature or appearance could well have been borrowed by the Jesus propagandists from what was known of the Baptist, whose execution took place during the terms of office of those figures we know from the Bible: Pilate, Caiaphas, Herod Antipas. Josephus does not anywhere describe the works and the execution of someone called Jesus of Nazareth.

Given the sparseness of the evidence, we may well ask whether the whole conception of Jesus is not a creation resulting from the syncretistic blending of several figures and ideas, built up in the imagination of the Hellenistically educated Jews as a personification of the expectation of redemption by the Jewish people. Since most of the characteristics attributed to him are not personal but rather of a supra-individual nature and indeed can be traced before his time, and since moreover they clearly express the desperate longings of the people of his age and the age that followed it, one need not be a "fool," as the philosopher Paul Deussen dared to say in 1913, to doubt the historical existence of the person of Jesus.[32]

Certainly it is not only Paul, and possibly Josephus, who lead us to the reflection that the Gospels could not have been written without some personal motive. Apart from Paul, the authors of the New Testament documents are persons historically unknown. Apart from John and Paul, they were men in whom we can discern no fully thought-out theology. Whence did the first collectors and suppliers create their faith in the early return of the Messiah, if not from the shock of experience? And where did they get their power to devise and develop the passion and resurrection of a purely imaginary figure?

Ernst Troeltsch, the religious philosopher whose ideas are labelled "historism," believed that a symbol only became a symbol for believers if it was embodied in a real man who had lived, fought and conquered. What has a progressive theologist to say to this truly considerable thought? This, in 1969: "Thus, historism gave way not only in metaphysics but at the same time in sociology. It was no coincidence that Ernst Troeltsch and Max Weber lived in the same house in Heidelberg." (Heinz Zahrnt, *It Began with Jesus of Nazareth.*)[33]

What distinguishes the Gospels from the cult legends of other religions is said to be their "interest in history." In them, "myth is subdued through history." The "Lord" to whom the Christians prayed was no cult god who may or may not have lived, but an historical human being, a carpenter's son from Nazareth. And Heinz Zahrnt can go back for this conclusion to Ernst Troeltsch and Max Weber; Troeltsch said the same thing better fifty years earlier.

Let us look for a first, provisional explanation. The Jewish people had been waiting for centuries as no others had for the man—Messiah, the Anointed, with whose help God would found his new, changed kingdom of earth. So the execution of a man could only become the basis of a new religion through a sudden change of ideas, through the shattering of their expectation of the Messiah. Clearly the carrier-rocket, Judaism, had to be fired at the right moment.

The young Christian brotherhood — and here is Ernst Troeltsch again — started off under better auspices than the other cult societies looking to Mithras, Attis or Osiris, because it was not true of them, as the neo-Platonist Sallust says of the ancient mystical religions, that their content "never happened, but ever is."[34] As a concrete centerpoint and cult symbol, as the means of unification and of witness, there was a man who only recently had lived and suffered. This — together with Paul — gave Christianity an advantage over competing religions.

If it is correct that "we know virtually nothing about the life and personality of Jesus" (Rudolf Bultmann),[35] we must still assume some personal nucleus that makes comprehensible the tremendous momentum of the early Christian movement, even though we admit that it would have been unthinkable without Paul and perhaps owes its success to him alone. Some man must have existed whom his fellow Jews, simple people no doubt, believed to be endowed with powers which they did not command, and whom they believed capable of bringing about a change in their conditions. This man was executed, or came to some other violent end, to the infinite, and in due course productive, disappointment of his followers. Out of this disaster came heavenly salvation and triumph. We can discern no more.

Death on the cross rather than by, say, stoning or beheading could be regarded as historically credible, since this peculiarly disgraceful and painful means of death was not the subject of any Old Testament prophecies. So could the name Jeshua-Jehoshua, since in the old Bible Isaiah announced the coming of a child called Immanuel, not Jesus-Jehoshua (Immanuel means "God is with us"). Any further indication, especially about historical dates, has to be sought in the "official" documents available to us, i.e., the Gospels accounted canonical by the church. There is also information to be gained from the later book called the Acts of the Apostles, which actually deals almost solely with the works of salvation of the apostle Peter and those of Paul, not recognized as an apostle — more a story than a report, and not especially creditworthy.

When do they say Jesus worked and died? Luke's Gospel says that John the Baptist was baptizing in the fifteenth year of the reign of the Emperor Tiberius, i.e. about the year 28 C.E., one year after the marriage of Herod and Herodias. He is said to have been arrested and/or killed in 29 or 30; the Gospels say this took place shortly before the execution of Jesus, which by their account must have been in Nisan of the year 29 or 30. If John's Gospel is right, the death of Jesus took place on 14 Nisan, the eve of the first day of the Passover and the day before the Sabbath. This would fit with the year 30, since on 8 April, 30 (and not again until 4 April, 33) the first day of the Passover (Mazzoth) coincided with the Sabbath, which by Jewish reckoning began at nightfall on Friday.[36]

The theologian Ethelbert Stauffer puts the death of Jesus in the year 32. Sejanus, the favorite of Tiberius, is said to have fallen and to have been executed in October, 31. The Governor Pilate, the Tetrarch Herod Antipas and the High Priest Caiaphas were likewise threatened through the fall of Sejanus and so found it advisable to cooperate with one another.[37] This too is only a supposition.

Since Jesus was baptized by the Baptist, and since he started his public ministry after the Baptist's arrest (or, according to John's Gospel, before his arrest), we must assume this to have been in the years 28 or 29. But the Gospels of Mark, Matthew and Luke agree that his ministry did not last more than a year: only the very late Gospel according to John gives a longer time, two or three years.

In the Gospel according to John, Jesus purged the temple at the beginning of his ministry; in the other three Gospels, at the end. In the fourth Gospel, he went five times as an adult to attend feasts in Jerusalem, three of these being the Passover. The other Gospels record only one such visit, his last Passover. While the first three Gospels give the impression that the bulk of his work was done in Galilee, the Gospel according to John suggests an activity mainly in Jerusalem.

There is no agreement between the different versions about the day on which Jesus died. In the first three Gospels, he died on a Friday, 15 Nisan; the last supper, which according to Mark, Matthew and Luke was a Passover meal, took place on Thursday evening, 14 Nisan, reckoning days from sunset to sunset. In the gospel according to John, however, the last supper was not a Passover meal, and he was crucified on 14 Nisan — according to John at noon, according to Mark at nine in the morning on 15 Nisan. Both dates depend on accounts that contain contradictions within themselves.

For instance, if Jesus had wished to celebrate his last meal as a Passover meal on the evening of 13 Nisan, the date postulated by John, then he would have had to do without unleavened bread and without the required ritual dishes. These kosher dishes are not given out for the Passover until the day before the Passover, called the Day of Preparation. We must therefore assume that the Gospel according to John has placed the crucifixion before the slaughter of the Paschal lambs at the sixth hour (midday) of the Day of Preparation in order to emphasize the symbolic parallel between the Paschal lamb and the sacrificial lamb, Jesus.

But if, as the other three Gospels will have it, Jesus was arrested during the night after the Passover supper, it becomes almost incredible that he should have been tried during that holiest of nights, delivered to Pilate on the firstday of the feast and actually crucified on the first feast day. All four versions refer to the need for haste because the Sabbath would begin when darkness fell; a corpse might not be left hanging during the night or taken down on the Sabbath. Yet, if the accounts of the synoptic Gospels agree, it would actually be the first day of the feast, 15 Nisan, that was desecrated by trial, execution and burial, which is impossible. The fact that the evangelists were not capable of correctly recording details of such immense importance to the Jews allows us to conclude that either they had no historically valuable material available to them or, if they had, being people educated on Hellenistic lines and possibly not even Jews, they did not know how to deal with it.

The term of office of the Roman prefect ("Procurator") in charge of Judea, Pontius Pilate, ran between 26−36; that of the High Priest Caiaphas, similarly responsible for Judea, between 18−37. Jesus could therefore not have died before 26 at the earliest or after 36 at the latest. If we accept the statement in the Gospel according to Luke that Jesus was about 30 years old "when he began," then he must have been born about the beginning of the new era.* Most researchers into the life of Jesus nowadays believe that he was born in the year 6 or 7 before the era named after him. Estimates range from 7 B.C.E. to 7 C.E.

It is not easy to see which of these considerations is conclusive. Every assumption has in it an element of choice. The census, the "taxation," which according to Luke's Gospel was ordered for the whole Roman empire by the Emperor Augustus, can still be given no definite date. Luke says it took place "when Cyrenius was governor of Syria." "Cyrenius" was identical with the Syrian

---

*Even the "Star of Bethlehem" which is said to have stood over the birthplace of Jesus is called in to help establish the time. It had already been investigated and evaluated by the astronomer Johannes Kepler (1671−1630). Kepler ascertained that in the year 7 B.C.E. there was a constellation of the planets Jupiter and Saturn such as recurs about every 800 years. This conjunction, he says, was not the star of the wise men; he only drew attention to it "in that it bears witness to the experience, that God himself does mark conjunctions of this kind with extraordinary wonder-stars visible in the high heavens." The view that the conjunction was actually the star of the three wise men breaks down because, to quote the *Theology and Church Lexicon*, current in 1964, "a conjunction cannot proceed in a north-south direction from Jerusalem to Bethlehem."³ᴷ

governor Quirinius, who had not yet become governor in Herod's lifetime, but who had almost determined the fate of the eastern half of the kingdom before Herod's death (4 B.C.E.) Since the king can hardly have ordered the killing of the little children after he himself was dead, the legend of the slaughter of the innocents at Bethlehem suggests that Jesus was born before the year 4 B.C.E. (This great king Herod had three of his own sons executed, but they had grown out of the years of childhood. The saying is attributed to Caesar Augustus that he would rather be a pig than a child in the house of Herod.[39])

The taxation of the whole of Syria, including Palestine, under the powerful eastern ruler Quirinius may well have lasted some years, with the usual interruptions and caesuras. In 6 C.E., when Judaea was a Roman province, the census may have been recommenced, or by an alternative interpretation, it may then have been brought to an end. That gives us 6 or 7 C.E. as the year of Jesus' birth. The Hamburg Furche Press Bible, translated by Ulrich Wilckens, has this to say in its commentary: The "first basic registration of goods and property in Judaea" was carried out in the years 6 or 7 C.E.[40] So we are still left with some time between 7 B.C.E. and 7 C.E.

The birthplace is unknown. Enlightened theologians have long accepted it as no more than a pious legend that Jesus was born in Bethlehem, although the acceptance has been marked by some really extraordinary struggles. There is nothing on the subject in the earliest Gospel, that bearing the name of Mark. The Gospel according to Matthew gives Bethlehem as the birthplace, but immediately goes on to say why: "for so it is written by the prophet." The reference is to Micah 5:2, which reads:

But you, O Bethlehem Ephrathah,
who are little to be among the clans of Judah,
from you shall come forth for me who is to be ruler in Israel,
whose origin is from old, from ancient days.

But the Gospel according to Matthew quotes Micah's prophecy differently:

And you, O Bethlehem, in the land of Judah,
are by no means least among the rulers of Judah;
for from you shall come a ruler
who will govern my people Israel. (Matt. 2:6.)

Is Ephrathah in the land of Judah, called Bethlehem and said to be the birthplace of King David, southwest of Jerusalem, different from an Ephrathah to the northwest of Jerusalem in the neighborhood of Rama, where the ancestress Rachel is said to be buried? The question is still doubtful and proves not to be greatly significant, since Matthew has before him a tradition which already identifies Bethlehem with Ephrathah.

A descent as humble as that described in the Gospels does not come from the golden material beloved of the legend, thinks Ernst Bloch.[41] But the humble descent is only to be found in Luke, a born storyteller; he makes the holy "domestic and intimate" (Kurt Kusenburg);[42] it is he who put in the crib, and indirectly the stall, and the story that there was no room at the inn. In Matthew's version, the mother and child are in a "house." Ox and ass, draught animal and riding animal, were later borrowings from the prophet Isaiah, who said: "The ox knows its owner and the ass its master's stall; but Israel, my own people, has no knowledge, no discernment." Luke was educated in Greek: the heavenly child is a Hellenistic mythical figure, the savior who comes to this world unknown and in lowly circumstances. Since the circumstances of the coming of Jesus were unknown to Luke, he made up the romantic details. Kierkegaard gives us the theology: "The Savior is veiled in poverty and lowliness so that only he can find him who seeks him with infinite passion."[43]

In the latest Gospel, that of John, certain Jews cast doubt on the possibility of Jesus' being the Messiah with the argument: Surely the Messiah is not to come from Galilee? Does not scripture say that the Messiah is to be of the family of David, from David's village of Bethlehem? Certainly Bethlehem Ephrathah is not in Galilee. The gifted theologian David Friedrich Strauss, on whom the young Friedrich Nietzsche vented his rage in no small way in one of his *Unseasonable Observations*, noticed this *ad usum Delphini* birthplace of Bethlehem as early as 1835, when he wrote: "Our author (Luke) knew perfectly well what she (Mary) had to do there (in Bethlehem): she had to give birth to the Messiah in the city of David in accordance with the prophecy of Micah 5:2."

This was one hundred and twenty years before the theologian Ethelbert Stauffer wrote: "On the other hand, the Davidic descent of Jesus is an argument for Bethlehem"[45] — though the descent is no more firmly established than the birthplace. The scriptures said that the Messiah would be a son, i.e. a descendant, of David. The Lord had promised David: "And your house and your kingdom shall be made sure for ever before me; your throne shall be established for ever." (2 Samuel 7:16.) And:

Once for all I have sworn by my holiness;
I will not lie to David.
His line shall endure for ever,
his throne as long as the sun before me.
Like the moon it shall be established for ever;
it shall stand firm while the skies endure. (Psalm 89:35−37.)

Yet house, kingdom and throne had not existed since the captivity in Babylon half a millennium before. Reason enough to trace the Messiah back to David, to promise him the throne of his father David, as the angel of the Lord does according to Luke. To this day, pious Jews pray in hope to "the Messiah, the son of David," and they don't mean Jesus.

Luke makes the parents of the boy-Messiah move from Galilean Nazareth to Judean Bethlehem on account of the census or taxation. (Stauffer: "Joseph belonged to the tribe of David and so had a share in hereditary possessions in Bethlehem."[46]) In Matthew's Gospel, they have to leave because the boy is threatened first by King Herod; then, after their return from Egypt, the family moves into Galilee for fear of Herod's son, "king" Archelaus. This son of Herod the Great ruled as ethnarch, grand duke, over Judaea, Samria and Idumaea, from 4 B.C.E. to 6 C.E., when his dukedom was taken from him on the creation of a Roman province. He had no more claim to have inherited his father's title of king than had his brothers, the tetrarchs Herod Antipas and Philip, who had been in office longer than he.

The flight into Egypt is not found in Mark, the earliest Gospel, nor is the murder of the children, nor the adoration of the Magi, who concern themselves with kingly offerings and do not trust "King Herod." All this has been inserted in Matthew's Gospel so that Jesus can come back from Egypt, thus fulfilling the prophecy (Hosea 11:1): " . . . out of Egypt I called my son." Israel is the first-born of God. Israel prays to God:

Thou didst bring a vine out of Egypt. . . .
But let thy hand be upon the man of thy right hand,
the son of man whom thou hast made strong for thyself! (Psalm
80:8−17.)

The evangelists set out to represent Jesus as the second and last
Moses. As in the story of Moses, the birth of Jesus arouses un-
easiness in the rulers. Each time they consult the wise men, each
time there is a slaughter of children and a miraculous rescue.[47] The
flight to Egypt in Matthew's Gospel ends when Joseph reaches
Nazareth with the child and his mother. But Luke says that Mary
was already living in Nazareth when the angel Gabriel announced
the birth of the Savior. It is worth noting that Jesus has gone down
in history not as "Jesus of Bethlehem," as one might expect if that
had really been his birthplace, but as "Jesus of Nazareth."

Are we then to take it that he lived in a place called Nazareth
until the start of his ministry? Apparently not. To judge from
Mark's Gospel, his disciples lived by the Lake of Gennesareth,
probably in Capernaum; this is the place of which it is said with
regard to Jesus and his followers: "then he went home" (Mark:
3:19). The "family," who according to Mark said he was out of his
mind and "set out to join him" in order to lock him in the house,
could not have been brought all the way from present-day
Nazareth, more than twenty-five miles.

In Matthew's Gospel too, when Jesus is coming back to Capernaum, it is said: "So he got into the boat and crossed over, and
came to his own town." (The modern commentary to the *Luther
Bible*, 1964 edition, gets around this by explaining that Jesus had
regular lodgings in Capernaum when he returned from his travels.)

But did he perhaps come from a place called Nazareth before he
began to work with Capernaum as his headquarters, or had he arrived from there some time earlier? How does he come to be called
"Jesus of Nazareth," a name which so stuck to him that, according
to John's Gospel, the soldiers twice answered his question "Who is
it you want?" with the words "Jesus of Nazareth"? And how does
it happen, again according to John, that the words inscribed in
three languages on the cross were: "Jesus of Nazareth King of the
Jews"?

What is written here in almost all the Greek manuscripts is not
"Jesus of Nazareth" but "Jesus the Nazarite" (in Greek, Ἰησοῦς ὁ

Ναζωραῖος). The *Greek-German Dictionary of New Testament Scriptures and other early Christian literature** (1963) holds that the verbal step from Nazareth to Nazarite is "hard to defeat." But it must not be overlooked "that Ναζωραῖος meant something else before it came to be used in connection with Nazareth."[48]

Paul, whose experience on the road to Damascus is described in the Acts of the Apostles (22:8) hears a voice saying: "I am Jesus of Nazareth whom you are persecuting." In the Greek manuscripts, however, there is nothing of the sort, but "I am Jesus the Nazarite whom you are persecuting." The *Jerusalem Bible* reads likewise. A little gentle retouching?

Of course, all four Gospels and the Acts mention a place called Nazareth as the place from which Jesus hailed, but Matthew and John know only, and Luke prefers, the description Nazarite. In Acts, the first Christians are called Nazarenes and Jesus is himself called a Nazarite six times. Paul knows nothing of either the origin in Nazareth or either of the descriptions.[49]

What sort of town is this which will not fit with the surname derived from it and which at the same time can serve as godmother to a rapidly expanding sect — a town indeed at the expense of which, according to John's Gospel, they are already making snide jokes ("Can anything good come out of Nazareth?")* as if it was not only not unknown, but known only too well. In contemporary Jewish literature apart from the four Gospels and the Acts it is never mentioned, nor is it in the Old Testament. But even in the letters of Paul and in the other New Testament letters written to individual apostles, it occurs as seldom as the designation Nazarite for Jesus and his followers.

Hardly any place would be less fitted to make Jesus popular than this quite unknown Nazareth, if indeed any unknown place can serve to make a man better known. There are 63 places mentioned by name in Josephus, but the name Nazareth or Nazarat or Nazarath or Nazara or Nazaret never occurs. (All these forms are found in the manuscripts.) Galilee in those days covered an area as big as Berkshire, and according to the synoptic Gospels, the place

---

*John 1:46: "Can anything good come out of Nazareth?" says Nathanael, seeking to become an apostle, to the apostle Philip, when he shows him "Jesus, Joseph's son, of Nazareth." Philip answers: "Come and see!" ("a sovereign remedy for prejudice and doubts," opines the *Luther Bible Commentary*, 1964).

called Nazareth even had a synagogue in which Jesus read.

The first reference to Nazareth as the place from which Jesus came is in Mark's Gospel, which persistently uses the term Nazarite. But it is doubtful whether Nazareth was ever mentioned as a place in the original text of Mark. This is how it appears in the Gospel: "In those days Jesus came from Nazareth in Galilee and was baptized by John in the Jordan." (Mark 1:9.) But the same passage in Matthew, who follows in Mark's footsteps, speaks only of Galilee, not of Nazareth. The place may have been inserted during the copying of Mark's text. When Jesus, by Mark's account, comes "into his father's city," where he is not accepted, he does indeed come to Nazareth in the sub-headings both of the Catholic *Jerusalem Bible* (1969) and of the Protestant *Mustard Seed Bible* (1971), but there is nothing about in Mark's original text.

This visit to his home town is surely an "ideal scene"[50] developed out of the double proverb: "A prophet is not made welcome in his homeland, and a doctor has no success among those who know him." Luke, who also makes use of the second part of the proverb ("Physician, heal yourself!"), extends the narrative dramatically, transferring the entry of Jesus into the synagogue at Nazareth to the beginning of the work of Jesus among the people.

Jesus is given the scroll of the prophet Isaiah. As if by chance, he opens it to Isaiah 61:1−2 which according to Luke's rendering reads:

> The Spirit of the Lord is upon me,
> because he has anointed me to preach good news to the poor.
> He has sent me to proclaim release to the captives
> and recovering of sight to the blind,
> to set at liberty those who are oppressed,
> to proclaim the acceptable year of the Lord.

Here he should have gone on to read " . . . and a day of vengeance for our God," but he leaves that out. Instead, he sits down and says: "Today this scripture has been fulfilled in your hearing." He is the proclaimed Anointed, Messiah, Christ. Now they all applaud him (Wilckens), speak in his favor (*Mustard Seed*), agree with him (*Jerusalem Bible*); they are astonished at his gracious words (Wilckens), are amazed at such words of grace from his mouth (*Mustard Seed*), wonder at the words of grace (*Jerusalem*

Bible), and ask: "Is not this Joseph's son?" (and not, as Mark has it, "Is he not Mary's son?"). How does it happen, in view of such amazed approval, that they switch to the "rejection" similarly described to us?

All his hearers fly into a rage because he can (Mark), will (Matthew), may (Luke) not perform miracles in Nazareth; they drive him out of the city and want to throw him down from an overhanging rock of the hill on which the city is built (*Luther Bible*, 1964, "a rock twelve meters high"). "But he passed straight through them and went away." At any rate, his exit provided a miracle.

It is Luke who, writing later than Mark and Matthew, endows Nazareth with the additional description, "where he had grown up." But although Luke deliberately establishes the connection, there is still no reference to Nazareth in the original life history of Jesus that is available to us. An expert, Dr. Brückner, found in 1911 that Nazareth "could not be definitely traced in the matrix of Mark's Gospel."[51] What can be traced, though, is a conflict between the terms "Nazarene" and "Nazarite" which cannot be cleared up with any certainty.*

The Gospel according to Matthew, which is particularly careful about the fulfilment of the old scriptures, makes a clumsy attempt to mediate. We learn (2:23) that the nickname Nazarite — the *Revised Standard Version*, among others, writes "Nazarene" — comes from an Old Testament prophecy. It says in Matthew (2:23): " . . . there he settled in a town called Nazareth. This was to fulfil the words spoken through the prophets: 'He shall be called a Nazarite.' "

Matthew should have started with Isaiah's text (11:1-2):

There shall come forth a shoot from the stump of Jesse,
and a branch shall grow out of his roots.
And the Spirit of the LORD shall rest upon him,
the spirit of wisdom and understanding,
the spirit of counsel and might,
the spirit of knowledge and the fear of the LORD.

---

*A Nazarite is possibly identical with a Nazirite: Samson, the strong man (Judges 13:5-7), was such a Nazirite, one "consecrated to God." The Nazirite was forbidden to have his hair cut and to drink wine. He is often regarded as the type of the ascetic. The verbal distinction between Nazarite and Nazirite has given rise to a conflict about ascetic ways of life. The anti-ascetics have brought up their surname Nazarene against the ascetics' password Nazarite, to "paralyze" their asceticism or Nazarism (John M. Robertson).[52]

The Hebrew word for "branch," "shoot" — also "scion" — is *neṣer*. From the stock of Jesse, King David's father, there springs a shoot, a new hope for Israel, a Messiah-figure. Isaiah says about the servant of God: "He grew up before us like a shoot, like a root from parched earth." From the top of a cedar of Lebanon, says Ezekiel, a great eagle with bright feathers will pluck a tender shoot (17:34). Jeremiah (33:15) prophesies a "righteous branch," and the monks of the monastery at Qumran call their "Messiah of Justice,"[53] whom they too long for, the "Branch of David."

In the (German) Catholic hymn the shoot (*Reis*) becomes a rose (*Ros'*), a little rose, sprung from a tender root. In just that same way, Nazareth might have found its way into the creed, either because a prophecy of the scriptures (*neṣer*) had to be fulfilled, or because some definition to rival the codeword Nazarite was needed; perhaps because an evangelist or a copyist thought up a suitable place-name, perhaps because he was grafting an available place-name on to the life history of Jesus. Shalom Ben Chorin, a specialist in Jesus who has a sharp ear for events on Jewish ground, considers that Jesus became a Nazarene because he had to fulful the neser prophecy.[54] Since Jesus was, on the one hand, at home in Capernaum, and, on the other, had to fulfil the scriptures with a Davidic birthplace, there was not much left for Nazareth except that the nickname from this village could just about be traced.* There is today a town in Israel called an-Nasira, with 44,000 inhabitants, mostly Arabs. Tourists are shown the workshop where Mary's husband worked at his carpentry.

The theologian Stauffer argued nimbly in 1957 that there could be nothing more ordinary than to assume that Bethlehem was Jesus' birthplace and Nazareth his home town: "For Joseph was a construction worker. Even in ancient Palestine construction work was not a very stable occupation."[56] Even Bornkamm writes: "Nazareth is the city of his fathers."[57] It seems to be an old tradition that Jesus was a carpenter or the son of a carpenter (both ver-

*It is true that none of the evangelists has been able to satisfy our Orientalists, who have long complained that there is a voiced *s* in the Greek transliteration of the name Nazareth and an unvoiced *s* in the Aramic and Syrian forms of the name, and also, in the modern Arabic. The problem was familiar to the church father Hieronymus (d. Bethlehem about 420), who translated the New Testament from Greek into Latin. He points out that there is no voiced *s* in the Hebrew form of the name (*scribitur autem non per z litteram, sed per hebraeum sade, quod nec s nec z littera sonat*).

sions appear in the manuscripts of Mark),[58] and there is no objection to this, except that he was possibly not a carpenter at all. In those days there was certainly a saying: "Is there a carpenter or a carpenter's son among us?" when there was a difficult problem to solve.[59] He may have been put to work as a carpenter because he was not a learned rabbi.

We know nothing about Jesus' ancestors. Since, according to the prophecies in the scriptures, the Messiah was to inherit the throne of David, the authors of the Gospels according to Matthew and Luke furnish Jesus with two quite different family trees, both of which in fact go back beyond David, one as far as the patriarch Abraham, the other all the way to Adam, the first man. Both authors commit the idiotic mistake, to be explained, perhaps, by Jewish adoption customs, of presenting the family trees in such a way that the foster-father Joseph appears to be the real father.[60] Joseph, in Luke's words, was "taken for the father of Jesus," and according to Matthew was "the husband of Mary" but not entitled to be considered the father of Jesus. [61] Luke says Joseph was the son of Eli, Matthew says of Jacob; Luke gives him forty-one ancestors going back to David, Matthew only twenty-six. In his book *Jesus*, Stauffer assures us "Jesus came from a family poor but proud of its ancestry" — a family that had apparently kept its blood pure for a thousand years.[62] But how these two pure-blooded pedigrees manage to diverge so incompatibly is something Stauffer does not explain. In his book *The Messiah,* the publicist and theologian Diether Lauenstein has recently sought to master the difficulties by working up Rudolf Steiner's idea of two boys called Jesus, one of the royal blood of David who died young and one, who was crucified, from a collateral branch.[63]

The earliest Gospel, that of Mark, knows nothing of Jesus' ancestors, nor of his father Joseph, nor of his descent from David. Acccording to Mark, Jesus is the carpenter, the "son of Mary," a common formula in cases of illegitimate birth.[64] Paul, the earliest witness, does not mention the name either of Mary or of Joseph. In the light of later determined attempts to resolve the controversy, it is hardly surprising to find in some of the Luke manuscripts that both Joseph and Mary are of the house and tribe of David.[65]

But there is another well established version, that Joseph came from the (kingly) house of David and Mary from the (priestly) line of Aaron, of the tribe of Levi. Says Stauffer: "Mary was most probably a Levite of the house of Aaron."[66] Luke uses the simple phrase "daughter of Aaron" to make her related to the mother of John the Baptist. John never mentions Mary by name but simply calls her the mother of Jesus. Standing beside the mother of Jesus beneath the cross, there was also her sister Mary, the wife of Cleophas; so if Jesus' mother was also called Mary, both sisters must have had the same name. In this last Gospel, the question as to whether Jesus was of the house of David no longer plays any part, since according to John, Jesus is already one with God the Father, which King David never was. (We cannot help being suspicious when Stauffer coolly boasts of the "Davidic descent" of Jesus[67] as though this non-fact was even credible.)

According to the three later Gospels, the father of Jesus — who of course was not his real father — was called Joseph. This first witness, whose fatherhood cannot be admitted, leads an existence in the shadow of "higher realities" (Karl Kerényi). Originally perhaps anonymous or quite unknown, he plays, according to Matthew and Luke, two quite different roles. Luke, although he too says that Jesus was descended from David, obviously attaches no importance to royal blood. The parents of the child, when the two of them go to be purified* (Luke doesn't know the rites), appear in Jerusalem and present the so-called poor people's offering,[68] two doves. Only Mary speaks when there is anything to be said. It is she who "kept all these things in her heart." Joseph has only a walk-on part.

Not so in Matthew's Gospel. He describes the dangers to a child of the royal house, and Joseph becomes a kind of court chamberlain. The name may have been borrowed from the Egyptian Joseph who is described as the great dreamer in *Genesis* 37:19 and who saw himself as a symbolic figure for the journey to Egypt. The name Joseph does not occur very often in the Hebrew Bible, but is prominent in the case of the Egyptian Joseph, who also maintained his chastity in the delicate affair of Potiphar's wife.

---

*Only the pregnant woman, not the man, has to be purified by a sacrifice, and that after forty days if she has borne a boy and after eighty if a girl.

Since the "foster-father" Joseph cannot be considered as a flesh-and-blood father, Matthew's Gospel makes him stir up suspicion against his young betrothed. He learns the real state of things in a dream which exonerates his betrothed. In dreams too he learns of the need to flee to Egypt and later to return, but to Nazareth, not home.

There are Egyptian associations too for the betrothed, Mary. The elder sister of Moses, she who draws the attention of Pharaoh's daughter to the sleeping suckling in the basket in the rushes, is described in the Hebrew Bible as *alma* and is named Miriam, i.e., the young woman Mary. (Incidentally it is Miriam, this sister of Moses, who sings the victory song against Pharaoh when the Israelites have passed dryshod across the Red Sea.) The description *alma,* rare in the Hebrew Bible, possibly accounts for the dream existence of the non-father Joseph; the word means young woman, and occurs most notably in Isaiah 7:14. The prophet has foretold a sign to King Ahaz, somewhere about the year 730 B.C.E. "Behold, a young woman (*alma*) is with child and she will bear you a son and will call his name Immanuel." Even Catholic scholars agree that the young woman referred to here very possibly just means the queen — which mans of course that the prophet was thinking of a sign in the near future.[69]

The Greek translation of the Old Testament, the Septuagint, translates *alma* not as "young woman" but, in accordance with Egyptian myth, as "virgin":[70] and this Greek text was the source used by the evangelists who themselves wrote in Greek. This gives Matthew a chance to point out yet another prophecy fulfilled, the birth of Jesus by a virgin as foretold by Isaiah. The *alma* called Miriam in the Old Testament might simply have passed on her name to the mother of the new, the second and last, Moses, the wrongly translated *alma* of Isaiah standing godmother to the virgin birth.*

It is virtually indisputed that Jesus came from Galilee. Günther Borkamm wrote in 1971: "Jesus' home is the semi-heathen, despised Galilee . . Jesus' mother-tongue is Galilean Aramaic, the same dialect by which Peter is recognized when he denies Christ in

---

*It is true that in many well-preserved manuscripts Matthew makes only Jesus, Mary's first son, immaculately conceived and born. No one need wonder that Stauffer regards the virgin birth as "historic fact." But even Karl Barth declares as an "ordinance of the church": "It is essential to the true Christian faith to accept the doctrine of the virgin birth."[71]

Jerusalem."[72] Galilee was only finally conquered by the Jewish king Aristobulus I, in 104/103 B.C.E. It was then forcibly converted to Judaism (including compulsory circumcision). Judaea, with salients towards Samaria and Galilee, regarded itself as the heartland of orthodox Judaism. Aramaic was the current speech in all three countries, with Greek for those with some education. Hebrew was only used for the law and for worship. In the Gospel according to Mark (14:70), some of the soldiers say to Peter: "Surely you were one of them, for you are a Galilean and your speech betrays you." (This in only so by implication in the *Revised Standard Version.* — Editor's note)

This first of all the Gospels is actually a Galilean gospel. The author is known to have inserted the references to Galilee in Mark's Gospel in the course of editing.[73] Galilee is presented as the scene of Jesus' works, not an unusual way of proceeding when we bear in mind that in John's Gospel exactly the reverse is done: the works of Jesus are as far as possible located in Jerusalem, and during the denial scene, which this evangelist also transfers, Peter is not recognized by his Galilean accent or by his speech at all.

"Is the evangelist (Mark) simply relying on memories — which indeed never go wrong historically?" asks the New Testament scholar of Münster, Willi Marxsen; and he does not think it likely.[74] For, according to Mark, even after the resurrection Jesus is to go ahead to Galilee, and his angel explicitly sends the disciples there, once more in line with a prophecy of Isaiah, that the future "prince of peace" should "bring Galilee of the heathen to honor." 8:23

The exhortation to go to Galilee is not found in Luke, who is addressing Gentile Christians. In Luke's version, the disciples were to stay in Jerusalem until they were endowed with strength from above.

Marxsen raises the question whether the writer of Mark wished to call the Christian communities to concentrate in Galilee. In this connection, it should be borne in mind that this Gospel named after Mark is considered to have been written just before or just after the destruction of Jerusalem (70 C.E.), i.e. during the Roman war against the Jews. "Galilee" was a byword for lack of orthodoxy and rebellious spirit.[75] The area had such a bad reputation for unrest that the members of the Jewish resistance party, the Zealots, were sometimes simply called "the Galileans."[76] Was the editor really only putting in the punctuation-marks? The very mention of the place in his Gospel would arouse suspicion as tendentious, and the coming of Jesus to Galilee would appear in that half-light that blurs the outlines. So whether Peter denied his master and whether both of them were Galileans would simply depend on the prejudices of that first Gospel writer, who had already dreamed up and incorporated the surname "Nazarene."

Did Jesus live? Did his actual life have any connection with the events that have been associated with him? Or was the human face completely invented out of the myth, the religious fantasy of the early Christians? A mythical interpretation, only indirectly determined by historical events, has taken on the Galilean associations, and so unravels relationships which otherwise would have had to remain unexplained. We are dealing here with the legend of the "Galilean Messiah."

The name Joseph does not definitely derive from the Egyptian references. Joseph could be linked with a Jewish Messiah tradition. The rabbinical exegesis includes accounts of a Messiah ben Joseph — a Messiah, son of Joseph. He is one of two Messianic figures, and later is even called the "Galilean Messiah."

After the end of the northern kingdom in the year 722 B.C.E. the nine and a half tribes settled there were officially regarded as lost. After that time, there remained officially only the tribes of Judah and Benjamin and half the tribe of Levi. (They shared the priests between them.) The "Galilean Messiah" was to gather the lost tribes in Galilee and lead them to Jerusalem against the heathen, and it was recognized that he was to die in battle.

The Talmud calls him "son of Joseph."* According to a later rabbinical writing, this "Messiah ben Joseph" will "sacrifice himself and give up his soul in death, and his blood will bring peace to God's people." He will restore what has been destroyed by the division of Solomon's kingdom. Then comes the second, the kingly Messiah, "Messiah ben David."[78] He fulfills the promises made to the Jews; he it is of whom it is said in the Psalms:

---

*The Messiah ben Joseph is first traceable in rabbinical literature of about the middle of the second century after Christ. But the oral tradition is considerably older, and the theologian Joachim Jeremias thinks it "very probable that the expectation of the Messiah ben Joseph goes back to the pre-Christian era." [77]

Ask of me, and I will make the nations your heritage,
and the ends of the earth your possession.
You shall break them with a rod of iron,
and dash them in pieces like a potter's vessel. (Psalm 2:8-9.)

This reference very strikingly suggests why Jesus came from Galilee, why he had Joseph for a father, why he told his disciples that he would rise again and return to Galilee and said that they should return there too. It suggests why Joseph had to emigrate into Egypt and come home again. It would not be foolish to regard the whole conception of Jesus as a myth, so unreal is it and so reminiscent of Joseph in Egypt, of Moses, of Joshua — Jehoshua. Even the name Jesus — Joshua — Jehoshua could be contrived out of an association with Joshua; Ernst Bloch has written of "Joshua of Nazareth."[79]

As Jesus is formally recognized as founder of the new outward sign of the covenant, baptism, so did Joshua ceremonially introduce circumcision as the sign of the old covenant. At the end of the journeying through the desert, Joshua circumcised all the men of Israel with flint knives, as the Lord had commanded him; so the rite is clearly very old.* Joshua ended his activities at the Passover, like the crucified Christ. For Joshua the sun stood still; for Jesus, hanging on the cross with dislocated arms, darkness fell in the middle of the day. In Book Five of the Sibylline Oracle, a Jewish book of sayings dating from the second century after Christ, Joshua, "who once made the sun stand still," is named as the one still awaited.[81]

But a Joshua has already appeared, in the book of the prophet Zechariah, over five hundred years before Jesus, where it tells of the two Messiahs, the two consecrated with oil ("two sons of oil") who stood before the Lord of the Earth. One of these two is the high priest Joshua (Ἰησοῦς in the Septuagint), who accused Satan before Jehovah. But the angel of Jehovah says of this Joshua: "Is not this man a brand snatched from the fire?"

Joshua — Jehoshua, the "man of the omen," is also significantly

---

*Moses is thought to have been uncircumcised. When Jehovah wanted to kill Moses in an encampment on the road back from Midian, Moses' wife Zipporah cut off the foreskin from her eldest son (Exodus 4:24-26) and "touched the cruel man's genitals with it," as Thomas Mann has it, whispering a mystic formula to herself; or in the *Jerusalem Bible* version, pretended to circumcise her husband, "touching his limb with her son's foreskin."[80]

called "my servant, the branch" (Hebrew *semach*), which reminds us of the shoot, *neẓer*, and the Nazarite. "Branch" is the name given to the man who "will shoot up from the ground where he is and will build the temple of the Lord." He, Jehovah, *will wipe away the guilt of the land in one day*. The Christian development goes further: the guilt of all men in the world is wiped away through the redeeming death of Jesus — Joshua.

Joshua the high priest may well have been an historical figure. A high priest of this name restored the temple in Jerusalem after the exile in Babylon, together with the secular leader Zerubbabel, who had led the Jews back out of exile. In dealing with this sort of material, one always finds that the nature of the "anointed," half-past, half-future, half-mortal, half-supernatural, has only the most blurred and shifting outlines. The original single figure soon splits in two in line with the ancient distinction between the priesthood and the kingdom, and both halves later join together again.

Ever since Zechariah, two Messiahs have been awaited in religious circles. They are also indicated in the literature of the Essenes, notably that of the Qumran monastery: a "Messiah out of Israel" (Israel stands for the secular community, so this would be the royal Messiah of the house of David) and a "Messiah out of Aaron" (a descendant of the brother of Moses, the ancestor of all priests). As presented by the Qumran community, the secular Messiah is subordinate to the priestly; but he is nonetheless the "prince of all the people." He will "establish the rule of his people for ever" and renew the "covenant of the people" (i.e. between Israel and God). Once more we encounter the formula of the "shoots from the root of Aaron and Israel."[82]

The Qumran *Manual of Discipline* states that a prophet is to go before, or beside, the two Messiah-figures.[83] The evangelists present John the Baptist as such a prophet, heralding their Messiah; but John's followers thought he was himself the Messiah, appearing for the second time after a first coming. In the "testament of the twelve patriarchs," already partly influenced by the Christians, a Messiah of the (priestly) tribe of Levi is promised together with one of the (Davidic) tribe of Judah,[84] which fits in with Luke's account of the descent of Joseph from the house of David and that of Mary from the tribe of Levi. Millar Burrows says that Christian theologians explain both these patriarch—Messiahs as one and the same person.[85] The text speaks, however, rather of a tendency to make the two figures coalesce.

42

According to this procedure, of which there are frequent examples, the evangelists would have fused the two Messiah-figures (the "dying Messiah ben Joseph" and the "victorious Messiah ben David") once more into a single person. Jesus must consequently appear twice and must rise again before the general resurrection of the dead so that he can return after his passion and death as the triumphant Messiah. If he is to return out of the clouds, he must already have risen into the heavens.

What Albert Schweitzer wrote in 1913 is still valid: "Modern Christendom must now reckon — has always had to reckon — with the possible surrender of the historical existence of Jesus."[86] Even before Schweitzer, the theologian Martin Kähler had reduced the complex position to a concise formula, that the factual personality of Jesus "is not unassailable on purely historical grounds."[87] Certainly, Ernst Bloch maintains that the manger, the carpenter's son, the visionary among the simple people, are all historical material, not fashioned from the golden stuff beloved of legend. But the golden legend of the nobleman appearing in the guise of a poor man is a favorite among fairy tales and myths. When we seek for Jesus in the flesh, we find his traces less on earth than in heaven, less in the history books than in the folk-myths.

2. What he might have wanted

*The beginning of every great thing on
earth is thoroughly and lastingly
steeped in blood.*
— Nietzsche

*. . . Without the shedding of blood
there is no forgiveness of sins.*
— Letter to the Hebrews, 9:22.

Imagine a Jewish preacher, about the year 30 of the present era, making the following public statements about himself in the country of the Jews:

- ° Break down this temple and I will build it up in three days.
- ° The Son can do nothing by himself, but only what he sees the Father do; and what he does, the Son does likewise.
- ° For the Father judges no man, but has given all judgment to the Son.
- ° I am the resurrection and the life.
- ° He who eats my flesh and drinks my blood has everlasting life, and I will raise him up on the last day.
- ° He who believes in me, as the scripture says, from his body will flow streams of living water.
- ° You are from below, I am from above; you are of this world, I am not of this world.
- ° Which of you can charge me with a sin?
- ° If I were to say, I do not know him (my Father), then I should be a liar, just as you are.
- ° Before Abraham was, I am.

    °   I have power to lay down my life and have power to take it up again. This commandment I have from my father.

    °   I and the Father are one.

Jesus said all these things, according to the Gospel named after John, the fourth and last of the Gospels accounted canonical by the church. If he had really made such statements, what would have happened? Going by every account in the Gospels and by one's normal, human judgment, the Jews would have risen up and lynched him without trial: he would have been stoned.[2]

The theological world is pretty well agreed nowadays that Jesus did not in fact make the statements attributed to him in John's Gospel. It has long been accepted for the other three Gospels that the teaching given to Jesus in them "is very largely not authentic, but is an expression of the faith of the early Christians at different stages of development." (Ernst Käsemann, Tübingen, 1906, an innovator among the elders)[3]; so we can say with regard to John's Gospel that "scarcely one word comes originally from Jesus" (as Luise Schottroff wrote in 1934).[4] Indeed, "scarcely" is no exaggeration.

What this evangelist puts into the mouth of Jesus is no different from the sayings he ascribes to John the Baptist, or indeed from his own sayings. The extended monologue form of Jesus' speech is "un-Jewish," says the head of the Mainz school, the biographer of Jesus, Dr. Herbert Braun,[5] and belongs to a manner of speech "not of the Palestinian but of the Hellenistic-Oriental religion." Braun writes: "I am not mistaken in supposing that the sermon has nothing to do with the historical Jesus and his style."

The Jesus of John ("My Lord and my God," as doubting Thomas calls him, 20:28) has departed so far from the level of an historically possible Jesus that anyone may say without fear of contradiction: This Jesus is certainly not a Jew and certainly not a man, but a spirtual artifact filled with poetic intensity, created by an inspired poet of genius or drawn by a supersensitive seismograph. He has already become the God–man.

It is consequently no wonder that the leading churchmen show a decided preference for this fourth Gospel according to John, though the Catholics less so, and with a proper caution. Luther calls it "the one tender, true, chief Gospel and far, far preferable to the other three." Rudolf Bultmann, who seeks to unearth all historical evidence for the Jesus-figure exclusively from the synoptic Gospels, has a preference for the historically unimportant fourth Gospel that could almost be called tragic, because in it Jesus "as the revealer of God reveals nothing except that he is the revealer," he and none other ("I am that I am," old Yahweh used to say on such occasions, and old Heidegger: "Existence is itself.").[7] For those great churchmen most eagerly concerned with the sharpening of the faith, right up to Kierkegaard, Barth and Bultmann, the most fertile of the Gospels is John's. It derives its special tension from the contrast between the God—man who has foreknowledge of everything and the mortal man dying on the cross. It has nothing to do with any historical figure, as Bultmann makes quite plain when he writes that as a source for the preaching of Jesus it "is hardly to be considered."[8]

Nonetheless, John does sort out the historical reasons for the death of Jesus more plausibly than the other three evangelists. He makes the Jesus affair, as they say nowadays, comprehensible. As George Bernard Shaw discovered, his account is very often nearer to the reality of the public life of Jesus "than the simple chronicle of Matthew or the sentimental romance of Luke." This evangelist, he writes, was "more a man of the world" than the others; he knew "what really happened beyond the books and the writing-desks, which mere chroniclers and poets never know."[9]

Let us not overdraw the logical strength and knowledge of the world of John the evangelist, still less the homogeneity of his Gospel.* But it is true that he does present a plausible conflict. Jesus is too popular and too unpredictable; he alarms not only the temple aristocracy but the whole country. The Pharisees and high priests — the Sadducees were leading party in the high council at the time of Jesus — put it like this: "This man makes many signs. If we leave him to go on like this, the whole populace will come to believe in him. Then the Romans will come and sweep away our temple and our nation." John also envisages a Messianic movement of considerable proportions. The high priest Caiaphas, presiding over the high council, sums it up: "It is better for you that one man should die for the people than that the whole people

---

*The evangelists are not bothered by literal contradictions, John least of all. In John 5:31, Jesus says: "If I bear witness to myself, my testimony is true, for I know whence I have come and whither I am going . . .". John 3:17 says: "For God sent the Son into the world, not to condemn the world, but that the world might be saved through him."; but in 5:22: "The Father judges no one, but has given all judgment to the Son . . ." Mark 9:40 makes Jesus say: "For he that is not against us is for us," but Matthew 12:30 nonetheless finds it possible to put into his mouth the "current profane proverb" (Bultmann [10]): "He who is not with me is against me   ."

should be destroyed." We might well suppose that this experienced high priest could have reached this cynical political decision on his own. But theology is against us. The evangelist cannot openly impute a divine influence over the normal channels and authorities. So he adds this:

He did not say this of his own accord, but being high priest that year he prophesied that Jesus should die for the nation, and not for the nation only, but to gather into one the children of God who are scattered abroad. (John 12:51-52.)

We know now the Jewish leader's reasons — the decisive reasons, we could suppose in the normal run of things. But over and above that, Jesus had wounded many religious sensibilities. If he had made only a fraction of the statements the evangelist ascribes to him, he would have been liable over and over again to the death penalty under Jewish law. More than once the Jews wanted to stone him, but they never did. He for his part appeals to the good works he has done for them in his Father's name. They answer (10:33): "We stone you for no good work but for blasphemy; because you, being a man, make yourself God." The reproof could well have flowed easily from the evangelist's stylus, since he himself had actually elevated his Jesus into a god.

But he seems to have had some inhibition here. Jesus' answer looks highly rabbinical, not at all in John's manner; it has as it were a false bottom. The evangelist makes Jesus dodge the issue: "Is it not written in your own law, 'I said: You are gods'?" In Psalm 82:6 it actually says: "I say, 'you are gods, sons of the Most High, all of you.' " But verse 7, which the crafty evangelist does not quote, goes on: " . . . 'nevertheless, you shall die like men, and fall like any prince.' "

It is virtually out of the question that any Jew in Galilee or Judaea in those days would have thought himself, or declared himself, to be the son of God. He would have been thought crazy. But the Jesus of John's Gospel does just that, so it is only natural that the Jews should bring their complaint before Pilate (John 19:7): "We have a law, and by that law he ought to die, because he has made himself the Son of God." Nowhere but in John's Gospel does Jesus put the catch question to the Jews so simply: He, Jesus, is the voice of God; "He who is of God hears the words of God; the reason why you do not hear them is that you are not of God" (8:47).

What matters is not the message itself, but that the messenger should be believed to be the messenger; as in our present-day philosophy, the existentialist Karl Jaspers asserts always that he "asserts nothing, but merely calls the roll" — the medium is the message. "What shall we do," the Jews ask Jesus in John's Gospel, "to do God's work?" To which he replies: "It is God's will that you believe in him whom he has sent."

The Jesus of John's Gospel is the divine principle. Before his incarnation, he was with his Father in Heaven. He has come to this world to lead the erring children of light to the Father, unknown and uncomprehended by the rulers of this generation. They have to execute him in order to fulfill a plan of salvation that is hidden from them. There is no information to be looked for from this evangelist about a Jesus as he might actually have lived. But what about the other evangelists? Do they give us any hints about Jesus the man and so about the origin of the Christian religion?

None of the four evangelists is known, either by name or in any other way; all four of the Gospels have been handed down to us anonymously. It was the Phrygian bishop Papias who first named Mark, about the middle of the second century; he saw Mark as a travelling companion and interpreter of Peter.[12] Another version says that Mark was for a time one of Paul's companions. The content of Mark's Gospel makes it evident that the author was neither the one nor the other, and it is generally accepted today that Papias was trying to reinforce the credibility of this Gospel by appealing indirectly to an apostle. In early church circles — the evidence again comes from Papias[13] — Matthew's Gospel was similarly given enhanced credibility by being ascribed to the apostle Matthew, who, if he existed at all, is quite certainly not the author ("He modestly conceals in his Gospel that this" — a tax-gatherer and Essene with Jesus — "was his standing, and that this was his house," to quote the commentary to the *Luther Bible* of 1964).[14]

The first to give a name to the evanglist Luke, also reputed to be a travelling companion of Paul's, was Bishop Irenaeus of Lyons, about 180.[15] But it is possible that the Gospel preached by Paul was not based on Luke's account. "Luke" is also generally accepted as the author of the report of the activities chiefly of Peter and Paul which later came to be called *acta apostolorum*, the Acts of the Apostles.

48

Church tradition, again relying on Irenaeus, has linked the Gospel bearing the name of John with "the disciple of the Lord who leaned upon his breast."[16] In the Gospel itself the author does not mention his name but refers to himself as the disciple whom Jesus loved; but this nameless disciple scarcely saw his master. The anonymous disciple-author has a double function: he is said to have been specially favored by Jesus, and to have seen everything himself. So it is he whom Jesus loved, who leans on the breast of the Lord and asks him who is to betray him. It is he who is acquainted with the High Priest and "brings Peter in" to the High Priest's courtyard. It is he, whom Jesus loved, who stands beneath the cross with Jesus' mother, who is not present in the other Gospels; and Jesus entrusts his mother to him. The account of the crucifixion ends with these words (19:35): "He who saw it has borne witness — his testimony is true, and he knows that he tells the truth — that you also may believe."

He, the disciple whom Jesus loved, goes with Peter to the empty tomb, but outruns Peter and gets to the tomb first; Peter and he both see, but he believes.* The "beloved disciple John" goes back to Irenaeus, who has ascribed the Gospel to that apostle, specifically naming him among the twelve as one of the two sons of Zebedee, — who, according to Mark, were nicknamed by Jesus "Boanerges." In Aramaic this means "hot tempered," freely translated by Mark as "the sons of thunder." He is said to have died a martyr's death between the years 50 and 70. Paul names him together with Peter and James as one of the "pillars" of the congregation in Jerusalem.

It is not certain whether one author at a time was at work on each Gospel; in Matthew, collaboration certainly appears possible. But John's Gospel too is reckoned to have been revised and corrected by scholars, and parts of it actually to have been replaced by substituted material. The end is obviously by an editor.

---

*The editors of the Gospel add yet another scene that suggests a certain rivalry: when the risen Jesus commands Peter to follow him, the disciple whom Jesus loved comes too, and Peter says: "Lord, what will happen to him?" Jesus answers: "If it should be my will that he wait until I come, what is it to you? Follow me." The word got round among the brotherhood that Jesus had said: "This disciple will not die." But in fact Jesus did not say: "He will not die" but "If it should be my will that he wait until I come, what is it to you?" Meanwhile the Lord had still not returned, but the evangelist had already died, mourned by his scholars and editors.

However this may be, the scriptures have been transcribed a number of times before reaching the form in which we have them. The oldest fragments to have reached us date from the second century, and even so they are only fragments. The oldest, part of the text of John, is dated at the earliest 125 C.E.[17] There are no authentic original texts. "Mark" writes a clumsy Greek, full of mistakes, shot through with Aramaic constructions. He does not mind employing vulgarisms. Matthew writes more smoothly and correctly. Luke is an excellent master of Greek but takes over certain stylistic imperfections from his sources, imitating the manner and style of the Septuagint, that translation of the Old Testament into Greek said to have been completed by seventy-two translators in seventy-two days between the second and third centuries B.C.E. in Alexandria. This translation was also used by the evangelists.[18]

The oldest account of Jesus is that of Mark, who may have had Greek or Aramaic fragments available to him. Matthew and Luke knew Mark's text and to some extent base their texts on it, so that these three are called the synoptic Gospels: their texts can be laid side by side and compared with one another.[19] The old church said that Matthew's Gospel was the first, perhaps because it was their favorite. But chronologically it was written after Mark and before Luke. Research has led to the almost certain conclusion that Luke knew Matthew's Gospel as well as Mark's; but I will nonetheless add a slight element of doubt here. The synoptic Gospels show more similarity to one another than to John. Luke, the last of the synoptics, has more in common with John, who wrote after him, than with Matthew or Mark.

However, about a third of the material which Matthew and Luke have in common is closely similar in both Gospels, yet is not found in Mark. It has been deduced from this that there was a collection of sayings attributed to Jesus which was used by both authors independently, the source of *logia* or sayings that has been called *Q*. *Q* is a philosophical construction, which has not prevented Ethelbert Stauffer from enthusing over it as "the oldest book about Jesus in Christendom."[20] But even such a theologian as Rudolf Bultmann has gone so far as to explain what was in *Q* and what was not. He knows, for instance, that *Q* was originally written in Aramaic and that it was translated into Greek several times.[21] For a long time, no one doubted the existence of *Q*. No doubt it will comfort the laity, who are always less inspired by what cannot be proved, to read in the latest work of the Göttingen theologian Joachim Jeremias of his doubts whether the source of the *logia* ever existed.[22] For our purposes, it is enough to assume that it did not. What is not found in Paul and Mark and what cannot be accommodated in the construction of *Q*, that peculiar property of the evangelists writing later than Mark, we shall ₅uspect of not belonging to the oldest tradition.

The original dates of the four Gospels accepted by the ancient church into the official canon can only be determined roughly. Willi Marxsen of Münster[23] (1964) puts them as follows:

- ° "Mark" between 67 and 69
- ° "Matthew" in the eighties
- ° "Luke" somewhere about 90
- ° "John" towards the end of the first century.

The date of composition of the three Later Gospels keeps on slipping further away from Mark. Ulrich Wilckens,[24] in the commentary to his translation of the New Testament (1971), assumes a date for Matthew "probably towards the end of the first century," for Luke "at least twenty to thirty years later than Mark's Gospel" and for John, a date between the turn of the century and, at the latest, the year 120. Wilckens puts Mark's date at "shortly after 70" and the date of the Acts of the Apostles around the year 100.

Where were the Gospels written? Marxsen[25] assumes for John "in the East," for Luke "not in Palestine or Syria," for Matthew "probably in Syria, possibly in Transjordan"; as for Mark, the church fathers of old agreed, and the present-day Bibles still do, that it was written in Rome, a hypothesis that goes back to the Emperor Constantine's court theologian, Eusebius.[26] Eusebius keeps on cropping up when history is to be made rather than written; (see the references to Jesus in Josephus). But it is true that Mark's Gospel is familiar with everyday Latin military technical terms.[27]

Marxsen nonetheless believes that the author was writing in or near Galilee, "since such a colorful description of this landscape can hardly be explained otherwise — for do you write a 'Galilean gospel' without visiting the region?"[28] This too, as we can see immediately, is no more than a conjecture, for we already have another explanation of the significance of all the Galilean references in Mark.

Perhaps Mark wrote in Palestine but it may be that none of the evangelists did. We cannot clearly make out whether he was addressing the Gentiles rather than the Jews. We do believe that in Matthew we can discern that he lays special emphasis on the rejection of Israel and is writing for Jewish Christians, or former Jews. But even such a meticulous theologian as Wolfgang Trilling of Leipzig believes that a Jewish-Christian coloring in Matthew has been balanced by later editing by Gentile Christians.[29]

Luke is probably Greek, and is writing for Gentiles, and all one can say about John is that he is well informed in Jewish-Hellenistic philosophy. Whether he himself is a Jewish or a Gentile Christian one cannot tell, but, like Paul, he is certainly a born theologian. His Gospel is saturated with the *"Gnosis,"* the knowledge, which we shall discuss later and which Hans Conzelmann, the disciple of Bultmann, has called "a monstrous mixture from Iranian, Babylonian and Egyptian ideas."[30] The evangelists share with their master the fate that what we can most easily find out about them is what they were not.

Obviously they did not set out to tell everything as it was. They are trying rather to add force to their teaching, which they equate with the teaching of Jesus. To illustrate how hard the old, false traditions die, be it noted that the *Jubilee Bible*, prepared in 1964 using the text newly revised and approved by the German Evangelical Church Committee (the *Luther Bible*, with commentary *not* by Martin Luther), describes Matthew and John as two of the twelve apostles. Of the first, it says: "Matthew was originally called Levi and did not receive his name Matthanja (God's gift) until he was received or accepted as an apostle." And of the other: "the son of the fisherman Zebedee and of Salome, and brother of the elder James."[31]

The *Luther Bible* printed in 1966 is more cautious in its comments, but even so it makes Matthew tell the story of "his calling" to be an apostle, and in John the indications point to "the disciple John, the son of Zebedee."[32] The exceptionally carefully edited Bible of the Catholic Herder Press passes on the (false) traditions and finds the (false) assertions "confirmed and more closely defined from interior evidence."[33] The *Luther Bible* of 1964 feels it can say of the evangelist Mark that he was "not improbably" that young man who, when Jesus was arrested, was seized by the linen cloth that was all he wore, and who slipped out of it and ran away naked (Mark 14:51-52): "For only Mark reports this event, so it is not unreasonable to conclude that he himself was this young man. He was also really at home in Jerusalem."[34] On which the Franciscan theologian Dr. Gerhard Dauntzenberg has the laconic comment (1970): "None of the Gospels was written by an eyewitness."[35]

The books of the Bible are not by nature such as to lead the latest discoveries of the theologians to a breakthrough. But since the Second Vatican Council, the Low-Church-leaflet style commentary (like this from the *Luther Bible* of 1964, on Herod: "*Aussen schwimmert's, innen wimmert's*"[36] (shining outside, whining inside) has become rare among both confessions. The new translation of the Gospels by Ulrich Wilckens issued in 1970 permits itself a frankness in the commentaries, also by Wilckens, that was quite unknown until recently, even if there is still some edifying trash. Even the *Jerusalem Bible* can be displayed, though the dogmatic restrictions have not yet fallen. Its commentary still explains the numerous unbridgeable contradictions in the four Gospels with the pious argument that the Holy Spirit meant to prepare a nourishment of faith, "which the faithful would be capable of receiving."[37] Good old Martin Luther!*

So now we have three synoptic Gospels from which we cannot learn much about the person of the man Jesus, and one other Gospel which tells us nothing at all. And we have Rudolf Bultmann, who embodies in his own person the essential inability of present-day theology to find a way out. Seeking after the truth more earnestly than anyone, he has spent a lifetime investigating the synoptic Gospels. As Ernst Bloch says, he has in an empirical fashion "put to the sword" everything at all strange, everything unnatural, indeed everything that is wonderful.[38] He has made it as it were a life's work out of the most meticulous historical research. Yet he still declares it to be a theological error when anyone questions the identity of the earthly Jesus with the Christ of the church's teaching.[39] The conflict between Bultmann the believer and Bultmann the scientist has tragic and paradoxical, but admittedly sublime, features.

---

*In (the original German text of) this book, the texts of both Testaments are mostly quoted from the *Jerusalem Bible* (1969) or from the Protestant *Mustard Seed Bible* (1971). Since the Protestant Ulrich Wilckens has only translated the New Testament, his translation was not generally used, but only taken into account from time to time, in the case of quotations, so indicated. No serious Bible researcher can, for the rest, avoid the need to make his own translation from time to time.

Bultmann says that we can know virtually nothing more than we do about the life and the person of Jesus. Christ in the flesh "does not concern us; what went on in the heart of Jesus I neither know nor want to know."[40] That leaves us with the problem of tracing back the teaching of a man who, as a human being with a curriculum vitae, never existed. If we want to attempt that, we must first ask, how did this man regard himself? And Bultmann, as with a hammer-stroke, tells us — and more and more theologians agree with him — that, in his personal opinion, Jesus did not think of himself as the Messiah.[41] If not as the Messiah, then as what?

The Gospels, all four of them, leave no doubt in their teaching that Jesus knew himself to be the Messiah and, sooner or later actually said so. What truth can there be in them, if they regard Jesus as the Messiah when he himself does not; if they put their own doctrines into the mouth of one who considered himself, and confessed himself, to be the Messiah in the opinion of the evangelists but not in his own? Bultmann shrugs this question off as "trivial": "Whether or not he knew himself to be the Messiah is neither here nor there."[42]

By way of explanation, he seeks a "meeting with history" — his own highly personal meeting, certainly, but still with history.[43] How can he do that when he knows nothing about the life and person of Jesus? He is not looking for a personal Jesus, but for what Jesus willed, the correlation of sentences he spoke, of thoughts to which he gave expression. Bultmann is looking for the teaching of Jesus.[44] But again, how can he do that when he tells us himself that hardly a single word ascribed to Jesus, literally not one, can be recognized as having been beyond doubt uttered by him?[45] How can he expect to pick out the coherence of the teaching when he does not know the most important thing about it, whether or not Jesus regarded himself as the Messiah or as being in any other way supernatural?

Says Bultmann: "It is essential to the tradition of the kerygma" (this foreign word of the theologians gives such a false security, though it means no more than sermon or proclamation) "that the authenticity of what has been handed down should not be questioned."[46] One is not to base one's belief in God on historical research. Faith is obedience: "The word of the proclamation comes to us as God's word. We cannot question its legitimacy; it asks us only whether or not we want to believe" — as Heidegger explains to us, the questioning of existence is man's answer to the

54

demand of existence.[47] And it is folly to question the necessity, the correctness, the foundation of belief. There will be no answer: "Else the word would not be the word of God."[48] And Bultmann's opposite, Karl Barth, tells us exactly the same: "It is not the right thoughts of man about God that make up the content of the Bible, but the right thoughts of God about man."[49] Man is nothing, achieves nothing: the power of God can harden his heart, the witness of the Holy Spirit can "put him in the wrong." Once again we meet this conception: "Grace would not be grace if we had gone astray in God's eyes."[50] Barth and Bultmann, the two great theologians (as the *Frankfurter Allgemeine*[51] calls them) are entirely at one on this: there must be no questions, we must believe without questioning, to ask is to reject. Is that also going astray? Presumably not. Anyone who asks ceases to believe.

For Barth, what matters is the covenant concluded by God with all "who are in the faith of the children of Abraham" and sealed by him "once and for all in Jesus Christ."[52] That is how we are to believe it. For Bultmann, the point at issue is not the person of Jesus but the lessons ascribed to him, the complex of thoughts handed down to us in an age-old cloak of tradition, of which Jesus is the bearer. ("It is overwhelmingly probable that it really was he," says Bultmann.)[53] He is concerned with a lesson which he sees as an historical phenomenon and whose author he does his utmost to establish as the "cipher" Jesus.[54] Once again, how does he resolve this contradiction between a person who appeals to us and a lesson that is completely impersonal? Does it make no difference, then, whether Jesus taught the lessons attributed to him or whether they were created by the earliest tradition out of other lore and simply put into his mouth?

Perhaps it would make no great difference today if a new ethic were to be preached in the name of Jesus. Bultmann demonstrates, and we can support his argumentation, that that is out of the question.[55] The commandment of love, which "is generally held to be the essential Christian demand," occurs "remarkably seldom" in the words of Jesus.[57] Neither Jesus nor his followers, Bultmann states drily, considered the commandment of love to be a new demand; neither Jesus nor his followers had it in mind to found a particular system of ethics based on the commandment of love. As Bultmann never grows tired of emphasizing, Jesus really gives us no absolutely compulsory theory of what one should and should not do.[57] It is only in Luke that his portrayals of the rich and powerful carry, as it were, a somewhat sour after-taste. He does not condemn property as such, nor marriage as such, nor does he call for sexual or any other asceticism.

He sees mankind, says Bultmann, facing the decision: man must now determine, and must fully determine, to do the will of God, and he, Jesus, transmits God's will.[58] Jesus, says Bultmann, has thought the old Jewish ethic of obedience through radically, to the end; but what does "thought through to the end" mean? However generously it is interpreted, it still shows us only the limits of Bultmann's own thought and presumably of every theological search for historical or any other kind of truth. For who decides what is the will of God? Who defines the ethic of obedience? These questions are clearly answered in John's Gospel. Obedience consists in acknowledging the one who demands obedience — Jesus — as being the one who has the right to demand obedience. Only the gnostic Gospel according to John, argues Ernst Bloch, seems to Bultmann to be reconcilable with the modern world scene, in that in general it has nothing to do with it, but, in would seem, "only with the solitary spirit of every age."[60]

Bultmann, who tries to discern the teaching of Jesus not in the deeply religious John but in the other three Gospels, inquires about the "work." The work of a Plato or a Jesus, a Dante or a Luther, a Napoleon or a Goethe — these are all names mentioned by Bultmann[61] — the work regarded not as what has been achieved but as what the doer "essentially willed," cannot be determined without some knowledge of the living conditions and of the personality so generously swept aside by Bultmann. We "know" Luther, Napoleon, Goethe; they have lived and written, people met them and spoke with them. But Jesus we do not know. We do not know what he "willed." We do not know whether any of what he willed "can be relevant today as a demand of his historical existence" (Bultmann), simply because we do not know what he willed and what attitude he would have taken to our historical existence. As preacher, Bultmann sees this dichotomy in such a way that he preaches about Matthew 11:28 ("Come to me, all who labor and are heavy laden . . .") as if it were a saying of Jesus, although as a Bible researcher he knows that this is "a quotation put into the mouth of Jesus from a Jewish prophetic scripture."[63] What can Jesus have willed? We can approach the question impressionistically, like Adolf Holl, in his recent book *Jesus in Bad Company.*

Jesus was a utopian, thinks Holl,[64] a rebellious young man — that is beyond doubt. Clearly he was, since he wished, perhaps to enforce, perhaps to proclaim, the kingdom of God on earth. Family, religion, property, education were, according to Holl, regarded by Jesus as "dying conceptions"; socially he cannot be placed, cannot be classified. Well, this may well be so.

But did he not come to any sort of accommodation with the world and its material organization "in kinship and family, religion, class and social level, property and influence and education"? Here we must pause. If these things did not (or did no longer) interest him, can we therefore say that he had not learned to live with them? We know, or we believe we know, that he did not see eye to eye with some of the representatives of the ruling school of thought. But is he always to be found among the dissatisfied, among the prisoners and the condemned, among the oppressed, among the poor? And his sympathies always with the outlawed, the neglected, the forgotten? Does he side with the poor as a matter of principle? Is he one of those children who ran away from home? Or do social conditions not interest him so much because the eruption of the kingdom of God demands his whole attention?

Jesus is certainly not the "father of all revolutionaries," and if we could track down his relatives we should understand why. He is "unfortunately not very conscientious," and this rather casual observation of Holl's strikes us as somewhat novelistic. He wants to "change thought" — but no, he wants to abolish it. Thought is to be left to him and his heavenly father. What is needed is to refrain from thinking; to believe, to obey. Did Jesus have "an eye for the obvious"? Yes and no: he had the end of the world in his sights. He does not want to get his name in the papers, writes Holl artfully, but perhaps that is just what he does want. He certainly has an urgent item of news to communicate.

We can throw the Gospels away at once. If we do not think it possible that Jesus proclaimed the coming of the kingdom of God. A Messiah, or some other holy person, would shortly bring the world to an end, judge all men and bring in the final salvation upon earth: too much precision is not to be looked for here. But the matter is urgent, for in the teaching of Jesus, the time at which this decisive turning-point would be reached was in the quite near future. It could be perceived from the signs of the times as the weather is read from the meteorological conditions or the approach of spring deduced from the state of the vegetation. The change has to be accomplished in time for this ending of the world, this last judgment and final salvation. To survive the judgment men must stake their all on one card. To forget the approach of the end is to act foolishly, "like a man who with a cloudburst in sight still builds his house without adequate foundations" (Herbert Braun).[65]

Did Jesus, then as Holl[66] says, invite men to a "life of the least possible security"? On the contrary. In fact, he was able to offer the best life insurance obtainable, a policy against wailing and gnashing of teeth in the darkness, if the kingdom of God really was just around the corner. The Gospels are soaked in the idea of punishment and reward. Jesus was something of an anarchist in the name of the kingdom of God, denying all established forms of power here and now.

Jesus, thinks Holl, proclaimed an early end to all forms of government, chains of command and pecking orders and reserved a place in hell for them all. But what is the point of attacking the establishment if you are going to replace it with a new pyramid with yourself at the peak? For where does Jesus seek alliance with those reasonable establishment figures, with the "liberals," with or without a prefix, with those Pharisees who refused to believe that the cosmic catastrophe, the revolution in the kingdon of God, had already begun?

Does he respect the authorities? No, he certainly does not. Is he a rebel? Yes, if he existed; then yes. Did he declare that the kingdom of God was at hand, or did he with to bring that about by his own actions? We can no more find an answer to these questions by studying him than we could in the writings of Karl Marx. Who can ever know from the higgle-piggledy evidence offered us by the Gospels whether he wished to bring peace or a sword. Would he have fired a machine-gun for the Vietcong? Would he have had the H-bomb manufactured? No, we must really keep our speculation within bounds; we must be moderate.

Was he, to take Ernst Bloch[67] at his word, simply a man who went about doing good? Was all that he said and did right, without blame or error, as Gollwitzer says?[68] I am not so sure. It would be equally true to say that he set people against one another unnecessarily, perhaps even out of a desire for self-aggrandizement (Gore Vidal: "demagogic joiner")[69]; for while we may concede that he carried out the unique special task of God, we shall never get

58

beyond that without the aid of the theologians. If we take shelter behind those Jesus-formulae available, we shall find that they do not all work.

It is true that the biblical words of the biblical Jesus, even the Old Testament references of the Bible, have inspired many earthly revolutionaries, outstandingly the peasant-priest Thomas Münzer, whose comparison of himself with the person of the Savior strikes us immediately. If we wished to envisage Jesus as an earthly revolutionary (which he may have been though the Gospels say little or nothing about it) then Thomas Münzer offers us a vivid pattern, and as a forerunner of Münzer, Jesus takes on a form by no means blasphemous. Everything that Jesus left as his trace along the road, writes Ernst Bloch in a book on Münzer that has survived the years, all that has been detested in the German peasant-priest.[70]

There is the thundering against the "scribes": they declare, says Münzer, that God no longer reveals himself to his dear friends through visions and voices,[71] and he damns them for it in Allstedt before the Saxon prince. He, Münzer, has seen visions and heard voices; he calls for a new John the Baptist who shall sound the trumpets. No man on this earth shall be spared who strives against God's word — if he opposes him.[72]

There is the doctrine of the transformation of things. The days and the hours of the final battle between darkness and light have dawned, the time is fulfilled, the time of the reaper is come, "now even the weed cries out that the harvest is yet distant". Münzer swings the sword of Gideon against the "bigwigs who have blasphemously made God into a little painted man."[73] The Lord will pour out his most intense anger upon them. They have stolen the scriptures out of the Bible like artful thieves and robbers, [74] but: "He alone shall have the government, to whom all power is given in heaven and on earth."[75] The conversion of the whole world is at hand; power will be given to the common people. God's conspirators, not "Brother Fat-pig and Brother Soft-life," are the representatives of the revolution.

Let us remember that even Luther, [77] Münzer's original mentor, expected the judgment of the world in his own lifetime, at any rate at the time the confusion among the brotherhood was at its height, so we can comprehend the apocalyptic preaching to which Münzer was inspired by the New Testament. True, the forty-year-old Luther reacted extremely half-heartedly, perhaps even a little treacherously, to Münzer's native violence: "For if he says that God and his Spirit have sent him like the apostles, let him show the same with signs and wonders, or let him restrain his preaching: for when God wishes to change the order of things, he always shows it by miraculous signs."

Münzer, who "from his youth up always ran like a storm against the wind" (Ernst Bloch), "who preached before the princes in Allstedt more boldly, more daemonically than was spoken before any Nebuchadnezzar",[78] reminds us of Jesus of Luke who "saw how Satan fell, like lightning, out of the sky" (Luke 10:18). The certainty that we cannot find in Jesus, Münzer has in excess. Both of them believed that their words would move mountains. Münzer was tortured and executed at the age of 35, after the slaughter of the peasants at Frankenhausen in 1525. We can see what it was this Jesus redivivus wanted; but not what Jesus wanted.

His message, like his person, remains extremely unclear. If we can believe that he was an eschatological prophet looking forward to the last things and wishing to mark the divine transformation of things, then perhaps we are not far from the truth, but we still cannot picture the man because we can hardly feel empathy with an eschatological prophet. Even if we could get clear what the followers of the dead Jesus — in their eyes the reawakened and risen Jesus — really believed themselves to be, would we be able then to clarify what he himself was and what he believed himself to be? It is precisely this that seems impossible.

The evangelists, we hear recently, have given to him everything in the way of titles to supremacy that they could find: Messiah, son of God, son of man, son of David. Stripped of these honors, he would have been just another prophet. But the other prophets certainly did not associate salvation with their own persons. They saw themselves as God's messengers; they were understood as personifying the actions of God. Jesus on the contrary associates his person with the coming of the end: he announces it, he claims obedience under the will of his Father, whom he interprets, he assembles the congregation of salvation, he promises salvation to his followers. How can he do that unless he sees himself as the Savior, one specially chosen by God, one indeed to whom full power and might have already accrued? As Bornkamm says, Jesus has "the astonishing certainty that the decisions that face him and his word here will be confirmed by the judgment of the world".[79]

His inability to declare himself openly as the Messiah although he already believed that he was, or soon would be, finds a natural explanation when we consider what would commonly be expected of the holder of that title, what had always been taught and understood about the two Messiah-figures in esoteric circles, even if the Messiah was awaited as the king of an ideal future. If any man declared that he was the Messiah, he would have been expected to bring about an immediate end to the Roman domination. The Messiah was quite essentially thought of as a war Messiah; he could not establish the kingdom of peace without the use of force. That is why the descent from Israel's most illustrious warrior king ("son of David") was so important.

We do not know whether Jesus was the man to make such a claim look absurd. But the material circumstances were by no means favorable to the appearance of a Messiah. It sounds rather like a joke to hear from our theologians that Jesus refused the political kingship,[80] that he "consciously opposed. . . any striving for political domination" (Martin Hengel), that he "renounced the easy road of public approbation" (Joachim Jeremias). How could he have set about becoming king of the Jews? What sort of picture do our divines have of the Roman empire?

The Messiah is the *ideal* Anointed, but not necessarily therefore the son of God. In the Coronation Psalm (Psalm 2:7) God speaks to the kings of Israel, to the *actual* Anointed: "You are my son, today I have begotten you." But it would never have occurred to any king on that account to believe that he had been begotten by God; that would have made the number of God's sons pretty considerable. "Son of God" was not a usual description of the Messiah in Judaism. Hans Conzelmann, second after Käsemann among the disciples of Bultmann and recognized as such by the master, says unequivocally that Jesus "did not claim to be the son of God according to the the texts available."[81] Hardly any theologian worth mentioning still says that Jesus declared himself, or believed himself, to be God's son, although "the whole of Christendom," as Cardinal König maintained against Adolf Holl, stands or falls by the dogma that he was the son of God. (Holl had to explain to the Cardinal in answer to this inquiry that, on the question of whether Jesus was God's son, he believed what was in his book — he calls it there a "form of words." But, after all, he is the lecturer on religious knowledge in the Faculty of Theology in the University of Vienna and presumably will continue as such).

"You live from the church," it says appropriately in the Cardinal's *Monitum,* "but do you also live in the church?"[82]

How do things stand, then, on this question of the title of Messiah or Christ? To quote Conzelmann again, it can be immediately recognized "in most places" that it has been inserted by an editor. Conzelmann draws attention to three particular passages in Mark's Gospel, which cannot be immediately recognized as spurious, and then proves that they cannot be considered as authentic;[83] yet the theme of Mark's Gospel is the gradual self-revealing of a Lord who knows himself to be the Messiah and the son of God. What are proofs worth if they are emptied of their contents in this way?

Certainly the strangest title that Jesus is said to have given himself is that of "son of man." Fifty-one times altogether in the four Gospels, not counting the parallel passages, Jesus speaks of himself in the third person as the son of man, and all four evangelists leave us in no doubt that they associate this title with supreme powers of supernatural dimensions. The Aramaic language knows the word "son of man" in the simple sense of "human being," but it also understood in a religious, supernatural sense.[84] The texts of the Gospels, written in Greek, give us no elucidation: they call the son of man ὁ υἱὸς τοῦ ἀνθρώπου "the son of the man," and the children of men (see Mark 3:28) are called οἱ υἱοὶ τῶν ἀνθρώπων. Therein lies the poverty of every translation, which has to be literal and meaningless when it cannot get at the true meaning.

There is a ring about the mysterious name. Even more in translation does it give the impression of someone foreign yet at home, someone cast away like Mowgli among the beasts of the jungle, above us and yet of us, child of human parents and yet son of God. But behind this facade of sound lies empty bombast. "How simple this word would be, " muses Ernst Bloch, "if there was nothing at all behind it but a somewhat superfluous description of something that has nothing at all concealed in its mind but simply, in Aramaic, goes on two legs." Bloch, then, believes that in using the expression, Jesus had something at the back of his mind, as if when he used it it "would be of great value with men, of greater value indeed than anywhere else."[85]

If that is so, then the conception of the son of man is outstandingly well adapted for the see-saw between a bombastic I-am-one-of-you attitude and that superman still to be portrayed. But who says that it was Jesus who chanced upon it? The evangelists could have made just as good, or better, use of such an idea.

Paul does not speak of his Lord as the son of man but as the one born of David's stock (Romans 1:3). In the sayings of Jesus contained in the *Gospel of Thomas,* parts of which may well be very old, the son of man occurs only once, and then as one who does not have to hide his head.[86]

We could easily work up a cross-examination act. Question: What does Jesus mean when he speaks in the third person of the son of man? Answer: He probably never spoke of himself as the son of man at all. Question: What does he mean when he describes himself as the son of God and the Messiah? Answer: He probably never described himself as such. Question: Did he believe he was the Messiah? Answer: What is the Messiah? Question: Did he believe he was the son of man? Answer: Which version of the son of man?

The prevailing opinion today is that Jesus took up and put about the title of son of man as a description of his essential nature but that he never really believed himself to be such. One could say with equal justification that he never spoke of the son of man, that this title was conferred on him later because it sounded well and fit in with the program. That is what Conzelmann does: he regards the whole idea of the son of man as folk-theology.[87] The Biblical commentator Wilckens, on the other hand, affirms that Jesus refers to himself as son of man in a great many speeches and that he claims heavenly authority for it.[88]

The Messiah is a strictly national figure; the Jewish tradition seems to have taken over the "son of man" from the Persian apocalyptic, the announcement of the coming end of the world, and to have amalgamated it with the idea of the Messiah; he is the transcendental man of heaven concentrated on Israel. (The evangelists could not clearly differentiate between the Messiah and the son of man. No wonder, considering the airy substance of both those mythical figures.) The oldest of the Jewish scriptures in which a religious son of man appears is the Apocalypse ("revelation") of the book of Daniel,* written about the year 165

---

*The name Daniel was borrowed from a hero of olden times. The protagonist of the book of Daniel was deprived of his rank in the time of Nebuchadnezzar and stood out against him as Thomas Münzer withstood the princes in Allstedt, though he was certainly better supported by the heavenly hosts.

B.C.E. after the high priest Jason had gone ahead with Hellenization and the Syrian king Antiochus IV Epiphanes had introduced the worship of Zeus into the temple of Jerusalem, an unexampled humiliation which touched off the rising of the Maccabees.

The apocalyptic writings, steeped in Persian influences, were circulated as a kind of esoteric teaching among the unofficial circles of Jewry and quite certainly among the sectarians of the Qumran monastery. It says in the book of Daniel:

> I saw in the night visions,
> and behold, with the clouds of heaven
> there came one like a son of man,
> and he came to the Ancient of Days
> and was presented before him.
> And to him was given dominion
> and glory and kingdom,
> that all people, nations and languages
> should serve him;
> his dominion is an everlasting dominion
> which shall not pass away,
> and his kingdom one
> that shall not be destroyed.
>
> (Daniel 7:13-14.)

The kingdom of God will come, but he will rule, not directly, but through a mediator who comes increasingly to resemble a man. He was not thought of as a universal ruler, as countless theologians have convinced themselves,[89] but as a Jewish ruler, a ruler of the world having power over the heathen peoples. (The heathen are called in the Gospels ὁ ἐθνικός, from ἔθνος — people.) The *Jerusalem Bible* sees this as the last link in the chain of Messianic promises. Jesus, king of the dawning kingdom of God, will call himself "son of man" and "thereby make it clear that he has come to fulfill the promises of the book of Daniel":[90] the redeemer as the final, ultimate deliverer.

What do the Gospels believe about the son of man? When the congregation has reached its highest point, he will come down from heaven like lightning, expected by no one. Shrouded in clouds, surrounded by hosts of angels, he will appear in heavenly glory. He seats himself on the throne on the right hand of God and sends his angels forth to gather together his chosen people from the four winds. He sits in judgment with twelve representatives of the twelve tribes as his assessors.

That is how Jesus describes his role according to the Gospels. Clearly it would be very difficult today to vindicate a man who cherished such expectations even if he envisaged, not himself, but someone else in the role of the coming son of man. How much more so if Jesus thought of himself as the coming son of man, as is stated quite explicitly in the Gospels! It certainly takes courage to put forward such a view today, and it is refreshing to read in the year 1971 the quite firm opinion of Joachim Jeremias,[91] the Göttingen theologian, that when Jesus speaks about the son of man in the third person, he does not mean two different persons, one human (himself) and one supernatural (someone else), as Bultmann rather suggests.[92] Moreover, he has two different situations in view: he differentiates between his present and his future *in statu exaltationis*, and it is this secret relationship to which he draws attention by the use of the third person: "He is not yet the son of man, but he will be raised up to be the son of man."

If Jesus was neither the Messiah nor the son of man nor the son of God, and if he did not even think he was any of those, what is left? What remains apart from a handful of ethical principles? We still have his reported readiness to give up his life to reconcile God with all mankind. According to church doctrine as delivered by Gustav Heinemann as leader of the synod, God has concentrated "the anger and the judgment at all our disobedience into a death sentence on one single man," and Jesus willingly submitted to the sentence.[93] It certainly cannot have been so.

Once more we are groping in the dark with nothing to hold on to. If he does not believe himself to be either the Messiah or the son of man, nor yet a second Judas Maccabaeus, an earthly king of the Jews, what good could his death do? The good shepherd who gives his life for the sheep certainly does not do it for nothing, but because he expects a reward, or punishment if he does not deliver the sheep unhurt in time for the slaughter. (The equation of these proverbial sacrificial animals with the salvation of mankind has a characteristic flavor of the perverse.)

Given the poverty of the sources, it was only to be expected that someone would come up with the idea that Jesus, although not educated after the concepts of his time ("wandering preacher"),[94] modelled his life according to the old prophecies, and undertook on his own body a kind of heavenly woodcarving. Rudolf Otto, the theologian who died in Marburg in 1937, is the begetter of this version and of all its subsequent variants. Jesus, says Otto, had drawn his guiding principles mainly from two scriptures, the book of the prophet Deutero-Isaiah, written about 540 B.C.E. (the "second Isaiah," the first having been written about 700) and the book of Enoch,[95] which appeared piecemeal between 170 and 30 B.C.E. and which had long been held in the highest esteem by the early church fathers until it was finally ejected from the list of apocryphal scriptures by Hieronymus in the fourth century. The book of Enoch thus became a "hidden," an unrecognized book; it is no longer disputed that it had great influence in the writing of the New Testament.

The prophecies of Deutero-Isaiah contain a passage about a suffering servant of God who gives his life as a sacrifice for sin and is crushed by Jehovah. He meets death for the sake of other men's sins; he possesses "no beauty, no majesty" and has "no grace to make us delight in him":

He was despised and rejected by men;
a man of sorrows, and acquainted with grief;
and as one from whom men hide their faces
he was despised, and we esteemed him not.

Surely he has borne our griefs
and carried our sorrows;
yet we esteemed him stricken,
smitten by God, and afflicted.
But he was wounded for our transgressions,
he was bruised for our iniquities;
upon him was the chastisement
that made us whole,
and with his stripes we are healed.
All we like sheep have gone astray;
we have turned every one to his own way;
and the LORD has laid on him
the iniquity of us all.
He was oppressed, and he was afflicted,
yet he opened not his mouth;

like a lamb that is led to the slaughter,
and like a sheep that before its shearers is dumb,
so he opened not his mouth.
By oppression and judgment he was taken away;
and as for his generation, who considered
that he was cut off out of the land of the living,
stricken for the transgressions of my people?
And they made his grave with the wicked
and with a rich man in his death,
although he had done no violence,
and there was no deceit in his mouth.

Yet it was the will of the LORD to bruise him;
he has put him to grief;
when he makes himself an offering for sin,
he shall see his offspring, he shall prolong his days;
the will of the LORD shall prosper in his hand;
he shall see the fruit of the travail of his soul
and be satisfied;
by his knowledge shall the righteous one, my servant,
make many to be accounted righteous;
and he shall bear their iniquities.
Therefore I will divide him a portion with the great,
and he shall divide the spoil with the strong;
because he poured out his soul to death,
and was numbered with the transgressors;
yet he bore the sin of many,
and he made intercession for the transgressors.

(Isaiah 53: 3-12.)

Jesus, says Otto, expressly quoted from Isaiah: he wished to be understood as fulfilling this concept, he recognized it "from the very beginning as a prophecy about himself."[97] Perhaps then he might have been what the Viennese heretic Adolf Holl will not allow him to be, a "tortured intellectual."[98] It is very hard to imagine how someone with such an obsession found any followers. But perhaps he did not have any followers at all, or very few; as Bultmann opines, only a "small band."[99] The essential point of this famous passage from Isaiah, is simply that he must make it his object to be brought to his death by his enemies, whoever they might be. Was that the prospect he had before him? Millar Burrows, professor at Yale University, following Otto, now actually believes that Jesus "found in Isaiah 53, the pattern for his life of self-sacrifice, his vicarious death and final victory."[100] Let us just note briefly that this passage, unique in the Old Testament, came out of the Jewish exegesis on the people of Israel. The prophet is writing in Babylon, where many of the Israelites had been carried off. So it is Israel that is the "suffering servant of God."[101] The second prophecy which Rudolf Otto regards as setting a model which Jesus adopted as his pattern[102] is the book, full of apocalyptic images and visions, written under the name of Enoch — a book that would have been very much more difficult of access in Jesus' time than Deutero-Isaiah. Enoch, like Daniel, is a hero from the murky past. According to the book of Genesis, he was 365 years old; it may well be therefore that he reflected old representations of the sun-god. Like the prophet Elijah later on, he never dies; God takes him to himself in a secret way, and Rudolf Otto does not hesitate to suggest that Jesus also had in mind a "translation and raising-up like those of Enoch" right up to the time of his death.[103] Enoch too was raised up to God.

All these apocalypses promise a blessed life to the contrite and righteous man, but stubborn sinners and the heathen end in eternal terror. Enoch, the "Jewish prototype of the Catholic Dante,"[104] is guided by angels on a journey through the world and the underworld. He meets the ghosts of just men who have died and of the fallen angels in their dungeons; he discovers an immense number of cosmic secrets and he prophesies the coming of the Messiah — son of man, also called "the just" and "the chosen." Messiah and son of man have already flowed together to form one. In the middle of the book, Enoch himself becomes the son of man, but finally he returns to the earth and tells his son Methuselah about his visions. In the judgment of Georg Beer, who has edited the book, it contains a "great deal of stupid gibberish."[105]

The part played by the Messiah—son of man is described at length. His enemies are the kings and mighty ones of the world; it is to them, the heathen beasts and birds of prey, that his judgment is directed; for them the instruments of torture are being prepared.

The heathen, specified by name as Medes and Persians, gather together to storm Jerusalem, but are led astray so that they kill each other. Their downfall makes an entertainment for the righteous. God's sword wreaks havoc before the face of the son of man; it becomes drunk with the blood of the enemy. The son of man makes the sinners and those who have led the world astray vanish from the face of the earth; he annihilates them. The righteous dead are raised up and the Jewish Diaspora returns home. The son of man, who was already in God's house before the creation of the world, now becomes a staff for the righteous and holy and a light of the people for ever and ever (and if he has not died, then he is still alive today).

How any Jew, or anyone at all, could have believed that there existed at the same time both the suffering servant of God who lets himself be led off to the slaughterhouse without resistance and the pre-existent lord of judgment of Enoch's fantasies is beyond our imagination. But we have to recognize that not only Rudolf Otto but also the no less expert Millar Burrows have stated just that: that Jesus "deliberately and consistently" set out to follow what was written about the son of man,[106] i.e., that he should suffer greatly and should be despised. It says so specifically in Mark (9:12), though it looks there as if the evangelist has combined Enoch and Deutero-Isaiah. The Messiah—son of man of Enoch is not one to suffer, still less to be despised, any more than the one described in the book of Daniel. His countenance, on the contrary, "is filled with sweetness like that of the holy angels" (46:1). He is pre-existent, not a man or a community of this world like Isaiah's servant of God. Let us say it straight out: any Jew who believed himself to be Enoch's Messiah or son of man must have been raving mad.

How does it happen, then that intelligent scholars can combine Enoch's son of man with a suffering servant of God? A confusion, natural enough in the tangled, third-hand translation of Enoch, can explain the error. In chapter 38, "the righteous man" appears before "the chosen righteous man." The reference here must be to the Messiah. But in chapter 47 — not necessarily from the same traditional source or by the same writer — it says:

69

In those days will the prayer of the righteous *ones* and the blood of the righteous *one* rise up before the Lord of the Spirits.

In these days will the holy ones who dwell above in the heavens intercede with one voice, pray, praise, thank and glorify the name of the Lord of the Spirits on account of the blood of the righteous ones, that it be not in vain before the Lord of the Spirits, that justice be done for them and that it be not delayed for ever.

In those days I saw how the Ancient in Years sat upon the throne of his majesty, and the books of the living were opened before him, and his whole army stood before him, which is on high in the heavens and round about him.

The hearts of the holy were filled with joy, because the number of righteousness was approaching, the prayer of the righteous *ones* was heard and the blood of the righteous *one* was avenged before the Lord of the Spirits.

We can now comment, very much against the spirit of the metaphor, that the righteous *one* whose blood was shed and was avenged before the Lord of the Spirits (God) is identical with the son of man. But since the suffering servant of God had already been concentrated into a single person, Enoch's reference to the righteous *one* can hardly mean anything but the host of martyrs massacred under Antiochus IV and later under the Jewish king Alexander Jannaeus. He is really speaking of the righteous *ones* and of the righteous one. We ought not to look to a Jesus for this combined gift of our theologians.

Apart from the fact that the Messiah—son of man in the pre-Christian era was not one who suffered, no reference to Isaiah's name of "servant of God" is to be found in the earlier periods of the Christian tradition: for example, there is none in the whole of Mark's Gospel, and even in Matthew 8:17, (which quotes Isaiah 53:4), no allusion to the servant of God or the passion of Jesus is to be found. In spite of this, Joachim Jeremias holds that this combination by Enoch of the son of man and the servant of God is fundamental to Jesus' consciousness of power.[107] We, on the contrary, recognize that the evangelists drew on Enoch in quite a different way; we are approaching the conclusion that it was they, and not Jesus, who swallowed Enoch's tales, they and not Jesus who had their eyes on Deutero-Isaiah. Their Messiah—son of man was a man who suffered *because*, and *after*, he died suffering. It fits into the picture that in Acts 3:18 Peter is made to affirm, quite incorrectly, that God "had foretold by the mouth of all the prophets, that his Christ should suffer."

Did Jesus wish to "sacrifice" himself, whatever the motive and whoever should benefit, and whether or not "commanded" by his heavenly Father? Did he expect to be raised up to God immediately after his "sacrifice"? If he was the pre-existent son of God from the beginning, how much was his sacrifice worth? "If a man knows that he is to be raised up after three days," Bultmann affirms, "then death will not mean much to him!"[108] If we are to reach any conclusion here, we must bear in mind that, while the idea of a suffering and dying God was always foreign to the Jews' original conception of God, the idea of sacrifice in any form was not. Blood sacrifice to appease God, the vicarious sacrifice of the guiltless and pure, the sacrifice of the firstborn and of only sons or eldest sons, these bring benefits to the community in the Jewish religion as they do among other peoples. The blood of the Paschal lamb, according to the old rabbinical teaching, is the blood of the covenant which atones for the sins of the past; Jesus, the new high priest, is at the same time the new Paschal lamb, atoning for the sins of all mankind.[109] The evil that every wrong deed brings upon its doer will be turned away by him through the act of atonement, after the redemption by human sacrifice; turned away by the blood of the sacrifice.

But nowhere in Judaism does God sacrifice himself. That the one, personal Yahweh, capable as he was under non-Jewish — Persian, Egyptian, Canaanite — influence of being emancipated from the status of a tribal god of Israel to become a world god, could also be capable of sacrificing his own, personal son: all this is very far from being a Jewish thought; and the sacrifice only for thirty years of life, two days' rest in the grave and one day of bodily torture is even further.

But Jesus cannot have had the same thoughts as Yahweh. To what ideas could a Jew of his time have been exposed? First of all, there is the idea that God's favor can be won through blood sacrifice, perhaps to gain some advantage, perhaps for the forgiveness of a sin against God's holy being. Firstborn children are sacrificed to the Lord (who had long ago given up devouring his own sons). Originally the firstborn sons, later the firstborn cattle, were sacrificed, as we see clearly in the fury of the angel of death against Pharaoh and the Egyptian firstborn and against all the firstborn of Egyptian cattle.

Yahweh himself, even when he no longer wished to admit it, had permitted ritual murder. True, he spared Isaac and was able to explain that he had only wanted to test Abraham's obedience (what a ghastly joke!). God will provide himself with a lamb for a sacrifice, says Abraham to Isaac when he inquires, seeing only the firewood and the knife but no beast for sacrifice. Let us remember Karl Barth, who reminds us that in the faith we are all Abraham's children! The Lord concluded the covenant with Abraham, on the evidence of the Bible (Genesis 22:16), because you have done this and have not withheld your son, your only son." This was the first act of blessed obedience.*

Isaac survived, the Bible tells us. But the daughter of Jephthah, the judge, had to die. The judge (at that time commander of the army) had promised God to bring him as a burnt offering whatever came first to meet him out of the door of his house, if God would send him victory over the Ammonites. His daughter, his only daughter, was the first living being to meet him after the victory, and things did not turn out as they do in fairy tales: he sacrificed her to the Lord as a burnt offering. (To lessen the shock of this horror to the reader, the daughter is granted a respite of ten days, to let her go over the mountains with her playmates and "bewail her innocence"; after which she dies "willingly." As in the myth of Iphigenia, it was thought necessary to tone down the cruelty of the happenings.)

Sons were sacrificed to the Lord as an act of vengeance. When Saul strove to exterminate the Gibeonites, "in his zeal for Israel and Judah," the Lord was displeased, since the Gibeonites had concluded a pact with the children of Israel. David, Saul's successor, asked them how he could make amends. They answered:

---

* The legend is told of the Pharisee leader Simon ben Shetach (about 70 B.C.E.) that his son had been condemned to death on deliberately false evidence. Shortly before his execution, the lying witnesses confessed their crime. Thereupon the son said: "My father! If you will bring salvation to Israel, take my body and sacrifice me." According to another reading, by a different translator: "If you wish to conquer, let me be the springboard." The story does not relate whether Simon's son actually was killed.[110]

'. . . let seven of his sons be given to us, so that we may hang them up before the LORD at Gibeon on the mountain of the LORD.' And the king said, 'I will give them.' (2 Samuel 21:6.)

Two sons and five grandsons of Saul were thus "hung before the LORD." The old God of Israel was a complex lord, a politician, for politics was always complex in the times of men and beasts. Mesha, king of the heathen Moabites, knew a means of saving his capital city in the battle against King Jehoram of Israel, according to the Second Book of Kings:

> Then he took his eldest son who was to reign in his stead, and offered him for a burnt offering upon the wall. And there came great wrath upon Israel; and they withdrew from him and returned to their own land. (2 Kings 3:27.)

Human sacrifice, unthinkable (Mesha — see Chapter 8 — describes it quite differently)! But we no longer get worked up about the backwardness of the people of old. Priests and kings in times past were simply not allowed to die a natural death. The father had to be killed so that his strength might be passed on, perhaps originally by eating him.

All sacrificing has a tendency to become, first vicarious, then symbolic. The son is sacrificed instead of the father, and the sacrifice of the firstborn children substituted by the firstfruits of livestock and crops; in place of the people's eldest sons, the members of the tribe of Levi are dedicated to God as priests. Vicarious suffering, vicarious death of the innocent: these have a redeeming, propitiating, healthgiving power. This thought is found often among the Jews and later among the Christians; so that even the innocent children murdered by Herod were claimed among the sacrifices, as the Catholic Schott Missal declares: "With the innocent children, sacrificing themselves in death for Christ, we too in an earnest spirit of sacrifice avoid the snares of the world, the devil and the flesh."[III]

It is nowhere recorded that the one to be sacrificed goes to the sacrifice willingly, with no concrete object and of his own accord, and it may well be that Jesus was far from thinking that he would reconcile the whole Jewish people with God through his passion and death. Apart from Yahweh's cruel test of Abraham, there has always been some concrete motive in all the examples we have quoted; the desired benefit was not abstract but plainly obtainable and actually necessary. It could hardly occur to any man who was not a Christian, but a Jew, to think he could reconcile the whole Jewish community, not to mention the whole of humanity, through an aimless death sought almost wilfully.

Now, of course, we do not at all know whether Jesus foresaw his passion and death and knew he must bear them. There are well-known theologians such as Bultmann and Wrede who deny this.[112] We can only say that he must have known the risk he was running if he behaved anything like the way described in the Gospels. There are people, of course, who simply want to know what will come next, not considering the consequences until it is too late. In such a case we could not speak of a "judicial murder," as Ulrich Wilckens does in the *Furche Press Bible* published by him.[113]

If Jesus had not admitted any motives that can be explained other than psychologically, then he must have had some purpose in view with his death, assuming, that is, that he was actually working for it. Here we must abandon the source material on Jesus, though not quite yet the earlier parallel prophecies. We cannot proceed from Barth and Bultmann, because Jesus quite certainly did not wish to redeem mankind. An impressionistic character-sketch a la Adolf Holl gives us something to think about, but does not lead to a Jesus of flesh and blood. Our look at Thomas Münzer gives form to a Messianic being, but probably the wrong form. Jesus, if we are to get any picture of him at all, must be seen in the apocalyptic climate of his Jewish period. Just as in the books of Daniel and Enoch, an oracle-text grows out of the dreadful days of Antiochus IV Epiphanes which is later mixed in with the so-called *Assumptio Mosis* to make an apocalyptic fantasy that can be placed about the year 10 of the present era.[114]

We hear of a person known as Taxon, which can be roughly translated as "the organizer." This eschatological Taxon speaks to his sons:

> We will fast for three days, and then we will go to a cave in the desert and die there rather than transgress the commands of the Lord of Lords, of God our father. For if we do that and we die, then our blood will be smelt before the Lord . . . then his rule will appear over all his creatures, then the devil will come to an end and sorrow will be taken away with him.[115]

The apocalyptic Taxon, a Levite, is the last martyr. Through his martyrdom, and that of his seven sons, he completes the measure set by God of the sins of the fathers (Jesus, in Matthew 23:32: "Fill up, then, the measure of your fathers"), the last drop falls into the barrel, the measure overflows and God's intervention is set in motion.

It says in Enoch that "the number of righteousness" is near, which means that the predetermined number of martyrs who will have to die before vengeance comes is reckoned to have been nearly reached. (The same image occurs in the Christian Revelation of John, 6:11.) The martyr thus prepares the way for the kingdom of God, removing to some extent the last barrier in the way of the kingdom of God, which is already pressing in on us. By his death, the righteous man starts off the period of collective suffering; following the time of need comes the final time of salvation. It has to be supposed, of course, in the case of this Taxon that someone does demand that he transgress the commands of the Lord, something that no one ever required of Jesus. On the contrary, he seems to have approached the borders of Jewish legality spontaneously.

Did Jesus, then, want to sacrifice himself? Did he want to be the "last martyr"? We don't know. But he might well have had ideas similar to those of the organizer Taxon, inspired by the Apocalypse, even though he may not have spoken Hebrew or Greek and had never read the texts then presumably current among the sectarians. (Joachim Jeremias makes the plain suggestion that Jesus considered himself to be the last prophet of God, whose murder should make the measure of guilt set by God to overflow.)[116] The idea that, as the only begotten son of God, he wanted to die, and had to die for the redemption of mankind, is a thought that certainly stems from Hellenistic Christian theology, as we shall see. No Palestinian Jew of that period could have had such an idea, unless it were somone quite removed from normal human thinking who had in mind some superhuman works of salvation, the meaning of which we cannot comprehend even today.

Everyone who wants to know how Christianity grew out of the consequences of the death of Jesus must clearly come up against the obvious decision: was Jesus "a man and nothing but a man," as the Dortmund professor Hartmann[117] states, perhaps an "immeasurably great man," in Albert Schweitzer's words, the only man "who had the strength to conceive himself as the spiritual ruler of all mankind and to take the histories by storm"[118] — or was he a divine being?* Paul and the evangelists, with the partial exception of Mark, answered the questions unequivocally in the way it has been impressed on us for eighteen hundred years: however well the desirable human qualities might fit into the heavenly frame, Jesus was nonetheless a divine being from heaven. It will soon be fifty years since Rudolf Bultmann, a professing and practising theologian, pronounced his personal opinion that Jesus did not consider himself to be the Messiah.[120] Bultmann thereby erased the whole picture painted by the evangelists of what Jesus thought himself to be, and only white space remained, from which theology has been laboring ever since to build up a written page.

Bultmann had formulated his epoch-making declaration subjectively and cautiously. But recently it has become a passport to modern thought to declare with a trance-like certainty that Jesus was not interested at all in the claims to sovereignty made for him, and thought of himself neither as the Messiah, nor as the son of man, nor as the son of God, nor as a descendant of the house of King David. The Protestant Herbert Braun wrote in 1972 that it is certain that Jesus did not require his hearers to accept him as the Messiah, that probably "he did not think of himself in this way."[121] Naturally, both of these things are nothing less than certain, not merely probable. Hans Conzelmann declares, even more succinctly: "Certainly Jesus did not in fact think of himself as the Messiah."[122] Whence this oracular certainty? We don't know what Jesus thought himself to be; we never can and never shall know.

---

*In a poll organized in West Germany in 1967, 42 per cent thought that Jesus was the son of God and was resurrected from the dead, 39 per cent believed thar Jesus was only a great man, 15 per cent thought he had no significance and 3 per cent believed that he had never lived. Thus 57 per cent did not believe him to be God's risen son.[119]

The Catholic Joseph Blank, director of the Institute of Theology at the University of Saarbrücken, wrote in 1971: "The Gospels certainly stick to the fact, no doubt historically unexceptionable, that Jesus never applied the description of Messiah to himself."[123] "No doubt historically unexceptionable," when we know nothing about it? And how can anyone say that the evangelists did not consider him to have claimed to be the Messiah, when he did after all in Mark's Gospel charge the disciples that they should tell no man that he, Jesus, was the Messiah; when in Mark's Gospel he answered the high priest's question whether he was the Messiah, the Son of the Blessed One, with the words: "I am."

The *Wilckens Bible* is quite right to comment: it is the main theme in the Gospel from the start, the theme to which Matthew always brings his readers back, that Jesus is the Messiah."[124] Who would have had the faith in the church if it had had no more to offer nineteen hundred years ago than a just man unjustly executed? The theologians were to be feared when, dogmatically and with evil consequences for the doubter, they put forward the sovereign claims. But the clairvoyant certainty with which, in the light of circumstances no longer clearly perceived, they now hold the opposite to be proved does seem rather depressing. Joseph Blank even calls the various claims to sovereignty ascribed to Jesus in the Gospels the "surplus values" which gave Jesus more significance than other men,[125] and Stauffer again parades his marksmanship with the ingenious statement: "Jesus did not love the Messianic idea."[126] As the Jesuit convert George Tyrrell wrote in 1909, a "liberal use of the pruning-hook" has occurred.[127]

3. What he did not want

A theologian told me that everything
would be made easy and permitted to
me if I would only submit myself to the
Council, and he added: If the Council
said you only had one eye, even though
you had two, it would be your duty to
admit to the Council that this was so. I
answered him: Even if the whole world
said so, since I have my senses — as I
still have — I could not yield to them
without conscientious objection.[1]
—Jan Hus

"It would do no harm to my inmost religious convictions," said P.W. Schmeidel, New Testament scholar, in 1906, "if I had to convince myself today that Jesus never lived at all."[2] This thought calls for no divine or human person to bear witness to the spiritual development from the Old Testament to the New. Reading of, and research into, the Bible has only "the aim of making better men" (Kant). As Albert Schweitzer demands, the individual is left alone with the sayings of Jesus[3] — "above all his (Jesus') appeals for fellow-creatures who need help in different ways, by which I am affected" (Herbert Braun).[4]

If Jesus is only a religious fiction created out of the longings of his time, does that make any difference? If the first lessons of the Christian believers, the first conversion of the Graeco-Roman west, were dominated by foreign religious ideas streaming westward from the Orient, does that make any difference? Ethically and morally, it makes none.

It does make one difference, though, for such a faith no longer needs a church. It crosses out the creeds of both confessions. The person of Jesus then becomes a particularly memorable theme which stimulates the imagination. If we regard it as irrelevant whether or not he existed, then at the same time all that he personally did or said or taught becomes meaningless.

But even the opponents of this form of reasoning come to much the same conclusions. Martin Kähler wrote in 1892: "The true Christ is the Christ we preach. But the Christ we preach is the Christ we believe in."[5] It is not the historical Jesus, the man himself, who has had the historical effect, not the Jesus who preached and as he was believed in. The Jesus of history, "this uncertain remainder of the critical subtraction sums," must be looked for in his "works." "Works" here does not mean, as it does in Bultmann thirty years later, what Jesus wanted, but exactly the opposite, what has resulted from it without him and with regard to him.

If the disciples believed in Jesus and preached the recognition of this belief, then, to go along with Martin Kähler, "the true historic value" is to be sought in a "significant form," in the impact which that one man made through his life. What that one man wanted is not exactly known, only what men wanted him to want, what they could hope for by using his authority.

But now suppose the historical Jesus had actually "wanted" something quite different from what his disciples later thought, said and preached, though indeed, as described earlier, we have not handed down the thoughts, words or preaching of a single actual disciple. Suppose the thoughts of Jesus, as far as they can be traced, are not his thoughts at all but were put into his head by Paul and the evangelists.

The churches have always suppressed the distinction, sometimes with cavalier *panache*, sometimes with a hermit's carefulness. In support of their legitimatization, they call in the word of their "heavenly founder" though it cannot be denied that Jesus did not wish to found any church, and founded none; though the words of Jesus are without question sayings thought up for him after his death by the congregation. Here the bravest innovator must quail. And so we hear the words of Jesus echo from the chancels, words which not only are not his but which say the reverse of what he might have done and thought. (The heavily printed verses in the *Luther Bible* of 1964, on whch the existence of the churches rests, could well be proved to be post-Jesuanic throughout.)

The fewer the words of Jesus that can be traced back to him with any certainty, the more substantial becomes the difference between Jesus presented to us in the Gospels and the Christ figure of the Christian church. From the well-known images we receive from the Jewish apocalypse and from the texts of the Gospels, we can at least be sure that the Jesus presented to us by the churches and the theologians never lived.

The most significant, undenied and indeed undeniable fact of Paul's letters, and also of the synoptic Gospels, is that the early Christians expected the Lord to return soon, very soon. This goes back to the similar expectation of the Jesus figure in the Gospels, no less clearly proven: the kingdom of God (of heaven, of the Father) is at hand, or is already here. Naturally, we cannot make out afresh what Jesus really must have said and thought about it, only what the oldest available tradition available to us believes he said and thought. That is all the foundation we have. What the church has subsequently determined to endow the Christ figure with is of no importance whatever.

Joachim Jeremias, a leading and learned Protestant of the con- servatives — the school of thought that regards the Jesus figure as authentic — suggests how we are to envisage the expectation of the kingdom of God in association with the name and person of Jesus in the Gospels.[6] In his recently published work, *The Preaching of Jesus* (1971; the first part of a planned two-volume New Testament Theology), he gives new argument for how that expectation cannot be divorced from the role intended for Israel in God's plan of salvation, as seen by all religious viewpoints among the Palestinian Jews of that time.

"The attempt to sketch Jesus' picture of coming events," writes Jeremias, "must start from the fact that he was convinced that his mission was the prelude to the coming of the eschatological time of trial." The murder of God's last messenger, which he himself is, will make the measure of guilt set by God overflow. God's patience with the "prophet-murderers of Jerusalem" is exhausted. The hour of darkness has come. The generation now living will fill up the measure; they must atone for the guilt of all Israel.

God will desert his temple; the "abomination of desolation," the "pseudo-Christ" will appear. He reveals himself in holiness and is glorified by false prophets. But his time is limited. At last the temple will fall in ruins, no stone will remain upon another. Within three days — this short time is not to be taken too literally — a new temple will arise. Only he who does not succumb to the attack will be saved: therefore, fly from the place of danger, for no man knows whether he will withstand the onslaught.

The kingdom of God comes amid terrible suffering, but this is only the prelude. The angels of God execute the judgment; the final, flaming hell (Aramaic *gehinnam,* Hebrew *gehinnom,* Greek γέεννα) opens its throat. Its place is the valley of the same name, south and west of Jerusalem. It gathers not only the souls for whom it is to serve until the last days as Hades, but also swallows the souls and bodies of the godless forever. Originally a place of dreadful cold and darkness (weeping and gnashing of teeth), fire soon joins forces with it: the judgment, following the pictures in Enoch, takes place "in darkness, chains and blazing flames." Jeremias soothes us: "Only Jesus will have authority to give expression to the fearful severity of God's judgment; there is no appeal against his sentence." Many (that is, all) are called to the Redemption, but only a few are saved. The call is infinite, but those who do not follow him risk their salvation for ever.

Existence in past ages under the conditions which formerly reigned does not deserve the name of "life." Outside the kingdom now beginning there will be nothing but death and the dead. Jesus, Jeremias believes, sees in the approaching catastrophe not a national disaster in the distant future, like the fall of Jerusalem in 70, but a danger that threatens his hearers here and now. Destruction hovers over them. All prayer about the coming of the kingdom "has as its theme the intervention of God very soon, not after thirty or forty years." Soon the roles will be exchanged, and those who now sit in judgment on Jesus will stand before his seat of justice. God can even — Jeremias praises this as unexampled — relax his holy will and shorten the period of trial of his own people; he can lengthen the sentence on the infidels.

The preaching of such an urgent program is naturally confined to the lost sheep of the house of Israel. The disciplines are not to take it to the Gentiles and the Samaritans. The world is at present under the rule of the devil; malice triumphs. Jesus is gathering the people of God to lead them into the kingdom on the last day. Only a remnant will be saved, the "holy remnant" whom Paul calls "the remnant chosen by grace" (Romans 11:6). The salvation of each is determined in obedience to the word of Jesus, but the disciples too will judge (that is, rule).

Few indeed will be chosen, but those few may be sure of becoming the children of God, of a share in the coming happiness, through Jesus. Their father has prepared power for them, a happiness beyond all imagination.

"And the kingdom and the dominion
and the greatness of the kingdoms under the whole heaven
shall be given to the people of the saints of the Most High;
their kingdom shall be an everlasting kingdom
and all dominions shall serve and obey them. (Daniel 7:27.)

Israel shall rule, represented by its saints. The rule of God and the rule of the heathen over Israel are an intolerable contradiction. The eternal sovereignty of God rests in his being king over Israel. True, he created all the other peoples, but they have once more rejected the covenant with God offered them on Sinai; only Israel has submitted to him and since then God has been Israel's king.

What part is Jesus himself expected to play in the events of the last days? The secret relationship between his earthly appearance and the future son of man has been described: "He is not yet the son of man, but he will be raised up to become the son of man." As such he appears, flying amid the clouds of heaven, appears on Mount Zion, hurls the kings and mighty ones from their thrones, seats himself on the throne and holds court. He destroys the armies of the enemy with the fiery breath of his mouth. Then he descends from the mountain and calls an army of peace to himself. He will be the support of the just and holy, the light of the peoples, the hope of the distressed. The righteous and the chosen people will eat with him and be his companions.

This Jesus, looking for the last days, as sketched in detail for us by Jeremias, is a narrow-minded visionary, imprisoned within the limitations of Jewish egocentricity; the apocalyptic promises with which Israel recoups itself for all its international and religious humiliations have gone to his head; he believes himself to be the future son of man and judge of the world. We observe two things: that he is not once mentioned in the history of his contemporaries, and that, in spite of this, he could become a little later the central figure of a primeval human dream, the dream of the return to the — also dreamed — primitive state, to the mother's womb, to Paradise.

Perhaps it is no accident that not one of the followers of Jesus who knew him in his lifetime left any personal account of himself after his death. There is not a line about any one of them. With the exception of the quite indefinable Peter, who is presumably indispensable as the figurehead of the tradition, they remain pale shadows of a melancholy bankruptcy. Anyone who believed in Christ during his lifetime must have received a jolt to his life, and must certainly have had trouble in reaching an accommodation with the newcomers who never knew Jesus in the flesh. None of the bold fantasies of the living Jesus had come true; he himself had been executed or otherwise killed; life went on. We are entitled to be genuinely curious about the skill with which present-day theology has dealt with the problem of presenting this Judaism-fixated, Gentile-subduing Jesus, this Jesus in the Jewish tradition promising the near end of the world, as author of a worldwide Christian mission, bringer of a timeless ethic and a contemporary religious impulse; of turning the shattered redeemer of the orthodox Jews into the savior of a community that tramples the Jews in the dust.

We read the relevant evidence not without a certain perplexity, because it is all so diligently sewn together and because, despite the most careful needlework, faulty seams still show between the Jewish Jesus and the Christian faith. The genesis of an error of monstrous proportions can be descried. Initially, indeed, it was not only a question of whether Jesus was raised from the dead and whether his death had thus been converted into a victory. Much more, the resurrection was the start of the events of the last days (this is Ulrich Wilckens, born 1928)[7]; it was the "definite beginning of the final happenings," "the beginning of God's last acts, that lie just ahead of us," and soon "the final events, already begun, would overtake the entire cosmos." The original Palestinian community saw in the resurrection "the conclusive confirmation of Jesus' unique revelation of himself through God" — the confirmation of a self-revelation, as contemporary theology increasingly accepts, that was dictated to Jesus retrospectively by this very community.

Those who believed that Jesus had risen again believed also, like the rest of the world up to that time, that the world would soon come to an end. Only in the light of this second self-deception can the first be explained. The cosmic final acts were no more to be observed now than they had been before the triumph of the earthly Jesus. The disciples "understood" thereby, says the Franciscan father Gerhard Dautzenberg, born 1934 (in *Rabbi J.*, his rejoinder to Johannes Lehmann's *Report on Jesus*),[8] that his resurrection "was already associated with the coming of the kingdom, that, having risen, he would be the Messianic ruler." So "his rule" (his purely imaginary rule, notable only for its absence) was also to have been extended beyond the national borders of the Jews (it had been promised, remember, that he would return immediately and for ever).

Now hear Josef Blank, born 1926, progressive Catholic university lecturer[9]: Jesus had latched on to the ideas of the eschatological expectation of an early coming "in a purely superficial way." He was "already realizing the kingdom of God for his own period in his works." Jesus interpreted (notice the vagueness of the phrasing) "the salvation to come in such a way that, out of the future, it already affected men in this world. In a final, radical way Jesus was putting into effect the expectation of the future, that God desired the salvation of his people and of history, and therefore required men to live out their lives at that time in the light of presence of the heavenly purpose of salvation, although against the appearance of existing circumstances." Clearly it was not Jesus interpreting here but the theologians, and in the face of a science — or conscience — better than theirs.

There is a useful tip in the book of Deuteronomy for prophets whose predictions are not fulfilled:

> When a prophet speaks in the name of the LORD, if the word does not come to pass or come true, that is a word which the LORD has not spoken; the prophet has spoken it presumptuously, you need not be afraid of him (18:22).

Nothing had come out of what Jesus had spoken in the name of the Lord; it had not come true. So the importance of Jesus is not now "primarily for his promises of the future" but for his announcement of a fulfillment already present" (Blank). Easter, says Blank, the resurrection of the Lord, is "God's conclusive Yes."

84

Can God's conclusive Yes rely at the same time on the idea of the first Christians that Jesus had risen, and on the later idea that he would soon return to bring about the end of the world, to judge the whole world?

The confusion of ideas swims back and forth without a lifebelt: Easter is the evidence that "the fundamental secret of God" is bound up with the story of Jesus, "that this Jesus belongs so much at the side of God that from now on we can never think of the idea of God without the name of Jesus of Nazareth, and conversely that God is to be found for all time in the story of this man and therefore throughout the whole story of mankind." Those who do not agree may console themselves, says Blank, with the thought that they suffer from "superficial factual positivism."

Helmut Gollwitzer, born 1908, believes the words and acts of Jesus invite us to a life "that already expresses the joy of the kingdom of God." So it is no longer: "The kingdom of God is at hand," but: "Act as if it were already here." Jesus' apocalyptic message of judgment has become the "joyous message of happiness."[10] But this is not found in the scriptures. Indeed, in the Acts of the Apostles (17:31.), Paul says:

"because he has fixed a day on which he will judge the world in righteousness by a man whom he has appointed, and of this he has given assurance to all men by raising him from the dead." (17:31)

Discussion with churchmen is still difficult, especially with the avant-garde Protestants and most especially with their outrider, Herbert Braun. He holds that important parts of the teaching of Jesus retain their validity "even if the apocalyptic horizon sinks."[11] You are welcome to understand that if you like. The horizon of the last times, which will "bring the new state of the world" (says Herbert Braun), gives us a system of reference within which we can perhaps understand the events of Jesus' life; all the rest is conjecture. But certainly Braun, born in West Prussia in 1903, has set up an advanced position which his colleagues are still far from accepting. He surrenders the very heart of the Christian faith, the resurrection of Jesus ("a form of expression imposed by circumstances"). It is no longer a criterion of his faith that Jesus was the son of God. Those who suggest that he is thereby abandoning the Christian faith are well justified. For what remains, while it may be "true," is something that cannot be attributed to the teaching of Jesus without yet further distortion of the facts, namely: "The proper service of God is the service of man, of man in his need." Two thousand years in the church — for that!

The Franciscan Dautzenberg says that it should not even claim its foundation through the earthly Jesus and should be careful that such ideas are not nourished among the churchmen."[12] This opinion will surely find its way to Rome. His equally Catholic colleague Blank seconds him: "Jesus of Nazareth did not, of course, want to found a new religion." Jesus did not wish to preach an "eternal, timeless truth, but addressed himself immediately to the people of his own time."[13] Unfortunately we don't know what he said to them; we don't know what his views may have been.

"The Jesus affair goes further," Willi Marxsen, born 1919, persuades us. But we keep on asking what this affair of Jesus is. Marxsen says he gave out hope all his life long: "We see that the Jewish idea, which was focused on the future, was anticipated by him, and he already appeared as a son of man."[14] It could not be more vague, for how *does* a son of man appear? Karl Rahner, born 1904, probably the most important spirit among the Catholics today, sees in the resurrection "God's victorious promise of himself to the world."[15]

Hans Conzelmann, born 1915, has observed "that the eschatology of Jesus, the announcement of the nearness of the kingdom of God, is not consistent with the idea of an organized church." An illuminating remark, but at once it is dark again. Conzelmann states specifically why there has to be a church: "If the salvation of God in Jesus is declared valid, is offered as a present possibility even after his death, if the revelation is understood not as the teaching of lessons but as an actual event, then its continual live discussion in the course of preaching is a part of the revelation, and with it also the place where it is preached, the church visibly gathered together to hear."[16] Definition of a church: the place where the errors of previous generations of theologians are corrected.

According to Wolfhart Pannenberg, born 1928, the resurrection is "even historically, a questionable event."[17] But Conzelmann has signed this brilliant sentence: "The question of the historical truth of the resurrection must be excluded from theology as misleading."[18] Why must it? And why is it misleading? It leads directly to the heart of the matter. We learn from Dautzenberg that the existence of the church is "based on its association with the risen Christ".[19] Association with what Braun calls a "form of expression imposed by circumstances"? Why not simply get it clear that the church owes its existence to the urgent fantasies of men in need of consolation? That their reliance on the man Jesus is understandable but in no way justified?

For these are the probable facts: Jesus

° did not set out to call the sheep of the house of Israel, and us other sheep, to baptism; unlike John the Baptist, he did not baptize; he did not institute a supper ("folk legend from Hellenistic circles of the Pauline sphere," says Bultmann[20]); did not want to found a sacrament of marriage; did not decree monogamy;

° did not know in advance the stations of his passion — delivered to the Gentiles, mocked, spat upon, scourged, crucified — as the evangelists believe, required no one during his lifetime to take up his cross and follow him, did not prophesy that he would suffer and die and would rise again after three days, did not (says Bultmann) represent his passion and death as the will of God and necessary for salvation,[21] did not regard himself as omniscient nor declare himself to be omniscient (the science of theology has found for the foreknowledge of Jesus the splendid expression *vaticinium ex eventu*, prophecy of events *after* they have happened); the assertion of the incarnation of God would have been regarded by Jesus as blasphemous, so Karl Jaspers surmises;[22]

° did not forgive sins, and shared no heavenly power to forgive sins. Paul still knows nothing of this, the most powerful weapon of the early Christian church. By the time Mark's Gospel was written, the community already felt it worth while to trace their right to forgive sins back to Jesus;*

---

*The earliest instance in Mark (2:1-12) makes it quite clear that the interests of the community have been inserted into the story of a miracle. Four people let a man sick with palsy down through the roof on his bed to Jesus in the room below. At first he does not heal him, but when he sees *their* (the four men's) faith, he says: "Your sins are forgiven." In justification of his forgiveness of sin, Jesus then says: "Is it easier to say to this paralyzed man, 'Your sins are forgiven' or to say 'Stand up, take your bed and walk'?" Clearly, it is the forgiveness of sins that is easier. When he can actually heal, why should he not also be able to forgive sins, argues the evangelist. And so the man sick of the palsy is also healed.

° did not promise his disciples the coming and the support of the Holy Spirit; he had never heard of this Holy Spirit, still less that he himself and the Holy Spirit would in days to come be said to be constituent parts of a Holy Trinity. In the Hellenistic Gospel of John, the Spirit is introduced in the simplest possible way. Jesus says there: "It is for your good that I am leaving you. If I do not go, your Advocate will not come, whereas if I go, I will send him to you."

The descent of the Holy Spirit is described only by Luke, in the Acts of the Apostles. The legend is evidently adapted from a text in the prophet Joel, imaginatively re-written by Luke:

And it shall come to pass afterward,
that I will pour out my spirit on all flesh;
your sons and daughters shall prophesy,
your old men shall dream dreams,
and your young men shall see visions.
Even upon the menservants and maidservants
in those days, I will pour out my spirit. (2:28-29.)

The Holy Spirit had a long way to go before he arrived at an equal status in the Holy Trinity. Hans Conzelmann says that, in the prologue of John's Gospel, "the image of two gods" shines through.[23] The Logos of this Gospel, translated as "the Word," is the "Son" and not the Holy Spirit. It is interesting to observe that the Hellenistic Jewish philosopher Philo of Alexandria, one of the godfathers of the idea of the Logos, calls his own Logos on the one hand "the firstborn son of God," and also "the second God," yet on the other hand, he also describes him as the $\pi\alpha\rho\acute{\alpha}\kappa\lambda\eta\tau o\varsigma$, correctly translated as advocate, also as helper and comforter. The $\pi\alpha\rho\acute{\alpha}\kappa\lambda\eta\tau o\varsigma$ is in John's Gospel called the Spirit of Truth, whose coming is spoken of by Jesus. Uncertainty reigned about the theological meaning of this "Paraclete" up to the time of the council of Constantinople; then, for the first time, the Paraclete became holy, uncreated and an object of prayer.*

---

*Logos and Paraclete might be thought of as a concession to the need for polytheism, as well as a defense of the heavenly wisdom, regarded as female, the daughterly Sophia, who according to Jewish ideas was the first creation before the beginning of the world, the loved one by God's side. According to Conzelmann, she is the *Doppelgänger* of the Logos, or more accurately the forerunner — for in the Christian figuration she no longer appears, losing her substance partly to the Son and partly to the Holy Spirit.[24]

The legal support and the Holy Spirit coalesced to form the support of the Holy Spirit, and so the Spirit became the third of the Three in One. Countless men have gone to execution because they preferred to believe in a different number, or even no number, instead of this mythical, archaic, numerical hocus-pocus. The number three is blessed with much deadly significance.

Reduced to a denominator, Jesus wanted neither to found a church nor to be like God nor equal with God; what is more, he would have said about such presumption what, according to Mark (10:18) he perhaps actually did say (or, of course, perhaps did not say) when someone addressed him as "good master": "Why do you call me good? No one is good but God alone."*

Dautzenberg criticized Johannes Lehmann's *Report on Jesus* as being "journalistic and commercial."[25] But the Christian religion, too, like every relative truth or untruth, has spread commercially and journalistically. Whether the first lessons of its missionaries were "properly" written and checked — as the Sunday-paper theologian Zahrnt says without a hint of irony — or whether they were "given over to Hellenism,"[26] is a pretty ominous alternative. What is true of the Jesus of John's Gospel (Conzelmann: "He is the envoy, no more") is just as true of the important missionaries: the medium is the message.

Two factors determine the years in which the Christian religion was established: first, the world of Greek speech and ideas into which it was born and from which its witnesses came, and secondly, the man Paul. He who looked forward longingly to the end of all history is one of the truly great key figures of history. Like Marx and Freud, he is one of those spirits without whom history is unthinkable. If we ask ourselves who influenced history most powerfully, Caesar or Augustus or Saul of Tarsus, the question is just not worth answering.

---

*Or he might have said what the Jews said to him in John's Gospel (8:41), when he stressed his heavenly origin. They replied: "We were not born of fornication; we have one Father, even God." John's Jesus answered them (in that spirit of charity so favored by this evangelist): "You are of your father the devil, and your will is to do your father's desires." The father-son pattern has to be applied to the opposition as well.

This theology of the media was itself the message. Pauline Christianity, with its hostility to the body and its sense of sin, its predestination and its missionary zeal, is so characteristic that we just cannot imagine a non-Pauline Christianity. The less we can grasp of Jesus, the more formative becomes the man from Cilicia, in the south of present-day Turkey, even if we rely on those of his epistles which can be said with certainty to have been written by him.[28] In the whole of ancient literature you will not find such a storm of self-justification like that of Paul in Chapters 11-12 of his Second Letter to the Corinthians. When Paul protests that he has achieved more in his missionary work than all the other apostles (what, all together? — 1 Corinthians 15:10), we may take that quite literally. As Freud wrote, he was "a man with a gift for religion, in the truest sense of the phrase. Dark traces of the past lay in his soul, ready to break out into the regions of consciousness."[29]

For him, an historical Jesus remains amorphous. Paul seems to have been glad not to have known "Christ in the flesh." He uses the title of honor "the Anointed" as a given name or a surname according to the context.[30] He claims to have received his inspiration directly, never from anyone who knew Jesus; the Lord informed him of his opinions himself. Jesus' command to his disciples to go forth as missionaries ("Go out into all the world"), first made known in a relatively late version of the Gospels, Paul understood immediately after Jesus' death. He takes the absurdity by the scruff of the neck, forces the negative into reverse and draws up a theology of wreckage. Credo quia!

Whatever things were true, honest, just, pure, lovely, of good report, what was virtuous and honorable: all this was commonly accepted without the teaching of Christ, says Conzelmann with his eyes on Paul. "Christians are not in dispute with Jews about lifestyle but about whether Jesus was the Messiah."[31] Paul — Shaw calls him "more Jewish than the Jews, more Roman than the Romans"[32] — adapts the Jewish Messiah to the circumstances of the Roman Empire; he carries him over the river as Saint Christopher carried the Christ-child.

We don't, of course, know what it was that suddenly struck him. But it is quite credible that he, a young man of perhaps twenty to thirty years old, was venting his hate on the early Christians in the land of the Jews because he himself was pregnant with a new theology, but still did not know to whom to attach it. Before his eyes, there hovered a son of heaven, replete with powerful qualities but still without reality on the human level. That there had been this Somebody, and that he need no longer be in dispute with him — this blissful realization came as a sudden shock of enlightenment to him. What a good thing he did not know the object of his new life. For him, the only good Jesus was a dead Jesus.

Jesus was now not a man to him: he had simply, as it were, entered into the outward form of a man. He who enjoyed the divine nature had stripped himself of it to assume the nature of a slave (Philippians 2:6-7), was sent by God in a form like that of our own sinful nature (Romans 8:3), became poor although he had been rich (2 Corinthians 8:9), came from heaven (1 Corinthians 15:47). It was "early Christian conviction," says Wilckens, that "Christ was with God in heaven before his birth."[33] It is Paul who defined and developed, even if he did not lay down, this early Christian conviction.

According to 1 Corinthians 10:4, Christ travelled with the Israelites through the desert as a rock, a somewhat idiosyncratic interpretation of the book of Exodus, in which the rock on Mount Horeb from which Moses struck drinking water is a stationary one. Christ was the holy rock from which the Israelites drank. Like the ancient Jewish "wisdom of God," Christ worked on and in Israel invisibly and successfully before his incarnation.

Christ was born "under the law" (Galatians 4:4); this is a key clause in Pauline theology. For he freed all Jews, and all men, and especially Paul, from the "curse of the law" (Galatians 3:13). If we consider how Paul strove for thirty years to get rid of the law of Moses, we cannot conclude that Paul was only trying to drag it from its pedestal because it so obviously stood in the way of the spread of the Gospel. Paul's own ideas are also in question here. Paul seems to have suffered unspeakably from the law and the impossibility of satisfying its six hundred and thirteen precepts and prohibitions. More than anything, he wanted to abolish the law, rather than set it aside. To break free from the law and its prescriptions, he was prepared to run the risk that everyone would misunderstand him, as if he had abolished all the ethics and morals to which in fact he clung more than most.

The law, Paul says, is a curse. On the one hand, it distracts people from recognition of the existence of sin — mankind loses the innocence of ignorance — while on the other, it opens up no way out from sinfulness. You can have all of it or none. Applied to life, it brings the sinners eternal death. No mortal can be justified by keeping the law; no man can fulfill it. But the law is a dying conception of this fleshly world. It belongs to the exhausted forms of government of this world, which have served their purpose. The law is like a rich man's slave put in charge of the growing boys; it has no function when they reach their majority. Those who are under the law are sons of the maidservant and not free. They cannot inherit the kingdom of Christ.

Admittedly, the law was also the condition for Israel's existence. But Israel too is a dying conception. In Christ, the law has been fulfilled. Christ has abolished the law. Christ by his death has delivered Paul personally from the curse of the law. Paul ceases to observe the law. Read only the sad perplexity that comes over him when he realizes that communities he has founded in the Gentile countries have accepted the Jewish calendar and no doubt other things as well: "You observe days, and months, and seasons and years! I am afraid I have labored over you in vain." (Galatians 4:10-11). For how can a non-Jew look forward to the new age — Paul "presses towards it" like a competitor in the arena (Philippians 3:14) — and still voluntarily accept the old calendar, the old unfulfillable rules, the thousand unpleasantnesses of the old law from which, thanks to Christ, man has escaped? At a time when the dawning of the utterly new is but a breath away, how can anyone want to bring back all the old nonsense that divides Jews and Gentiles, instead of fusing both together in readiness for the Day of Judgment? He, the Jew, had broken through the egocentricity of the people of Jerusalem and gained the open field. How could non-Jews want to return to the old captivity?

At first, Paul had believed the return of the Lord to be so near at hand that his preaching had not taken into account the idea of an earlier death; see his first letter to the congregation of Thessalonica (4:13-18). Later, he assures the Corinthians (1 Corinthians 15:51-52): "We shall not all sleep, but we shall all be changed, in the twinkling of an eye, at the last trumpet." It is those who go to sleep as Christians who will be awakened.

The Hellenistic world understood by life after death the continuation of the soul with no material body. The idea of the resurrection of the body was strange to most non-Jews, as it was to the old Israelites. In Jesus' time, it was still denied by the Sadducees, the ruling party in the temple. Paul inherited it from the Pharisees and linked it with his son of heaven. Christ is the "firstborn of the dead" (letter to the congregation in Colossae, in Phrygia, possibly not all written by Paul). Paul concludes from Jesus' resurrection, "for reasons of pastoral-theological considerations" (Wilckens),[34] that God will awaken those who have already fallen asleep as Christians. He assures the Thessalonians (1 Thessalonians 4:14) that "through Jesus, god will bring with him those who have fallen asleep." All? By what criterion? That is still obscure. Paul, like many Jews and Christians, is a believer in predestination. God shows mercy as he chooses but also makes men stubborn as he chooses (Romans 9:18). God rules over "vessels of wrath," those who are objects of retribution due for destruction, and "vessels of mercy," who from the first have been prepared for this splendor (Romans 9:22-23).

Paul takes all that for granted. But he is also an inveterate moralist, as he shows in his second letter to the Corinthians (5:10): "For we must all appear before the judgment seat of Christ, so that each one may receive good or evil, according to what he has done in the body." When must we appear, the moment we die or not until the general resurrection? Paul sheds no light on this. He himself, as paladin, presumably goes up to the Lord immediately.

Theologically, a man can only be justified by faith in Christ; but a life displeasing to God can get a man into serious, if transitory, difficulties. It seems there is someone among the Corinthian community living with his father's wife. We are not told whether she had been divorced, or had run away, or whether she simply was a widow. Paul (1 Corinthians 5:5) says "you are to deliver this man to Satan for the destruction of the flesh, that his spirit may be saved in the day of the Lord Jesus." Hardly a message of blessing. Root out the wicked from among you, Paul exhorts them, and now we hear clearly enough that he is not speaking in the spirit of his Lord Jesus Christ. Obviously Paul is now counting on the early death of those cursed in this way. At the last judgment, then, would the good or bad deeds judged be only deeds of faith, and not wicked conduct — unchastity perhaps? Here again, Paul sheds no light.

Of course he was bound to be attacked by his Jewish adversaries, Christians as well as non-Christians, on the grounds that he condoned immorality in abolishing the yoke of the law. But how wide of the mark was the reproach levelled at Paul! In the delights of the third heaven, of which he gives us an account, the lusts of the flesh seem to have had no part. He gives a lot of advice on good living but never once claims to be speaking from his own experience ("I wish that all were as I myself am" 1 Corinthians 7:7). Or is he perhaps referring to evil desires when he writes that "a thorn was given me in the flesh, a messenger of Satan, to harass me, to keep me from being too elated" (2 Corinthians 12:7)?

Very few experts would agree with that.[35] He calls his Jewish Christian opponents, to show his scorn for them, the "people of mutilation," the castrators, banking on the ignorance and prejudice of the Greeks against the Jews. (The (German) *Mustard Seed Bible* is shy and always speaks of "false circumcision.") ·

The world of Paul, like that of John later, is fallen creation. The material is bad, the spirit is good, but only the spirit of God; he would like to see the arts of reason ($\lambda o\gamma\iota\sigma\mu o\iota$) and the wisdom of this world destroyed. The earthly state, the flesh, must be overcome, and woman is the embodiment of this earthly state. Although, according to Galatians 3:28, man and wife are "all one in Christ Jesus," Paul permanently established the inferior status of the wife. She belongs to the husband, to put it a little unkindly; she is "his own vessel," to be held holy and in honor. (The *Mustard Seed Bible* plays that a bit too hard: its translation reads that the man should "seek to prevail over his wife in holiness and propriety" — 1 Thessalonians 4:4). Anyone who does not yet have a wife should not look for one; it is no longer worth the trouble. True, marriage is no sin, but one runs a risk of troubles in the future, troubles against which he, Paul, must gladly have warned the congregation.

Though Paul still expected to experience the coming of his Lord, he had already found his first excuse to continue to act as if:—.

The appointed time has grown very short; from now on, let those who have wives live as though they had none, and those who mourn as though they were not mourning, and those who rejoice as though they were not rejoicing, and those who buy as though they had no goods, and those who deal with the world as though they had no dealings with it. For the form of this world is passing away. (1 Corinthians 7:29-31)

From this first "as if" of Paul's there grew the church's final "as if": Act as if only a short time was left. Act as if the existence of the world was passing away. This second "as if" is a rattdifficult one with which to conform.

Christianity rose like a three-stage rocket, each stage an explosive error: first, the error of Jesus that the last days of the Jews had come, then the error of his apostles that he had risen again, and finally the error of Paul and the synoptic Gospels that he would soon return and judge all men. No other dogmas presented such massive errors, yet they were allowed time to transform themselves quite quickly into contradictory illusions.

We do not know how Paul died, [36] though the death of his opponent James is on record in Jerusalem in the year 62.[37] From the few lines we have describing this "brother of the Lord," and from the tradition we have of him we get the picture of a highly persuasive and unwavering man. At some time, though we do not find it in the Acts of the Apostles, he must have replaced the not very clearly defined, or all too clearly defined, Peter, who then disappears into legend. James seems to have regarded it as his life's work to keep the law of Moses and to represent his brother Jesus as one who had kept that law.

James seeks to preserve circumcision, "the passport (*Ausweis*) to absolute religious preference above all other peoples" (Wilckens);[38] but people like him, especially when they try to extend their influence outside Israel, are called "dogs" by Paul, "evil workers" and "castrators" (Philippians 3:2), even "lying apostles" (2 Corinthians 11:13).* Paul watches over the purity of

---

*Paul hates the Jews sometimes, as we can see from his first letter to the congregation in Thessalonica, where the Jews assailed him violently — as the *Jerusalem Bible* puts it, "with embittered fury":

> These also killed the Lord Jesus and the prophets and drove us out; the Jews who are heedless of God's word and enemies of their fellow-men, hindering us from speaking to the Gentiles to lead them to salvation. All this time they have been making up the full measure of their guilt, and now retribution has overtaken them for good and all. (2:15-16)

To many Bible commentators (including Wilckens) this passage seems so hostile that they doubt whether Paul really wrote it.[39]

the congregations he founded, such as that in Corinth, like a father over his daughter's virginity, as he says in his second letter to the Corinthians (2 Corinthians 11:2). This was not entirely possible when even Barnabas, Paul's ally during the debates between the Jewish Christians and the Gentile Christians in Jerusalem, when even this leader of the Christians in Antioch had accepted and submitted to James' wish that Jewish and Gentile Christians, although bound to one another in the faith, should live apart from one another; which shows how great James' authority was. One gets the feeling that Christianity might never have existed if Paul and the other Gentile apostles had agreed to stick to circumcision and James' other principles. Neither Paul nor James is prepared to say what attitude the earthly Jesus would have taken. Maybe it was all one to them. Jesus has already become the object of this controversy rather than its inspiring subject. On a higher level, each of them had some right on his side: Paul against James in his view that Jesus was not a fanatical follower of the ancient religious scriptures, and James against Paul in his acceptance that his brother Jesus was not the son of heaven, existing since the beginning of the world, but a man chosen by God, a new type of Messiah. James, who had not been among the disciples during Jesus' lifetime, would naturally find it hard to think of him accompanying the Israelites on their flight out of Egypt in the form of a holy rock, of his being pre-existent before his earthly birth by his heavenly Father.

After the destruction of Jerusalem, which James did not live to see, his congregation was dispersed. The "Ebionim," the "poor," who are gathered as a Jewish Christian sect in the land east of Jordan, regard Jesus not as the pre-existent son of God but as a prophet and Messiah; they reject the cult of Mary. Such "radical circles among the Jewish Christians of Palestine" (Jeremias)[40] deny to Peter the "protophania," the first appearance of the risen Lord. Paul mentions James in his list (1 Corinthians 15:7) as at least the second-named witness of the resurrection. In the four Gospels, however, and in the Acts of the Apostles, this Easter appearance to James is not mentioned. What a lot of wrangling there has been over these mutually competing catalogues! The Gospel of Thomas, in which we can follow a Jewish Christian trail back to the beginnings of Christianity, contains as Logion 12: "The disciples said to Jesus: We know that you will go from us. Which of us then shall be the greatest among us? Jesus said to them:

96

When that time comes, you will go to James the Just, for whose sake heaven and earth were made." The Ebionites were numbered among the heretics as early as about 200 C.E. We can only wonder whether the church founded in the name of the living Jesus might not have brought down the heretics' ban on him a great deal more quickly.

It is certainly not by chance that the Ebionites with their Jewish Chosen stayed in one place as an insignificant sect, whereas Paul, Hellenistically minded and literate in Greek, was able to get a foothold almost everywhere with his heavenly son of God. Of course, Paul did not "destroy" Christianity, nor did he "hand it over to Hellenism." It was rather that something whose begetting is still obscure was settled in him and in the Hellenistic language and culture. The redeeming death of Christ, an event he at once expressed theologically, was adapted by him for the Greeks and those who spoke Greek and thought as Greeks, and his theology grew from their ability to understand.

The religious lessons of missionaries are highly informative in feedback, in their constant reaction against the opposition to their dissemination. Sacraments dictated by Jesus created themselves spontaneously as it were; most significantly, next to the forgiveness of sins, that of the Eucharist, which brought to life again in a sensual-symbolic way archaic customs in which a man may have eaten (murdered?) his father in order to receive a share of his strength (to reconcile himself with him?).[41] It was logical that Jesus in the flesh should remain in the picture.

This mysterious sacrament was Hellenistic. But even the Gospels, written long after Paul, reached us written not in Aramaic but in Greek, the language "which at that period of Graeco-Roman history was normally used for letters, business and other everyday affairs" (Millar Burrows).[42] None of the four editors-in-chief seems to be at home with the orthodox ritual of the Jews. Even the Gospels, despite their Jewish origin, are filled with Hellenistic influence. The Jesus portrayed in the Gospels is already exalted in such a way that he was bound to rise directly to become a partner and co-ruler with God.

Under the influence of the gnosis which had flooded in from the East over the whole inhabited world, including Palestine, the man Jesus, who was not raised up to be the son of God until his resurrection, as even James may perhaps have believed, became the son of God from the beginning of time. Daemonic forces, the "powers of this age" (1 Corinthians 2:8), rule the world. Godhead is something entirely unwordly, something that belongs to the other side. The redeemer comes down as a stranger, unknown to the powerful ones of the world; he deceives the rulers and finds out the souls of light, who, like him, are strangers. He brings heavenly food for the hungry, is doctor for the sick, and leads the lonely soul through the hostile spheres back into the world of heaven. Thus, theologically minded persons as different as Paul and John the Evangelist are irresistibly attracted in equal measure by this hope of surrender of the world to chaos, hope of its utter decline, by the gnostic ideas of revelation and redemption.

The first man, who fell from the kingdom of light into darkness and chaos, is redeemed and led back by a second primal man to his place of origin. (Paul calls Christ the "second man," the "last Adam.") The first Adam is of the earth, earthy; "the second man is from heaven" (1 Corinthians 15:47). Paul's son of heaven had to suffer and die for everybody, Jews and Gentiles.

A man can be God, and God is willing to be a man. This was something new to the Jews, but not to the far more numerous Gentiles. The idea of a dying god was as current among them as the man who is united with him in the mysteries. "Not only," says Bultmann, "do the heathen mysteries know the conception of the dying god of redemption, but the heathen-gnostic mythology above all knows the idea of a pre-existent heavenly being who, in obedience to his father's will, puts on this world's clothing and takes poverty and want, hatred and persecution upon himself in order to lead his people along the path to the heavenly world."[43]

All the mystery-gods of the Hellenistic world are gods who suffer. The mystery cults regarded with suspicion by the Roman state as early as the second century B.C.E.,[44] continue in the form of the sacraments of the Christian religion. The dreadful punishments of hell were lovingly drawn up, not by the Jewish apocalyptic writers, let alone the early Christians, but by the Orphics, that movement traceable in Greece as long ago as the fifth century B.C.E.: their consecration, their calling to repentance, and their ascetic rules of life had as their goal a happy lot on the other side. It was not the Christians who first began fishing in the hereafter.

So the Christian religion, freed from the fetters of the law, shaped itself in the forge of countless religiosities. Bornkamm is not surprised that Graeco-Jewish religion occupied "most of the room" in the early church's teaching, "that the real Christian message can therefore remarkably recede"[45], or, to put it more plainly, that it does remarkably recede. What seems to us to be the central theme of Christianity, the conscience, is a non-Christian, pre-Christian acquisition. It is not to be found in the Gospels; Paul (Romans 2:15) took it over as a "non-Christian tradition taught already" (Bornkamm):[46] the tiresome, incorruptible, unsilenceable knower of all human deeds. Paul speaks (Romans 2:15) of the conscience and the thoughts of the non-Jews, "which argue the case among themselves, accusing and even defending them."

Seneca, Nero's tutor, recommended a searching of the conscience every evening.[47] Philo, the Jewish Hellenist, sees in the name of conscience God's own word sent into the souls of men.[48] The ancient Jewish culture could not conceive of the conscience: it would cut down God's judicial sovereignty and freedom to grant mercy. The Gospels speak of reward and punishment, but not of conscience. "Most emphatically," declares Günther Bornkamm, "the New Testament does not know the idea of the good deed which brings its own reward. Why not? Simply for this reason, that God is present and he cannot resign his judicial office to anyone else."[49]

Corresponding with the "suffering God" of the mysteries are the "suffering just men," a theme of the sages' teaching even before the death of Socrates. "The just man," writes Plato, Socrates' pupil, "is scourged, tortured, bound, blinded with fire, and when he has suffered every misery is finally strung up * on the cross."[50]

In the *Book Of Wisdom*, by an Alexandrian author of the first century B.C.E., the godless rise up and plan their impious assaults. "Let us, " says the book (2:12-20), "lie in wait for the just man, for he troubles us. He opposes our actions; he accuses us of violation of the law. . . He boasts that he has knowledge of God and calls himself a child of the Lord. . . he dares to call God his father. Let us just see whether what he says is true; let us try what sort of an end he will make. For if he is the true son of God, then God will take him to himself and deliver him from the hand of his

---

* Other possible translations: "impaled," "hung," "nailed," "beaten."

adversary. We will test him with insults and with mishandling, so that we can find out about his gentleness and try his patience. We will condemn him to a degrading death. . . " Who would not think here of the accounts of the Passion in the Gospels?

The just man is tried by God like gold in the furnace, and is accepted as a sacrifice. And when God visits the just, they are transfigured and fly up like sparks in the stubble. They judge the heathen and rule over the peoples. What fools we should be if we considered the just man's life to be mad and his end without honor! For now he is numbered among God's children, and his inheritance is among the blessed.

If we suppose that Jesus wanted to relate all these ideas to himself and to carry them out himself, we shall go a bit crazy: the figure will crumble into dust and blow away. But it is different if we try to project ourselves back into the period when Paul (on the instructions of the High Priest Caiaphas, if the Acts of the Apostles can be believed) was persecuting the disciples of the dead Jesus. Jesus had been killed without any great public commotion. The frustration of his— few — many? — followers may have been so tremendous that most of them recanted. But a few gathered together, heard the allusions of the women to the event, had visions, and told their friends — pen-friends perhaps — of their experiences, and their friends gave them a helping hand. Only in the brotherhood of like-minded spirits could the shock of the disaster they had experienced work itself out fully.

They were ashamed now of those weeks and months after his death, when they had thought his life crazy (see the passage in Mark 3:21 about Jesus' family) and his death dishonorable. Now indeed, they may have looked into the scriptures and found what they wanted there, and sought for what they wanted to find: an account, partly in code, partly in plain language, of the life and passion of their Lord. There was the pattern. They had only to take it up again and proceed with the weaving of their fantasy.

True, there was nothing in the Jewish tradition about a resurrected Messiah, only the resurrection of all men for the Last Judgment. But the Jewish tradition also had nothing about a crucified Messiah, so it had to be adapted. It was indisputable that a man chosen by God could "return," like Elijah or Enoch, even if one helped a bit by having him first, not dead, but "carried up into heaven." This man had died; so the scripture had to be adapted again. But how does the somewhat incomprehensible phrase "descended into hell"[51] find itself in the Christian creed? How did Jesus get into the underworld between his death and his resurrection? Did he go there as a dead man, or as a prophet?

There is a previous example. Enoch, that proto-Dante, tells practically at the beginning of his wonderful exploits that he was empowered by God as the "writer of justice" to make known God's sentence to the fallen angels, that they should know no peace for all eternity. "Angelology," the science of angels, is essentially indebted to the book of Enoch. What fallen angels were these, condemned to stay in one place, desolate and dreadful, until the day of their final annihilation? Taught by Enoch, the New Testament tells us of one.

According to the Second Letter of Peter (2:4) "God cast them into hell and committed them to pits of nether gloom to be kept until the judgment."* According to Peter's first letter (3:9) Christ must preach to them in their captivity, and the eternal condemnation described by Enoch is changed into a sign of redemption. (It is not denied that the descent of Jesus into Hell also fulfills an ancient myth. When the Babylonian fertility and mother goddess Ishtar goes down to Hell to bring back her beloved, Tammuz, the god of vegetation, from the kingdom of the dead, all fertility ceases until she comes up again.)

* What crime had they committed? In Genesis (6:14), they do not appear as traitors, but quite impartially as the sons of God, who courted human women, and one wonders why the flood has to break in at this point. Enoch gives us a more logical version. By his account, two angels had treacherously left God's heavenly capital to have intercourse with the daughters of men, whose beauty had inflamed them. By this act they defiled themselves and begot giants 3,000 ells long, They taught men all manner of secrets, including the painting of the eyelids with cosmetics, so that much godlessness and sin came into the world. The book of Genesis suppresses this fall of the angels from God because it conflicts with the story of the fall of Adam and Eve. The sons of the angels and the daughters of men, who Enoch says consume the produce of mankind and mankind itself, are called in Genesis the "heroes of old, men of renown." According to Enoch, God sends the great flood to bring to an end the abominations that have arisen from the fall of the angels.

We are always being told that the evangelists do not set out to give us a factual historical account but to propagate the teaching of their faith; and that is literally true. Indeed, the "fact" of the resurrection, always so described by theologians of every persuasion, arises from a classical defence mechanism: events must be undone, denied, changed to the opposite. There was a path leading from the crippling melancholy that had made the "I" poor and empty, and it restored healing, understanding and value: The disaster must be only apparent, unreal; Jesus must not have died. These things must not be, too, if we read the scripture of the fathers rightly, such as the Psalmist:

> For thou doest not give me up to Sheol,
> or let thy godly one see the Pit. (16:10)

Or still more clearly from the prophet Hosea:

> Come, let us return to the LORD
> for he has torn, that he may heal us;
> he has stricken, and he will bind us up.
> After two days he will revive us;
> on the third day he will raise us up,
> that we may live before him. (6:1-2)

Had Jesus not himself prophesied that he must suffer and die and would rise again on the third day? For that, too, appropriate passages were found in the scriptures of the fathers; they were so thoroughly edited that Rudolf Otto found the relative tradition of the Gospels "strong and sure as diamond."[52] The "third day" reflects ancient ideas by which the souls of the dead lie three days near the grave before vanishing into the heavens.[53] Matthew (12:40) makes Jesus prophesy that the son of man must be "three days and three nights in the heart of the earth," just as Jonah was three days and three nights in the fish's belly. (The story of Jonah is an ancient myth; the three days could just as well have been borrowed from the resurrection story of the cult-god Attis. In any case, the three days and nights are not corroborated by the Easter stories, according to which Jesus would not have been in the grave more than a day and a half.)

The Gospels actually make a point of declaring signs and wonders to be superfluous. Anyone who can be brought to believe only by signs and wonders has a minimal faith. And yet a contrary tendency can be discerned. As the date of composition of the Gospels grows later, we find they report the miracles with greater emphasis, culminating in the story in John's Gospel in which a four-day-old corpse, already "stinking" (11:39), is brought back to life. And this from the very evangelist who tells us: "Blessed are they who have not seen and yet believe" (20:29). "Mere miracles," comments Ulrich Wilckens, are "in truth" a means of shutting oneself off from Jesus.[54] But, in truth, the church is founded on mere miracles. David Friedrich Strauss indeed maintained that without faith in the resurrection, "a Christian community could hardly have been got together."[55] Without the resurrection of Jesus, this miracle of miracles, there would have been no church and no Christianity.

The evangelists, especially Matthew, make us share in the process of working backwards from newly activated prophecies; they quote the old texts from their Greek prototypes and never bother about accuracy. "The coastlands wait for his law" says a verse in Isaiah (42:4) about the servant whom God chose for himself and on whom his favor rests. From this, Matthew produces (12:21): "and in his name will the Gentiles hope." The book of the prophet Isaiah was a great storehouse; so was that of Zechariah. The vicarious death of the innocent for the guilty is a "ransom" (Mark 10:45; Matthew 20:28) and a "sacrifice for the countless hosts of the lost" (Joachim Jeremias) — notwithstanding the doctrine, also propagated in the Gospels, that only a "holy remnant" will be saved at the imminent Last Judgment.

"The word of God is in the Bible," Karl Barth has told us again and again, with great emphasis.[57] But it is interesting to know how God's word got into the Bible. If, as Barth and Bultmann say, God's word asks us only whether or not we wish to believe it, then we should not want to accept this conglomerate of worn-out wishes, fears, prejudices and idiosyncrasies as being without question the sole and exclusive last word of God and the Holy Spirit. How do even Barth and Bultmann know which word of God had ever asked us this? Has this been revealed to their sensorium? We have never heard that the Protestant churches have disavowed the Trinity, that heavenly Triumvirate, even though the Holy Spirit only achieved promotion to the third godhead by a parliamentary trick when he coolly took advantage of his privileged position as inspirer of the Catholic Councils. It was not until 381 that he finally succeeded; all the same, it took him 1,500 years to reward the Pope with infallibility.

At Christmas 1572, in the market place at Heidelberg, Johannes Silvanus, the superintendent of Ladenburg, was beheaded in the name of the Holy Spirit and in the shadow of the Church of the Holy Ghost. He had disputed that "the one God is in three persons." [58] To this day, the Jesuit Father Karl Rahner calls everyone a heretic who does not believe in the Holy Trinity. The Trinity nmay be a matter of indifference to us, but it cannot be a matter of indifference that with the help of the Trinity an authority has been set up which, for example, forbids the use of the pill and so aggravates famines.

What would Jesus have thought in his lifetime, Father Rahner, if someone had read out to him the 1870 definition of infallibility? Rahner[59] has asked this question himself, and has also answered it: "Jesus would probably only have been puzzled and would not have understood it at all." That sounds clear enough, but with this voluble theologian, we soon see the devil's hoofmark: Jesus would have considered "his message about the imminence of the kingdom of God to be no less unanswerable" — a message, remember, that simply did not come true, about a kingdom of God that was not imminent. "And, " says Father Rahner, "we can presumably concede that he envisaged the later invincibility, the indestructibility of the church and with it of all the offices of the church."

Here is one who knows in his attractive way that what he says is wrong. His speech betrays him. Jesus never thought about his church, this church or any other church. Of that much, at least, we can be sure. Perhaps Father Rahner SJ merely does not dare to know. Another writer, less inclined than Karl Rahner to justify Papal infallibility, has written: "The church differs from other human organizations — and the difference is absolutely crucial only in this — that to it, as to the brotherhood of those who believe in Christ, is given this promise: that it shall endure all mistakes and all failures, all sins and all burdens; that in all times of disturbance its truth shall never be confounded or destroyed, that in it the message of Jesus Christ shall endure, that this Jesus Christ himself shall remain within it in the spirit and will preserve it in Christ's truth through all errors and confusion." God takes care that " if ever it strays or wanders, the church still finally maintains its course and passes on Christ's truth."[60]

This speech, too, is deceitful. Whoever gave the church this firm promise, which message is Jesus Christ's, and how does Jesus remain in the spirit in a church he never dreamed of in his lifetime? The quotation is from the book, *Infallibility: An Inquiry*, by the dauntless Swiss adviser to the Church Council, Hans Küng, born 1928. But are we now, like a hard-line Communist or a Swiss lieutenant, to rest content that the "course" of the church is the right one? From the viewpoint of his friend Rahner, Küng has already gone too far with his half-and-half accommodation. Rahner — and Küng too, presumably, if it should come to an oath in Rome — still maintains that "there are infallible, definitive lessons of the Popes and Councils." For this is what the second Vatican Council laid down in 1965: ". . . it must be recognized of the books of scripture, that they teach certainly, faithfully and without error that truth which God wished to have recorded in the holy scriptures for our salvation."[61]

Those who still appeal to Jesus will have to admit in all honesty that the Ladenburger superintendent, Silvanus, was nearer to the historical Jesus, the Jesus who lived and suffered, than the whole of the Roman church. Küng's "course" was not the right one in 1572, nor in the year 100, nor is it now under Pope Paul. If the Holy Spirit of the Roman church existed, one ought to assess the effectiveness of his commitment to support it by whether he can move Küng's church, first to modify, finally to abolish all the fossilized errors and misdirection right up to the enthroning of the far from infallible Holy Spirit as one of the Holy Trinity.

The church, urges Küng's pupil Josef Nolte, born 1940, must "take on a degree of intellectual honesty," confess its "fallibility" and accept the growing consequences of it.[62] But if it wished to abandon the mother-ship of its dogmas and hurry out to meet an unknown Lord across the open sea, it would sink, as did Peter of old.

4. His lessons?

*If the world has been found worthy to
bear the man Jesus Christ, if a man
like Jesus has lived, then and only then
does living have a meaning for us men.
If Jesus had not lived, then our own
lives, despite all the other men we
know, honor and love, would be
meaningless.[1]*
— Dietrich Bonhoeffer

Millar Burrows, the American
professor of theology, who was one of the discoverers of the *Dead
Sea Scrolls*, those pre-Christian manuscripts written on leather,
papyrus and even copper which were found in 1947 near the
former monastery of Qumran, wrote in 1958: "The question is not
whether any of Jesus' words had really been preached before or
whether anything he did had been done before .... The most
important thing is not that the words of Jesus should be new, but
that they should be true."[2]
   That was said in reply to all those Qumram enthusiasts who saw
the uniqueness of Jesus disappearing in the light of the monastery
scrolls. But the question does still remain, which of the "true
lessons" come from him and which were formulated by others
before him. Can we be certain which are lessons that have been
ascribed to him but did not originate with him, though they were
used by him and held by him to be correct, and which are "true,"
i.e. words unquestionably spoken by him as his own? One must
answer that not one lesson exists which can be attributed to Jesus
with any sort of confidence, as was already known before the
discovery of the *Dead Sea Scrolls* and was finally proved through
Qumran. For once, Helmut Thielicke is right in a way when he
says that Jesus himself "hardly spoke a word that could not

already be read in the rabbinical literature before him, substantially in the same form."[3]

No one took down in shorthand what Jesus may have said. Those who went about with him for a short time — if any did go about with him — were simple, illiterate people who spoke only Aramaic. After the death of their master, their reaction was not to write down his words but to make up a rhyme about what happened. At least we should expect them to have a good memory. What seemed right to them at the time, they turned into his lessons. They made lessons *about* him into lessons *from* him. There is thus, affirms Martin Dibelius, "no Aramaic source about the life of Jesus."[4]

So no "genuine word of Jesus," no "parable going back to Jesus himself," no "very probably genuine, old word of Jesus," no "probably genuine parable" such as is still suggested by the above-named theologians, exists. The genuineness is never "guaranteed." When Herbert Braun, head of the Mainz School of Theology, asks us nonetheless to accept such assurances[5] (although with the general reservation that there can be no absolute certainty, only a greater or lesser degree of probability) then, of course, this appearance of truth is often enough mere groping.

What is written in the Gospels and other New Testament writings can all be confirmed, not however through a single person, but by references to the very extensive body of writings of a specific Jewish tradition which took its own way, branching off from the main highway of the official Judaism of the temple. The discoveries of Qumran have given this overwhelmingly apocalyptic tradition a clear form, but the difficulty of establishing a firm connection between Jesus and such a continuity remains insuperable.

There have been many attempts to connect him with the Qumran sect of Essenes, who were expecting the end of the world, from King Frederick and Voltaire down to Johannes Lehmann's book *Report on Jesus*.[6] The Essenes, the third most significant group after the established Sadducees and the Pharisees whom we know from the scriptures, are most surprisingly not mentioned in the Gospels. Since the discoveries in and around Qumran, we may well doubt whether those striking omissions are accidental.

Flavius Josephus, our most important witness about Jewish events in the time of Jesus, by his own account studied with the Essenes as a very young man.[7] Their movement was the most radically affected by the desecration of the temple by Antiochus IV Epiphanes, in which Jewish leaders had taken part. The Essenes had completely withdrawn from the Jerusalem temple and its bloated priests, inflamed by the ardent vision of reconciling themselves with the God of Israel so that he might once more recognize them as his chosen people and redeem them from slavery. The name "Pharisees" means "segregated," but the only truly segregated group was the Essenes, chosen ones who went to live as monks in the desert.

The Qumran monastery lay within sight of what has always been supposed to be the place where John baptised in the Jordan, within sight too of the fortress of Machaerus, on the eastern side of the Dead Sea, where the Baptist was executed by the Tetrarch Herod Antipas. It thus required no great effort of imagination to associate that reputed "forerunner" in some way with the monks of Qumran.

The undertaking suffers from the heavy camouflage with which the Christians have endowed the Baptist. All the same, the similarities in vocabulary and doctrine between the Qumran and the New Testament texts are striking and significant. The moral command of brotherliness, the praise of poverty, humility and chastity, the forbidding of swearing and bad language, the love of one's enemies, absolute love within the brotherhood — everything we now think of as essentially Christian teaching was already taught by the Essenes.

Their songs of thanksgiving tell us that the Essenes wished to preach "to the poor the joyous message of the fullness of thy (God's) mercy"; they wished to be "heralds of good news."[8] They wanted to conclude a new covenant (or, as Luther translates it, "a new testament") with God. Like the Christians, they have a not entirely comprehensible master, their "Teacher of Righteousness" who was brought before the Council by the "priest of sacrilege" and tortured or executed. (The Qumran commentary on Habakkuk writes of the Teacher and the priest of sacrilege: ". . . they inflicted on him vindictive sentences of scourging and the terrors of painful sicknesses, and vengeance on his fleshly body.") Like the Christians' Jesus, he came as the new lawgiver in the place of Moses. At the end of time he will "teach justice."[9] As with Jesus, the question arises whether he thought of himself as a Messianic personality.

108

The object of the Habakkuk commentary is to show that the events foretold by Habakkuk for the last days had already come to pass in the time of the founding of the community, and that they came true in a special way in the life of the Teacher of Righteousness. "The founder of the Essene community," writes Joachim Jeremias, "was convinced that justice and salvation were established in his message," a message that "only he embodied." The parallel with the Jesus of the evangelists is unmistakeable.[10]

Gert Jeremias, son of Joachim Jeremias and an expert on Qumran, finds the "immense self-confidence" manifested in the message of the "Teacher" to be "almost frightening." Both the Teacher of Qumran and the Jesus of the Gospels "know themselves to be the last messenger sent by God." The Jesus of the Gospels was not the first, but the Qumran Teacher before him was "the last prophet before the end." He also "has almost taken the place of God." It is said of him too that at the last judgment he will absolve "all who believe in his message and live according to it."[11]

The Teacher of Rightousness — if he is not a mythical figure — certainly died long before Jesus. Like the Biblical Jesus, he called down judgment on Jerusalem and disputed with the officials of the temple. To him, as to the Biblical Jesus, "all the secrets of the words of his servants the prophets" were revealed by God. Like Jesus, he was betrayed and ill-treated. God had commanded him "to establish the community of his chosen."[12] Of what he did or taught or said, we know no more than we do of Jesus. He lived, if at all, a hundred or a hundred and eighty years before Jesus. The French Jesuit Father Jean Daniélou, since 1969 one of Pope Paul's cardinals and one of his hard-line supporters, wrote of this rather shadowy figure in 1957 as "one of the great religious figures in the history of man." Millar Burrows sees in him "a man of independent prophetic spirit, resolved to accept suffering for his view of truth and right." Daniélou even declares* that, if Christ were not

---

*This may have been one of those passages that laid the professor of early Christian history open to the charge of less than complete orthodoxy. Today he sees himself exposed to other charges: "Theologians like Daniélou, who would have been prosecuted by the Inquisition, yet who now set themselves up as pseudo-scientific Grand Inquisitors, are appointed cardinals by the Holy Roman Church and realize their expectations" (Hans Küng in his book *Infallibility: An Inquiry*).

God, then the Teacher of Righteousness would stand higher than he.[14] This great Jewish prophet is said to have foretold the coming of the Messiah, and actually that he would come in the form of Jesus Christ. "How could the genuineness of a prophecy be disputed when it is an established fact that it has been fulfilled?"[15] Checkmate: we are disarmed.

That the community the Teacher of Righteousness was required to build up for God has striking resemblances to the early Christian church and community, was observed some time ago by Gfrörer, Vicar of Stuttgart, who had never heard of this Teacher. He wrote in 1831: "The Christian church arose out of the Essene community, whose thoughts they developed and without whose rules their organization would have been inexplicable."[16]

It was a community whose members, like the early Christians, believed that the last times had dawned and that they had an active part to play in them. Apocalyptic writings such as were in fashion after Antiochus' desecration of the temple, writings set forth under the name of a Daniel or an Enoch, were the Qumran monks' favorite quotations, if indeed they had not actually been composed in the Essene sects. But like the first Christians, the Essenes had to live year after year in expectation of the last time, for "the last time is extended and delayed beyond all that the prophets have said."[17] Thus, the Qumran community also needed a fixed hierarchical order and rules, and these stood godfather to those of the Christians.

The word for "church" in the Aramaic texts of the first Christians is the same word used in Qumran for "community,"[18] just as the expression "council" in Qumran was taken over for the council of the church. Daniélou writes: "The Qumran hierarchy consisted mainly of the Council of Twelve."[19] That number sounds familiar: there are twelve tribes of Israel, twelve administrative areas under King Solomon and twelve signs of the zodiac. Twelve apostles followed the Lord on earth (Conzelmann: "The 'twelve apostles' never existed"[20]); twelve persons, not identified with the apostles in the context, form the Twelve of whom Paul speaks in his first letter to the Corinthians. Why precisely twelve? There was a council of twelve in Qumran, too. The warden (Hebrew *mebaqqer*), Greek ἐπί σκοπος, the bishop, was subordinate to them. It is said of the Council of Twelve: "This is the trusty battlement, the costly cornerstone; its foundations shall not shake nor yield place."[21] To the Christians, the "cornerstone rejected of the builders" is Jesus. In

Matthew's Gospel (16:18), as is well known, and not in Mark, the oldest of the Gospels, Jesus promises Peter: "And I tell you, you are Peter, and on this rock I will build my church, and the powers of death shall not prevail against it." In the songs of praise and thanksgiving of Qumran, the just man speaks in the name of his community:[22]

> Thou settest me up like a strong tower,
> Like a soaring battlement,
> Buildest me firmly on rock
> And settest me firmly upon eternal foundations
> And all my walls upon the trusty battlement,
> Which can never be destroyed.

The trusty battlement and the costly cornerstone go back to Isaiah (28:16), where he is speaking of Zion's foundation-stone, be it a trusty stone or costly cornerstone. The community is the strong tower, the soaring battlement founded upon rock. The "gates of hell" are in Qumran the "gates of death" and certainly mean the same thing. (It was in Christian usage that the Greek word Hades first changed its meaning from "the underworld" to "Hell"; perhaps we should picture the pillars, the gates, as the greedy, gaping jaws of a monster.) The just man of Qumran had already reached the "gates of death" when he saved himself in the community of God, in the "fortified city" with its "soaring battlement," "founded upon rock."[23]

It was not Jesus who loved Isaiah, as Jeremias tells us;[24] in any case, we know nothing about it. But Qumran loved him: the "trusty stone" of Isaiah becomes in Qumran the community, and a "trusty battlement." In the Gospels, Isaiah's "costly cornerstone" is rejected by the builders. Jesus, according to Matthew, wishes to build a community; the teacher of justice, according to Qumran, must do so; in Qumran, to the glory of God and in obedience to his commandment, in Matthew's Gospel, of his own free will: "I, Jesus, will."

The Essenes lived in cities only when so obliged; whether they lived in Jerusalem, we do not know. Their chosen people in the monastic community of Qumran lived without women. They might keep their personal property for the first year but no longer. Outside the monastery, a high tax was levied for the poor. Anyone who gave false information about his property was excommunicated for a year. (The Christian couple Ananias and Sapphira, found guilty of the same offense in the early Christian community, die on the spot — Acts of the Apostles (5:1–11).[25] The Christian proto-Communism in Luke's Acts is idealized scene-painting, but in Qumran, it was the real thing.

The precepts put into the mouth of Jesus by the first Christians (Matthew 18:15-17) can be matched in the canon of the Qumran sect, the *Manual of Discipline:* No one shall bring a dispute with his brother before the Council until he has discussed it before two witnesses.[26] In Matthew, the dispute has first to be discussed with the brother alone, then in the presence of one or two witnesses and only then before the whole council. If the brother will not listen to the council, then "treat him as you would a pagan or a tax-gatherer," says Jesus as reported in this gospel of love.

The men of Qumran, like the Christians, prayed three times a day, not in the direction of the temple in Jerusalem but towards the East; they renewed their vows (as the Christians, their baptism) every year; the novice received a white robe in both communities; Herod Antipas, according to Luke, made them put a "gorgeous" robe on Jesus when he sent him back to Pilate, and the clothes of the "transfigured" Jesus became "dazzling white" or "exceeding white as snow."

John the Baptist, if he was something more than just closely connected with the men of Qumran, came himself from their esoteric circles. His baptism, also vouched for by Josephus,[27] is, like the Christian baptism, formally called a baptism of the return to the forgiveness of sins. In the course of it, those prepared for the return were under John's guidance immersed in the Jordan. The early Christians, like the Qumran community, equated repentance with entry into the community. Before John, if he did indeed baptize, the Jews did not practice baptism. As we have seen, the mark of membership was circumcision. The Qumran people likewise did not practice baptism, but they did have a custom of ritual washing. They had a holy meal in which only initiates might take part; the priest said a prayer before and after a meal. Only men shared the meal, and they sat in strict order of precedence. Luke takes up this question of the dispute about seniority at the Last Supper, and in John's Gospel a washing of feet takes place at the Last Supper as well as the argument about *placement*, mirroring the ritual washing and strict precedence of the Essenes. There are also suggestions among them of the order of precedence of a Messiah-meal

112

on the final occasion, and in Luke it says a propos of the Last Supper:

You are those who have continued with me in my trials; as my Father appointed a kingdom for me, so do I appoint for you that you may eat and drink at my table in my kingdom, and sit on thrones judging the twelve tribes of Israel. (22:28-30)

We read in Josef Blank's book, *The Man From Galilee*, that the characteristic symbolic ceremony of the message of Jesus is "the formal meal at which the presence of the eschatological kingdom of God is symbolically represented."[28] It seems to have been overlooked that Qumran originated the rites of the Gospels. We cannot definitely say that Jesus would have celebrated the brotherhood's membership of the coming kingdom in the "formal meal," even if it is so set forth in the Gospels. That was something straight from Qumran. By the rules of Qumran, the priest had to be the first to stretch out his hand and "pronounce a blessing over the first of the bread." At the Messianic meal of the last times, "the Messiah of Israel must stretch out his hands towards the bread" after him, as the second one.[29] But in Luke's Gospel it says:

But behold the hand of him who betrays me is with me on the table. (22:21)

The theology of the Essenes is similar to that of the gnostic Gospel of John, and also to that of Luke. The "sons of light" stand implacably against the "sons of darkness." The "prince of this world" is entirely Essenic; the Qumran community have an "angel of darkness" and a "prince of light" — to the Christians, Jesus.[30] The phrase "children of light" in Luke (16:8) is characteristic of the Essene writings, as is the speech Jesus is said to have made to the priests and officers of the temple: "But this is your moment — the hour when darkness reigns." John says that Jesus goes by night, "when no man can work." The idea of the final battle between the forces of darkness and light can be found throughout the Essene texts as it can throughout Luke and John.

The *Manual of Discipline* calls on men to hate all sons of darkness and iniquity,[31] and John's Gospel cannot arouse any different feelings against those who do not believe in Jesus. He speaks continually of the "hatred of the world" for the disciples,

113

and does not enjoin love for those outside the Christian community: "I pray, not for the world, but for those which thou hast given name." The Old Testament also preached hatred for the evildoers (Psalm 26:5) and for those whom the Lord hates (Psalm 139:21), but Qumran cuts itself off more strictly. All the same, it does say in Leviticus: "You shall not nurse hatred against your brother" (19:17).

In John's Gospel, as among the Qumran community, "truth" is a key-word. Both know the phrase "do the truth," the phrases "eternal life" and "light of life." John speaks of the "children of light," Qumran, like John, of the "spirit of truth." To both, Qumran and Christians, "the way" of their faith is "the truth and the life."[32]

It says in John's Gospel: "In him was life, and the life was the light of men. The light shines in the darkness, and the darkness has not overcome it." (1:4—5.) This is an exact *leitmotiv* from Qumran. The "spirit of truth" which Jesus promises in John's Gospel is called in Qumran "angel of truth." He is the "helper" of the "prince of light," as the Christian "spirit of truth" is also called "comforter" or "helper" or, in Greek, $\pi\alpha\rho\acute{\alpha}\kappa\lambda\eta\tau o\varsigma$. The image of the well as a source of faith (including Jacob's well — John 4:1—30) is common to both the evangelist and the Essenes, and both say that "living water" flows out of him. At the end of time, says Qumran, God will cleanse men by pouring out the spirit of truth over them; and in Matthew's Gospel, John the Baptist says the same about the one who shall come after him.[33]

What has come to us almost unintelligibly in Matthew, the first sentence of the Sermon on the Mount — literally, "Blessed are the poor in spirit" — appears intelligibly in the Qumran teaching. The subject here is the *anije ruach*, those who have remained poor for the sake of the spirit. The people of Qumran called themselves a "community of the poor," their members the "poor of the spirit," "poor of grace" and "poor of redemption."[34] "Especially striking," thinks Millar Burrows, although he is concerned to work out the differences between Qumran and the Gospels, "are the parallels in the Sermon on the Mount."[35]

But these parallels are not only with the writings found in Qumran but also with the apocalypse of Enoch, which may have originated in the misty circles of the Essenes. Do the nine beatitudes in Matthew's Sermon on the Mount really go back to Jesus? Not exactly. First, they are quite different in Luke; second, they do not appear at all in Mark; but third, we are told by Günther Harder, professor of New Testament studies at the Ecclesiastical High School and Director of the Institute for Church and Judaism in Berlin, that the verses in Matthew's Sermon on the Mount are "not an original speech by Jesus, not even Jesus' original words, but a part of the early Christian interpretation of the (Mosaic) law."[36]

We cannot help but gasp at the thought that the sermon on the mount is "not an actual sermon . . . but a collection of sayings," and that we do not know "to whom these sayings were addressed nor on what occasion they were uttered" (Martin Dibelius).[37] Theologians like Bultmann and his pupil Ernst Fuchs have always doubted that the "beatitudes," the so-called "macarisma" (from $\mu\alpha\kappa\acute{\alpha}\rho\iota\varsigma$ = fortunate), really go back to Jesus.[38] They certainly did not form part of the earliest sources. But they are found in the book of Enoch; and the Qumran community also had a series of beatitudes beginning with the word "blessed," which have not yet been edited. It would be a great surprise if they did not turn out to resemble the beatitudes of the apocalypse of Enoch, in which, for instance, it says: "Blessed are you righteous and chosen ones, for your lot shall be glorious," or "Blessed be he who gives clothes to the naked or gives his bread to the hungry"; or "Blessed be he who has compassion in his mouth and meekness in his heart." The theologian Rudolf Otto saw "a close relationship between Jesus and the tradition of Enoch."[39] We might rather say that the later Gospel tradition has helped itself liberally from the Enoch apocalypse. Among the Qumran community, as later in the Gospels, property is called "Mammon";[40] the Qumran commentary on the prophecies of Habakkuk turns the prophet's warning against wine into a warning against wealth. But it said about the priest of sacrilege that "he did not cut off the foreskin of his heart but went astray on the ways of drunkenness." The vessel of God's wrath will destroy him.[41]

Matthew's "Love your neighbor, be good to them that hate you," reads in the sacred book of the Essenes: "I will not take vengeance upon anyone for his evil deeds. I will deal with him with good will. For judgment over all living men is with God."[42] To turn the left cheek when the right is struck, this rule of life which neither the Essenes nor Jesus nor his disciples nor the first Christians were able to follow, was not laid down by Mark; it first appears in Matthew and Luke. For the weaker — i.e. the first Christians — it was the most important precept of all.*

The *Damascus Document,* related to Qumran although partially known before, says that every man should love his brother as himself and should care for the poor and needy and the stranger[44] (all to whom the "gleaning" of the fields and the vineyards are allotted in Leviticus, for what it is worth). Bultmann really did show an instinct when he maintained, even before he knew about the *Dead Sea Scrolls,* that a new ethic was not really preached in the Gospels.[45]

With the help of the Essenes, we can make sense of the "men of good will," the *homines bonae voluntatis* of the Latin Bible (the "Vulgate"), who first crop up in Luke's account of Christmas and also, prematurely, in various places. In the *Mustard Seed Bible,* the heavenly host wishes "good will to men." But it does not mean to men of good will, men whose will is good and who are good-natured to others, but to "men in God's grace," men "with whom God is satisfied." And in the Qumran hymn of thanksgiving, we find just this meaning; to be precise, "the sons of his good will." The *Manual of Discipline* speaks of the "chosen of goodwill," i.e., "those chosen people who do Thy will." The men of God's will are thus the chosen, and the Protestant Bible published by Furche in 1971 translates: " . . . and on earth peace among the men of his grace." They themselves are blessed and praiseworthy because they have devoted themselves to love, poverty, meekness, chastity, the right road. They, the poor, who welcome the time of trouble, are the meek who shall inherit the land, says the Qumran commentary on the 37th Psalm.[46]

They are the "sons of light"; the desert is not only their physical but their spiritual home. The Messiah will come out of the desert; God made his pact with Israel in the desert. It is into the"desert of the peoples" that they have emigrated. They have "cut themselves off from the community of the men of evil" as they were commanded. They have voluntarily broken away from the normal

---

*The postscript in Matthew (5:48): "You therefore must be perfect, as your heavenly Father is perfect" is an ancient Jewish commandment which reads: "You shall be holy: for I the LORD your God am holy" (Leviticus 19:2). The word "good" is peculiar to Matthew. In Luke, Jesus says: "Be merciful, even as your Father is merciful" (6:36), and this too is not a saying of Jesus. It existed before in Aramaic: "As your father in heaven is compassionate, so be ye compassionate on earth."

forms of Jewish life. In days to come, they will return to the "desert of Jerusalem," which meanwhile they consider so destroyed that they no longer turn towards its temple when they pray.[47]

The desert, as we have seen, is not mere landscape, neither is it the uninhabited, unclean, unholy space into which the scapegoat is sent. Here it is a symbolized region of salvation. The Essenes, oppressed by the "priest of sacrilege", were exiled about the year 60 B.C.E. in the region of Damascus, to fulfil, as the so-called *Damascus Document* suggests, a prophecy of Amos (5:27): "And I will drive you into exile beyond Damascus." (It may be, of course, that Damascus too is only used symbolically, intended as a spiritual place and materially perhaps identical with such places as Qumran.)[48]

Now in the last verse of his first chapter, Luke says of John the Baptist: "And the child grew and became strong in spirit, and he was in the wilderness till the day of his manifestation to Israel." But why was this son of Zacharias, a priest of the temple, again according to Luke, in the desert from his childhood up? The passage remains puzzling. "We could not imagine this boy simply thrown out into the desert" (Daniélou). Now we can imagine it: either actually or symbolically, he was in the desert of the holy ones, for the Qumran research worker William Hugh Brownlee thinks it possible that the Baptist was adopted as a child by the monks of Qumran. And indeed Josephus reports:

> . . . (they) choose out other persons' children, while they
> are pliable and fit for learning; and esteem them to be of
> their kindred, and form them according to their own manners.[49]

All the Gospels make Jesus begin with John the Baptist, by whom he was baptized. Mark states simply: "In those days Jesus came from Nazareth of Galilee and was baptized by John in the Jordan" (1:9). John was presumably preaching along the same lines as Jesus a little later: Repent, for the kingdom of heaven is at hand. But in Matthew, he already declares himself a herald: " . . . he who is coming after me is mightier than I, whose sandals I am not worthy to carry" (3:11). He already adopts the attitude to Jesus: "Do you come to me? I need rather to be baptized by you."

In Luke, we have gone a step further. The Baptist has now found himself a birth-legend of his own, similar to that told of

Jesus (but not by Mark). John, a child in the womb of his mother Elizabeth, leaps for joy when his mother catches sight of Mary the Mother of God. Zacharias, his father, prophesies about him: "And you, child, will be called the prophet of the Most High; for you will go before the Lord to prepare his ways . . . " (1:76).

In John's Gospel, we go forward another step. When John the Baptist sees Jesus coming to him, he says: "Behold, the Lamb of God, who takes away the sins of the world! This is he of whom I said, 'After me comes a man who ranks before me.'" He who has sent him (John) to baptize with water has said to him: "He on whom you see the Spirit descend and remain, this is he who baptizes with the Holy Spirit." And now he has seen the Spirit descending on Jesus "like a dove from heaven." We shall meet the dove again.

Back to the simple Mark. In his first chapter, verses 2-5, he tells us that the following is written in the prophet Isaiah:

"Behold, I send my messenger before thy face,
who shall prepare thy way;
the voice of one crying in the wilderness:
Prepare the way of the Lord,
make his paths straight . . . "

"Herald" is also translated as "angel." But the Lord speaks in the prophet Malachi (3:1), saying that the way shall be prepared for him — i.e., the Lord — by a herald or angel. And in Isaiah (40:3) there is no voice crying in the wilderness, but a voice cries:

"In the wilderness prepare the way of the LORD,
make straight in the desert a highway for our God."

The Septuagint, the Greek translation of the Old Testament, has it wrong, and Mark has followed the wrong translation. Before Qumran, theologians like Karl Ludwig Schmidt and Rudolf Bultmann believed that "in the wilderness" was a later insertion, like that other verse of Mark:

Now John was clothed with camel's hair, and had a leather girdle around his waist, and ate locusts and wild honey. (1:6)

which is intended to characterize John as a desert preacher so as to fit the prophecy of Isaiah. But desert does not just mean rocks or sand, and locusts are not just locusts; they must be roasted if they are going to be eaten, and it says as much in the *Damascus Document*. Desert and locusts alike are attributes of the Essenes.[50]

So it was not the evangelists who painted the Baptist in desert camouflage in order to fulfil the verse of Isaiah but, on the contrary, the Essenes who looked to Isaiah[51] — the *Damascus Document* is witness — when they retreated to the desert before the priests of sacrilege. John (his previous history, says Bultmann, "obviously had nothing to do with a coming Messiah"),[52] called to repentance and conversion "in the desert." It was in the desert that the way should be prepared, not, as the evangelists will have it, for a Messiah, but for "the Lord." The annihilation of sinners through eternal fire is foretold by Qumran and preached by the Baptist.

Very cautiously, Millar Burrows gives his opinion that there are certainly many points in which the thoughts of John resembled those found in the Dead Sea Scrolls: "Like the sectarians (Essenes) he dedicated himself in the wilderness to the task of preparing the way of the Lord. His baptism of repentance could have had some spiritual connection with the ritual bathing of the Qumran sect. Like the *Manual of Discipline,* he emphasized that a bath in water cannot wash away sin unless there has been some previous spiritual purification."[53] Here is the Baptist, reported by Luke: "You vipers' brood! Who warned you to escape from the coming retribution? Then prove your repentance by the fruit it bears." (The soldiers who rather surprisingly make this pilgrimage to Luke's Baptist in the desert, he tells to be content with their pay. Once more we are reminded that the earliest fragments of the Gospels we have were written in the second century.)

The Baptist's prophecy that he who comes after will execute judgment with fire is in the Qumran *Hymn Scroll*. Millar Burrows writes: " . . . brightly painted with pictures of the torrents of Belial, which will consume in their flames the very foundations of the mountains. The scrolls even have a representation of a Messianic baptism through the Holy Spirit."[54] Unlike Jesus, the Baptist does not drink wine, nor do the Essenes.

Things are now clearly critical for Jesus. There existed before him, at least as an idea, a Teacher of righteousness who seems to have anticipated most of the Gospel lessons. He was tortured by the priests of the temple after a judicial sentence, if not actually executed.

The followers of the Teacher of righteousness are described in detail by Flavius Josephus, but the followers of Jesus are not. He himself is mentioned, if at all, only in a subordinate way. John the Baptist, described in the Gospels as Jesus' forerunner, declaring himself not fit to take off his sandals or to unloose their strap, seems in fact to have been a figure in his own right, well substantiated by Josephus and having no connection with Jesus. "With good reason," says Gert Jeremias,[55] we have assumed a direct link between John the Baptist and the Qumran community, whose teaching undoubtedly shaped the Gospels more than did that of the earthly Jesus, whom the theologians have torn apart into a "historic" *("historich")* hardly comprehensible, figure and a comprehensible "historical" *("geschichtlich")* figure.

Was he no more than an invention of the early Christian community? Was it really not he, but only John the Baptist, who was executed? Or was he an Essene? What evidence, asks Johannes Lehmann, is there to disprove "that Rabbi J. lived in one of the caves in or around Qumran?" The Qumran community had a two- or three-year novitiate. What evidence is there, asks Lehmann, to disprove "that Rabbi J. passed his novitiate in a cave outside Qumran?"[56]

Astonishing as it may seem, there is evidence against it. There is nothing at all to show what Johannes Lehmann regards as "in the highest degree probable," that "Rabbi J. was influenced in his teaching and his speaking by the Essenes of Qumran."[57] Jesus, if he was not a Messianic "loner," could still have stood very close to the liberal left wing of the Pharisees. That he should have attacked the Pharisees' hypocrisy and hardness of heart appears doubtful when we consider that he seems to have shared many attributes of the Pharisees, and that until the outbreak of the Jewish war it was not they but the Sadducees who exercised political power. The Sadducees are hardly mentioned as such. It is the Pharisees who are always quoted as Jesus' classic opponents; "they are always on the spot when the editors need them" (Bultmann),[58] even when their own writings are used against them as if they were not theirs at all.

We have found ample proof that many of the lessons contained in the Gospels could have been based on the apocalyptic writings, and specifically those of the Essenes of Qumran which have recently been discovered. We should now consider the fact that the Essenes, to whose lessons the New Testament owes so much, are never mentioned in those lessons, and that John, who at the least was closely connected with the Essenes, is only allowed to appear as the herald of Jesus. Anyone who knows only the New Testament — Johannes Lehmann's *Report of Jesus* is right on this point — gets no idea from it that, in addition to the Pharisees and Sadducees, (with both of whom Jesus seems to have been at odds), there also existed the Essenes.[59]

So far, so good. All the same, there is something distinctive about the teaching of the Gospels, an important and at the same time refreshing vagueness, insignificant to us but beyond all measure significant in Jesus' time; they do not express themselves clearly about Jesus' attitude to that commandment common to Sadducees, Pharisees and Essenes: Torah, the Law, the Law of Moses. Yet no one observed the law more radically and more strictly than the Essenes, above all in the one area of it in which the attitude of Jesus is given shape and color in the Gospels: the keeping or breaking of the Sabbath.

The keeping of the Sabbath distinguished Jews from Gentiles. In the teaching of the Pharisees, the Sabbath commandment was as important as all the other commandments put together. Scrupulous observation of the Sabbath is a virtue in itself, allowing of no concessions; it is God's will. Even Yahweh himself observes the Sabbath with strict ritual with his angels in heaven. The chosen people of Israel are allowed to take part in it. To them "the proper honoring of the Sabbath commandment is ordered by God in an outstanding way" (Herbert Braun).[60] The Law, the Torah, is a cosmic power which fundamentally holds the world together. But Jesus' attitude to the Law is described in the Gospels as quite antagonistic. As Dautzenberg writes in *Rabbi J.*, his reply to Lehmann's *Report on Jesus*, "he was in fact not a teacher of the Law, but seems to have taken up a position from one case to another in accordance with his own individual and unorthodox charismatic authority."[61] He who should above all others teach us did not even have a firm attitude to the Law.

As less orthodox people, we may assume that Jesus is not himself speaking in all those places where he strictly stands up for the Law. It is not in Mark's Gospel, only later in Matthew and Luke that he says that heaven and earth must pass away before a jot or tittle disappears from the Law. ("Quite certainly spurious," according to Braun.)[62] His attitude to the Law both in speech and in practice, ambivalent to say the least, unthinkable in a rabbi or lawgiver, seems to us to be exactly the most important evidence that he really lived and worked. However much the evangelists may have twisted his words to mean the opposite of what he said; however much they have interpolated, he existed.

The Jews sought to kill him because he broke the Sabbath; it says so in as many words in John (5:18) and, by implication, in the synoptic Gospels.

Now what interest would the authors of the Gospels have in telling the "Gentiles" about Jesus' breaches of the Sabbath if in the view of the first Christians he had not committed any? And this although the tendency is not to exonerate the Jews but to pile on their guilt?

The *Damascus Document* of the Essenes tells us what the orthodox Jew might *not* do on the Sabbath:[63]

° speak a foolish or vain word
° speak of the next day's business
° prepare food
° go into the field and think about the week's work
° open a sealed vessel
° make a journey of more than 2,000 ells (about 1,100 yards, still called a Sabbath day's journey)
° pick up the baby to carry it about
° lead restive livestock out of the stall
° assist at the birth of livestock
° pull livestock out of a ditch or well into which it has fallen
° pull out a man who has fallen into a pool with the aid of a ladder, a rope or any other instrument.

You were allowed to help him out, which gave an opportunity for interpretation to the less extreme among the Pharisees. It was still doubtful whether you might pass water on the Sabbath, according to Josephus.[64] One is tempted to conclude that all these impossible rules had been decreed by Yahweh to give him an opportunity to be angry with his people all the time.

Let us just see what Jesus said and did about this. Again, nothing really revolutionary, because there was of course a rabbinical school which opposed the strictly orthodox interpretation of the Law and the hypocrisy that necessarily went with it. It was, in fact, the philanthropists among the Pharisees who brought on themselves the reputation of duplicity, because they always had a justification ready for every occasion.

Whether Jesus was only claiming that he himself was superior to the Sabbath laws, to his own greater glory, or whether he was aiming at a general relaxation, is still doubtful. Only in Mark, and indeed only in one part of the Marcan manuscripts, is he reported as saying: "The sabbath was made for man, not man for the sabbath" (2:27). The saying has its rabbinical parallel before Jesus, in the saying: "The Sabbath is given over to you, not you to it." On the other hand, Mark 2:28 — "so the Son of man is lord even of the sabbath" — is in Conzelmann's judgment a dogmatic assertion by the Christian community.[65]

When we hear of what Jesus did on the Sabbath, we do not want to blow up again the old discussion of whether or not he did really, permanently, heal. However this may be, Mark tells us that he was accused of having healed on the Sabbath day a man with a "withered" hand. In Luke, there were also a crippled woman, the nature of whose illness we can only guess at, and a sufferer from dropsy, both of whom he healed on the Sabbath. In his justification, Mark begs the question in a quite characteristic way:

"Is it lawful on the sabbath to do good or to do harm, to save life or to kill?" But they were silent. (3:4)

But it was not a question of saving a threatened life, only of whether it was permitted to heal on the Sabbath a hand that had been lifeless for years. A hundred years after the Qumran instruction, there was a school of the Pharisees which sought to relax the strict rules of the Law, not only in Qumran. In the Gospel according to Matthew, who knew the scriptures, this school makes itself heard. Some of the answers directly contradict some of the precepts of the *Damascus Document,* as when the evangelist (12:11) makes Jesus say: "Suppose you had one sheep, which fell into a ditch on the Sabbath; is there one of you who would not catch hold of it and lift it out?"

Or according to Luke (14:5), who may not have known Mark but who probably knew of the rabbinical discussion: "Which of you, having an ass or an ox that has fallen into a well, will not immediately pull him out on a sabbath day?" It was the practice of Jews that the Sabbath-breaker, if he would not be warned, must die. Not so among the Essenes. The *Damascus Document* forbids the killing of the Sabbath-breaker.

123

Of course, there are scholars who declare that according to the text of the four Gospels Jesus did not commit a single offense against the Sabbath laws; in particular, David Flusser, professor of New Testament studies at the Hebrew University in Jerusalem, has come into prominence with this thesis.[66] That Jesus' disciples plucked the ears of corn on the Sabbath because they were hungry (Mark 2:23-28)— Flusser will admit this one offense — appears at once in a different, more legitimate light if we accept the possibility of a mistranslation. The disciples may quite likely only have rubbed the ears; even that, if it was done with the hands and not between the fingers, was not looked on with favor by the law-abiding. But it was not an offense.

He is an attractive figure, this Jesus who does not go everywhere with the Torah under his arm. Unfortunately, though, we have to suspect that the episode of the rubbing of the ears of corn was not invented until after his death, in order to defend the first Jewish Christians against the attacks of the orthodox. That is something we can always assume when only the disciples are blamed, although their Master was among them. Also, the disciples were not, as Flusser declares, "laxer in their religious observances than their Master"; but the community was reluctant, in defending itself against accusations, to lay the revered Master open to unnecessary charges.

But what would have happened if Jesus had told one of those healed on the Sabbath to take his bed back home? The Jews objected to it, according to John: "It is the sabbath, it is not lawful for you to carry your pallet" (5:10). No breach of the sabbath? Or when, on the Sabbath day, he made a paste with spittle and earth (John 9:6) to heal a blind man? Some of the Pharisees, says John, came out against it, and with good reason. For even by the liberal interpretation of the law, healing on the Sabbath was allowed only if there was some possibility of mortal danger. No breach? "This fellow is no man of God; he does not keep the Sabbath," said some of the Pharisees, according to John. Others disagreed with them, for a sinful man, a man not from God, could not work such signs.

The evangelists agree in expressing their proven opinion that Jesus aroused hostility through breaches of the Sabbath and was proceeded against for that cause. Why could he not put off his healing for a day? Did he have to be on his way in a hurry, or did he intend it as provocation?

Joachim Jeremias sees a flouting of Torah unheard-of in the spirit of the time,[67] in the pattern of antitheses in Matthew 5:21-48: "You have heard that it was said to the men of old ... But I say to you ... " According to which, by Matthew's account:

° not only shall one who commits murder be brought to judgment (i.e. condemned to death) but also one who is angry with his brother and calls him a villain; one who says to him: "Thou fool" shall be condemned to hell fire

° it is not only one who commits adultery according to the Law of Moses (with another man's wife) who commits adultery, but anyone who looks on a married woman with a lustful eye

but also
° a woman can only be divorced by her husband with a note of dismissal for unchastity (presumably adultery)

° not just the breaking of an oath, but all swearing, is forbidden

° the principle of "an eye for an eye, a tooth for a tooth" shall give way to the principles of turning the left cheek when someone strikes you on the right; of giving away your coat if someone sues you for your shirt; of going two miles with someone if they require you to go one mile

° it is not enough to love your neighbor, your relatives; you should also love your enemies within the people.

So massive a contradiction of Torah would indeed have been unheard-of for the contemporaries of Jesus, who still lived under the administrative theocracy of the temple in Jerusalem, whose authority reached beyond the borders of the Roman province of Judea. The contradiction would be less unheard-of at the time when Matthew's Gospel was written, at least twenty years after the destruction of the temple in Jerusalem, and outside Palestine ("perhaps in Syria"). So it is not mere chance that only Mark, who had compiled his Gospel shortly before or shortly after the fall of Jerusalem, does not give us these unheard-of principles. Jesus certainly never uttered these commandments, the first of which contains sheer, merciless rubbish. Matthew, writing for Jewish Christians, still does not demand that we should love the enemies of our people and our faith. The Gentile Christian Luke is the first to extend the commandment to love our enemies to include all men without discrimination. *He* is the cosmopolitan, not Jesus.

No, Matthew's Jesus cannot possibly have lived under the administrative theocracy of the temple of Jerusalem. That "But what I tell you is" speaks not of an authority that "arose beside and against that of Moses," as the New Testament scholar of Tübingen, Bultmann's pupil, Ernst Käsemann, proclaims; it is rather, as Günther Harder makes clear in response to Käsemann, a matter of "a characteristic added formulation typical of the evangelist."[68]

Matthew's Gospel adapts many of the sayings from the Qumran writings and the closely related *Apocalypse of Enoch*. What could the ban on swearing or that on bad language, taken over from Enoch or Qumran, mean under the shadow of the imminent kingdom of God? What is being formulated here is not the ethic of Jesus but the ethic of the community, dear as it was to the communities of Qumran and likewise to the first Jewish Christians. Are we to imagine an eschatological Jesus, who "thought domestic ties a snare for the soul" (George Bernard Shaw),[69] who could not even spare time to bury his dead father and who nevertheless lays down rules for marriage for the last days?

What the Marcan text has to say about marriage actually furnishes the *Wilckens Bible* with the discovery that Jesus had taken "Graeco-Roman legal conditions" into consideration.[70] Very likely! Paul, long before Mark, commanded that the wife should not leave her husband ("yet it is not I that command, but the Lord"). Very likely! What really is likely is that the author of Matthew's Gospel based himself on Jewish legal conditions and therefore permitted divorce. According to the dogma of the honorable Rabbi Hillel,[71] otherwise a liberal, a man ought to give his wife a note of dismissal is she so much as lets the food get burnt. This teacher of the Law was liberal towards the husband, but not towards the wife. But Matthew says that the wife must be charged at least with unchastity, and this very limitation of the man's freedom of action appears to the male disciples in Matthew as wrong (" . . . then is it not good to marry").

On this question of covetousness and the purity of marriage, the Qumran community was notoriously more Mosaic than the Law of Moses. They write of the "eye of unchastity" where Matthew (5:28) has "a lustful eye." The *Damascus Document* reads: "Unchastity is a pitfall when anyone takes two wives in their lifetime, for the original order at the creation was: 'He created them man and wife.'" The passage is not entirely clear. Does it mean to forbid divorce, or have we here, as Gert Jeremias thinks, for the first time in Jewry "the requirement of lifelong monogamy"? For the author continues: "And those that were in the (Noah's) ark: two and two they came into the ark." David Flusser, who as a non-Christian has more feel for the Old Testament than for the New which is his subject, thinks: "There are signs that the Essenes completely abolished divorce."[72]

This is startlingly similar to the passage in Mark where he makes Jesus turn around the Law of Moses that a wife might be divorced by a note of dismissal:

> But Jesus said to them, "For your hardness of heart he wrote you this commandment (i.e., that Moses permitted divorce). But from the beginning of creation, 'God made them male and female.'"

The evangelist then makes Jesus quote Genesis 2:24:

> 'For this reason a man shall leave his father and mother and be joined to his wife, and the two shall become one.' So they are no longer two but one. (10:7-8)

By Jewish law, the husband can never commit adultery. Monogamy was not required among the Jewish Christians, only among the Gentile Christians, and consequently in the letters of Paul. The Jews regarded the wife as the husband's property, "and adultery in consequence as a particularly bad form of theft" (*Wilckens Bible*).[73] The law does not allow the wife to leave the husband if he is "unchaste" and brings home a strange woman instead of his wife. There is no sanction open to her. But what Mark and Matthew put into Jesus' mouth on the question, surely that is just Mark's and Matthew's opinions. Mark, just like the Essenes of Qumran, forbids the married couple to separate, but he probably has an eye on the Greco-Roman legal sphere. Matthew, on the other hand, allows the wife to be turned out if she is accused of "unchastity" (who judges whether she is?) but actually, this minimal protection given to the wife is already pretty widespread among the Jewish Christians.

It is laid down in Deuteronomy that the king of Israel shall "not acquire many wives" (17:17) — a not very exact prescription. The

Jewish scriptures maintain from the beginning a prudent double outlook on this ticklish problem. The family nucleus based on monogamy had long been customary by Jesus' time, but it was still legal for the husband to have relations with other women, and he might dismiss his wife. (This happens in Jewish communities to this day, requiring only the formula "I divorce you").

Marriage as a monogamous institution is praised, for instance, in the Talmud: "He who has no wife lives without happiness, without blessing and without kindness . . . without knowledge of the law and without company . . . without peace . . . he who has no wife is not a man."[74] The difference between this and the lessons of Qumran, of Paul and of the first evangelists (with which we should not associate Jesus), is striking.

The contradiction between the eschatological Jesus and Jesus teaching a way of life has of course occurred to the theologians. Joachim Jeremias gets out of it with the explanation that the ban on the dissolution of marriage is only valid until the moment of the full revelation (!) of the kingdom of God, for then there will be no more marriage.[75] On such shifting sands rather than on the authorship and authority of Jesus are the churches' moral rules founded. "Jesus goes back to the original order of the creation," is the way the *Luther Bible* of 1964 comments on Matthew.

With the aid of the particularly flexible laws on marriage, we have now shown what is in general to be regarded as having been taught by Jesus. We have gathered together fragments from which the mosaic of a fantasy Jesus can be composed, a combination of John the Baptist, whom Herod had executed at the age of about 30, and the Teacher of Righteousness, whom the priest of sacrilege tortured or killed and who is much less clearly defined historically than Jesus. We cannot harmonize this imagined Jesus with that miracle-doctor who provoked all the law-abiding by his non-observance of the Sabbath, nor with the despiser of his family (all this is in Mark), nor above all with that far from ascetic figure of the three later Gospels who sits at table with tax-gatherers, sinners and unclean persons, with Gentiles, in short, as Adolf Holl has it, "in bad company."

Here, of course, we must clear up an image that has become generally beloved. In the first Gospel, that of Mark, he sits at table with gentiles and prostitutes. He even eats and drinks in a way that makes the people remark: "Look, this fellow is a glutton and a winebibber, a friend of tax-gatherers and sinners." The real Jesus was obviously not what the evangelists later made him out to be, either because they are supporting the fashion of a non-ascetic, non-Nazarite Jesus, or because they wanted to build up the appeal of their propaganda in the marketplaces and the media, or because the evangelist did not want to mortify himself.

But it may be right enough that Jesus "was no Pharisee zealot" (Walter Bauer),[76] that, unlike the Pharisees and the followers of the Baptist, he did not fast. There were many Christian circles, too, where they did not fast. So we find in Mark the answer to the question put to Jesus, not, why did he not fast (the evangelist would not have dared to put that) but why did his disciples not fast. Mark's Gospel makes him reply: "How can the wedding-guests fast while the bridegroom is still with them?" And we could only wish that that really was his answer. Alas, we can only allow that it is *ben trovato*.

Jesus may not have been interested in religious purity and ritual correctness, particularly under the shadow of so many eschatological prophets with their eyes on the last things. Our problem remains that Jesus the apocalyptic, who announces the last judgment here and now, disappears behind the ritual pronouncements of the apocalyptic tradition. We must take the evangelists' word for it that Jesus foretold the last days and, unlike earlier prophets, linked them with his own coming. But with the individual clues, it is quite otherwise. If we may not assume that Jesus cared little for the Sabbath laws and the customs of the scribes, and that he treated sick-people with magic treatment on the Sabbath, then and only then, the whole historical Jesus, no matter whether or not there had been a brother of James executed, might indeed be only a mirage reflecting the wishes and interests of the community. Then, this community might have "gone astray after a timeless myth, even if for one reason or another they had endowed the central figure of the myth with the name Jesus" (Bornkamm).[77]

But we do believe that he, Jesus, existed; that he was not just anybody. Such a man, who upset the orthodox Jews, must — as it is stated in Mark's Gospel and nowhere else — have been out of his mind. His followers must have been worried about him. That they really would have acted as is described to us is of course nothing less than certain.

If Jesus was an Essene, then he must have been an escaped, a former Essene, a runaway Essene, and this theory has been advanced before.[78] This would explain why Essene teaching dominated the Gospels while they themselves were never mentioned. Now, we who seek to throw light on the adventurous theories of the church fathers set foot ourselves on the very land of adventure, and there is no turning back. That he observed a different calendar, that of the Essenes, so that what he did on the Sabbath was in his eyes done on days that were not the Sabbath — that seems to us too frivolous an interpretation, not really worth discussion.[79]

Another possibility has more facts to support it. It strikes us that the parallels between Essene lore and the statements of the Gospel according to Mark are very slight, notably slighter than those in the work of the other three evangelists. These last wrote long after the destruction of Jerusalem,* but Mark, probably either in the middle of the Jewish war or just after it. In the middle of the Jewish war, in 68 C.E., the Qumran monastery was abandoned by its inmates. The terrible defeat had also made a definite change in the spiritual background of the Jewish sects: the whole Apocalypse had to be rewritten. Essenes (from Qumran) and Christians could have got to know one another in the distress and confusion of the downfall of Israel. That could have happened in Syria, in Egypt and Asia Minor, even in Rome. That could explain why the Essenes left their mark more clearly on the three other Gospels than on Mark's. But it must be said that the apostle Paul is already full of Essene sayings and ideas, long before the destruction of Jerusalem. By a notable coincidence, he was converted at Damascus, where the Essenes had their (symbolic?) exile and later, perhaps, a settlement. In Damascus, if we wish to take the place literally, he received his first instruction (" . . . I will make you be carried off beyond Damascus").

Paul's conviction of the hopeless sinfulness of man, which he never tires of stressing theologically while refuting it through moral appeals, is surely something he does not have in common with the more superficial synoptics, but rather with Qumran. Similarly, his hatred of the flesh (Qumran: "mass of erring flesh"),[80] his certainty that man is foredoomed to salvation or

*The steadily growing pro-Roman tendency is surprising in view of the misdeeds of Titus and Vespasian; but not so surprising when we consider where the new teaching was spreading.

damnation, his faith in "predestination" (which he proclaims theologically and manages to dodge through the practice of his ministry).

Like Paul, the *Manual of Discipline* attributed redemption to a choice; the Qumran psalmist trusted in "acquittal in God's justice." The Habakkuk commentary speaks of those who are saved from the judgment "on account of their labors and their faith in the Teacher of Righteousness."[81] Paul defines redemption as "the righteousness of God through faith in Jesus Christ for all who believe" (Romans 3:22).

As a theologian on a grand scale, Paul denies that man can be redeemed by good works, although he continually urges such good works on the recipients of his letters. The Qumran people seem to have been less great theologians, yet on that account more reasonable and, on this point, more Jewish. To their way of thinking, good works lead to redemption, and the following of the Law at any rate is no hindrance to the acquisition of grace.

Paul writes: "But we have this treasure in earthen vessels, to show that the transcendent power belongs to God and not to us" (2 Corinthians 4:7). In the Qumran scriptures, we can read: "I thank thee, Lord, that Thou hast done wonders through the dust, Thou hast done mighty works through a fragile vessel."[82] Paul writes: " . . . giving thanks to the Father, who has qualified us to share in the inheritance of the saints in light" (Colossians 1:12).[83]

How can light and darkness agree together, asks Paul, like Christ and Belial? There is no other mention of Belial in the whole of the New Testament. But this prince of darkness is familiar to the people of Qumran, and so is the expression "Satan's angel", which Paul also knows. The little sermon in 2 Corinthians (6:14−18), in which he recommends the faithful to segregate themselves strictly from the unbelievers, is in atmosphere and in conception a piece of Qumran. "For you are all sons of light and sons of the day; we are not of the night or of darkness," writes Paul in his first letter to the Thessalonians (5:5). Paul, John and Qumran, which at first sight we should hardly connect with one another, prove despite all variations in revealed Christology to have strong Essenic features in common.

It has often been observed that the New Testament scriptures reflect a rather different type of Judaism from that of the rabbinical approach. We have found in them a spirit partly Greek, partly Iranian. But both of these are amalgamated in Paul, the spirit of the Greeks and the Iranian, Persian spirit of Qumran and Enoch. Who will now say that the study of dry parchments is not exciting?

Jesus, Bloch's "fanatic among little people," whom we must envisage not in the jet-set of the will-o'-the-wisp movement of the middle and last years of the first century, but in the year 30, forty years before the destruction of Jerusalem, has the least possible traceable connection with Qumran. His ostentatious refusal to observe the Sabbath, thinks Adolf Holl, must have "led immediately to his death."[84] Anyone who brought the authority of the temple in question at that time, under that theocracy, oppressed and oppressive and trembling with strain, was doomed and insane. That goes without saying. But was it a sane man who, according to Mark, spoke the following words:

> Truly, I say to you, whoever says to this mountain, "Be
> taken up and cast into the sea," and does not doubt in his heart,
> but believes that what he says will come to pass, it will be done
> for him (11:23)?

Faith — and Mao's Chinese have taken this literally — moves mountains. This eschatological saying seems also quite acceptable to the critical exegesis, although of course there is no evidence that it came from Jesus. The same figure of speech can be found in Paul (1 Corinthians 13:2), and he can hardly have got it from the apostles, for what we are looking at here is a rabbinical saying.[85] The moving of mountains, like Luke's withering of trees, seems to reflect the expected events of the last times. "In those days," says the Book of Enoch, "the mountains will skip like rams and the little hills like lambs" (51:4).

But does not this visionary phrase (whether or not Jesus uttered it) point to a man whose expectations are pitched too high, a man overstrained, an "inspired agitator" (Morton Smith), a dangerous fanatic, given his personal position and the circumstances of his people — a man endued with an exaggerated self-esteem, who feels that he is free from sin, for Father Daniélou, "an extraordinary puzzle"?[86]

Jesus is not really our pocket-oracle; he does not teach us how we should live, however much trouble the churchmen take to instruct us. The churchmen have even introduced the idea of an "interim ethic," to persuade us that Jesus could quite probably, on the one hand, have had the imminent coming of the kingdom of God in his heart, but on the other hand, have had in his head the forbidding of divorce and of swearing and other special precepts intended for an ordinary human life-span.

Did Jesus really "identify himself with the poorest," as Walter Dirks thinks?[87] Did he ever speak to the poor other than as the poor, did he intercede for "those of his fellow-men in various kinds of need" other than as an eschatological prophet, and did he intercede for them at all other than verbally? We learn nothing about it. The despised and harassed peasantry, the *Am-Haaretz* do not seem to have taken part in the supper, the ceremonial meal, "the ceremony that characterizes his mission" (Josef Blank).[88] The Gospels do not contain a single word against the basic evil of the Israelite community, slavery. We should have liked to hear a protest from Jesus against the handy custom of turning old or sick slaves out of doors. But we don't hear it.

No, the Gospels contain the lessons of the evangelists, no more; and those in turn contain the lessons of the Essenes, the Qumran community, the apocalyptics, the liberal Pharisees, the strict Pharisees, the Jewish Christians, the Hellenists and nothing else. What still appears most reliably Jesuanic is Jesus' position on the very borders of the legality of Torah. His teaching settles down somewhere between the submissive: "The kingdom of God is here," and the egocentric: "I have come," and nothing else is to be got from it. How deeply must a theologian have penetrated when Jesus becomes viable to him "as the religious realist in a people of quietists and Utopists, profiteers and desperados" (Stauffer)?[89]

If this "religious realist" was not simply an idealized derivative from John the Baptist or a man more fortuitously executed, if he was really an historic figure, then he must have been a turbulent man, prey to wild ideas, angered by the ordinary rules of conduct, a *provocateur* who imagined that the coming down of the kingdom of God depended on him and on no one else, who wished to bring down heaven to earth, who knew himself to be the instrument of a higher will, a man with the same uncompromising nature and contempt of life, perhaps, as Janis Joplin, no longer capable of such exaltation, no more open to spiritual ecstasy. Jesus, about whose life we quite seriously know not a word, could never grow old: so much we can sympathize with. It is no coincidence that today's theologians want to preserve his uniqueness by stressing what commands a quick sale today, his apparent companionship with gluttons, boozers and whores. It never says in the Bible that he ate with the poor and the sick and with women.

Perhaps it is credible that he was sorry for the rich because they could not follow the turbulent multitude into the innocent country of the primal days, into Israel's Paradise, now brought forward in time; they had too much on their plates. It is credible, if anything is, that he did not fast, that he had neither the time nor the inclination to fast, that, as one of the sayings in the Gospel of Thomas suggests, he simply did not want to make a show.[90]

"To recognize the world as self-dependent, essentially perfect," as Hegel demands from grown men on pain of their ruin[91] — that was something he did not want, something he was not capable of, as little as Kleist and Hölderlin, as little as Che Guevara. The later Hegel would have unhesitatingly declared him "spiritually sick."[92] We have now come into the field of poetry; but such is the opaque wall of cloud surrounding him that no one can be certain of anything about Jesus who is too blase to go on with an old story.

There are only traces of him in the Gospels, gestures against rather than for the seam of Essenism and related rabbinical teaching: traces of anger, rage, hate and joy; traces of an unconventional refusal to conform, a fanatical madness; traces, too, of an inner arrogance determined to perform the impossible here and now, convinced, as Rudolf Bultmann says, "that fate will arrange things in his favor."[93]

He did, says Ernst Käsemann, "what was required at the time."[94] But the kingdom of God did not come. And all the acrobatic exercises of theology (otherwise, ecclesiastical science), which converted the expectations concentrated in the Jew Jesus on a specific point into a long-drawn-out expectation for all mankind, and turned Jesus himself into "the last herald — after him, only God comes" (Zahrnt)[95] —all this is really rather embarrassing.

Simon Bar Kochba, leader of the last Jewish resistance to the Romans (132−135 C.E.), who certainly believed he was doing "what was required at the time," was named as Messiah by the Rabbi Akiba who died under the iron combs of the Romans. Bar Kochba was actually called Simon ben-Koseba (son of deception). But the rabbi applied to the man he honored the 17th verse of the 24th chapter of Numbers:

I see him, but not now;
I behold him, but not nigh:
a star shall come forth out of Jacob,
and a sceptre shall rise out of Israel;
it shall crush the forehead of Moab,
and break down all the sons of Sheth.

In Simon ben-Koseba, whom the synagogue later recognized as a
"pseudo-Messiah," the rabbi saw the star — hence, the title Bar
Kochba, son of a star. The people of the Damascus Document,
too, saw the star in the expounder of their law,[96] as Matthew and
John the divine did in Jesus.

All had seen the shining of his star.
All had come their gifts to bring.
Of Jesus and of Mary sing.

5. A prophet enters Jerusalem

Only let no one think he has been awaited as the Savior.[1]
— Goethe

Why Jesus went to Jerusalem, what he intended to do there and what he did, what happened to him there — of this, we know nothing. That he was there and that he was put to death in some violent way, we may well accept. There is, though, a passage in Luke that makes us wonder and raises some doubt whether he went up in person or only symbolically:

> At that very hour some Pharisees came, and said to him, "Get away from here, for Herod wants to kill you." And he said to them, "Go and tell that fox, 'Behold, I cast out demons and perform cures today and tomorrow, and on the third day I finish my course. Nevertheless I must go on my way today and tomorrow and the day following; for it cannot be that a prophet should perish away from Jerusalem.'"

He will "be at his goal" (*Mustard Seed*), "reach an end" (*Luther Bible* 1964), "finish" (*Jerusalem Bible*), "be finished" (*Wilckens*). As a "Galilean Messiah," did he have to go up to Jerusalem?

Did he have to "end his kingdom . . . here, at the place chosen by God" (Walther Zimmerli, born 1907, Old Testament scholar in Göttingen)?[2] Jerusalem is the place of fulfilment, the goal of the third (resurrection) day — that might well make one sceptical. A martyr killed in Galilee or executed by Herod in the fortress of Machaerus would have consequently have had to be transferred to Jerusalem in the subsequent process of deification. In Mark, though, Jesus prophesies to the disciples on the night of Gethsemane (14:28): "But after I am raised up, I will go before you to Galilee," as if Galilee has some concealed significance, perhaps as the actual, the non-symbolical, scene of events. But rather than create complete confusion, let us assume that Jesus was killed in Jerusalem.

We must content ourselves for a start with this rather meagre guesswork. We do not know whether Jesus had any purpose in mind, or what it was if he did. Did he wish, as Conzelmann believes, "to call the people as such — under his leadership — finally to repentance,"[3] without any sort of Messianic ambitions? Did he want to settle something, and if so what, or did he wish to die simply in accordance with his mission? Was he, as George Bernard Shaw quite seriously supposes, "overwrought" by all that had happened so that he "at last went mad as Swift and Ruskin and Nietzsche went mad"?[4] We do not know. We do not know whether he was condemned. We do not know who condemned him, whether it was the Council or Herod Antipas the Tetrarch or Pilate. With Bultmann, we are not even certain about the cross.[5] If he breathed his last on the tree, that certainly points to an execution at the hands of the Romans. If we hold the Romans responsible, then we can regard the stake or the cross as historical. Or did he never hang living from the tree at all?

Whatever strikes us as definite in the accounts of the evangelists seems to have been worked up from the prophecies and psalms of the ancient scriptures with a force of poetic imagination which would be incredible if the scriptures of the Old Covenant had not stood as a stimulating godfather, a religious poem worked on and added to uninterruptedly for more than eight hundred years. Psalms and prophecies told "even more about the suffering of the Lord than fleeing disciples or terrified women could tell" (Martin Dibelius).[6] The people of Qumran, too, revealed to themselves the fate of the mysterious Teacher of Righteousness from the prophecies of scripture.

But the imaginative powers of the disciples would hardly have sufficed for them to invent the figure itself, if they had not been inspired by the violent death of a man whom some of them had themselves known and honored. Just consider what it would have meant in the year 30 to regard oneself as one who, in Wolfhart Pannenberg's words, "ascribed to the relationship of mankind with himself the character of the eschatological verdict on their salvation or damnation."[7] Without simplicity, without the foolishness of a Parsifal, such a quasi-Messianic claim with regard to a united kingdom of all the children of this world in Jerusalem is unimaginable. Remember that the Talmud contains the instruction that the High Priest must exceed the rest of the priesthood in wealth. Yet Jesus came from no well-known family, he was not an educated man, he came from the country, it may well be from the half-heathen Galilee. He seems never to have stayed in Tiberias, the Galilean capital of the "fox" Herod Antipas, although it is almost impossible to traverse that country without touching Tiberias.

There is something primitive, something elementary in the stories of Jesus. Let us be clear that he is definitely said above all to have driven out devils, a business in which the recognized rabbis of that time no longer felt at ease. They tried to suppress this always unaccountable trick of popular faith (or superstition). But the post-Marcan Jesus sees in his power to drive out evil spirits the decisive proof that the kingdom of God has overthrown the rule of Satan. See Matthew:

> But if it is by the Spirit of God that I cast out demons, then the kingdom of God has come upon you (12:28)

In Luke, the spirit of God has become the finger of God (11:20). It is as the conqueror of Satan that Jesus drives out the devils. In that period, people believed in demons and in whole hierarchies of demons. Even sickness and various kinds of illness were attributed partly to the sins of the afflicted, partly to devils. Not until the very late edition of John's Gospel do physical suffering and infirmity, such as blindness from birth, serve to illustrate God's deeds (9:11 ff.): the high point of one of the miracles descending verbally step by step, a piece of factual yet glorifying theology.

Not only Jesus himself, but also his disciples, had "power over unclean spirits." He commanded them, according to Matthew(10:8 ff.): "Heal the sick, revive the dead, cleanse the lepers, drive out devils." The power is transferable, too. Peter, according to Acts (9:40), goes all the way and restores the dead to life. Jesus also commands the winds and the waves as if they were possessed by devils: "Peace, be still!" (Mark 4:39). The demons for their part, according to Mark (1:34; 3:11 ff.), "knew him" and were therefore strictly charged not to address him by his true titles so as not to make him known to all the bystanders.*

When he drives out devils, Jesus works only through the spoken word. It is not so when he heals the sick. On one occasion, he makes a paste of clay and spittle and smears it on the eyes of a blind man, as the Emperor Vespasian is also recorded to have done, with equally positive results.[10] His signs and wonders are meant to convince those not convinced by the word he preaches.

No doubt miracles were attributed to Jesus by report, and no one today should be so positivist as to apply the yardstick of science to every single healing. The legends may well have snowballed. Matthew sometimes uses the doubling technique, putting "two blind men," "two possessed of devils" where Mark is content with one. Whether Jesus wanted to work miracles is just a question of whether you think it likely. I for one accept it.

In any case, miracles were obligatory; they were reckoned to be signs of the day of salvation (which is also a day of vengeance), as described to us in the book of Isaiah:

Strengthen the weak hands,
and make firm the feeble knees.
Say to those who are of a fearful heart,
"Be strong, fear not!
Behold, your God
will come with a vengeance
with the recompense of God.
He will come and save you."

Then the eyes of the blind shall be opened,
and the ears of the deaf unstopped;
then shall the lame man leap like a hart,
and the tongue of the dumb sing for joy.
For waters shall break forth in the wilderness,
and streams in the desert . . . (35:3–6)

---

*It really calls for a great sense of piety to recognize with Professor Josef Blank, anno 1971, that: "Where men are freed from the power of devils, then they are restored to true humanity as God intended it; then we can see what Jesus meant by the salvation of men." Blank sees in Jesus' driving out of devils not myth, not demonology, but "demythologizing, de-demonizing."[9]

139

To bring good news to the humble, to proclaim liberty to captives and release to those in prison; to bind up the broken-hearted, to comfort all who mourn, that is the task of the true prophet, according to Isaiah (61:1−2). Jesus, according to Luke, quotes him in Nazareth. The dead will live, their bodies will rise again (Isaiah 26:19) — there's a program. In Matthew and Luke, but not in Mark, the Baptist sends to ask Jesus whether he is the expected one, or whether they should look for another. Jesus sends the Baptist the reply: "Go and tell John what you have seen and heard: the blind see, the lame walk, the lepers are cleansed, the deaf hear, the dead are raised up . . . " If Jesus had not himself believed in his signs and wonders,* they would still have been attributed to him. Bultmann believes that miracles were also reported of John the Baptist,[12] understandably, even if they are not mentioned in the Gospels.

We can easily believe it possible that the self-confidence of Jesus was in contrast to the rather sensitive nature of the Baptist. We must also take into account that many educated people mistrusted or disliked this style of declaring the kingdom of God. Unless the Gospels are pure fantasy, Jesus thought of himself as a sign of the kingdom of God that he preached.

In such men, religion and simplicity come together, and the appeal to childlike, credulous simplicity runs as a continuous thread through all four Gospels (and not only the Gospels; so modern a theologian as Herbert Braun praises the parable of equal pay for unequal work, "where by this argument man is initiated into the role of the gifted child").[13] Certainly there were many who were expecting the Messiah, but scarcely anyone among those people, with their Hellenistic education, was able to envisage this Messiah, scarcely anyone was inclined to see himself as the Messiah. or even as one for whom, as our theologians say, "fate is decisive."

---

*Blank gives a "general" afirmative to the question "whether the historical Jesus actually performed miracles." He counts it to Jesus' credit that he steadily refused to perform Satanic miracles. A repeat of the miracle of manna, for example (when the Lord saved his people from starvation in the desert by a rain of manna), or the effective appearance in the temple (after hurling himself from its pinnacle) or the Messianic rule over the whole world ("All this will I give you"), he refused as temptations of Satan. Blank concedes that Jesus did not abolish all the evil in the world with his miracles. But "he had clearly pointed a way which is valid for believers, namely, that the relief and, as far as possible, the elimination of all human distress, of sickness, hunger, ignorance, bondage and every kind of inhumanity is the continuing and the first task of man for man." So the miracles can also be seen as a kind of lesson.[11]

140

Indeed, there was nothing divine attaching to the Messiah, even if God did say to him, as to every newly anointed king of Israel: "He said to me, 'You are my son, today I have begotten you'" (Psalm 2:7). The Messiah is only the anointed, no more, "a human creature, flesh and blood like all mortals. He is only the best of the race of men and the chosen from among his people" — so writes the Jewish historian Joseph Klausner.[14] Anyway, who ever thinks of himself as the best of the race of men, "only" the best? Even Jesus, as we have seen, possibly or probably did not regard himself as that.

The dramatic color of the Gospels has often been admired, so that it was some time before the authenticity of the accounts was queried. The wealth of relevant detail had been taken as proof of a high degree of authenticity. But it is precisely those relevant passages, for instance in the Passion in Mark's Gospel, which seize with poetic force upon earlier prophecies from the old scriptures. They are richly endowed with "creativity" and "poetic force," those qualities which Martin Dibelius will not allow the first of the Jesus-propagandists;[15] the term "biology of legend," following the epic laws of folk poetry, has justifiably been used.[16]

Mark's account of the dialogue between Jesus and his heavenly father in the garden of Gethsemane, immediately before his arrest, cannot have been overheard by any of the sleeping disciples:

And he said to them, "My soul is very sorrowful even to death; remain here, and watch." And going a little further, he fell on the ground and prayed that, if it were possible, the hour might pass from him. And he said, "Abba, Father, all things are possible to thee; remove this cup from me; yet not what I will, but what thou wilt." (14:34-36)

The cup of suffering is a frequent motif in the Old testament. Here the evangelist suggests that Jesus had nothing else in mind than to do the will of his heavenly Father and to be offered up as a sacrifice for sin in Jerusalem, where the healing power is presumably strongest. The Psalmist, in the lament of a Levite in exile, sings three times running, Psalm (42:5&11) and in Psalm (43:5):

Why are you cast down, O my soul, and why are you disquieted within me?

141

We see the soul cast down and disquieted even unto death in a different light in the story of Jonah. Jonah is mortally angry because the Lord first makes a castor-oil plant grow for him and then lets it wither, so that the sun scorches his head. We always have to reckon with the creative power of re-interpretation in the Gospel story-tellers. The mortal distress of Jesus satisfies the vision of the first Christians, who looked on his prayerful struggle, part doubting, part obedient, as a proof that he was the Messiah, a fulfilment of the prophecies. Thus, it says in the so-called letter to the Hebrews, which may have been written by an unknown author towards the end of the first century:

In the days of his flesh, Jesus offered up prayers and supplications, with loud cries and tears, to him who was able to save him from death, and he was heard for his godly fear. (5:7)

Bultmann regards the night on the Mount of Olives as an "original, separate story of quite legendary character." The disciples have to sleep, for dramatic reasons: "the contrast between their dullness and Jesus' fear of death is thus made most effective."[17] The well-known verse: "Watch and pray that you may not enter into temptation; the spirit indeed is willing, but the flesh is weak" (Mark 14:38) is an interpolation of Christian construction, however "genuine" it may sound in the ears of churchgoers. Only the Holy Ghost can have told the evangelist what it was that Jesus prayed, or else the author has created it out of the scriptures. There are already plenty of passages dealing with the tension between heavenly will and human lowliness.

If we read the texts in this way, against the background of the older writings, then we must soon doubt again whether Jesus really went up to Jerusalem to make a demonstration and yet at the same time to keep the Passover. The Messiah was generally expected at precisely this festival, which had to be celebrated in Jerusalem and not in the other Jewish lands. The Passover supper, privilege of Jerusalem and the signal for the starting of the Passover week for all Jews, could only be celebrated in Jerusalem on the afternoon and evening of 14 Nisan; the celebration began after sunset (i.e., the beginning of 15 Nisan). There is scarcely one detail in the Passion stories that cound not have been adapted from the old Bible. Take only the purging of the temple, unlikely as it may have seemed to the church father Origen (he called Jesus' behavior, taken literally, "presumptuous and rowdy");[18] it emerges without any strain from the sayings of the elders.

So now we have two versions to choose from. *Either* Jesus conducted himself in line with the prophecies so that he might fulfil them, an assumption which is elaborated to the point of caricature by Hugh Schonfield in his best-seller *The Passover Plot*[19] ("we must next get it clear that Jesus included his resurrection in his planning just as much as his execution"); *or* the reports of the evangelists have been woven from the texts of the prophets and psalmists.

In support of his reading, Schonfield tells us that Jesus consciously followed a plan of life so ordered as "to fulfil what the prophecies required of the Messiah in accordance with their conceptions." Thus, even as he hung from the Cross, he borrowed from Psalm 22 the words: "My God, my God, why hast thou forsaken me?" But even a theologian like Burrows declares that it is "quite clear that Jesus deliberately and consistently directed himself towards 'what was written about the Son of Man.'"[20] What was it that the first editor came on to describe the entry of Jesus into Jerusalem, and how did he come upon the entry? We can find the whole plan for the Messianic entry in the prophet Zechariah, who so often serves us as advance announcer:

> Rejoice greatly, O daughter of Zion!
> Shout aloud, O daughter of Jerusalem!
> Lo, your king comes to you;
> triumphant and victorious is he,
> humble and riding on an ass,
> on a colt the foal of an ass.

Since the real kings behaved like Oriental despots, there was an age-old wish for a king who as a sign of his moderation was depicted as riding on an ass. It is maintained, but not verified, that Zerubbabel, who rebuilt the temple in Jerusalem at the side of Zechariah, was regarded as such a king of peace, riding for symbolic reasons on an ass.[21] In any case, he vanishes without trace from the history of Israel.

The editor of Matthew tries to be more precise than Mark; with a literalness worthy of the good soldier Schweik, he makes them bring Jesus a she-ass and a foal. In the Hebrew text of Zechariah, the ass is described as a foal, the young of a she-ass; the evangelist has got the duplication from the Septaugint, which he relied on and which is written in Greek (" . . . rides upon an ass and the foal of an ass"). So now Jesus has to sit on both animals, Matthew does not tell us how. He is no more forthcoming on the question of whether anyone could make any progress on a foal anyway. Bultmann at any rate finds it an "absurd" idea that Jesus should have ridden into Jerusalem on a relatively untried foal of an ass simply to fulfil the scripture.[22] But the *Luther Bible* of 1964 does not find it absurd at all: it tells us that Jesus wanted to remind the people of the fulfilment of this heavenly prophecy. So we must decide: either for a Jesus who, like a yachtsman, rounds all the buoys which mark his course, or for evangelists who are not so much recreating events as creating them from the scriptures.

Zechariah prophesies the entry and the people's rejoicing. But was there any such entry, and did Jesus have more than a handful of people with him? Did his arrival perhaps, as Maurice Goguel, the biographer of Jesus, wrote in 1932, "pass practically unnoticed in the middle of the crowd"? The circumstances described by Mark, as has been illuminatingly pointed out by Shalom Ben-Chorin in his book, *Brother Jesus*, suggest not the Passover but Succoth, the popular Feast of Tabernacles, which is celebrated to this day in the Jerusalem sanctuary as a combined harvest thanksgiving festival and pilgrimage in the autumn.[24] Succoth is reckoned to attract more pilgrims than any other feast in the Jewish calendar. The branch of palm, *lulab*, was, and still is, swung together with a kind of citrus and with osier and myrtle in a kind of festival bouquet in procession round the altar, while Psalm 118:25 was and still is recited:

Save us, we beseech thee, O LORD!
O LORD, we beseech thee, give us success!

after which it goes on:

Blessed be he who enters in the name of the LORD!

and one verse later:

Bind the festal procession with branches,
up to the horns of the altar!

Here it is, the procession with branches in hand. "Deliver us" is in Hebrew *hoshiana*, whence we get the Greek ὡσαννά (English "Hosanna") of those who take part in the procession. The Marcan evangelist's knowledge of Jewish ritual appears here in a dubious light:

> And those who went before and those who followed cried out, "Hosanna! Blessed is he who comes in the name of the Lord! Blessed is the kingdom of our father David that is coming! Hosanna in the highest." (11:9-10)

The branches of palm turned into green branches or, in Wilckens's translation, "bundles of leaves":

> And they brought the colt to Jesus, and threw their garments on it; and he sat upon it. And many spread their garments on the road, and others spread leafy branches which they had cut from the fields. (11:7−8)

If the entire entry had been invented in order to fulfil the words of the prophets, that would tell us little except that the author had a close acquaintance with the scriptures. But is it perhaps not wholly invented? Is Jesus perhaps coming, not to the Passover, but to the Feast of Tabernacles, which the tradition has converted into the Passover? Is this interpretation meant to signify the symbolic Paschal lamb, with its link with Isaiah, who says of the "suffering servant of God":

> All we like sheep have gone astray;
> we have turned every one to his own way;
> and the LORD has laid on him
> the iniquity of us all.
> He was oppressed, and he was afflicted,
> yet he opened not his mouth;
> like a lamb that is led to the slaughter,
> and like a sheep that before its shearers is dumb,
> so he opened not his mouth. (53:6−7)

That would at least make it possible to explain how it is that the disciples have not yet managed to describe to comrades learned in the scriptures, and to give date to, the evening of what was apparently their last meal with the Master in accordance with the order for the Passover. We should at least know when the supper,

145

the Passover and the Sabbath were. That, if nothing else, must have stayed in their minds as a lasting memory.

Both traditions, of the Synoptics and of John, reveal such serious gaps here that they must both be suspected of having given preference to the symbolic significance of (in the Synoptics) the Passover supper and (in John) the slaughter of the Paschal lamb, rather than the actual events (of the Feast of Tabernacles?). Perhaps it is putting the cart before the horse to suggest that the evangelists did not feel, or no longer felt, like Jews and that they used materials from people who were not on the spot. Thus from what was perhaps an annual meal in remembrance of the death of the Lord and in expectation of his return, a last supper before his death was evolved; from that again, a symbolical Passover meal, and from that, a seminal supper for the setting up of a Hellenistic-Christian sacrament, the Eucharist.

We may speculate further: no Jew in any way instructed in the law, says the expert Gustav Dalman, would speak, as the Marcan evangelist and the scripture-obsessed Matthew speak, of the first day of the feast if he meant the day of preparation for the feast.[25] In John's Gospel, Jesus already stands before Pilate while the slaughter of the Paschal lambs is being prepared. There, as also in Paul, the Last Supper is not a Passover meal. Even Mark's supper, many theologians think, is not a Passover meal in the texts nearer the original. During the Passover, everyone must have his own bowl before him. Mark (14:20) states that the traitor Judas takes from the same bowl as Jesus. To the question who it will be, Jesus answers: "It is one of the twelve, one who is dipping bread in the same dish with me."

It may be that the writers of the Synoptics combined the Passover, which was right to them on symbolic grounds, with the Feast of Tabernacles for the benefit of their Hellenistically educated readers, considering that Jewish ritual would not be specially important to them. What mattered to the writers of the Synoptics was the cult, that founding of a mystic and unifying spper in remembrance of Jesus (Bultmann: "a cult-legend"). They certainly made use of recollections of the Passover supper, itself a memorial meal for the suffering and deliverance of Israel in Egypt, even if they confused the "cup of blessing" of the Passover with the chalice of the New Covenant, the (ox-)blood of the Old Testament (Exodus 24:8) sprinkled by Moses over the people with the blood of Jesus, and the memory of their deliverance from the hand of the

Egyptians with the memory of the salvation of Jesus and of his act of salvation.

But they could make good use even of the Feast of Tabernacles. Like the Passover, it was originally a seasonal festival. Its name is derived from the huts they lived in during the fruit harvest, then from the tradition that Yahweh had made the Israelites live in arbors during the flight out of Egypt. (Leviticus 23:43: Luther speaks of the "summer leaves or tabernacles".)[26] In the Messianic end-time that the prophet Zecharias foresees, "then everyone that survives of all the nations that have come against Jerusalem shall go up year after year to worship the King, the LORD of hosts, and to keep the feast of booths." (14:16)

Whatever feast he may have been going to, or perhaps to no feast at all: Jesus, says Mark, goes "up" to Jerusalem, a thousand meters difference in altitude from the Lake of Gennesaret, two hundred meters below sea level, to the city of David set eight hundred meters above. He beholds the temple, perhaps for the first time, goes out through the gate to Bethany, spends the night there and returns next day to Jerusalem. On the way, he curses a fig-tree which bears no fruit ready for him when he is hungry, since it is not yet the season for figs: "May no one ever again eat fruit from you!" (Mark 11:12–14).

See the trickle of symbolism: Jerusalem is to be destroyed, and there are even theologians who consider it "unhistoric" that the fig-tree had "withered away to its roots" (Mark 11:20). But after all, it is still shown to pilgrims on their way to the Mount of Olives. Mark reads:

And they came to Jerusalem. And he entered the temple and began to drive out those who sold and those who bought in the temple, and he overturned the tables of the money-changers and the seats of those who sold pigeons; and he would not allow anyone to carry anything through the temple. And he taught, and said to them, "Is it not written, 'My house shall be called a house of prayer for all the nations?' But you have made it a den of robbers." And the chief priests and the scribes heard it and sought a way to destroy him; for they feared him, because all the multitude was astonished at his teaching. And when evening came they went out of the city.

To get this narrative in proper perspective, we must picture to ourselves the temple of Herod in all its pomp and glory, the equal of the seven wonders of the world — the Holy of Holies set deep within, behind walls, forecourts and courts, the innermost room which even the High Priest might enter only once a year, on the greatest of their feast-days, the Day of Atonement (Yom Kippur). This concentration in Jerusalem of the entire worship, the temple and the offerings, of all Jews was something unique; there was no center of worship like it anywhere in the inhabited world. If a heathen entered the inner courts, he incurred the death penalty and, as an inscription discovered there reads, "himself bore the responsibility."[27] Adolf von Harnack saw in Jesus' purging of the temple his "first unequivocal Messianic action," and also "his last."[28] The money-changers and dealers did not sit in the temple but in the semi-profane forecourts around the temple. The current coin with the portrait of Caesar had to be exchanged for temple coinage with no image on it, which could be used for the purchase of beasts for sacrifice on the spot. Ben-Chorin writes: "The idea that Jesus, armed with a whip of cords, overturned the tables of the money-changers and chased out the officials of the temple bank is too fantastic to be true."[29] Jesus always does everything alone; none of the disciples ever does anything beside him or with him. The temple police do not intervene, not even in John's Gospel, which puts this scene at the beginning of the activity of a still entirely unknown Jesus. He has a "whip of cords," a kind of cat-o'-nine-tails. The scene has been worked up from several prophecies, such as the temple address of Jeremiah (7:11) with its accusation: "Has this house, which is called by my name, become a den of robbers in your eyes?" Or from the close of the prophet Zechariah:

> . . . and every pot in Jerusalem and Judah shall be sacred to the LORD of hosts, so that all who sacrifice may come and take of them and boil the flesh of the sacrifice in them. And there shall no longer be a trader in the house of the LORD of hosts on that day.

— from Psalm 69:9 ("Zeal for thy house has consumed me"), and Isaiah 56:7 ("for my house shall be called a house of prayer for all peoples"). No, we may comfort ourselves with Origen: it is only in the highly-colored versions of the evangelists that the Lord behaved in this "presumptuous and rowdy" way. But he had to go

148

into the temple, according to Malachi (3:1−3): and the Lord whom you seek will suddenly come to his temple" and will "purify the sons of Levi and refine them like gold and silver." The scene, which Bultmann calls "a probably historical happening" and Braun "an actual event from the life of Jesus,"[30] is an imitation, and not even a realistic one.

We could not begin to describe all the deviations that have been printed in connection with the purging of the temple. One interesting opinion is that of Rabbi Victor Eppstein, based on a historic conflict of the year 30 C.E. Caiaphas, as High Priest, had introduced the sale of beasts in the courts of the temple and thus come into competition with the sales on the Mount of Olives, which were controlled by the Council.[31] That can obviously have nothing to do with Jesus. Stauffer on the other hand envisages a Jesus who is a rigorous maintainer of the Sabbath and manages to bring about a ban on transportation within the temple and its courts[32] — a somewhat odd idea applied to such a notorious Sabbath-rationalizer. Joachim Jeremias, again, has declared that the tables of the money-changers were not set up all the year round, but only for three weeks before the Passover, and during the Passover;[33] he has an indication of time here, and he believes in it.

Anyway, the people the temple priests were so worried about never seem to have played any part on Jesus' side. They were not there when Jesus was taken before Pilate. And not even the crucifixion during the feast brought about what seems to have been so greatly feared: there was no sort of disturbance, not even the threat of it. Jesus goes into the temple premises and talks like a street-corner preacher, even with the High Priests, among whom we understand were also the former High Priest and his clan. If the scenes described by Mark were "genuine," then Jesus would have been making fun of the *pilpul*, the sharp-witted, penetrating speech of the rabbis. He would seem to have been enjoying it, neither threatening nor threatened.

Two persons are described to us whose conduct could in a penetrating light have expressed opposite sides of his being or of his later *imago*: Judas and Peter. In the epic story we are trying to unravel, the disciples figure as human chips off the Ego of the Jesus-figure, who has been turned into a superman; they give life to the Passion Play. "On the first day of unleavened bread," meaning the day of preparation for the Passover, Jesus celebrates the

Last Supper with the twelve disciples (clearly without wives, who would have been allowed to be present during a Passover meal). But first we have a fairy-tale, as we did just now with the ass's foal ("the Master has need of it"). Two disciples go into the city, meet a man carrying a jar of water, follow him into a house, speak to the landlord: "The Master says, 'Where is the room in which I can eat the Paschal lamb with my disciples?'" and find everything just as their Master foretold.

Judas sits at table with them. But in Mark's story, Jesus gives no indication which of the twelve is the traitor (he does, though, in Matthew and in John's Gospel, where the opportunity is taken once more to draw attention to the author, the "disciple whom Jesus loved"). But the betrayal looks quite senseless. Jesus has remained in a relatively small area, surrounded at least by his disciples, for several days. It needed no expert to point him out and say: "That is he."[34] The writer of John's Gospel has seen how illogical this is. He makes Judas show the authorities where Jesus hid himself overnight; Judas "knew the place". In John's Gospel, Judas is specifically the man of the night, in which only he can work; he is the angel of Satan, the angel of death of the Passover night in Egypt, only this time he destroys the righteous. John says: "As soon as Judas received it (the bread that Jesus had given him) Satan entered him." To get himself into the picture, the beloved disciple-evangelist overlooks the illogical fact that he, the beloved disciple, already knows who is the traitor, yet when they were still at table no one knew the meaning of Jesus' words: "Do quickly what you have to do."

The scene gathers episodes as the years pass. In Mark, which does not describe him as the treasurer, Judas says only: "Rabbi" and "kisses him"; kisses the life from the lips of the anointed.* In Matthew, he actually asks the temple priests about the reward, and Jesus speaks to him: "Friend, do what you are here to do." In Luke, who has already made the devil enter into him, Jesus asks him: "Judas, would you betray the Son of Man with a kiss?" Finally, in John, the devil enters into him as soon as Jesus gives him the piece of bread. According to the beloved disciple, even

*The army commander Joab, fallen into disgrace with King David on account of the murder of Absalom, kills his rival Amasa with his sword while he kisses him ("Is it well with you, my brother?" (2 Samuel 20:9-10)).

Judas and the men he brought with him — incidentally, there were six hundred of them — fall to the ground when Jesus answers the question, whom were they looking for, by saying: "I am he." The kiss, together with all other symbolic kisses, is not found in John. This evangelist makes Judas a greedy criminal: "... he was a thief; he used to pilfer the money put into the common purse."

The opinion of the most knowledgeable Catholic expert, the professor of theology Josef Blinzler, that "this sinister, dark figure" remains "a psychological puzzle which not even poetic fantasy can illuminate" sounds innocent, when everything tells us that it is to poetic fantasy that this superfluous traitor owes his entire existence. In 2 Samuel (1:16), David, the rival of Saul, says to the camp-follower who reports that on his orders he has killed King Saul: "Your blood be upon your head; for your own mouth has testified against you, saying, 'I have slain the LORD's anointed.' " David has the man killed; Judas, according to Matthew, "hanged himself." King David was also betrayed by his chancellor Ahithophel in the case of the rebellion of his son Absalom; he had to flee over the Mount of Olives and the brook Kedron, but escaped because Ahithophel's plan was not followed. Ahithophel, who betrayed David, hanged himself (2 Samuel 17:23) like Judas who betrayed David's son: the only suicides in both Testaments.[36]

Much the same thing happens to Judas, only in the reverse direction, as happens to the Virgin Mary: the more highly this anonymous lady was honored in Christian teaching at the start, the more spiteful and wounding becomes her legend in the Jewish writings. (Mistress of a Roman legionary called Panthera, hence "Panther-cat," "hairdresser," she conceived her illegitimate son during menstruation, he is a bastard of impurity, a so-called "Mamser ben Nidda" etc.)[37] Judas, on the contrary, ever more blackened by the Christians as the very picture of human degradation, grows in Jewish literature to become an angelic counterpart and milk-brother of Jesus, with whom he battles in the heavens. An Islamic legend, found in the Koran, even relates that Judas suddenly received the same face as Jesus and was crucified by the Jews in his place.[38] In the Jewish collection of legends, *Toldoth Jeshu*, written down in Hebrew before the eighth century, Jesus is beaten by Judas in a contest of magic. Both fly in the air, but Judas soils Jesus by urinating on him and thereby vitiates the miraculous power of the misused word of God which Jesus has sewn up in his flesh.[39]

The Freudian, Theodor Reik, obviously influenced by such legends, pictures Judas for us as "Christ's *alter ego.*"[40] After Jesus' death, he says, a lasting impression was made on the subconscious of his followers to the effect that their Master had committed a crime against God, the ancient father, or at least against the law of Yahweh. The scapegoat is the part of the Ego which should be repressed. For Jesus' followers Judas is the other Ego of a Jesus who may have wished to follow different paths from those described, a Jesus from whom his followers had to drive out the consciousness that he had betrayed the Yahweh of the Law; that he, not Judas, is the traitor to God. Actually, there is a function of exoneration, of a scapegoat, shown by the increasingly frightful end pictured for the Judas figure — in Acts (1:18) he tears open his stomach so that all his bowels gush out; in later accounts he decomposes, hurls himself into the sea with a millstone hung round his neck, swells to so monstrous a size that he cannot pass down any street.[41] He carries with him into the desert not only all the temptations and omissions of the disciples but also perhaps the thoughts and actions of the Master. Consistently enough, the evangelist John finds a fulfilment of scripture even in the treachery of this "son of iniquity" (Gollwitzer).[42] Paul, surprisingly, does not mention him, though a betrayal is always theologically productive; but perhaps as a renegade himself he was concerned to conceal this wretched sort of political turn-coat? Surely that would be to underrate Paul.

In the non-canonical *Gospel according to Peter,* written later than the four canonical Gospels, the Lord is mourned and wept for by his *twelve* disciples after his crucifixion.[43] Bultmann diagnoses "legendary coloring" in the Judas story[44] — although the similarity of Judas with Judah* with Jew has contributed to appalling pogroms for a millennium and a half. (Even those who believe virtually nothing else still believe that Judas betrayed Jesus to his enemies — 91% in the 1967 poll).

*(It should be noted that these words are even more similar in German than in English: Judas, Juda, Jude. — Editor's note.)

Ben-Chorin thinks that we cannot doubt the historicity of Judas, because the original community could hardly have invented a figure so exceedingly painful.[46] I do not agree. The Gospels are playing on the double-bass the whole time; they get their inspiration for it from the scriptures. It is there in the Psalms (41:9): " . . . Even my bosom friend in whom I trusted, who ate of my bread, has lifted his heel against me."

Matthew has been through the old Bible particularly carefully and constructed his account without any thought of plausibility or comprehensibility. In Zechariah (11:12−13):

> Then I said to them, "If it seems right to you, give me my wages, but if not, keep them." And they weighed out as my wages thirty shekels of silver. The LORD said to me, "Cast it into the treasury" — the lordly price at which I was paid off by them. So I took the thirty shekels of silver and cast them into the treasury in the house of the LORD.[47]

The evangelist does not bother to check the context. He slaps the passage down on to a very superficial key-word and serves it up like this:

> When Judas, his betrayer, saw that he was condemned, he repented and brought back the thirty pieces of silver to the chief priests and the elders, saying, "I have sinned in betraying innocent blood." They said, "What is that to us? See to it yourself." And throwing down the pieces of silver in the temple, he departed; and he went and hanged himself. (Matthew 27:3−5)

Here they are, the thirty pieces of silver, and Judas throwing them "into the house of the Lord, into the treasury."

Even more strikingly, Matthew puts together the next five verses from Zechariah and Jeremiah. In Chapter 32, Jeremiah is talking about the purchase of a field in his birthplace, Anathoth, as a pledge for the redemption of the Jews. Yahweh has ordered him to buy the field as a sign of his promise that, despite the disaster brewing up over Jerusalem, there is still hope: "Houses, fields and vineyards shall again be bought in this land." Jeremiah paid seventeen silver shekels (pieces of silver), not thirty.

What does Matthew make of it?

But the chief priests, taking the pieces of silver, said, "It is not lawful to put them into the treasury, since they are blood money." So they took counsel, and bought with them the potter's field, to bury strangers in. Therefore that field has been called the Field of Blood to this day. Then was fulfilled what had been spoken by the prophet Jeremiah, saying, "And they took the thirty pieces of silver, the price of him on whom a price had been set by some of the sons of Israel, and they gave them for the potter's field, as the Lord directed me." (27:6—10)

Confusion reigns. The passage comes, not from Jeremiah, but from Zechariah. In Jeremiah, there are not thirty pieces of silver but seventeen; it is not the children of Israel who have sold the ground but the prophet who has bought it, on Yahweh's orders; it is not a "blood acre" but a field of promise. Matthew calls the field the Potter's Field either because the Lord had told Jeremiah: "Take these deeds, both this sealed deed of purchase and this open deed, and put them in an earthenware vessel, that they may last for a long time" (32:14); or, because in the Hebrew text the prophet Zechariah gives the thirty pieces of silver (about the price of a slave)[48] not "into the treasury" but "to the potter."

The evangelists did not always compose in this slovenly way. Yet nothing is left of the figure of Judas but this fictitious mirror image of the Lord, the son of darkness. The dramatic function of Peter has long been recognized; all that is disputed now is whether the object of the story of his denial of Jesus is to distinguish him or to blacken him. While before the Council of the Jews Jesus is admitting what he is, Peter, the disciples' representative out there in the courtyard, is denying him. The contrast with the Lord, steadfast in his sorrow, is obvious. Peter too, like Judas, takes on the role of a kind of scapegoat, though in more positive colors. The flight of the followers of Jesus, their shame that they had not made the slightest effort to rescue the Lord or even to be present, if only at a distance, at his death, even to bury him, as John the Baptist had been buried by his disciples: was it not natural that they should humble themselves in an "ideal scene," an imagined scene of symbolic character?

In Mark, Peter begins to weep; in Matthew, he goes out and weeps bitterly ("This is how Peter himself described the events to Mark," claims the *Luther Bible*). In Luke, the Lord turns and looks at Peter just after he denies him. Finally, in John, one of the servants recognizes in Peter the man who struck off the ear (only Luke knows that it was the right ear) of the High Priest's servant (who by now actually has a name: he is called Malchus). And although the servant who recognizes Peter is a relative of this Malchus, according to John nothing at all happens to Peter, nobody asks him any questions; in Mark, whose version the others only elaborate, it has not yet become even a disciple who strikes out, but "one of the party."

The denial three times and, in Mark, the cock's crowing twice (in the other Gospels, the cock only crows once) are folk-tale motifs. Bultmann believes that the whole story of the denial is legendary and literary.[49] He has actually held learned debates on whether the crowing cock is historical.*

The arrest in the garden of Gethsemane contains nothing that does not arise quite naturally from the situation: the dressing-up is taken from the old prophecies. The disciples run away, for it stands written, according to Mark (14:27): "I will strike the shepherd and the sheep will be scattered." And here is the passage itself, again from Zechariah:

"Awake, O sword, against my shepherd,
against the man who stands next to me,"
says the Lord of hosts.
"Strike the shepherd, that the sheep may be scattered;
I will turn my hand against the little ones." (13:7)

The flight of the disciples is "simply a literary motif," thinks Bultmann's pupil Ernst Fuchs.[51] Certainly some scholars see in the text of Mark traces of a quite early, almost pre-Marcan tradition according to which Jesus' followers could have tried to resist the arrest of their Master:

---

*Wilhelm Brandt thinks it unhistorical because in Jerusalem, unlike the rest of Palestine, the keeping of poultry was forbidden in Jesus' time. But, says Dalman, "the Sadducees (as the temple party) and the people did not take much notice of such prohibitions." Jeremias even thinks it "probable" that poultry were sold in the market in Jerusalem. The keeping of poultry, says the Strack-Billerbeck commentary, was only allowed in Jerusalem if the birds were not given a chance to flock together; if they flocked, worms developed on the surface of the ground, and worms are "unclean beasts." One could go on like that pretty much forever.[50]

And they laid hands on him and siezed him. But one of those who stood by drew his sword, and struck the slave of the high priest and cut off his ear. And Jesus said to them, "Have you come out as against a robber, with swords and clubs to capture me? Day after day I was with you in the temple teaching, and you did not seize me. But let the scriptures be fulfilled." (14:46–49)

These verses can actually be read as if Jesus had been taken by surprise, in the view of Ernst Haenchen.[52] But verse 42 contradicts that:

"Rise, let us be going; see, my betrayer is at hand."

But, again, verse 42 is thought to be an editorial interpolation in Mark's text. Luke neutralizes the action of the anonymous follower who has struck off the ear of the policeman by having Jesus immediately heal the ear again.

Mark suggests that there might have been an original tradition that an attempt was made to arrest those who were with Jesus:

And a young man followed him, with nothing but a linen cloth about his body and they seized him, but he left the linen cloth and ran away naked. (14:51–52)

But the prophet Amos (2:16) can actually improve on that:

"and he who is stout of heart among the mighty shall flee away naked in that day," says the LORD.

Mark says they all ran away, not only this one young man. "Why was Jesus alone arrested?" asks Bultmann, "was there no intention to arrest the disciples, or did they manage to thwart that intention by running away?"[53] Very strange indeed, if there really was talk at this time of the "Passover revolt of the year 32" (Stauffer).[54]

A number of critical readers, from Reimarus, the contemporary of Lessing, down to Joel Carmichael, have repeatedly, almost at regular intervals, put forward the theory that Jesus was an armed insurgent against the Roman occupation, and that the Gospels have done everything possible to gloss over that fact. Johannes Lehmann, too, in his *Report on Jesus* assumes that "Rabbi J." or his followers were involved in violent resistance to the Roman power.[55] The Swiss theologian Oscar Cullmann particularly names

Judas as a resistance fighter, a zealot, as though he did not agree with Jesus' peaceful methods. We should like to see the proof.[56]

Luke, the story-teller, makes one of the two disciples walking with Jesus to Emmaus say to him (24:21): "We had hoped he would liberate Israel"— Martin Hengel's translation. This dramatically graceful version is always tempting, but it has not been and cannot be proved. Certainly there are some relevent passages in the New Testament writings which have been exploited on these grounds, but there is only one which really makes us prick up our ears. Immediately before the general move to the garden of Gethsemane on the Mount of Olives, Luke makes Jesus say:

And he said to them, "When I sent you out with no purse or bag or sandals, did you lack anything?" They said, "Nothing."
He said to them, "But now, let him who has a purse take it, and likewise a bag. And let him who has no sword sell his mantle and buy one. For I tell you that this scripture must be fulfilled in me, 'And he was reckoned with transgressors'; for what is written about me has its fulfillment." And they said, "Look, Lord, here are two swords." And he said to them, "It is enough." (22:35–38)

Characteristically, the disciples went to sleep straight after this warning. From this slightly muddled passage in Luke, can we deduce that Jesus' followers were arming themselves? And, lacking further proof, that he had issued a call to a general march out into the desert (Robert Eisler, 1930)?[53] There is no substantial evidence for it.

Except just this: that it was the Romans who hung him on the tree and who presumably therefore saw him as an agitator. But who was an agitator by their way of looking at things? Anyone who acted in a way judged to be against the Roman people and their security; anyone who, as a private citizen, deliberately and with malice usurped the functions of an official; anyone who willfully made enemies out of friends of the Roman people. Thus Mommsen, *The Roman Penal Code*.[59]

It follows that someone who claimed, no matter how peacefully, to be the Messiah, or even just a prophet of the end-time, could quite easily have been punished as an enemy of the Roman people. It needed no rattling of swords, no call to obtain weapons. The common conception of the Messiah included acts of violence, no matter how peaceful the prophet himself might sound. This is the picture drawn for us by a psalmist of the first century before Christ's birth, whom we know in a Greek version (*Ps. Sal.*17):[60] The kingly Messiah ($\chi\rho\iota\sigma\tau\acute{o}\varsigma$), as "the son of David", will liberate Jerusalem from the heathen; will rule over the sinners of his people — thus over Caiaphas & Co. — over those whom Ezekiel calls "the shepherds of Israel, who care only for themselves." He will gather together a holy people and found a kingdom in which no more wickedness is committed and he will put down the heathen peoples. How could such a one enter into Jerusalem peacefully, without excitement, if not actual disturbances, arising wherever he went? Jesus, writes the Tübingen dogmatist Josef Rupert Geiselmann, was "hailed by the people as the political liberator" — but how does he know that?[61]

Of course, there is another question, whether Jesus was not taken by surprise, and whether the disciples, equally surprised, had not armed themselves from the start. Then there would certainly have been a $\vartheta\acute{o}\rho\nu\beta o\varsigma$, a disturbance, and certainly there would have been more blood shed than flowed from the right ear of the servant Malchus. Also, the events would have stood a very much better chance of being noticed by historians like Josephus and Philo. Following the normal practice of Pontius Pilate, whom only Stauffer calls "blood-shy," a thousand people would have ended their lives on the cross instead of just one.

We know virtually nothing, so anything is possible; but we must admit that we cannot get beyond groping and speculation. There are traces in the texts which suggest some kind of resistance, but that is all. So the attempts to paint Jesus as a world revolutionary will never end; as the patron saint of secular liberation fronts, he is indispensable.

6. The trial

No particular excitement was generated over the case of one Jesus of Nazareth. "Jerusalem, such and such a date: the ringleader of the riots on which we recently reported was today sentenced to death and immediately executed."
—Max Horkheimer (as Heinrich Regius)[1]

Jesus before Pilate, the man not of this world standing before the ruler who is unwilling to sentence him but who cannot even understand him — that is one of the really great scenes in world literature. Anyone who doubts that poets have been at work here should read the first account, that of Mark, who draws the characters and the scene without any depth. Matthew adds nothing more than flourishes. Luke, the story-teller, puts a political sketch into Mark's account. But not until we get to John does the scene rise to the level of an intellectual discussion.

To Pilate's straightforward question "What have you done?" Jesus gives the surreal, eternally true answer: "My kingdom is not of this world." He is king in the kingdom of ideas; he has to bear witness of the truth, beyond all the laws of this world. Pilate, at a loss to know what to make of it, utters the casual, the absolutely insignificant phrase "What is truth?" One thing is clear: John has created a deathless scene, tremendous world-theatre.

Of course, there are people, and will continue to be, who insist that John was elaborating an old account. No criminal proceeding in history has had so much written about it as the so-called trial of Jesus, whose basis and framework remain unknown to us. Was there a trial at all? All that seems really certain is that Pilate was prefect of Judea for ten years. A crime-play has been put on without action or actors, with no judge to condemn and no accused to defend himself. "He (Jesus) may incidentally have been executed; that is most likely," thinks the Marburg theologian Ernst Fuchs.[2]

The more nonsensical the account, the fatter the exegisis. Professor Josef Blinzler of Passau published, in 1969, a new 520-page book, *Der Prozess Jesu (The trial of Jesus),* in which pretty well the same absurdity of the Gospel accounts is stretched out, pulled about and finally certified. Eleven closely-printed pages are devoted to the study of the problem: "Did Pilate take his seat on the bema (= judgment seat)?"

The question that John says Pilate put to Jesus, "Where have you come from?", is translated by Blinzler[3] as follows: "Are you of earthly or heavenly origin?" He even accepts the assumption that Pilate, who according to Matthew washed his hands as an assertion of his blamelessness, "has here adapted himself to a Jewish custom."

Blinzler explains the fact that Luke is the only one of the evangelists to report the episode with Herod (Jesus was sent by Pilate to Herod, who sent him back), by telling us that the evangelist had dedicated his work to some highly-placed person, "i.e., to a person presumably particularly interested in affairs at court."

If, concludes Blinzler,[4] Pilate was as corrupt, ignorant and cruel as he is made out to be by the Jewish historians Josephus and Philo, "then Tiberius would not have left him in office for ten years." Even in the work of those Jewish authors who deal with the problem with the help of the whole armory of scientific methods, Blinzler "is not always free from the impression that they would like to belittle the guilt of the Jews for the killing of Christ as much as possible."

But those of us who read the Gospels without Blinzler's spectacles must declare that we do not know what happened. All that is really certain is that it cannot have happened as the tradition tells us.

What still arouses the sharpest resentment is that the procurator Pilate should within two hours have (convicted? and) sentenced to crucifixion a man he knew to be innocent, under the pressure of the Jews whom he despised. Even if we accept that he merely confirmed a Jewish sentence, that is an impossibility.

But did the Jewish Council, the Sanhedrin, really pass sentence of death? It does not seem to be so; yet, if so, why did the procurator have to confirm the sentence? And why did Jesus then die a Roman death on the cross and not a Jewish death by stoning or by strangling? Death by burning — though Rabbi Eleazar ben Zadok, as a child riding on his father's shoulders, actually saw it happen to a priest's daughter condemned to death for adultery — was out of the question on religious grounds.

Whether the Sanhedrin was allowed to pass sentence of death at the time of Jesus' death no longer has to be settled. Mark's report of the trial, we can see at once, is absolutely conclusive; those written after him have added a certain amount, but never the salt of clarity. Had the disciples not received any report? That is hardly credible, unless the subject of the report had simply not happened. Actually, they had a good informant in Joseph of Arimathea, according to Mark a "respected member" of the seventy-strong Sanhedrin. He is said to have buried Jesus, but Herbert Braun has his views about that: "In view of the established Jewish custom of burying criminals secretly in a sort of knacker's yard, we cannot rid ourselves of doubt whether the present stories of the burial in the Gospels contain any historical germ at all."[6] But thank God we still have Stauffer, who assures us that Jesus was laid in an honorable grave and that Pilate and a number of Jewish judges never enjoyed an entirely clear conscience (!!) after that.[7]*

Mark says Joseph of Arimathea was "a man who was eagerly awaiting the kingdom of God"; Matthew says he was a disciple of Jesus; Luke makes him a Councillor "who had dissented from their policy and the action they had taken"; in John, he is "secretly" a disciple, secretly "for fear of the Jews." This fear clearly did not prevent him from asking Pilate (not asking the Jews!) for Jesus' body. In the uncanonical *Gospel of Peter,* he is actually presented as a friend of Pilate.[8] Fear cannot have stopped him telling what he had learned about the proceedings against Jesus, if indeed he was not actually present himself, unless, of course, there were no proceedings in Council. After the burial he disappears from history. Maybe he was only dragged into it because it says about the servant of God in Isaiah (53:9): "And he made his grave with the wicked, and with the rich in his death."[9]

*Stauffer continues what the evangelists began. Mark calls it "a grave," Matthew "a new grave," Luke "a grave in which no one had been laid before," and John " a new grave, in which no one had ever been laid."

161

There is a phrase in Mark's Gospel which reduces the Passion story to the lowest denominator:

> It was now two days before the Passover and the Feast of Unleavened Bread. And the chief priests and the scribes were seeking how to arrest him by stealth, and kill him. (14:1)

Passover, the Easter festival, took place only in Jerusalem, as we have seen; the celebration proceeded on to the general feast-days of unleavened bread. The hearing before the Council in verses 55—64 (Conzelmann: "not authentic") are regarded by Bultmann as "a secondary expansion of the short statement in 15:1"[10] (secondary in such a context means added by later editors, not derived from the primary, earliest tradition):

> Now the chief priests and the whole council sought testimony against Jesus to put him to death; but they found none. For many bore false witness against him, and their witness did not agree. And some stood up and bore false witness against him, saying, "We heard him say, 'I will destroy this temple that is made with hands, and in three days I will build another, not made with hands.'" Yet not even so did their testimony agree. And the high priest stood up in the midst, and asked Jesus, "Have you no answer to make? What is it that these men testify against you?" But he was silent and made no answer. Again the high priest asked him, "Are you the Christ, the Son of the Blessed?" And Jesus said, "I am; and you will see the Son of man sitting at the right hand of Power, and coming with the clouds of heaven." And the high priest tore his mantle, and said, "Why do we still need witnesses? You have heard his blasphemy. What is your decision?" And they all condemned him as deserving death. (Mark 14: 55—64)

The name of the officiating High Priest is missing in Mark's Passion story, is given correctly as Caiaphas in Matthew, appears in Luke's Acts of the Apostles wrongly as Annas (4:6); in Luke's story of the Baptist and John's account of the Passion both Annas and Caiaphas appear. The Frankfurt professor of theology Hans-Werner Bartsch[11] sees the whole story of the Passion in Mark's version as "an invention"; it is intended simply to act as a bridge

162

between the "historically verified" arrest ordered by the Sanhedrin and the trial before Pilate.* But is the arrest on behalf of the Sanhedrin historically verified? John, the latest evangelist, writes of a cohort, which he says took Jesus prisoner, and that would be six hundred men, or if we think of a maniple, from two hundred to three hundred men. (Stauffer makes it come to a thousand men.[13]) Where did the Jews get a cohort from, with a captain at its head? As so often, John brings his own logic into play, but there are still people who assume that he has sources of his own.

There are several improbabilities. Each has an answer to it, but the sum of them does not add up to a whole. Where do the "many" (Mark) witnesses come from so suddenly, and by night? If a trial was already being mounted, why were they not prepared in advance? Why do the proceedings take place at night? (Luke is the first to make the action take place by day.) Why not immediately after the feast-days, when the pilgrims will have left? Did a crucifixion present less of a reason for rioting than some kind of "protective custody" during the feast?

Why should Jesus express an opinion about the evidence of the witnesses, evidence which had collapsed under the weight of its own contradictions? Why does the High Priest question him "again," only this time putting, not the same, nor even a related, question, but asking him directly: "Are you the Messiah, the Son of the Blessed One?" The first of these accusations was not a blasphemy deserving death in itself. The Sadducees were not expecting a Messiah at all, the other members of the Council, if Jesus really appeared before them, not this Messiah. But the second accusation, that Jesus declared himself to be the Son of God, could only have been uttered by the High Priest through inspiration from above. Even to his disciples Jesus had never made any such claim, a claim utterly inconceivable to a Jerusalem Jew.

Let us not tangle with the Jewish code of law. It can, it is plain, be grossly underestimated. Thus the Pharisee Simon ben Shetach,

---

*Ferdinand Hahn regards only verses 57—59 of Mark's account of the trial, that is, simply the throwing down of the temple, as secondary; and Gerhard Schneider agrees. Martin Dibelius, on the other hand holds the account of the proceedings before the Council to be legend. Hardly any theologian today believes that Jesus thought of himself as the Messiah, or claimed to be such. It needed the authors of the Gospels to show that Jesus was condemned to death because of his admission that he was the Messiah. According to H.J. Holtzmann (1907), he admitted that he was the Messiah "and paid for this step with his life," "because in the general opinion of the people he was clearly not what he said he was."[12]

about 70 B.C.E., is said to have executed eighty Hellenistic "witches" in one day, although the law, the unquestionably valid Halachah, prescribed that only one execution per day was allowed. However, the records of this crime are not free from doubt.[14]

We do not know whether the Mishna, the later, liberal code of law of the Pharisees, was wholly or partially practised in Jesus' time.[15] The jurisdiction of the Sadducees was certainly harsh and cruel, and it was they who ruled the temple. They might have been able to claim that the special circumstances absolved them from the law which prohibited their pronouncing a verdict on the same day as the trial took place. But it is quite unthinkable that the Jewish Council would have assembled in court on the first day of the Passover, as the synoptics tell us without even tripping over the sacrilege. Their version "stands in complete and utter contradiction to what was laid down for feast-days in the law" (Eduard Lohse).[16]

Another difficulty crops up in John's Gospel. He introduces the Romans into his account of the arrest, a detail, if not correct, at any rate credible. But what is quite incredible is that the Roman captain should have taken Jesus to the former high priest Annas, whom the Romans had dismissed in 15 C.E. (Three high priests had followed him in quick succession; the last was dismissed by the Romans in 18 C.E. and then came Caiaphas.) Annas is said to have questioned Jesus, by John's account; and Annas' son Ananias, high priest for three months in the year 62, ordered the exectuion of Jesus' brother James "the just." He too, like his father, belonged to the party of the Sadducees, who, as Josephus observes, "were harder and more ruthless in judgment than all the other Jews."

Annas, who had already interrogated Jesus, now sent him with his hands bound to Caiaphas, who by that time had been in office as high priest for over ten years. Caiaphas does not interrogate him. We hear that he was Annas' son-in-law. When the Roman governor of Syria, Vitellius, removed Caiaphas from office in the year 36, Annas' son Jonathan became high priest. Have the son and the son-in-law got mixed up? John also seems to think that the high priest was exchanged each year in rotation, like the chief priests of the heathen religions of Syria and Asia Minor; he says of Caiaphas: "who was high priest in that year." The Holy Spirit, though on the whole a journalistic inspiration, is a poor reporter.

Among the charges brought against Jesus, one stands out which many people believe to be a later interpolation: that Jesus had said that he would throw down the temple built with hands, and in three days build another made without hands. Once more we come up against the magic figure three. The accusation, significantly the only one, makes us think of Qumran's Teacher of Righteousness and of the plans Robert Eisler attributes to Jesus of staging a march into the desert.[17] The phrase recurs obstinately, in different guises; is there perhaps a grain of truth in it? Stephen, too, said to have been stoned shortly before the conversion of Paul, was, according to the Acts of the Apostles, accused by the Jews of having said that Jesus the Nazarene would destroy the holy places (6:14). Mark speaks of false evidence. But if we look it up in John, it suddenly becomes true evidence. John has just driven the dealers and money-changers out of the temple:

> The Jews then said to him, "What sign have you to show us for doing this?" Jesus answered them, "Destroy this temple, and in three days I will raise it up." The Jews then said, "It has taken forty-six years to build this temple, and will you raise it up in three days?" (2:18−20)

"But the temple he was speaking of was his body," adds the evangelist, something which the Jews listening to him obviously could not have known. Even the disciples did not understand it in that way: only later,

> When therefore he was raised from the dead, his disciples remembered that he had said this; and they believed the scripture and the word which Jesus had spoken. (2:22)

It just shows what confusion prophetic utterances can cause. But John does not bring the destruction of the temple which he found in Mark and Matthew into his account of the trial; he leaves it out. Did he regard it as proved from the Jews' point of view? Did he know of the rabbinical prophecies according to which the temple would be destroyed and built anew by the Messiah? Could Jesus actually have boasted of such bold tricks: throwing down the temple built with hands (that is, with human hands) and within three days building another not made with hands, with human hands? Jeremias believes that Jesus described himself as the builder of the new temple and thus as the descendant promised to David in the scriptures (2 Samuel 7:12−13).[18]

It could be that every Messiah-candidate felt himself bound to make such election speeches. It could just as well be that it was not Jesus at all who said these things but the "Messiah" Menachem, the leader of the Jewish nationalists (the Zealots) during the first week of the uprising against the Romans in 66 C.E. (see Chapter 10). The original authors of the Gospels have simply transferred to Jesus what they came upon in a different connection; they have naively exchanged and amalgamated what they would like to have happened with what actually did happen. Mark's false evidence could have been borrowed from one of the Psalms:

> Give me not up to the will of my adversaries;
> for false witnesses have risen against me,
> and they breathe out violence. (27:12)

Several prominent law teachers also sat in the Sanhedrin, who spoke up more than once and who are on the record: Nicodemus,[19] for instance, who spoke with Jesus by night in John's Gospel, and who helped to bury him, and Gamaliel the Elder, Paul's teacher. Would they not have passed on some dying words about this interesting case, supposing the Council had really tried it? It is most unlikely. One outstanding thing about the associated scene of mockery in Mark is its impossible placement in the middle of the court scene (which Luke corrects):

> And some began to spit on him, and to cover his face, and to strike him, saying, "Prophesy!" And the guards received him with blows. (14:65)

Here behind the ostensible intention of jeering and mockery, the fundamental conviction seems to shine through that the Messiah could "smell out"[20] an evildoer without seeing him or knowing his voice, so that Jesus had to be able to "prophesy" who it was that hit him even with his eyes blindfolded. (Luke makes this clearer in 22:63−64.) There follows a second scene of mockery, this time with Roman soldiers, whose habit of picking out someone by lot for the sake of a bad joke and making them play the king for a time before having them executed, might have enraged Mark:

And the soldiers led him away inside the palace (that is, the praetorium); and they called together the whole battalion. And they clothed him in a purple cloak, and plaiting a crown of thorns they put it on him. And they began to salute him, "Hail, King of the Jews!" And they struck his head with a reed, and spat upon him, and they knelt down in homage to him. And when they had mocked him, they stripped him of the purple cloak, and put his own clothes on him.(15:16—20)

The pretend-king, sitting as if seriously on his throne, then no less seriously after not too long a reign executed, is an age-old, cruel invention of many religions. This seems to be the unholy origin of our king of the fools, Prince Carnival. But the evangelist may have known of an episode that happened some years after Jesus' death. When the Jewish king Agrippa I visited Alexandria in 38 C.E., the town mob, which was hostile to the Jews, made him look ridiculous by means of a pantomime which Philo describes for us. They took a harmless madman, a general butt called Carabas, and put a diadem of papyrus on his head, a blanket on him instead of the official robe, and gave him a piece of papyrus in his hand as a sceptre. A bodyguard stood beside him, while others came forward to greet him, to pray him for a judgment or to sue for an audience. And all round was the loud shouting of people addressing him in Syrian as "Lord."[21] (At the back of our heads we hear an echo: Release Carabas!)

It is notable that in Mark's account of the trial — and this is the only relevant account of the Passion — no charge of Sabbath-breaking is made against Jesus. If the required proofs were missing, he had still, so they said, occupied the temple and rebelled against the temple clergy. The Gospels, notably that according to Mark, ascribe actions to him for which he had certainly deserved the death penalty under Jewish law. They depict him effectively as a preacher of revolt, a false prophet and corrupt teacher, and one moreover who would not listen to warnings.

If he had blasphemed the name of God with his claim to be God's Son, actually before his judges, his body must be hung up on a pole shaped like a cross and taken down again before the close of the day on which he was executed. If possible, his execution should take place in public as a deterrent on the eve of a great public holiday (Feast of Tabernacles, Passover, Festival of Weeks).

But now John's Gospel declares, and the Synoptics imply, that the Jews would not have had legal power of life and death to allow them to execute Jesus. Jesus has to be sent before the Roman prefect, Pilate. He represented the Roman power; in him "the Roman state, with its questions about the young Christianity, could see itself as in a mirror," as the Catholic theologian Clemens Thoma[22] says. There, we sense again a little the longing for martyrdom. Jesus' kingdom is not of this world; there is the emperor and all that is due to him, so the scene becomes "an apology for the lords of the world" (Ernst Bloch).[23] Through the figure of Pilate, it is demonstrated to the Roman world that Christianity and the state can exist side by side. It is not Pilate but the Jews who are guilty of Jesus' death. Tertullian in the year 200 can actually call Pilate a "secret Christian," and in the Coptic Christian church he has been canonized as a saint.

Mark's description of the Pilate episode, to which the other evangelists add nothing in the way of facts, can be grasped better if we put aside the improbability of the time factor and disregard any connection with the Passover or the Sabbath. Let us take a relaxed view, and not compress all the events into the two hours between 7:00–9:00 a.m. Let us rather allow them the time they would normally take:

> And as soon as it was morning the chief priests, with the elders
> and the scribes, and the whole council held a consultation;
> and they bound Jesus and led him away and delivered him to
> Pilate. And Pilate asked him, "Are you the King of the Jews?"
> And he answered him, "You have said so." And the chief priests
> accused him of many things. And Pilate again asked him "Have
> you no answer to make? See how many charges they bring
> against you." But Jesus made no further answer, so that Pilate
> wondered. (15:1–5)

"He spoke Greek with Pilate," Stauffer tells us.[25] Pilate's question, "Are you the king of the Jews?" can either not have been meant seriously, or not have sounded so; let us therefore take it as an interpretation by the evangelist. "You have said so." Wilckens reads the sentence as a modern idiom, "*Thou* sayest it," with the implication: it is not I who say so.[26] After that, he apparently says nothing more. His silence before the High Priest and Pilate echoes a motif from Isaiah (53:7): like a lamb led to the slaughter, the servant of God does not open his mouth in complaint or defense.

So now Pilate has a prisoner who simply says he is the king of the Jews. Perhaps the procurator has not yet heard of any kind of Messianic prophecies. But the expression "king of the Jews" meant something to him, unless he took Jesus for a harmless lunatic. But that would not fit in with the fact that, according to Mark, he seems to have believed that the Jewish officials had handed Jesus over out of spite:

> Now at the feast he used to release for them one prisoner whom they asked. And among the rebels in prison, who had committed murder in the insurrection, there was a man called Barabbas. And the crowd came up and began to ask Pilate to do as he was wont to do for them. And he answered them, "Do you want me to release for you the King of the Jews?" For he perceived that it was out of envy that the chief priests had delivered him up. But the chief priests stirred up the crowd to have him release for them Barabbas instead. And Pilate again asked them, "Then what shall I do with the man whom you call the King of the Jews?" And they cried out again, "Crucify him." And Pilate said to them, "Why, what evil has he done?" But they shouted all the more, "Crucify him."

"Ignorant mobs" were at work, says Peter Ketter, in "impious bravado," says Blinzler.[27] Psalm 31:13 puts it this way:

> Yea, I hear the whispering of many —
> terror on every side! —
> as they scheme together against me,
> as they plot to take my life.

With the Barabbas episode the evangelist was able to show vividly how even criminals had been preferred to Jesus, so that he fulfilled the prophecy of Isaiah that the suffering servant of God would be "reckoned among transgressors" (53:12). But Pilate's so-called custom of releasing a prisoner to the Jews at the feast is not borne out by evidence, either for him or for any other Roman prefect. About this time Pilate had probably been in his post for three or four years. We need say no more than that the practice sounds "highly unlikely" (Eduard Schweizer)[28], doubly unlikely for a man with Pilate's particular reputation.

In some of the manuscripts of Luke, the usage appears as a Jewish "festival custom," which was thus independent of who happened to be governor at the time. But even as such there is no evidence for it. The absurdity of the text tempts us into speculations.* The words put into Pilate's mouth by Mark: "Do you wish me to release for you the king of the Jews?" words addressed to the people milling round him, cannot really have been spoken as they are reported, unless, of course, we believe that he was making a joke quite inconsistent with his official position. This mob, howling for Jesus' crucifixion — why does he suggest that they call Jesus "King of the Jews"? Arrogance on Pilate's part, or excess of subtlety on Mark's (which Matthew changes in both places)?

Of course, Pilate could have had reason to do the people a favor. Only why should he release an agitator for whom the cross was a certainty, and then hand over for crucifixion one who was not an agitator and whom he did not himself wish to have crucified? Why did he not hold the case over until after the feast-days? Can it have been that he did not even care that he should be compelled to take proceedings that he did not really understand by people who certainly had no powers to force him into precipitate action? By people moreover who knew themselves to be defiled if they so much as entered his office or his home?

Matthew contents himself with elaborating Mark. Pilate must now wash his hands, see Psalm 26:6:

I wash my hands in innocence,
and go about thy altar, O LORD.

So when Pilate saw he was gaining nothing, but rather that a riot was beginning, he took water and washed his hands before the crowd, saying, "I am innocent of this man's blood; see to it yourselves. . . . " (27:24)

---

*H.Z. Maccoby, in the periodical "*New Testament Studies*," (Cambridge), puts forward the theory that Barabbas means "Son of God" and "teacher," and that he was in fact identical with Jesus. It was Jesus the people were calling for. Another version will have it that the word *barnash* (= Son of Man) has been changed by a tiny error in copying to read *barbash* (= Barabbas), which leads to the same conclusion as in Maccoby. Paul Winter, in his book *On the Trial of Jesus,* supposes that Pilate had two men called Jesus in custody, Jesus Barabbas and Jesus son of Joseph; it actually says as much in a text of Matthew that was available to Origen. Pilate only wanted to make sure which of the two he was to release. The original accounts, says Winter, have been replaced by others.[29]

Moreover Pilate's wife warns her husband that he should not become guilty of the blood of this just man; she has been "much troubled in her dreams on his account." Objections to such touching fantasies are unnecessary (Blinzler: "Even a heathen woman recognized Jesus' innocence").[30]

Luke, the story-teller, spots the gaps in Mark's account and sets about jumping over them or filling them in. Luke tells us that the Jews prefer a charge that Pilate understands very well: they declare that Jesus has subverted the people and forbidden them to pay tribute to Caesar. But there Luke's imagination seems to run dry. This charge does not seem to interest Pilate at all; he just asks, "Are you the king of the Jews?" and when Jesus confirms that ("You have said so") he is content: "I find no crime in this man."

For the Jews too, Luke seeks an unequivocal accusation. They will not understand that Jesus is the Son of God, and therefore, says Luke, "all" the members of the Council ask him: "Are you the Son of God?" And for the first time Jesus answers clearly and beyond any doubt: "You say that I am." (Let us note in passing that the question and answer are quite unorthodox; as Lohse says, the Jews avoided "any expression about the Messiah's relationship as Son of God";[31] the thought of anyone's being physically a son of God was to them a heathenish abomination.)

Of course, it has also struck Luke that Herod Antipas, Jesus' provincial ruler, who is said to have conspired with the rulers of the temple against Jesus, has disappeared in Mark. Luke solves this problem by an insertion "of screaming improbability" (Goguel).[32] Pilate hears that Jesus comes from Galilee:

And when he learned that he belonged to Herod's jurisdiction, he sent him over to Herod, who was himself in Jerusalem at that time. When Herod saw Jesus, he was very glad, for he had long desired to see him, because he had heard about him, and he was hoping to see some sign done by him. So he questioned him at some length; but he made no answer. The chief priests and the scribes stood by, vehemently accusing him. And Herod with his soldiers treated him with contempt and mocked him; then, arraying him in gorgeous apparel, he sent him back to Pilate. And Herod and Pilate became friends with each other that very day, for before this they had been at enmity with each other (23:7–12).

171

The scripture — Psalm 2:2 — has to be fulfilled:

The kings of the earth set themselves,
and the rulers take counsel together,
against the LORD and his anointed...

The solution, transferring the prisoner to his provincial ruler in Galilee, strikes us as pretty crafty, but in fact we find ourselves crossing a Bridge of Asses.* Pilate, before whom Jesus has not spoken, can now appeal to Herod, before whom he has also not spoken; even Herod finds him not guilty. He, Pilate, wishes to flog Jesus and let him go.

Here in Luke, the whip has a particular object: as has often happened before, it is to take the place of the death penalty. And because the people will not venture on such a solution, Jesus is not flogged in Luke, nor does he wear a crown of thorns.

In John, too, the flogging and the crown of thorns have a motive: they are intended to conciliate the mob when they catch sight of Jesus. It is not until the third century — and in art, a thousand years later — that Jesus begins to wear the "crown of thorns" (a wreath of acanthus branches?) even on the cross.

The flogging motif, found also in Mark, cannot go back to Jesus Christ but may rather have been included from a later happening in the accounts from which Mark worked. Josephus reports that, four years before the outbreak of war between the Jews and the Romans, i.e., about 62 C.E. an unknown countryman came to Jerusalem, one Jesus son of Ananias, and cried out one lament after another, day and night, over Jerusalem and the temple, bride and bridegroom, the whole people. Some people beat him, but he would not be silenced. Josephus reports:

Thereupon the magistrates, supposing, as was indeed the case, that the man was under some supernatural impulse, brought him before the Roman governor (Albinus); there, although flayed to the bone with scourges, he neither sued for mercy nor

---

*The Arabic writer Abd el Jabbar, somewhere about the year 1000, set down all he knew of the different religions. His account of Christianity comes from Jewish Christian material older than Islam. In these accounts Pilate appears as a man who wants to find out something interesting about Jesus, thus taking over the role ascribed by Luke to Herod. The Jews crucify Jesus, and it is Herod, not Pilate, who washes his hands because he finds him innocent.[33]

shed a tear, but, merely introducing the most mournful of variations into his ejaculations, responded to each stroke with "Woe to Jerusalem!"

When Albinus asked him who he was and where he came from, and why he cried out, he gave no answer but continued with his lamentations, until Albinus, convinced of the man's madness, let him go. A stone from a Roman catapult is said to have ended the Cassandra-like life of this Jesus.[34]

Flogging, blows in the face, spitting and mockery — none of these should be taken literally without consideration for the Jesus of Josephus. Isaiah has moreover again stood godfather, when he prophesied:

I gave my back to the smiters,
and my cheeks to those who pulled out the beard;
I hid not my face
from shame and spitting. (50:6)

And in 53:5: " . . . and with his stripes we are healed." The "gorgeous" white robe put on him by Herod marks Jesus out as the true high priest, the mocking red robe of costly purple as the true king. At the feast-day of his own sacrifice, Jesus changes his robes as the high priest does on the great Day of Atonement (Yom Kippur), for which Jesus' own day of atonement stands; Shalom ben-Chorin makes us hear these consonances.[35] But Mark may have had pictures from the Jewish war in his mind's eye, for during the collapse of 70 C.E. Simon ben Giora, the Jewish usurper, had "returned to the temple place at daylight, in white robes over which he had thrown a purple mantle" (Martin Hengel),[36] after trying in vain to escape through an underground tunnel; he was later executed in Rome.

The tendency of the evangelists to play down or even to cut out completely the part played by the Romans, (becoming more unrestrained as the destruction of Jerusalem recedes into the past), has long been observed and explained from the point of view of the interests of the early Christian communities. With John's Pilate, we get the feeling that we are no longer looking at a Roman procurator at all, but at a busy lawyer bustling to and fro to execute his brief — even though Pilate takes his seat on the famous judgment seat. Three times Pilate finds Jesus not guilty. He seems completely at a loss what to think. He is worried, too, because

Jesus has been charged with making himself the Son of God. Perhaps he really is, Pilate seems to think, for what is truth?

John looks for the inner motive of Jesus for not defending himself (like so much else, it is impossible to prove with certainty that John knew the other three Gospels; the assumption is perfectly possible, and I assume it). He has elevated the confrontation between the temporal rulers of the world and the Logos from on high, the king of truth, to a spiritual plane. Each is essential to the other. The temporal ruler feels himself invaded by a dark presentiment of the kingdom of truth, inaccessible to him. So he asks Jesus, a little nervous, a little confused: "Where have you come from?" Since they could not understand one another, he does *not* ask, as Blinzler likes to explain it: "Are you of earthly or heavenly origin?" but simply "Where have you come from?". And this son of another world does not answer him.

> Pilate therefore said to him, "You will not speak to me? Do you not know that I have power to release you, and power to crucify you?" Jesus answered him, "You would have no power over me unless it had been given you from above; therefore he who delivered me to you has the greater sin." (19:10—11)

John is not consistent here: he betrays a theological conception such as we might rather have looked for in Matthew, who makes Jesus in the garden of Gethsemane eesay something that sounds more like John: "Do you suppose (speaking to the one who has drawn his sword) that I cannot appeal to my Father, who would at once send to my aid more than twelve legions of angels?"

If we read John (19:11) literally, it is the Father in Heaven, who has given Jesus into the hands of Pilate "from above," who has the "deeper guilt." It cannot be meant in that way, but that is how it reads. It also makes no sense that Annas and Caiaphas should have the deeper guilt; they too are acting on orders from above; and "the devil has entered" even into Judas, as the text says. It is Origen, condemned by the church as a heretic long after his death, who reconciles the theological contradiction in John (when he foresees the ultimate return to God of all the evil powers of heaven and all the rulers of the earth);[37] as was only to be expected, he was numbered among the heretics on account of this belief. Josef Blinzler brings us a version from the depths: "Because Pilate does not proceed against Jesus of his own free will but in execution of the special power vested in him by God, he bears less guilt than the Jews, who demand the death of God's messenger simply out of hate and wickedness."[38] I should not like to have met Josef Blinzler, born 1910, three hundred years ago if I had been a heretic or a Jew. But even the *Wilckens Bible* trips up in the case of Pilate: "It emerges rather that anyone who does not believe in Jesus will be forced into the school of unbelief." Well, they would not mind that.

What would have happened if Pilate and Caiaphas had flogged Jesus and let him go? Paul and the evangelists, notably John, do not let themselves get led away by the contradiction that, on the one hand, the rulers of this world did not recognize the secret wisdom of God — "if they had, they would not have crucified the Lord of glory" (1 Corinthians 2:8) — and that, on the other hand, they had to carry out the will of God (Caiaphas does not speak "of his own accord," (John 11:51). So men infinitely reproached for having killed Jesus, for the "murder of God," really had no chance not to kill him. How furious God would have been if his plan of salvation had been thwarted and Jesus had only been condemned, like Paul, to forty stripes less one.

John's Gospel emphasizes the logic of Luke, which at least has looked for and found some anti-Roman theme. Anyone who says he is king of the Jews is in competition with Caesar in Rome. And that is what the Jews tell Pilate, who in all four Gospels is not allowed to grasp this connection: "If you let this man go, you are no friend to Caesar." The unlikelihood only becomes greater with the decided emphasis. For Pilate, although he has taken his place on the judgment seat, has given no formal verdict on the charges. Sitting on the seat, says John, he told the people: "Here is your king." And "Shall I crucify your king?" And the Jews answered him, the Roman procurator: "We have no king but Caesar." Then, with a heavy heart, he handed over Jesus to them to be crucified. Suddenly it is the Jews, not the Romans, who crucified Jesus (which Luke leaves a little bit in the air).

It seems impossible to establish whether there was a trial of Jesus, and what happened at it. We do not know how he came to be executed. Jesus seems to have offended the temple party (that is, the Sadducees more than the Pharisees), and to have offended Herod Antipas the Tetrarch, through his challenge to their authority. He was handed over (?) by Pilate (?) to be killed (?), crucified (?) by Roman (?) soldiers (?): we can see nothing but

175

question marks. Was he perhaps stoned or strangled by the Jews and then hung after his death on a cruciform post? Or was he lynched, or was he secretly murdered with no trial by the Council, no trial before Pilate?

Tertullian (died after 220 C.E.) and Justin (executed in Rome about 165 C.E.), both Church Fathers, write in a way that leads us to believe that they had certain documents before them. Have any been forged, have they been allowed to get lost? However it may be, we have no such documents or reliable evidence before us today.

If, at the end of his life, (whenever that may have been), Pilate had been asked about that just man he reluctantly sent to be crucified in Jerusalem, he would probably not have understood or remembered. It was with good reason that in July 1971, the Supreme Court in Israel turned down the second proposal that the case against Jesus should be reopened, for this is an historical, not a judicial, problem. Not altogether consistently, in view of the lack of evidence, the plaintiff was referred to a court in Italy.

7. Raised from the earth

Behold, my servant shall prosper,
he shall be exalted and lifted up,
and shall be very high.
— Isaiah 52:13.

The legal punishment of crucifixion was unknown to the Jews of the Old Covenant; they were content with stoning, burning, beheading and strangling, in that order. Adultery with a betrothed girl was punished by stoning, adultery with a married woman by strangling. The Pharisees at the time of the evangelists were trying to get round the severity of the punishments; in the Mishna, their new code of laws, they laid down legal conditions that could hardly be satisfied.

In the Qumran texts, there is a "lion" who is said to have hung men up still alive,[1] which had never occurred before in Israel. The text may well refer to the Jewish king and high priest Alexander Jannaeus (103-76 B.C.E.) of the tribe of the Maccabees, who had eight hundred of his Pharisee opponents crucified in the middle of Jerusalem and their wives and children executed before their eyes, as we are told by Flavius Josephus.[2] This king also counts as a favorite for the role of the "priest of sacrilege" in the *Dead Sea Scrolls*.[3]

Crucifixion was not legal among the Jews, but the Law of Moses did contain the process of "hanging up on wood," a supplementary punishment for blasphemers already put to death by stoning, in accordance with Deuteronomy (21:23): "For a hanged man is accursed by God." He was therefore not allowed to remain hanging overnight "on the wood," presumably on a tree. Hence, even if the Sabbath had not been approaching, Jesus would have had to be taken down and buried before nightfall, if the

Romans gave permission to take his body. The Jewish punishment of subsequent hanging is not clearly differentiated, even in the Hebrew texts, from the capital punishment methods of their neighbors: to be hanged on a gallows, impaled on a stake, or bound or nailed to a cross or post.

To be hanged on wood, dead or alive, was regarded by the Jews as the most shameful of deaths. The Romans used the punishment of crucifixion as a deterrent against members of a subject people who had offended against the Roman state, and against slaves; it was not allowed by law to be inflicted on Roman citizens or on women — or at any rate, it was very rare. If Jesus died on the cross, then he died for rebellion against the Romans. If he was killed by the Jews, then he certainly did not die on the cross.

The followers of the risen Christ obviously saw a connection between the crucifixion and a hanging on wood. In the Acts of the Apostles, Jesus is spoken of as one "killed by hanging him on a tree" (Acts 5:30); and again, "They put him to death by hanging him on a tree" (Acts 10:39). "O foolish Galatians!" complains the Apostle Paul in Galatians (3:1): "Who has bewitched you, before whose eyes Jesus Christ was publicly portrayed as crucified?" And twelve verses later:

> Christ redeemed us from the curse of the law, having become a curse for us — for it is written, "Cursed be everyone who hangs on a tree . . . " (3:13)

Paul, the earliest witness, does not tell us who crucified Christ, or hung him up, whether it was the Romans or the Jews; "the powers that rule the world" would not have crucified (or hung up) the Lord if they had known the secret purpose of God (1 Corinthians 2:8). In 1 Thessalonians (2:15), he writes that the Jews had killed the Lord Jesus just as they had killed the prophets. Paul is not concerned with the immediate circumstances of the execution but with its theological side: he who freed men from the curse of the law himself hangs from the wood as one cursed by God.

The actual words used by Paul are not helpful. Κρεμαννύναι means originally to hang, the word used for to hang up, to hang on a post or to crucify, but equally for the hanging up on a tree or post of one previously put to death by stoning, as one accursed by God. The other word, σταυροῦν, means properly speaking to knock in posts, to erect palisades. It is rarely found before Paul with the transferred meaning of "crucify." It is found twice in the Septuagint in the sense of "hanging on the gallows." Haman, for instance, the enemy of the Jews in the book of Esther (7:9), is hung up, and the word used for it is σταυροϑήτω. The noun ὁ σταυρός, which is used by the evangelists for "wood of the cross," is originally a post put up in the ground.

If we had only Paul's letters to go by, we should not be able to say whether we should visualize Jesus as hanging dead or living. In the case of mass executions, for instance during the siege of Jerusalem, the means of death might have changed, since hanging up from a post called for less material then crucifixion and still inflicted the same torture. The delinquent was bound as often as he was nailed. The word used in Josephus[4] and in the letter to the Colossians (2:14), προσηλοῦν to mean "nailed" is not found in any of the New Testament accounts of the crucifixion. But Mark, who was well versed in the technical vocabulary of the Roman military, makes it clear that he is referring to a crucifixion, as the delinquent must not carry the wood (cross-piece, upright, both?) himself.

John makes Jesus say about his own future:

" . . . and I, when I am lifted up from the earth, will draw all men to myself." He said this to show by what death he was to die. (12:32-33)

If anyone gave Jesus a sponge soaked in vinegar as he hung on the cross, he would not have used a very long stick: the cross was not very high. A man hanging on the cross was only a little higher than a man standing on his own two feet, especially as he squatted with his legs stretched out on a wooden support (*sedecula*). The cross-piece was fitted to the top of the upright so that the cross was not a so-called "Latin" cross with a cross-piece cutting through the upper part of the upright (as distinct from a "Greek" cross, which had bars of equal length on all four sides). The limbs of the condemned man were most commonly bound with cords, which prolonged the death agony for days. (The bones of a man crucified in the neighborhood of Jerusalem during Jesus' time have been found; his feet were pushed over to one side and both fixed to the cross with a single nail.)[5] The head hung between the arms, perhaps so deep that a plate could be seen in the middle of the cross-piece bearing a description of the crime, supposing anyone had taken the trouble to prepare one. Cicero[6] says that crucifixion was the harshest and cruelest of all forms of capital punishment.*

We may permit ourselves some medical discussions, for instance whether Jesus could have held out for three or for six hours when he had been nailed to a cross without a *sedecula* for support, or whether blood mingled with water could flow from a lance-wound (Blinzler quotes commentaries which see this as a miracle; Bultmann regards it as purely symbolic and considers the attempt to find a medical explanation "comic.") [8]

Let us not speculate whether Jesus was nailed through the hands only (or, more probably, through the forearms), or also through the feet, supposing of course he was nailed at all. Luke speaks of scars; they cannot have been caused by nails. John makes doubting Thomas put his finger in the imprint ($\tau\acute{v}\pi o\varsigma$) and in the place ($\tau\acute{o}\pi o\varsigma$) of the nails in Jesus' hands, but also in the quite certainly invented wound from the spear. The accounts of the evangelists do not give us facts. Hence the thick piles of books of exegesis.

Anyway, the Romans were certainly familiar with crucifixion as distinct from the mere hanging up on a post or tree. So let us assume, in agreement with later Christian art, that Jesus was crucified and nailed through both hands and feet — the question of the *sedecula* could be discussed for years, but there is no point in discussing whether Jesus was nailed through the palms of his hands or through his wrists (or forearms), since the hands simply could not have supported the weight of his body.

For a long time the representation of the cross in works of art was not permitted. For a time there was no Christian art at all; during the Byzantine iconoclasm in the eighth century, painters often had their right hands chopped off. Until the fifth century they ventured only on symbolic representations, the lamb and the good shepherd, with a Latin cross; or there appear, for instance on Passion-sarcophagi, "the way to death as the road to victory," "the crown of thorns as laurel-wreath, the cross as the banner of

*The cross appears as a symbol in pre-Christian times, though not in its characteristic form as used for execution, which of course was not a cross. It was seen in the worship of Osiris as a "symbol of life." The tree of life can turn into the wood of death and torture. The Phrygian Marsyas is a god "hanging on a fir tree" (Bruckner). The late Martin Brückner found the hanging Marsyas displayed on an old candelabrum in the Capitoline Museum in Rome "and was astonished at the resemblance to the representation of the crucifixion in expression and attitude." The spirit of the god Attis, of this symbol of withering spring flowers, was transformed into a fir-tree — and this tree too has acquired a popular Christian function as the Christmas tree.[7]

victory" (Heinrich Lützeler in *Der Mann aus Galiläa*.[9] Not until
the first half of the fifth century do we find simplified pictures of
the crucifixion. It was still a long way to Matthias Grünewald, but
Passion poetry blossomed ("Jesus falls for the first time under the
Cross," "Veronica gives Jesus the kerchief," etc.).

Artists have been inspired by blood-offering and the myth of the
cross for over a thousand years. To get an idea of the self-
contradictory mixture of sublime spirituality and solid
commonsense achieved by the mysteries on the soil of the German
heritage, we should look at the Passion paintings of Albrecht
Dürer.[10] Christ, still wearing the crown of thorns on his already
transfigured head after his crucifixion, sits melancholy on a stone,
his head supported by his right hand. Could he be reflecting on his
Father's treachery?

Or the angels which hover round the crucified Christ like
helicopters, catching the blood from his five wounds in costly
chalices; one with a face like Gerhard Mauz, actually holds two
cups (Klopstock[11] has described this terrific scene in his impressive
way: an army of angels, a wide-encircling army, fearful servants of
the almighty purpose, spreads out far around Golgotha — a truly
great conception). Or Dürer's sacrificial lamb from the Revelation
of John, holding a flag with a cross in its near forehoof. Out of the
lamb's breast, caught in a cup by a high ecclesiastic, springs the
blood in which the chosen "make their robes white" (Revelation
7:14); the rejected are to be tortured for all eternity in fire and
brimstone, so that the "smoke of their torment" (Luther) rises up
to heaven, where the holy ones, branches of palm in their hands,
stand and gaze at them, touched but complacent.

In Dürer's *Trinity*, God the Father lifts the dead Son to himself.
The two look uncommonly like each other; God the Father wears
a papal tiara. Over the two hovers the Holy Spirit in the form of a
dove, his beaky head reminding us rather of a cockatoo, or of a
very famous French actor; even the great Dürer sometimes creates
farmyard stock. He is not afraid either of mixtures or of contrasts;
he gives us Jesus in the temple as the pitiless flogger and in Pilate's
court as the pitiful flogged.

The five stigmata can be inferred from all or any of the Gospels.
John makes the water of baptism and the blood of redemption
flow from a wound in the side, required also for other purposes, in
what the theologian Otto Baumgarten,[12] 1908, calls an "allegorical
conceit." German hymns have been inspired to an all-pervading

sweetness by religious painting. Here are some lines by Johann Rist, a priest at Wedel, near Hamburg, written in 1652:

> Five cellars here thou mayest see,
> Five cellars fill'd with wine for thee . . . [13]

Five tables, five wells, five doors, five caves, five apothecaries, five pearls — Jesus has the old familiar juice in stock, his body comes out of the winepress.

> Your heart stands open now for all to share:
> I only should have had the entry there.

— sings Mary Magdalene of the dead Jesus in Rilke's poem called *Pieta*.* And here is Johann Rist again:

> Creep in the Lord's sore-wounded flesh,
> For there thou canst be safe and fresh.[14]

That there were five wounds (Zinzendorf includes the circumcision as a Passion-wound)[15] and not, say, just two on the wrists, and that the scars on hands and feet were caused by nails, has been clearly perceived by a number of persons who bore the stigmata: their total number is variously put between a hundred and three hundred and thirty. Again, no proof of facts not available to us, but no doubt a proof of the imagination of impressionable people. The first to bear the marks of all five wounds was Francis of Assisi; for the rest, men are generally less susceptible than women, which is only to be expected.

We can imagine the shock to his followers of the accursed death of their Messiah. "His form, disfigured, had lost all the likeness of a man, his bearing changed beyond human semblance," as Deutero-Isaiah prophesies about the servant of God. To complete the humiliation, many of the Church Fathers seem to have attributed physical shortcomings and deformities to him, and it is not absolutely excluded that they may have been handed down in the tradition in some way.[16]

*Rainer Maria Rilke: *Selected Works* Vol II trans. J.B. Leishman © The Hogarth Press Ltd 1960. By permission of New Directions, New York.

He is said to have looked older than he was. In fact, according to John (8:57), the Jews say to him when he cannot have been forty: "You are not yet fifty years old, and have you seen Abraham?" The famous passage in Luke (4:23), "Physician, heal yourself," cannot refer to Jesus' physical defects. It takes a rabbinical proverb ("Physician, heal your own limp") and quotes it in connection with a sermon reported by Luke in Jesus' home town. It could well mean that a prophet coming from Nazareth should heal in Nazareth first before performing miracles in Capernaum, in Israel first before among the heathen.

We know nothing about his appearance, but in the so-called (Syrian) *Acts of Thomas*,[17] fragments of writings dating from the period after 250 C.E., there are references to a twin brother of Jesus called Judas Thomas, who is said to have been extremely short. According to Robert Eisler's research, Jesus was hunchbacked as a result of so much hard work in his youth,* he had little hair, a thin beard and a long nose.[19] "This general agreement is on record," confirms Origen in his attack on Celsus in 180, "that the body of Jesus was 'misshapen'"; though certainly not "ignoble," as Celsus thinks; also, it is not clearly and generally reported that Jesus was "short."[20]

Origen also regards as clear and settled the reports that Jesus was deformed. This version cannot in any way have accorded with reality. Certain deviants from the law, the Docetists, denied that Jesus had been made man at all: his physical being, his death and above all his Passion were nothing but illusion (Greek δοκεῖν, "seem"). Nothing more cogent seems to have been deployed to confute them than Isaiah's prophecies about the suffering servant of God; Tertullian, the North African (about 160−220), applies these literally to the "little body" (*corpusculum*) of Christ: he had no beauty, no majesty, he was despised, he shrank from the sight of man; but for ever and ever, cries Tertullian, "however inglorious, however ignoble, however dishonored, he will be my Christ!" *Si ingloriosus, si ignobilis, si inhonorabilis, meus erit*

---

*Blinzler writes that Jesus had behind him "an exceptionally deprived and exacting life," what with forty days fasting in the wilderness, staying awake all night to pray, irregular and unnourishing meals during ceaseless activity. How does the man know all this?

Christus.[21] So we know very little.* But we always have Stauffer, so we do know that Jesus had "at least the normal stature of the Jews."[23] It is beyond even Stauffer's powers to describe his voice. He recommends us to listen to Bach's St. Matthew Passion to get even the most remote idea of it. (Since Eusebius and the emperor Constantine, Jesus has stopped being ugly and is now uniformly beautiful.)

The humiliation of the Lord, not apparent but physical, is, as Tertullian never tires of telling us, "the disgrace essential for the faith."[24] But there is no account left of the actual circumstances of this death that we can regard as a direct eyewitness account. The evangelists compete, and they do not seem to have any alternative, in fulfilling the prophecies of scripture, though Blinzler[25] denies that "the witness of the prophecies is worked out in an historically formative way" in the crucifixion. That is something we cannot deny.

Blinzler calls in Paul Wernle, who has written about Mark, emphatically the least unreliable of the evangelists: "It is one thing to tell stories, quite another to write history to some purpose." The theme of our book here is that with the evangelists, not excluding Mark, it is no longer possible to sort out what they invented from time to time and what they put out for propaganda purposes: the significance they saw in the events they related.

As always, Mark serves us most sensibly. Clearly there were no eye-witnesses. No disciple sees the crucifixion even from far off, none of Jesus' brothers, nor his mother. Women who had followed him from Galilee and had looked after him (causing scandal to the righteous, no doubt, and not only those of Qumran) looked on from a distance. Some women are actually named, and besides them "many others who had journeyed with him to Jerusalem" looked on quite obviously a saving clause. Bultmann thinks the presence of the Galilean women entirely unhistorical.[26]

Once more, the fulfilment of the prophecies is enlightening. In Luke "his friends had all been standing at a distance; the women who had accompanied him from Galilee stood with them and watched it all." But the Psalmist says:

*Schleiermacher saw it as "heavenly guidance" that "neither a certain tradition nor an authentic picture of the appearance of the person of Jesus has come down to us," for every great theologian has known how to turn the scarcity into abundance, the gap into a cornerstone of providence.[22]

My friends and companions stand aloof
  from my plague,
and my kinsmen stand far off. (38:11)

The soldiers in Mark led or dragged him to the place of execution. Normally the condemned man went naked, and the wood was bound to his outstretched arms; both these things are reported differently by Mark, possibly on esthetic grounds. The evangelist gives us no positive reason why Jesus did not carry the wood himself:

And they compelled a passer-by, Simon of Cyrene, who was coming in from the country, the father of Alexander and Rufus, to carry his cross. (15:21)

The cross, the post, the cross-piece or whatever. Many experts see here a rudiment of an old tradition, because Mark fills in so little detail of that kind. But for just·that reason the passage is suspect. It could have been inserted because the example of following in the path of Jesus. "Take up your cross and follow me" had to be clearly represented in the flesh. Blinzler believes that the cross-piece alone whould not have been so heavy that Jesus could not have carried it;[27] still, he had been weakened by the flogging.

And they brought him to the place called Golgotha, (which means the place of a skull). And they offered him wine mingled with myrrh; but he did not take it. (15:22−23)

Apparently a custom of the women of Jerusalem, who wished, and were allowed, to ease the condemned man's last hours. No fulfilling of the scripture here, apparently. Matthew, however, makes this of it:

...they offered him wine to drink, mingled with gall; but when he tasted it, he would not drink it. (27:34)

basing himself on the Psalms:

They gave me poison for food,
and for my thirst they gave me vinegar to drink. (69:21)

...they divide my garments among them
and for my raiment they cast lots. (22:18)

Mark goes on:

> And they crucified him, and divided his garments among them, casting lots for them, to decide what each should take. (15:24)

According to verse 25 it must have been getting on for nine o'clock in the morning. The Romans evidently did not worry about the Jews' feast-day. The account of casting lots for the clothes indicates that John was fully familiar with one of the synoptic texts. Stauffer, a stickler for precision, points out the peculiarity that "his (Jesus') under-robe had no seam, but was woven throughout like the Chiton (the official robe) of the high priest."[28] How does he know that? He does not know it at all; and moreover he knows that the relevant passage in John, written down in the seventieth year after Jesus' death, is put in by the evangelist to make an Old Testament prophecy come true. John writes:

> When the soldiers had crucified Jesus they took his garments and made four parts, one for each soldier; also his tunic. But the tunic was without seam, woven from top to bottom; so they said to one another, "Let us not tear it, but cast lots for it to see whose it shall be." This was to fulfill the scripture,
> "They parted my garments among them,
> and for my clothing they cast lots."

John, too, is anxious to be precise, more precise than Mark. The tunic is seamless, woven throughout from the top, in order to supply a credible explanation for the fact that the soldiers "shared the garments among them," as it says in Psalm 22, but did not *share* the tunic but gambled for it. Here again, as in the case of the ass's foal, we find an exaggerated literalness. The detailed procedure of sharing out the clothes is broken down into two acts, dividing and casting lots, perhaps, indeed, as David Friedrich Strauss has worked out, to signify by the seamless tunic an undivided church.

Mark tells us that the Romans put a plate up on the cross:

> And the inscription of the charge against him read, "The King of the Jews." (15:26)

Many experts today no longer believe the inscription to be genuine; others, Bultmann among them,[30] regard it as the completion of the passage in Mark 15:2—which itself is not now generally considered genuine—in which Jesus confirms that he is the king of the Jews. Neither Jews nor Romans could have written such an inscription.[31] John, again following the trail of the synoptics, seems to have spotted the discrepancy, and so he goes on:

> The chief priest of the Jews then said to Pilate, "Do not write, 'The King of the Jews,' but, 'This man said, I am the King of the Jews.'" Pilate answered, "What I have written I have written." (19:21-22)

"For," says the book of Esther, "an order written in the name of the king and sealed with the royal signet cannot be revoked"(8:8).

In our poetry, we often find several themes combined wilth one another, and so we do in Mark's. "Thieves" on the right and the left, "the poor malefactors on the cross." The great one is visualized framed by the less great, who enhance his fame, just as the transfigured Jesus (Mark 9:2−7) is accompanied by Moses and Elijah. It applied equally at the time of his ruin. Jesus, who according to Isaiah 9−12, was "reckoned among transgresors" and in one version of Isaiah found his "grave among the wicked,"[32] had to die surrounded by criminals. Thus, in Mark:

> And with him they crucified two robbers, one on his right and one on his left. And the scripture was fulfilled which says, "He was reckoned with the trangressors." (15:27−28)

We see how the report is put together sentence by sentence with no regard for the actual events. The details that follow in Mark also sound unlikely. They could have been lifted not only from the Psalms but also from the book of the *Wisdom of Solomon* (a hundred years before Christ):

> And those who passed by derided him, wagging their heads, and saying, "Aha! You who would destroy the temple and build it in three days, save yourself, and come down from the cross! So also the chief priests mocked him to one another with the scribes, saying, "He saved others; he cannot save himself. Let the Christ, the King of Israel, come down now from the cross,

that we may see and believe." Those who were cricified with him also reviled him. (15:29–32)

The chief priests and the doctors of the law, Jesus' typical opponents, are not easy to visualize as visiting the place of execution on this high feast-day. Bultmann thinks this a "legendary growth."[33] The idea comes from the Psalmist:

All who see me mock at me,
  they make mouths at me, they wag
    their heads;
"He committed his cause to the
  LORD; let him deliver him,
let him rescue him, for he delights
  in him!" (22:7–8)

Matthew (27:43) adopts almost word for word the Greek translation of verse 8, though the parallel is less striking in translation: "He trusted in God; let him save him now, if he will have him; for he said, 'I am the Son of God.'" In the book of *Wisdom*, written under Hellenistic influence and in Greek, it says about the just man: ". . . and calls himself a son of the Lord. . . boasts that God is his father." And in Matthew: ". . . for he said, I am the Son of God." It is the ungodly who spoke in this way in the Psalms and the book of Wisdom; all the more impossible that the temple priests and doctors of the law should have used these words against the crucified Christ. This is how the ungodly in the book of *Wisdom* deal with the just man: "Let us see if his words are true; and let us test what will happen at the end of his life; for if the righteous man is God's son, he will help him and will deliver him from the hand of his adversaries" (2:17–18).

In Mark and Matthew, both the thieves or murderers taunt Jesus. So it is interesting to see what Luke makes out of Mark's story; both those crucified with Jesus speak in Luke's version, but only one of them mocks him:

One of the criminals who were hanged railed at him, saying, "Are you not the Christ? Save yourself and us!" But the other rebuked him, saying, "Do you not fear God, since you are under the same sentence of condemnation? And we indeed justly; for we are receiving the due reward of our deeds; but this man has done nothing wrong." And he said, "Jesus, remember me when you come into your kingdom. And he said to him, "Truly, I say to you, today you will be with me in Paradise." (23:39–43)

The scene has its model in the Egyptian Joseph. While in prison, he meets two fellow-sufferers, Pharaoh's chief baker and his butler. Joseph tells the baker that he will be hung on a tree in three days, but to the butler he says that in three days he will be reinstated in his post. Think of me when you are with Pharaoh, says Joseph to the butler, and think of me, says the malefactor to Jesus, when you come to your throne. Today, answers Jesus, you shall be with me in Paradise—comfort for so many long hours of dying, "promise of eternal salvation" (Wilckens).[34] The plea and the promise are obvious additions, yet still Stauffer can believe that the answer "is certainly not invented."[35]

No, it is not invented; it comes rather from Isaiah's prophecy (53:12) in which the servant of God "bore the sin of many and interceded for their transgressions"; in verse 34, Luke adds to Mark's text: "Jesus said, 'Father, forgive them, for they know not what they do.' " In Mark, Jesus speaks only once on the cross, but in the other three Gospels, there are seven last words. What was Jesus thinking about as he hung there? Was he "waiting till the very last moment for the miracle that never came" (Ben-Chorin)?[36] Had he really expected that his raising up to God through death would be carried through to the end (Rudolf Otto)?[37] We can only wonder. The words of Psalm 22:1 quoted by Mark sound so human, yet they reflect only the feelings of the disciples or the evangelist:

And when the sixth hour had come, there was darkness over the whole land until the ninth hour. And at the ninth hour Jesus cried with a loud voice, "Eloi, Eloi, lama sabachthani?" which means, "My God, my God, why hast thou forsaken me?" And some of the bystanders hearing it said, "Behold, he is calling Elijah." (15:33–35)

What it says in Psalm 22:1 is: "My God, my God, why hast thou forsaken me? Why art thou so far from helping me, from the words of my groaning?" To suppose that Jesus would have recited this psalm instead of a dying prayer is hopelessly off the mark. All the quotation shows is what the author of Mark thought must have been in the mind of Jesus as he died. Did the evangelist really aim to prove to us Jesus' "agreement with God's will" (Dibelius) or "death as fulfilment" (Conzelmann)?[38] Luke seems not to have taken the words in that way. He finds the speech unsuitable and leaves it out. In John, there is no mention of it at all. But in Luke, instead of Psalm 22, Jesus quotes Psalm 31: "Father, into thy hand I commit my spirit." Of course there are scholars who are quite certain that Luke had access to some special tradition. It would be interesting to know.[39]

Only now does Mark fulfill the scripture from Psalm 69 which we have already learned from Matthew ("They gave me vinegar when I was thirsty"):

And one ran and, filling a sponge full of vinegar, put it on a reed and gave it to him to drink, saying, "Wait, let us see whether Elijah will come to take him down." (15:36)

The drink of knowledge shall be withheld from the thirsty; in its place he shall have vinegar, says a Qumran psalm.[40] What knowledge was withheld from Jesus? He had not asked for anything to drink, and what has drinking to do with the return of the prophet Elijah, who according to the ancient Jewish belief must return before the Messiah appears? Was there perhaps some onlooker who wanted to preserve the ebbing life, to make a bit more time in which to get a miracle?

Every Roman soldier carried a sponge with him in his equipment. In John the cane becomes a sprig of hyssop, an obvious reference to the bunch of hyssop (or marjoram) with which the children of Israel smeared the lintel and doorposts with the blood of the Paschal lamb at the first Passover, so that the destroyer slew only the firstborn of the Egyptians (Exodus 12:22). Jesus' Passover has taken the place of the sacrifice of the Paschal lamb.

In any case, Mark does not write "Eli Eli lama sabachthani." He writes, in Greek script, "Eloi Eloi lama sabachtani." That is the Aramaic form of the sentence. "Eloi," with a long "o," cannot possibly have led to a confusion with Elijah. So Matthew alters the first two words to read "Eli Eli," the Hebrew form, and then continues with the Aramaic appeal "lema sabachthani." Joachim Jeremias concludes from this change between Mark and Matthew that Matthew made the alteration, not for the sake of euphony, but because he was able to draw on an older source.[41] Jeremias

190

concludes this, although everyone knows that Matthew's account of the crucifixion is based on Mark's.

Jesus' last words to his mother and the disciple whom he loved, as John records them, are subjective poetry. They could no more have been spoken than those words, from a Jewish Christian source, that we find in the Arab Abd el Jabbar: as he hung on the cross, Jesus is said to have told his mother and brothers: "Take your sons and go away."[42] John presumably wanted to suggest thast the synagogue's own sons were not made to take in the Jewish mother of Christianity.

Not even that last cry described by Mark:

And Jesus uttered a loud cry and breathed his last. (15:37)

is reckoned by all Bible critics to belong to the oldest tradition. Gollwitzer, very clinical, thinks it "hardly possible" that a man who had been hanging from the cross for hours could have cried aloud *twice*.[43] The Messiah comes, as the Apocalypse tells us, "with the sound of the archangel's voice," declares Paul in his first letter to the Thessalonians (4:16).

Was that single cry "a cry of obedience and trust, a cry of faith" (Gollwitzer)? Perhaps it is a little indiscreet to cross-examine this dying man right up to the moment of his death. Jesus relies on the promise, says Gollwitzer; but we reject this kind of interpretation, which must imply that he thought himself in some way invulnerable. We should think no less of Jesus if we knew that he died in inward collapse and utter confusion. We are opposed to all those who say that the feelings of the dying Jesus were any different from the feelings of any other man dying in that way. And, with all possible sympathy with the by no means slight difficulties that churchmen have to face, we cannot help bristling when we see the Bishop of Hamburg, Hans-Otto Wölber, exclaiming in delight because the London production of the musical "Godspell" has dared to make the dying Christ wink at the audience from the cross. "That is knowledge; it leads beyond the cross," says Wolber. The rest of us can never be quite as blasphemous as the men of the church.

Josef Blank sees in the abandonment of Jesus by God "the radical crisis of God himself,"[45] and that is a permissable interpretation. But can we say that Jesus "heard the question of the whole of humanity" (Heinrich Vogel, theologian)[46] — a humanity

191

of which he knew so little and which is certainly troubled by more than one question? Did he suffer what no one else ever suffered, because every one of us can suffer only our own pain, but not the pain of all and with all, the rejection of all by the source of life? Did he endure this from the beginning, and for all men, so that they should not have to endure it (Gollwitzer)?[47]

We simply do not believe that physical pain is made worse because it is endured "for all," and we hardly believe that anyone can feel any worthwhile comfort from such suffering. It shakes us a little when we hear the incomparable Thielicke, not in a speech from *Godspell* but in his latest book of sermons, speak of that God "who staged the enigma of Golgotha and caused his son to die abandoned, and who yet is present in the darkness so that at the end the crucified Christ can bow his head full of peace."[48]

We do not trust such a transfer-peace. We do not believe that Jesus died full of peace, any more than Mark believed it. In the silent abysses, the dark vales of the dying Son of God (not my words) and over and above the "higher thoughts" which press forward towards Easter (not my words): that tells us nothing more. God actually stages this bloody play since he can reconcile himself with his creation in no other way, and that is all this producer tells us. "What a primitive mythology," writes Bultmann, "that a heavenly being can become a man and atone for the sins of men with his blood."[49]

We cannot and will not elaborate this end on the cross. Bultmann thinks it possible that Jesus had completely given way. He is not sure that Jesus saw any sense in his death.[50] In his view, the historical Jesus stands no higher than those who, in obedient love, died as soldiers in the World War: "I have done nothing to hurt him and he has nothing to forgive me for."[51] What a contrast there is between Bultmann's honesty and hollow rhetoric, if he can do nothing to prevent the destruction of the Christian conceptions but can only promote it; for, if that is not true, how does he arrive at the sentence: "Christ is the word of the forgiving grace"?[52] That just establishes the tragedy of Bultmann, and, if we consider the subject, also his greatness.

Although there have been men who have hung on the cross for hours and still survived — Flavius Josephus reports an example — they have left us no account of their experience. In a person who had believed in a supernatural rescue, a *deus ex machina*, which never came, then physical suffering and spiritual despair would become virtually inseparable. It may well be true in the case of Jesus, as Ernst Bloch envisages the end, that his belief that he was the bringer of the Messianic kingdom "only failed him on the cross."[54]

We need not devote more than a few lines to the miracles that accompany the death of famous personalities — "Pure romantic inventions,"[55] as Bultmann calls them. They hardly belong to the oldest period of the tradition. See Mark:

> And the curtain of the temple was torn in two, from top to bottom. (15:38)

> And the curtain of the temple was torn in two, from top to bottom. And when the centurion, who stood facing him, saw that he thus breathed his last, he said, "Truly this man was the Son of God!" (15:39)

The Roman captain has his parallel in the Jewish records of martyrs. The bearing of the Rabbi Chanina ben Teradjon at his martyrdom so impressed his executioner that he jumped into the flames with the rabbi.[56] Matthew puts in even greater wonders. He has the prophet Ezekiel in mind and makes the bodies of the saints rise from their graves and walk about in Jerusalem (though the son of man is not resurrected; for the moment he has merely died). This is what he found in Ezekiel:

> Then he said to me, "Son of man, these bones are the whole house of Israel. Behold, they say, 'Our bones are dried up, and our hope is lost; we are clean cut off.' Therefore prophesy, and say to them, Thus says the Lord GOD: Behold, I will open your graves, and raise you from your graves, O my people; and I will bring you home into the land of Israel. And you shall know that I am the LORD, when I open your graves, and raise you from your graves, O my people. (37:11–13)

There is no reason to disbelieve the resurrection of these dead men if we believe in the resurrection of Jesus. Luke evidently thought it inappropriate that the heathen captain should have declared Jesus to be the Son of God, so he makes him say: "Beyond all doubt, this man was innocent." The heathen should not have known at the crucifixion what was not revealed to the disciples until after the resurrection.

Mark makes the man on the cross give way to human despair, Luke presents him as a model of goodness and understanding. But John dips the end of the crucifixion in the font of his theology. Jesus, the Son of God from the very beginning, expressly in order himself to fulfil the scripture says: "I thirst"

> my strength is dried up like a
>   potsherd,
> and my tongue cleaves to my
>   jaws;
> thou dost lay me in the dust of
>   death. (Psalm 22:15)

The vinegar that he is given to drink is thus at least motivated by a previously expressed wish. Jesus does not despair as he does in Mark and gives no loud cry as in Luke; he says: "It is finished" (19:30). He bows his head and dies.

If it was necessary to hasten the death of crucified men, their legs were broken with iron clubs (on the body found in Jerusalem, the feet, complete with nails and the wooden plank, were smashed). Reference to this custom enables John to fulfil some more prophecies. Since Jesus is found to be already dead, his legs did not have to be broken like those of the other two:

> But one of the soldies pierced his side with a spear, and at once there came out blood and water. He who saw it has borne witness — his testimony is true, and he knows that he tells the truth — that you also may believe. For these things took place that the scripture might be fulfilled, "Not a bone of him shall be broken." And again another scripture says, "They shall look on him whom they have pierced." (19:34—37)

In the book of Exodus, it says about the Paschal lamb:

> In one house shall it be eaten; you shall not carry forth any of the flesh outside the house; and you shall not break a bone of it. (12:46)

and in the Psalms:

> He keeps all his bones;
>   not one of them is broken. (34:20)

In the same way the wound in the side is "taken from the Old Testament" (Martin Dibelius).[57] Zechariah, who has shaped the Gospels so generously, prophesies:

> "And I will pour out on the house of David and the inhabitants of Jerusalem a spirit of compassion and supplication, so that, when they look on him whom they have pierced, they shall mourn for him, as one mourns for an only child, and weep bitterly over him, as one weeps over a first-born. (12:10)

The servant of God in Isaiah (53:5) is "wounded for our transgressions." To enable them to look on him whom they have pierced, the evangelist makes a soldier stick a spear or lance into the dead body's side, the origin of an incredibly fertile myth.* We cannot help asking why the favorite disciple who claims to have seen it all with his own eyes allows the Lord to carry the cross by himself, why he leaves out Simon of Cyrene and with him the only detail in the account that may perhaps be authentic. Just as Mark, or an earlier writer, may have invented Simon to illustrate the following of Jesus, John cannot make use in his representative theology of a representative of a representative.

Jesus, who was convicted of wishing to destroy the temple and overturn the law of Moses, was now dead. "If he had not died he would not have become historic," the worthy ex-theologian and Orientalist Wellhausen[59] has written. That is true enough, and yet it is only a half-truth. Jesus, who had been executed, had preached a message that seemed to be refuted when he died. His kingdom had not come, and did not come. To survive the catastrophe, to survive its own destruction, the message had to be verified over again. That was possible only if the death was not real, if it was "swallowed up in victory" (1 Corinthians 15:55): "O Death, where is thy victory? O Death, where is thy sting?"

Freud wonders whether Jesus really was a great teacher, or whether "it was not rather the fact and the circumstances of his death that were the decisive factors in his achieving importance."[60] Jesus must have foreseen his humiliating death, must have taken it into account, must have deliberately planned for it. Since that is not in human nature, he must have had advance knowledge of his resurrection, have included it in his plan of action. Indeed, in

---

*Augustine compares the wound in the side with the door in the side of Noah's ark, through which men and animals were saved.

John's, the last, Gospel, he must have deliberately brought it about. In Mark, he is raised from the dead; but in John, according to a witness, he has already power to lay down his life if he wishes to, and to receive it back if he wishes (10:18): "No one takes it from me, but I lay it down of my own accord. I have power to lay it down, and I have power to take it again; this charge I have received from my Father."

Only one thing was necessary: that he should rise from the grave; that he should be resurrected.

We simply do not know the details of what happened: how the belief grew in a Jesus no longer dead, in his appearance, transfigured or not transfigured; how he was able to rise in the first place, and what part was played by the women from Galilee. What we get from the Gospels is a highly incomplete substitute, as they never take any trouble or devote any space to the substantiation of supernatural happenings. There were miracles. Luther offers us a belated explanation: "But whereas the Gospel is now widespread, and has been preached to the whole world, it is not necessary to perform signs as it was at the time of the apostles. But if the need required it, and they would stir up and press forward with the Gospel, then we should truly set about it, we too should perform signs."[61] We remember that he had recommended Thomas Münzer to justify himself by working miracles. Münzer was in need of justification, and so were the first Christians.

Protestant theology has laid particular emphasis on the "empty grave" (Stauffer: "an objective and verifiable fact")[62] as if some demonstrable fact lay concealed here, simply because empty graves have occurred more frequently than ascents into heaven (Bultmann: "entirely secondary").[63] Belief in the resurrection was certainly established quite soon after the death of Jesus. Paul (literally, "the little one") seems to have come across it already at the time of his conversion, about the year 34.

The theological scholarship of both confessions decrees that the bringing back to life of Jesus by God is in a strict sense an object of faith. Says the Franciscan, Dautzenberg: "But we have the evidence of witnesses as historic fact that they saw him after his resurrection." But, really, we know of no witnesses who have committed any such experience to paper, as we do in the case of Augustus, from witnesses who, as Eduard Lohse says, "declared that they had seen how the dead man had risen up to heaven." No two of the reported "facts" about Jesus agree with one another.

Paul simply attests that the risen Christ appeared to him, the convert, years after the death of Jesus, and that it was from him when he appeared that he, Paul, had received the Gospel that he preached. He says nothing about when, where or how.[64]

Paul further reports that the risen Christ appeared before several of the disciples, to all the apostles together and to a large number of Christian brethren. He gives the number as five hundred. The Protestant Heinz Zahrnt calls the "happenings" of which Paul speaks "clear, agreed, historical facts."[65] But Paul leaves out the women mentioned in Mark and Matthew, and they in turn say nothing about an appearance before James reported by Paul.

The Gospels describe a palpable body, with bones and a stomach that can digest bread and fried fish, but which can nevertheless pass through walls and locked doors. Luke in his Gospel makes clear the agreed, historical fact that Jesus ascended into heaven on Easter day. The same Luke in the Acts of the Apostles describes the no less clear, historical fact that the resurrected Jesus showed himself among his followers for forty days and only then went up to heaven; forty days was the "usual time for embalming" (Genesis 50:3), the time that Joseph devoted to his dead father Jacob in Egypt. "It would go hard for the Christian faith," wrote Walter Pannenberg in 1960, "if the resurrection of Jesus were really not an historical fact."[66] That is true enough.

But then it would have gone hard for the Christian faith in the year 55. Paul, at the latest 25 years after the death of Jesus, still in the expectation of the Lord's immediate return ("We shall not all sleep, but we shall all be changed," 1 Corinthians 15:51), this Paul was preaching the program by which today the Christian church as a sole and divine institution falls rather than stands: "If Christ has not been raised, then our preaching is in vain and your faith is in vain" (1 Corinthians 15:14).

And there is a second, a fearful word in the same letter of this first and greatest of all propagandists (1 Corinthians 16:22): "If any one has no love for the Lord, let him be accursed."

We know of another dying man, and in his case we believe we can have some idea of the feelings that were uppermost in him in his last conscious moments: that splendid spirit, Giordano Bruno,[67] who may well have suffered more than Jesus, setting a standard for all men, conscious of his example up to the very moment at which he lost consciousness. The representatives of Jesus Christ (among whom we may confidently include Luther, Calvin and Zwingli) had kept him under arrest for seven years to get him to deny, for instance, that even Jesus sinned, or that the universe was infinite and there were other worlds in it. He did not oblige them, and so on the 17th February 1600, at the age of fifty-one, under the eyes of Pope Clement VIII and in the presence of fifty cardinals of the Holy Roman Church, he was burnt in the Campo dei Fiori, the place of flowers, in Rome. Before he suffocated, someone gave him the cross on the end of a long stick; but instead of kissing this sign of the victory of his executioners, with a last effort he turned his head in the opposite direction.

He might well be forgiven if he did not love our Lord Jesus Christ at that moment.

8.   The God
out of step

No need, however urgent it may be,
can make possible the impossible.[1]
—Schelling

At the beginning of the recorded history of Israel stands the religion of Moses. Whether men need religion today, whether religion can still offer us anything, may be a moot point. But it is beyond doubt that the men of ancient times needed a religion. Even the dance of the shamans, an institutional as much as a religious affair, represents, in the vivid phrase of Arnold Gehlens, "a grasping in the jaws of their own fear and greed" — fear of the weapons of the deadly animals, greed for their flesh as meat.[2] The dance charms and restrains; it "sublimates" the instincts for slaughter and gorging.

In their experience of sickness, hunger, sorrow and death, in natural disasters and the disasters of war, in oppression and slavery, the followers of shamanism needed protection. They needed to rely on others, a need oriented towards supernatural authorities. Man, says Alexander Mitscherlich, is a creature naturally hostile to men.[3] Religion was the first of all ideologies; it offered a system of control based on common values and convictions providing for all questions of doubt. Why were men living, and what was the right way to live? An answer could come only from an appeal to non-human authorities, observed and propagated on the Jewish patriarchal line of development by the prophet, the middle-man between man and the supernatural. Prophet and priest, the seer and the supervisor: it seems inevitable that they should come into conflict.

The prophetic answer to the religious question was always the exercise of power, political rule. Certainly the need for religion did not have to be created; it was always there. But it was not possible to submit to it, to fulfil it, without at the same time defining it. Once it was defined, the norms of control acquired with it had to be asserted, and it was also possible to make use of the controls thus established for the exercise of power in the "profane" fields outside the temple. Priests, prophets and temporal rulers — if they were not identical — were thus always in competition for power.

Religion stabilizes (or prevents) the establishment of power. Religion is power. The shepherd and the herd he must tend: that is the essence of religion, and at the bottom of it lies the childlike concept that our elders run the world for our benefit. But there was a special element in the case of the Israelite community. It was in actual fact founded by a political act which was felt to be a divine act of God. Religious and historical consciousness were thus one and the same. Moses the middle-man, who interprets the acts of God, is at the same time Moses the man of action who puts them into practice. In this respect, he was the model for the Jewish prophets Elijah, Isaiah, Jeremiah, and model too for Joshua-Jehoshua, the "son" of Moses, as also for Joshua-Jehoshua the Son of God. Myth, action and teaching are all inseparably combined in these prophets.

We can no longer discern what is mythical in the tradition of Moses and what is historical, and in particular whether Moses the leader of the flight out of Egypt was identical with the Moses who "received" God's commandments on Mount Sinai or some other holy mountain. We may just as well not worry about the name Moses. Most scholars today acknowledge that a substantial tribal group actually did leave Egypt during the thirteenth century B.C.E. to move into the land of Canaan, and it is often also accepted that this and other tribes or clans were often subjected to compulsory service in Egypt. Habiru (= Hebrew?) was in Egypt an expression signifying not a tribe but an inferior status, a class of people with lesser rights. An inscription on a memorial of the Pharaoh Merenptah, who is thought to have reigned 1234–1225, reads: "Canaan captured with all the tribes. Askelon is taken prisoner, Gezer is seized, Jenoam is destroyed, Israel — its people are few, its seed no longer exists. Syria has become a widow for Tameri (Egypt)."[4]

The fugitives, perhaps actual fugitives from a state of slavery, first established their federally organized tribal community on the soil of Canaan. Its members certainly did not appear right away as victorious conquerors; the plains did not yet lie open to them. As late as the time of Saul, the Israelites still had to have their swords and lances, their axes and ox-goads made by the Philistines, for "no blacksmith was to be found in the whole of Israel" (1 Samuel 13:19). They attributed victory and the conquest of territory to the guidance of Yahweh (the name means "I am that I am" or "He that is"). Egypt looked on them as "the inferior creations of the existing world" (Bloch).[5] Against the Egyptian god-king and his external power, they pitted the interior dictatorship of their absolute god: they saw religion as an integrating power.

Anyone who opposed the pronouncements of the covenant offended against the commandment of the Lord. Military organization and adherence to a catalogue of ethnic and cultural rules, even in everyday life, led to an indivisible union, which in turn had the result that disasters in foreign affairs could be explained by a failure to follow the everyday regulations. Fear, the primitive human experience (Freud: "Dark, unfeeling and loveless powers determine man's fate"; Bloch speaks of "nature's cold shoulder"),[6] was neutralized internally within the tribal and national community, and was turned aggresively outward. He who aroused these fears and made of them an outward-turned energy, who had "grasped fear and greed in his jaws," was no man, though such must have been the deeds of the man Moses; Yahweh had made use of Moses, Yahweh the indescribable god. Moses the sublimator, Moses the founder of institutions, may himself have received the "prize" for his boldness. It was attributed to Yahweh, so much so indeed that according to the Bible, Moses was not allowed to enter the promised land.*

The analysis of mythical events, the analysis of a figure that endures them and bears up under them on two levels, one as it were earthly, the other transcendental, becomes tremendously plastic when applied to the figure of Moses as it appears to us in the Bible. It is not Moses who gives the order to leave Egypt and march through the desert; he is only carrying out Yahweh's orders. And he can talk to Yahweh like this (Numbers 11:11−14):

---

*Could it be that Gehlen's "institutions" are due to Freud's "sublimation"? In 1938, a year before his death, Freud said to Salvador Dali: "Moses is sublimation made flesh."[7] But Moses is also institution made flesh. We are continually struck by the devotion of so many atheists to religion.

Moses said to the LORD, "Why hast thou dealt ill with thy servant? And why have I not found favor in thy sight, that thou dost lay the burden of all this people upon me? Did I conceive all this people? Did I bring them forth, that thou shouldst say to me, 'Carry them in your bosom, as a nurse carries the sucking child, to the land which thou didst swear to give their fathers?' Where am I to get meat to give to all this people? For they weep before me and say, 'Give us meat, that we may eat.' I am not able to carry all this people alone, the burden is too heavy for me.

Religion, says Feuerbach, is self-estrangement; and Marx, following after Feuerbach, speaks of the fact of religious self-alienation, the "division of the world into two worlds, one religious and one earthly." Man sees himself first as a limited individual, then as an unlimited, contrasting self, strange to that individual (God).[8]

Freud has combined Moses, his favorite historical figure, with his favorite ideal type-figure, the first ancestor of the first horde whose sons killed and ate him but with whom they afterwards try to affiliate and identify themselves. Freud sees the triumph and the crime of the past, the killing of the father, repeated in the person of Moses; he assumes "that the Jews, who even according to the Bible were stubborn and unruly towards this law-giver and leader, rebelled at last, killed him and threw off the imposed Aton religion."[9]

But Freud's theory of first ancestor of the horde has not finally been confirmed, so we are without any evidence of the murder of Moses. It is credible that an "eminent father-figure" led a group through the desert; much less so that it was on the instructions of Yahweh, whose name seems to have belonged originally to a god established in the conquered territory.* But was it a single man who uplifted the self-confidence of the people, ripe for integration, by the assurance that they were God's chosen people? Who made them a consecrated people, committed them to separation from the others? Was all this so much the work of a single man that Freud can say: "It was one man, the man Moses, who created the Jews"? Did he bring to the Jews the religion of the first ancestor,

---

*He seems to have been originally the heavenly bull, with a cow-goddess at his side; we often hear of the "horn of salvation" (e.g., in Luke 1:69) that God has raised up, certainly a metaphor for male potency.

"and the hope of reward, distinction, and finally world domination (which) is bound up with it"?[10] Or has some possibly important leader of an Israelite exodus from Egypt suffered the fate of being overshadowed in retrospect by the founder-figure of some other, no longer comprehensible and discoverable, historical process?

Moses, the father-figure, stands at the beginning of the mythically recollected history of Israel. The attitude of the child to the father has its parallel in the attitude of the Israelites to this figure who represents God, who never acts of his own accord. Moses is a channel for those feelings of guilt towards Yahweh which are no less formative to the children of Israel than was the safe deliverance from the land of the Egyptians. Unlike Freud, modern anthropology believes that the guilty feelings, and thus also perhaps the religion, grew out of incestuous desires and the prohibition of relations between persons of very different degrees of kinship, far more than out of the murder of a primitive ancestor (or even, if we disregard Freud, of Abel in the garden of Eden). Conflicts within the family might at any rate have been characteristic of the early communities, and feelings of guilt, diverted and controlled towards a godhead, were necessary for their settlement in order to get rid of the actual, worldly, temptations or offenses.[11]

But now there is the god of Moses, who chooses his people — rather a unique event — and so immediately "earns" a right to their absolute obedience. The details of this agreement between unequals must presumably remain obscure.

The idea of absolute obedience to Yahweh is the greatest advantage the Jewish religion had over that of neighboring tribes, thinks Max Weber, evidently assuming that only feelings of guilt towards God could secure the binding force of social rules. Guilty feelings towards Yahweh were certainly useful all round, to consolidate the establishment of a social hierarchy in the Israelite community. Originally a community with equal rights for all, under temporary military leaders ("judges"), the newcomers at once formed themselves into the poor-rich stratification that still persists in ancient Canaan. The invaders, Bedouin up till then, took over their agriculture from settled peoples, harvested cereals and wine, planted olive trees and fig trees. An aristocracy grew up in the towns, who demilitarized the peasants and shepherds and subjected them to taxation. They had to pay over half of all the oil and wine, a third of the grain, a quarter of the fruit. Solomon's splendid buildings would have been unthinkable without forced labor on the Egyptian model.

Non-Hebrews, bought or captured, worked as slaves (a word which does not appear in Luther's translation of either the Old or New Testament). But the practice of slavery was not confined to them. Anyone who got into debt could of course sell himself into slavery, nominally for six years. But what could he do at the end of six years, left without resources? And what if his master had given him a wife in the meantime? Wife and children remained with the master, and it was open to the slave to stay with him and continue as a slave (Exodus 21:4). As late as Jesus' time, and indeed long after it, the practice of debt-slavery persisted as a custom for native Hebrews, whereas in ancient Rome, debt-slavery for nationals had been abolished as early as 326 B.C.E.

One of the main functions of religion, to Marx as well as to Freud, is the provision of illusory compensations, socially binding and psychologically effective, offered as recompense for sacrifices extorted on earth. Religion, we repeat, was not only used as an instrument of domination; it actually was, and still is, domination in itself. It served to motivate and control the conduct of communities. The old Yahweh had done nothing, as far as we know, to disseminate any justice and humanity among his people that was not to be found all around them. The problem of slavery never seems to have dawned on him; it did not bother him in the least.*

No other people affords such a model analysis of the establishment of priestly rule. There were laws which had no basis outside the word of God, such as the directions for worship for the temple, the rules on cleanliness, the rules about food (not to be mistaken for hygienic precautions), and the rite of circumcision, whose origin is uncertain (since neighboring peoples also had it) but was certainly not a sanitary one (Freud: "a symbolic substitute for castration").[13] To have offended against the laws of God was a charge frequently brought in Israel. The cultivation of a guilt-complex standing at the disposal of a dominant caste and emphasized by eloquent prophets, could not be more carefully prepared. If ancient Rome had its *tribunitia potestas*, its power of the tribunes to uphold the people's rights against the aristocracy,

---

*It says in Exodus (21:20−21): "When a man strikes his slave, male or female, with a rod and the slave dies under his hand, he shall be punished. But if the slave survives a day or two, he is not to be punished; for the slave is his money."

Israel of old had the prophets, who watched less over the rights of the people than over those of Yahweh. What is once incorporated in the structure of the code of the law, even from the reservoir of the unconscious, is thenceforth built in to this power-station for the generation of guilt, this unceasing emotional machine. Rabbi Johanan ben Zakkai, a contemporary of Paul, formulated the principle with unsurpassable clarity: "In your lives, it is not the dead man that defiles, not water that makes clean; it is a precept of the king of all kings."[14]

If we accept the psychoanalysts' differentiation between introverted "guilt-culture" and outward-turned "shame-culture," then ancient Israel, unlike Israel today, was a model of a guilt-culture. It was not the consciousness of shame that foreigners ruled over Israel and oppressed the orthodox Jews that moved the people, but the constantly stoked-up feeling of guilt: the people were told they did not love Yahweh enough, did not honor, feed, follow him enough. In this inwardly-turned frame of mind, which constantly overcame external reality, the only help lay in a final, cosmic catastrophe from which a demigod Messiah must appear as a *deus ex machina*, the "anointed of the Lord," in Hebrew *meshiach-adonai*. He, the last mediator between man and God, has to redeem Israel, has to gain for the oppressed people, and guarantee them for ever a place at the forefront of all peoples in a new world order. He shall "rule them with an iron rod," as it says in the Revelation of John, or "shatter them like a clay pot," as the Coronation Psalm (2:9) has it. Nothing more then stands in the way of the eternal covenant between Yahweh and his chosen people. He will prepare a feast of fat things for all peoples out of mount Zion, with savory foods and clear wine upon the lees; he will wipe the tears from every face. Jesus, if he is discoverable, was the announcer of this cosmic overthrow, which never happened.

For however much he changed his nature under the influence of ideas from outside Judaism (Persian ideas, Egyptian, Canaanite) to that of a sole, universal God, Yahweh could never entirely shed the cocoon of his origin. Freud falls back on the classic method of analysis. The Yahweh whom the invaders (or, according to circumstances, the homecomers) met with in Canaan was a "rude, narrow-minded local god, violent and bloodthirsty." But the God whom Moses introduced to the Israelites out of the convictions dreamed up by the Pharaohs was already in Freud's view the one and only God.[15] We beg to differ. We see the one and only God as no great achievement if he is anything like a confusion with Pharaoh. And if we consult, not Freud's brilliant imagination, but the scriptures, then Yahweh appears as a tribal god, a god of war, of disaster, of the weather, a god indeed who promised his people conquest of the lands inhabited by other peoples. David's battle against the Philistines was the last in which Yahweh led Israel into battle. The scripture here calls him "Yahweh, Lord of hosts, god of the line of battle of Israel." Why should he have favored Israel? Because Israel had recognized and acknowledged him, and only him, as God; because Israel explained any failure on his part as punishment for actual offences against Yahweh; because Israel strictly followed Yahweh's commands, and if they were to be Israel's commands, they had to be distinguished from those of other tribes and peoples. Commands there had to be, either so that Israel should obey commands not obeyed by others and so prove their faithfulness to Yahweh, or so that they should not obey Yahweh's commands and thus cultivate their consciousness of guilt. Did that really make the Jew, as Ernst Bloch holds, "the morally most intensive man"?[16]

We hear — it may be the only known example — that a god has expressly concluded an agreement with "his" people, a somewhat one sided agreement, as we shall see. Gollwitzer is struck by the sharpness with which, here in the Old Testament, man is "spoken to about his guilt, his sins against God." Sins, judgment, forgiveness are to him always the "central content of the Christian faith." The old scheme for the control of requirements and interests does not strike Gollwitzer as the least bit dubious: the faithful God, but utterly faithful, and the faithless man.[17] The creation is actually faithless, the Creator only apparently so; he speaks through the words of Jeremiah:

for my people have committed two evils:
they have forsaken me,
the fountain of living waters,
and they hewed out cisterns for themselves,
broken cisterns that can hold no water. (2:13)

Man as comprehended by the religion of guilt sins not so much against his fellow-men as, above all, against God.

Sigmund Freud, who saw Moses as a revolutionary prophet of enlightenment, praises the "disdaining of magic and mystery, the encouragement of progress in spirituality and sublimations," which he believes have come into the world through the Mosaic religion.[18] Today we are not so sure. Moses and Aaron competed with the Egyptian sorcerers, who like them did tricks with snakes. Elijah, too, in his rain-making competition with the prophets of Baal on Mount Carmel, had no doubt that the god Baal existed; he was just trying to prove that his God was more powerful. King Saul's sons had Baal-names; the celebrated warrior Gideon was called Jerubbaal. David himself, during his time as leader of a rebel band, seems to have served in the army of the Philistines (1 Samuel 27—30) and to have borne the name "Baal-Hanan" (1 Chronicles 1:49).

Certainly Yahweh was angry with all who prayed to Baal; at one time he only allowed seven thousand men to survive in Israel (1 Kings 19:18): "all who have not bent the knee to Baal, all whose lips have not kissed him." He makes the prophet Jeremiah — or the prophet Jeremiah makes him — proclaim: The children of Judah set up their loathsome idols in my house, and build shrines to Baal to surrender their sons and daughters to Moloch; "it was no command of mine, nor did it ever enter my thought."

Yahweh would no doubt only reluctantly remember such a practice from the days when he himself was still "the cannibal in heaven" (Bloch);[19] he let it be recorded in the book of Judges (11:30—40) that he required the judge Jephtha to offer his still-virgin daughter as a burnt offering. It looks as if the abominations ascribed to the neighbor-gods were just those that the true God had put behind him.

Even the judge Jephthah does not seem to have assumed that there was only one god, his God, for he tells the king of the Ammonites (Judges 11:24): "Will you not possess what Chemosh your god gives you to possess? And all that the LORD our God has dispossessed before us, we will possess." Chemosh, the national god of the Moabites, and his companion-goddess Astarte, generally represented naked, had a shrine in Jerusalem almost until the destruction of the state of Judah. Beelzebub or Beelzebul was originally a god of the Phoenicians, until he became in Hebrew Baal Zebub, Lord of the Flies; and it was only in the development of a superiority complex by the God of Israel that he became a devil, or the devil.

"The unique achievement of Judaism," writes Reinhard Bendix in his book on the work of Max Weber, "can only really be assessed when we consider the immense task facing their religious leaders in their efforts to eradicate every foreign trace from the worship of Yahweh."[20] But the narrow-minded determination to see the gods of the "heathen" as nobodies means in itself no higher conception of God; it can only be explained as a symptom of a sickness, an attack of narcissistic mortification. When the religion of Yahweh came to be written down, the great days of King David were already only a distant memory. Israel's defeats, which were really the defeats of Yahweh, meant a deep, narcissistic outrage which had to be repulsed by a manic reaction; for God is a part of thee and of me, although an extremely idealized part. God himself was not held responsible, but the people were in some way to blame in the eyes of their God, most commonly through open or secret disrespect. Out of the wreckage, there came the plan of salvation. An obsessive quality derived from historical events is characteristic of religious phenomena, according to Freud;[21] the obsession is "in a certain sense a human prerogative."*

It is not for us to show that Jewish victories brought with them no less outrage and oppression, and no less cruelty, than Jewish defeats. The Bible tells us that the women and children of the Midianites were not treated with great consideration, mixed marriages with Midianite women being a capital offense, though not the rape of Midianite virgins (Numbers 25:8; 31:17−18). When Edom, Israel's hereditary enemy, was conquered in 125 B.C.E. — this was the Idumaea of the Romans, lying to the south of Judaea — the men were forcibly circumcised, and the ancient crime haunted the orthodox Jews traumatically: when the Idumaean Herod, circumcised indeed but highly profane and highly unpopular, became king, although according to Josephus he claimed to stand nearer to the Greeks than to the Jews, he had a family tree prepared going back to the time the Jews returned from exile. Some time between 458 and 398 B.C.E. the lawgiver Ezra (9:2−10; 10:17−44) ordered that all marriages of Jews with women of non-Jewish origin should be annulled. He named names, and it is a long list. The holy race had "become mixed with the foreign population." To placate Yahweh, the men dismissed their wives and children; it makes our heart bleed to read it. Anyone at that time

---

*The egocentric way in which many Israelites cultivated their view of the world is illustrated by an action of Paul's instructor, Rabbi Gamaliel. Although otherwise thoroughly liberal, he had an Aramaic translation of the book of Job (written in Hebrew) walled up in the forecourt of the temple, in order on the one hand not to destroy it, since it was after all a holy book, but on the other hand to withdraw it from circulation, so it should not get into the hands of the heathen.

who as a result of the confusion of war could not trace back his descent, who was not ready to prove that he came from the tribe of Levi, had to resign from the priesthood.

We cannot but be struck by the persistent conviction of persecution and ill-usage of a people that had for long persecuted and ill-used others, and we are tempted to see the effect of just those most significant of the Israelite prophets as "self-fulfilling masochism." The more servilely Israel depended on its God, the worse it was treated by him. Is that something to do with the father-religion of Moses, and of the fact that the mother, once drummed out of the cult, was rigorously kept at a distance?

Scarcely any culture of that age was without a female godhead in its pantheon, and eventually Christianity, too, found it could not do without one. There are even traces of some kind of matriarchal rule to be found in Stone Age remains in the land of Canaan. Zipporah, Moses' wife, circumcised her son with a stone knife and called him her "blood-bridegroom." And to this day the family, national and religious status of a Jewish child is determined after the mother.[22] The cult-type of the redeemer-son who loves his mother is often found outside Israel. It is striking that a change has actually been made in the Biblical account of the creation. The spirit of God hovering over the waters is transcribed in the original Chaldean text from Babylon as "mother of the gods": she broods over the abyss and brings forth new life. Father, mother and (redeemer-) son, the three persons in the drama of Oedipus, do not appear in that way in the Bible's *dramatis personae*; the mother, "cause of the whole conflict" (as Ernest Jones says in his biography of Freud), is replaced by the enigmatic figure of the Holy Spirit. He hovers there as a relic of the mother, always henceforth on the defensive if he is ever driven out of his neutral corner into the women's camp.[23]

A goddess of love and queen of heaven was even worshipped in Israel; the temple prostitutes, the Kedesh, were devoted to her holy service. In the written Bible, however, prostitution and the worship of idols were equated with one another. The Lord said to Jeremiah, who had emigrated from Egypt, in the seventh century B.C.E.:

Do you not see what they are doing in the cities of Judah and in the streets of Jerusalem? The children gather wood, the fathers kindle fire, and the women knead dough, to make cakes for the queen of heaven; and they pour out drink offerings to other gods, to provoke me to anger. Is it I whom they provoke? says the LORD. Is it not themselves, to their own confusion? (7:17–19)

But the people did not feel either hurt or ashamed:

Then all the men who knew that their wives had offered incense to other gods, and all the women who stood by, a great assembly, all the people who dwelt in Pathros in the land of Egypt, answered Jeremiah: "As for the word which you have spoken to us in the name of the LORD, we will not listen to you. But we will do everything that we have vowed, burn incense to the queen of heaven and pour out libations to her, as we did, both we and our fathers, our kings and our princes, in the cities of Judah and in the streets of Jerusalem; for then we had plenty of food, and prospered, and saw no evil. But since we left off burning incense to the queen of heaven and pouring out libations to her, we have lacked everything and have been consumed by sword and by famine." (44:15–18)

That was the time, says the Essenes' *Damascus Document*, when men served "the Astartes," the Ishtar of Babylon and the Astarte of the Western Semites. Ishtar, the queen of heaven, had as her symbol the crescent moon and star of Venus. Old Yahweh may not have been so terribly surprised to come across his former lady rival again, some centuries later, as a kind of sisterly daughter-in-law — this time under the name, not of Astarte or Ishtar, but of Miriam-Mary.

Theodor Reik in Berlin, another of Freud's biographers, saw in the suppression of goddess-worship signs of an "ever-strengthening feminine homosexual relationship with the heavenly father, Yahweh," of a relationship of "libidinous intensity," which certainly seethes with hatred where it relates to the forcible expulsion of the goddess, and can only be endured in sullen obedience.[24] The marriage between Yahweh and Israel becomes a favorite metaphor of the prophets from Hosea on:

"Surely, as a faithless wife leaves her
husband,
so have you been faithless to me,
O house of Israel, says the LORD."
(Jeremiah 3:20)

"I remember the devotion of your
  youth,
  your love as a bride,
how you followed me in the
  wilderness,
in a land not sown." (Jeremiah 2:2).

This unconscious hatred of Yahweh, swelling beneath the humble, obedient love, is compared by Reik to a compulsion-neurosis. Freud goes further: he sees the basis of Jewish ethics in the consciousness of guilt aroused by this suppressed hostility to Yahweh.

The account of the creation, written in the sixth century B.C.E., is not the oldest part of the New Testament; it seems to have been fed from Babylonian sources and to have been put in front of the five books of Moses by an editor. All the poetic stories of Abraham, (the first father of the people), of Isaac, of Jacob (the second father) and of the Egyptian Joseph, are legends — shadowy reflections of events that may have taken place in some form or other, uniquely sublimated in Thomas Mann's novel *Joseph and His Brothers*, as of now the last masterpiece of world-literature composed in German. This confession of faith was quoted in Israel before the Bible came into existence; it is repeated in the Bible in the Fifth Book of Moses (Deuteronomy 26:5—9):

And you shall make response before the LORD your God, 'A
wandering Aramean was my father; and he went down into
Egypt and sojourned there, few in number; and there he became
a nation, great, mighty, and populous. And the Egyptians
treated us harshly, and afflicted us, and laid upon us hard
bondage. Then we cried to the LORD the God of our fathers, and
the LORD heard our voice, and saw our affliction, our toil, and
our oppression; and the LORD brought us out of Egypt with a
mighty hand and an outstretched arm, with great terror, with
signs and wonders; and he brought us into this place and gave us
this land, a land flowing with milk and honey."

"My father was an Aramean," any ancestor, maybe Jacob, maybe not; he left here for Egypt to get away from bad living conditions. His followers were numerous, but became enslaved. That is how the history of Israel begins. Abraham is the "ideal" Israelite, Jacob is the "real" one, down-to-earth, full of cunning and wiles. The ancestral name Jacob is interchangeable with the religious name Israel, which means "contender with God."

It was not the God of the creation, taken over later from Egypt and Mesopotamia, Lord of heaven and earth, who led the Israelites out of Egypt, but the tribal god. He gives them a healthy distaste for the monarchical system from which they have just escaped, and a longing for another system than the monarchical in which he will take the monarch's place. Israel, at first, wished to be not the people of a king, but the people of their God Yahweh. The kings of Israel were to have a difficult time. And yet old Yahweh had to accommodate himself whether he liked it or not, for even Israel wanted to be "like other nations, with a king to govern us, to lead us out to war and fight our battles" (1 Samuel 8:20). Yahweh recognizes that the Israelites have disavowed him, "that I shall no more be king over you." He tells Samuel to warn Israel: a king will take their sons and daughters, their fields and vineyards, their slaves and servant-girls, their cattle and their asses—how right he was! But, seeing that he cannot persuade them, he locks the barn door after the horse has escaped, he "orders" Samuel to accede to the people's request. Politician and opportunist that he is, he wants to adapt himself to the kingship of Saul, David and Solomon (about 1030 to 931 B.C.E.). Israel not only wanted, it clearly needed the central authority of a king, and even Yaweh is made to undergo changes in his nature.

He was now no longer the god of a nomadic people wandering in the desert, having indeed a portable shrine, (the ark of the covenant), but still on the move between the tents of the tribes. No, David wanted to build him a temple, and God coyly sends his protest to the king through the mouth of the prophet Nathan (2 Samuel 7:5−6): "Go and tell my servant David, 'Thus says the LORD: Would you build me a house to dwell in? I have not dwelt in a house since the day I brought up the people of Israel from Egypt to this day, but I have been moving about in a tent for my dwelling.' " It was no good; he was locked up in a temple and changed himself after the pattern of an oriental potentate into the "God of Sabaoth," the god-king, a "Lord of Hosts" who "shines out" in his city against his enemies (Psalm 48:8; Psalm 50:2).

Gehlen has advanced a theory that an invisible god could only have been conceived among nomadic peoples, because he would need no established temple but his people would take him with them in their minds. But it was precisely during the wandering in the wilderness that Yahweh did become visible to privileged persons. They were not allowed to look at him. When Moses desired to behold the glory of his Lord (Exodus), the Lord said: "But you cannot see my face; for man shall not see me and live."(33:20). But he did not leave it at that:

> And the LORD said, "Behold, there is a place by me where you shall stand upon the rock; and while my glory passes by I will put you in a cleft of the rock, and I will cover you with my hand until I have passed by; then I will take away my hand, and you shall see my back; but my face shall not be seen." (33:21−23)

Yahweh, whose back side was allowed to be seen, assuming he made it visible,* had now settled in. The son of David, King Solomon, does service as a royal priest; later, the high priests' robes look like kings' robes. It is true that the capital city of Jerusalem under Solomon was an entrepot of heretical abominations. Canaanite and even foreign gods were worshipped in Jerusalem; Solomon built temples to the gods of his foreign mistresses, of whom the Bible, always generous with figures, concedes him seven hundred wives and three hundred concubines. No longer henceforth will two opposing currents stand still; inspired men, keeping foreign influences at bay, will demand strict faithfulness to the God Yahweh, who, for his part, continually and fairly treacherously transforms himself under those very influences. Thus, the saints of Qumran, insisting on the strictest adherence to the old law, still allow Persian ideas to break through in their writings.

The abstinence of Israel from any kind of sacred imagery, any pictorial conception of the gods, has a positively pathological side and could only have been kept up under rigorous self-discipline (plus unforced, unconscious hatred of Yahweh). There was, for instance, an enormous effort to pray to the sun and moon as

---

*Arno Schmidt would spot special relationships in this "appearance of God *a tergo*" (Bloch) and perhaps, who knows, quote Marcel Proust, who makes Jupien, the tailor, say to the Baron de Charlus: "*Vous en avez un gros petard!*"[27]

gods.* God had said, according to scripture: "Let us make man in our image and likeness." But man was not allowed to make an image of God. That was easier to order than to obey. Since, after a period of self-revelation, Yahweh was never again allowed to be spoken of by name, he was called Adonai (Lord); and so was the youthful god of Syria-Palestine, at once competing and identical with Baal, whose name goes back first to the Phoenicians and then to the Greek Adonis. Since the naming of Yahweh was punishable by death, the Jews were compelled to have other gods of whom they might speak.

Anything thought to have been defiled through contact with strange gods was firmly purified. So we read that King Hezekiah (716–687) cleansed the temple in Jerusalem from all foreign images and forms of worship. The "brazen serpent" set up by Moses in the desert fell victim to the purification because incense had been burnt before it. We can draw the conclusion that politics—centralistic politics—were partly if not wholly responsible when we read that Hezekiah's great-grandson Josiah (640–609) closed all places of worship outside Jerusalem, regardless of whether they were dedicated to foreign gods or to Yahweh. Even the ancient shrine of Bethel, which the Bible tells us (Genesis 12:6–8) was erected by Abraham, was destroyed.

Josiah sprinkled "the dust of the heathen images over the common burial-ground", and (2 Kings 23:1–20) "slaughtered on the altars all the priests of the hill-shrines" in Samaria, including the priests of Yahweh. ("Such words give us a significant insight into the circumstances of the time," Thomas Mann observed.)[28] The lament for the dead Josiah was "as great as the mourning over Haddad-rimmon," the youthful Baal-god who died and returned to life every year (1 Zechariah 12:11). The yearly ritual mourning was borrowed from the heathen Syrian god. The prophet Ezekiel gazes upon the sight from distant Babylon in 592 B.C.E.—the women at the northern gate of the Jerusalem temple wailing for

*We have only to read, for example, in Psalm 19:5-6:
"In them he has set a tent for the sun,
which comes forth like a bridegroom
leaving his chamber,
and like a strong man runs its
course with joy.
Its rising is from the end of the
heavens,
and its circuit to the end of them;
and there is nothing hid from its
heat."

the dead Tammuz—Tammuz, who died every year. The women of Canaan still lamented the death of their god Baal-Haddad-Adonis-Tammuz.

It is ironical that the religion more given than any other in history to pictures and likenesses should have developed from the Jewish community which had to attach the death-taboo to any representation of the true God, for fear of the imaginary gods of the surrounding world, without which they could never have been restrained. Not being allowed to call the true God by name was just one more temptation to worship strange gods.

Gollwitzer finds it no more than an uninteresting difference whether people pray to war-gods and fertility-gods or to a single god equally potent in all fields. But in Israel they lived differently, both inwardly and outwardly; this difference was decisive. To perceive the true meaning of creation in creation itself, to find satisfaction in living reality of any kind—that is just what was forbidden to the Israelites by the revelation of the living God.[29] But we find this interpretation difficult. The old Israelites seem not to have lived either inwardly or outwardly and "differently," any more ethically, than their neighbors; they lived only in a greater consciousness of sin, to which they were irresistibly drawn by their myths. "Remorse and repentance," writes Hans Kilian, "are substitutes for the historic change of concrete human existence which they foreswore."[30]

The old covenant between Israel and Yahweh, like the whole creation, was still unbreached. There was no duality between body and soul, no mortification of the flesh. There was still no need for the devil. Indeed, as Conway recognized in his devil-lore in 1879, the need was not felt because the God of the Jews "was held capable of every moral evil and was the more sought after for his authorship of it."[31] In 2 Samuel (24:1) the angry Lord incites King David against the people and gives him orders that Israel and Judah should be counted. But in 1 Chronicles (21:1) it says: "Satan stood up against Israel, and incited David to number Israel." The book of Samuel may have been written before the exile, and the corresponding passage in the book of Chronicles is reckoned to be more recent. First, it is the Lord who incites David, then it is the devil, and both times the Lord sends a pestilence throughout Israel that kills seventy thousand. Why such a counting of the men fit for military service should "bring guilt on Israel" (1 Chronicles 21:3)

215

we can only surmise. Did David just want to flex his muscles, and why shouldn't he? Or was he impelled by the basic evil of centralism?

At least to those who come afterwards, the introduction of monarchical rule, so glorious under David, seems to be *the* fall from grace in the history of Israel. During the monarchy, the "Old Covenant" is dissolved, again with a schizophrenic result. In contrast to their very worldly kings, they came to look for a holy one of God, an ideal king, a son of David, a Messiah, a Son of Man, who could do what the actual kings could not do, and could not, possibly, precisely because of continual prophetic irritation. Since the pious among the Jews did not like to see a man of war in the office of high priest, on account of the defilement of the temple through warlike deeds that necessarily resulted, the figure expected in religious circles was split into one kingly and one priestly Messiah, whose character and functions could not be strictly distinguished, indeed not even defined. Of course, this may not have been the actual reason. The age-old rivalry between medicine-man and tribal chief, between priest and king, is eloquently expressed here.   In 931 B.C.E. the Hebrew kingdom, after barely a hundred years of existence, split in two: in 722, the northern kingdom of Israel with its capital in Samaria was destroyed; in 587, the southern kingdom of Judah with its capital in Jerusalem. The ten, or nine and a half, tribes of the north "vanished" out of the sight of the south for ever. This is how the Lord saw these historic events, according to the prophet Jeremiah: he had punished Israel, the "apostate," because she "played the whore," and he had "put her away and given her a note of divorce." But did her sister Judah take any notice? Far from it: the "faithless woman" goes off and "plays the whore. . . defiles the land with. . . adulterous worship of stone and wood." In the book of Lamentations, probably unjustly attributed to Jeremiah, it says about the justice of the Lord (2:4−5):

> He has bent his bow like an enemy,
>   with his right hand set like a foe;
> and he has slain all the pride of our
>   eyes
>   in the tent of the daughter of Zion;
> he has poured out his fury like fire.

That was the great time of the prophets, the "pamphleteers and demagogues"* (Max Weber);[32] God acts, says the prophet Amos, through the visions of his servants the prophets. In times of prosperity, they foretell disaster, in times of misfortune, salvation. They were as often right as wrong, but they only recorded the prophecies that came true (a preference that they share with purely lay prophets like Tocqueville and Heine, in whose works, in order to give them their due as prophets, we have to encounter a choice of many prophecies that have not come true and one or two that have).

The social orientation of the prophets remains unclear. They condemned the conduct of the great as well as the rule of un-educated plebeians. They had no support among the peasantry because they were against the rural fertility cults; they looked on the religious customs of the people at best as routine. From Elijah to John the Baptist, they watched over the religious conduct of the great more than that of the masses.

The prophet Elijah attacked the king of the northern kingdom, Ahab, because for love of his Phoenician wife Jezebel he had erected a temple to the god Baal. Elijah was active in the ninth century B.C.E.; Malachi, an anonymous writer—possibly several writers (the name means "my message")— in the fifth century. This last of the canonical books of prophecy in the Jewish scriptures contains the prophecy: "Look, I will send you the prophet Elijah before the great and terrible day of the Lord comes." The Last Judgment, brought from Babylon, is announced and Elijah is its prophet. If the Messiah is associated with the Last Judgment, then he needs a prophet to proclaim him, a forerunner, a herald, who is promptly found in the literature of Qumran as he is in the gospels.

In the atmosphere of these prophets, miracles are regularly reported, supernatural happenings in which the men of God must have faith. Elijah is seen by his pupil Elisha to go up to heaven in a fiery chariot in a thunderstorm, not far from the spot where Jesus was to be baptized by his forerunner John (we may well ask why Elijah's ascent should be less credible than that of the Lord Jesus). Since Malachi had prophesied that Elijah would return before the

---

*For a time, prophetic inspiration seems to have been a kind of group-delirium; even King Saul, when the spirit of the Lord came upon him, stripped off his clothes and "lay down naked all that day and all that night" (1 Samuel 17:23−24).

Last Judgment, any prophet who wanted to foretell the end of days had to cope with the scribes' objection that Elijah must appear first.

The first Christians were prepared for the objection that the Messiah could not have come yet because Elijah, assuming he was not himself to return as the Messiah, had to appear before the Messiah. Matthew's Gospel (11:14) allows for it in making Jesus say about the Baptist: ". . . and if you are willing to accept it, he is Elijah who is to come." To this day the Jews put ready a cup of wine for Elijah at the Passover, to be prepared for his possible return. Many of Jesus' contemporaries made no distinction between what had been and what was still to be; in the synoptics, he himself is surrounded by the rumor that he is Elijah returned.

In the eighth century B.C.E., it seems that the prophets instituted the use of writing. The intellectual achievement of the earliest Jews is a historical self-portrait in their holy books. ("The Lord said to Moses: 'Write this for a memorial in a book' ". Exodus 17:14.) On top of the conviction of sin and guilt which the Jews have bequeathed to the Christians, there is added as a kind of second mortgage dependence on the scriptures, faith in the divine inspiration of the holy texts, so that in the Catholic church, as in the old Jewish interpretation of the law, no jot or tittle may be changed in what has once been set down. The text of the dogmas, like that of the law of Moses, is sacrosanct; only interpretation remains available if need arise.

Since the prophet and lawgiver Ezra in the fourth century B.C.E., the written word, though clearly emanating from the spoken word, has lived a life of its own; it has become, not the holy word, but holy scripture. Philo of Alexandria, [33] Jewish godfather of the Christians' Logos, actually held that the grammatical errors in the Septuagint (the translation of the Jews' holy scriptures into Greek) were divinely inspired and showed the way to valuable allegorical interpretations. Augustine[34] justifies the difference between the periods fixed for the city of Nineveh before its fall—three days in the Greek text, forty according to the Hebrew—in this way: Christ lived with his disciples for forty days after his resurrection, and there were three days between his death and resurrection. Thus both dates, "properly understood," are in accord with one

218

another; the deviation is only apparent.* The *Jerusalem Bible* sees it not so very differently when it declares, in the year 1969, that the Holy Spirit did not intend his interpreters to arrive at a precise unanimity in detail but actually wished there to be some divergence in the witness.[36] Arguments about which of the scriptures are holy and which are not are to be found in the Jewish as well as the Christian writings, and virtually nowhere else. The canon is a Jewish invention. It needed a non-Palestinian Jew, Saul-Paul, to set the law of Moses aside. Great theologian that he was, he explained that it had been fulfilled and abolished in Jesus Christ: the law of Moses as slave in the master's house, as a kind of tutor in charge until Christ should come (Galatians 3:24).

On Palestinian ground, theocracy and scripture combined to form a symbiosis; and what that can mean was not only experienced by the old Hebrew Kingdoms, but is still being experienced by the young state of Israel in her time. Often prophecies did not deal with what lay in the future but hastened to legitimize misfortunes that had already arrived as fulfilling an earlier prophecy ("retrospective prophecy"). Certainly in the time of the kings, and long past the time of Jesus, prophet meant, in effect, protest against the worship or conduct of the ruling class. The prophets preached against the suppressed natural wish of the people to yield to the worship of gods all around, and also against the rather less suppressed wish of the kings to concern themselves with politics rather than the utterances of the prophets. Those kings praised in rabbinical literature as messianic figures were those who scorned *Realpolitik.* Their memory was praised the more highly, the more unreasonably they were frustrated — Josiah of Judah for example.

This great purifier seems to have been no great realist in his external politics. He opposed the Egyptian Pharaoh Necho, who had sent to say to him that he would not fight against Israel but only against Assyria (Necho: "God has said, I must hasten"). Josiah did not listen to Necho's word from God and was fatally wounded by a dart in the plain of Megiddo in 609 (we know the historical references only from the Bible, and they seem to be contradictory; at any rate we should very much like to know why Josiah "throws

---

*Intellectual games are not a privilege of the ancients. The dogma of the Trinity appears in Hegel's Thoughts as a dialectical proposition: he sees a "kingdom of the Father" (thesis), "kingdom of the Son" (antithesis) and "kingdom of the Spirit" (synthesis).[35]

himself in despair against the superior power of Egypt," as Werner Keller[37] joyfully proclaims.)*

It was not easy for Jewish kings to trust or distrust their prophets. When Ahab, king of the northern kingdom, wished to march against Syria, all but one of his prophets supported him. But their advice did not come from themselves. In fact, God had decided to destroy Ahab, and so he sent one of his serviceable spirits to mislead Ahab's prophets and put lying counsel in their mouths. Ahab died standing in his war-chariot, as Josiah had been transfixed by a dart. Whores washed themselves in his blood, for, egged on by his Phoenician wife Jezebel, he had gone whoring after wood and stone.

As far as social conditions were concerned, the poverty and consequent enslavement of the peasantry, the classic criticism of the prophets that Israel must return to its beginnings, to a just order of society, was more than reasonable. But that was of course only indirectly what the prophets were getting at; they were more concerned with Yahweh than with the circumstances of the community. But we ought not to shrug off the social criticism of the prophets as no more than accessory, even if the offense to Yahweh was more important to them than the harm done to men. They are always drawing attention to grievances. The humble were oppressed and the poor trampled under foot, even by the concubines of the mighty. Tribute of grain was exacted from the poor. Who obtained justice for the orphans and helped the cause of the widows?

"But let justice roll down like waters,
    and righteousness like an
        ever-flowing stream." (Amos 5:24).

Shame on those who lie in bed planning evil and wicked deeds. They rob the fields and the houses, take man and house, master and property. They use false measures, false weights, false balances (Micah 2:1–3, 6:10–11).

---

*We can only consider the Bible as an historical source, at the earliest, after its accounts of King David. Mesha of Moab, who according to 2 Kings (3:27) could only save himself from the warriors of Israel by sacrificing his son on the wall of his beleaguered city (see Chapter 2), had the events engraved very differently on a memorial stele in 840: "I have had the ditches for (the capital city) Qerihoh dug by prisoners from Israel." Omri of Israel (885 –874) is named on the stele, the first mention of a Jewish king in a non-Biblical source. In the annals of the Assyrian king Tiglatpileser II (745–727), it says about Menachem of Israel: "I took possession of tribute from Menachem of Samaria."[38]

220

Certainly the prophets, down to and including John the Baptist, were concerned with the abuses of society, but still more with the improper marriage of a king or the religious practices of a queen from a strange country. What they really stood for was the unattainable—the purity of the old days, crystallized in legend; a return to the land of innocence which never existed, even in Moses' time. All that the prophets did flowed out into a "complete misconception of political reality" (Richard Bendix).[39] The prophet Micah (7:15) utters the master-prayer to Yahweh: "Show us miracles as in the days when thou camest out of Egypt."

Once more we should make clear the schizophrenic strain provoked by the fact that every process of political-cultural adjustment had to be condemned as not in tune with the true faith of Yahweh. Herod the Great, for instance, that commanding figure of a hundred years before the destruction of Jerusalem, only kept himself in power (which he shared with the Romans) with the aid of exceptional gifts and great cruelty. What the prophets thought Israel should have been able to preserve — the pristine form of the Worship of Yahweh — in those days when religion was one of a number of elements of political inflexibility, directly contributed to the downfall of the Israelite community. In every misfortune the prophets, those "Titans of the holy curse" (Max Weber),[40] kept their eyes fixed on the hope — popular, no doubt, but almost crazy — of world domination. Presumably we should even see Jesus in this tradition of prophetic messianic thinking, however unlikely his personal share in it may have seemed.

If it has been declared for eighteen hundred years that the Jews, and only the Jews, maintained the purity of the faith in the one God, and kept monotheism bright and in working order, to some extent as a vehicle for Christianity, that has been a false reputation. They have remained true under constant pressure to their one God Yahweh, to God their Father; the universal God invaded the Jewish tribal lands from outside. He made his sun to shine equally on the just and the unjust, but not equally on the Jew and the non Jew—not until the destruction of Jerusalem. The God of the whole world originated in the Hellenistic sphere of the collapsing oriental empire, and the God of the Christians has drawn on both sources: from the non-Jews the universality, from the temple the intolerance of all who believe in other gods.

What the old religion of Yahweh could offer the Jew was the direction of his conduct on earth. He could keep to the rules that had been laid down by Yahweh, could recognize God and so live in harmony with God and man, physically and spiritually healthy and in the expectation of a long life; like the righteous Job, he could die "old and full of days."

The dead lived on in some way as shadows in a shadow-world; they went down into the pit, into Sheol. There was no distinction there between the good and the bad; the good name that the good man left behind him when he died was all the reward he had. If the good man was to be rewarded at all, it could only be in the life on this side. There was no other. The messianic king Hezekiah, when he was on the point of death, complained to the Lord:

> For Sheol cannot thank thee,
>   death cannot praise thee;
> those who go down to the pit cannot
>   hope
>   for thy faithfulness.
> The living, the living, he thanks thee, as I do this day. (Isaiah 38:18–19)

He got better again.

Anyone who regards these simple attitudes to life and death as basically superior to later ideas of the other side must remember that the individual was formerly regarded as one to be raised and cared for collectively. The whole people had to be true to Jehovah and the individual must accommodate himself to this collective faith. Israel knew, as small communities do, the liability of the whole people for the actions or neglect of the individual. But Israel shared with other communities the hope of a communal future. Once the conception of the individual and his uniqueness was generally recognized, however, even Israel had to accept that the individual valued lasting relations with God, though by now with a God who had retreated so high that angels came into fashion as mediators — the Lord's messengers, personified actions of God.

The individual, thus made aware of himself, could not accept that death was the end. He was afraid of the idea of annihilation. Characteristically, the rich and powerful were the last to adopt this way of thinking, and adopted it least completely. In Babylon, during the fifty years of the captivity, the Jews learned Babylonian ideas, and when the Persian Cyrus destroyed the kingdom of Babylon in 538, Persian ideas as well. Cyrus seems to have adhered to the teaching of his East Iranian countryman Zoroaster, who saw the god of truth and goodness locked in an endless struggle with a wicked lord of this earth. When Cyrus let them return to Jerusalem the Jews brought with them, and enriched, what suited their own requirements: a somewhat dualistic outlook that departed from the strict monotheism of the Father. The good and evil principles fought for domination and in the end, the good would triumph in a final, fearful battle of cosmic dimensions.

They learned about, and adopted, the resurrection of the body, the Last Judgment, and also the idea contained in the Revelation of John of a thousand-year kingdom (of peace) interposed between the present troubled conditions and eternity. They even accepted the double judgment inherited by the Christians, an individual judgment after death and a general judgment at the end of the world. "Religion," says Freud, "is an attempt to master the mental world in which we find ourselves by means of a world of wishes";[41] immortality, forgiveness, the other side are conceptions of our psychic interior, "psycho-mythology."

The germs were implanted in Babylon, but it was centuries before the seed sprouted. In the year 332, in legend, anyway, Alexander the Great stood before the temple in Jerusalem. In Egypt he founded Alexandria, and it became the second, Hellenistic capital of the Jews. When the Syrian Seleucid ruler Antiochus IV Epiphanes submitted Jerusalem to his reign of terror in the year 167 B.C.E. — crucifixion for all who kept the Sabbath and circumcised their children, wrestling schools with naked wrestlers*, the sacrifice of pigs' flesh on the altar of the temple, prayers not to Yahweh but to Zeus — things had gone far enough to bring about the breakthrough into the world of the other side. Antiochus' efforts do not seem only to have set up resistance. Many Jews openly listened to the arguments of the collaborators: "Let us go and make a covenant with the heathen that are round about us: for since we departed from them, we have had much sorrow" (1 *Maccabees* 1:11). The readiness of many Jews for Hellenism only made worse the reputation of the foreign king.

---

*There had always been a flavor of the international in these contests, of the promotion of harmony between the peoples. But the fertility goddesses of Canaan which tempted Israel had been naked, and naked now were the Jewish wrestlers competing in the stadium beside the temple. Some of them, so 1 *Maccabees* tells us (1:15), "made themselves uncircumcised, and forsook the holy covenant."

Antiochus gave form and reputation to the "Antichrist," the Beast of the apocalyptics who were now springing out of the ground. Brave men were convinced that a true Jew must suffer death, if need be, for his faith; and they did so often enough, for instance during the Bar-Kochba rising of the Rabbi Akiba. But where was the reward for a god-fearing life when the righteous were being handed over to the executioner in droves? They could read in the book of Ecclesiastes (7:15—17), written in the third or second century B.C.E.: "In my vain life I have seen everything; there is a righteous man who perishes in his righteousness, and there is a wicked man who prolongs his life in his evil-doing. Be not righteous overmuch, and do not make yourself overwise; why should you destroy yourself? Be not wicked overmuch, neither be a fool; why should you die before your time?" With that little good luck commended by the Preacher, the Jews could stop circumcising themselves; but now that little good luck no longer existed. For the first time it was clearly laid down, in the book of Daniel (12:2): "Many (that is, all) of those who sleep in the dust of the earth shall awake, some to everlasting life, and some to shame and everlasting contempt."

Satan, who in the old Jewish teaching had belonged in the court of Yahweh as a professional prosecutor (Luther still calls him the "ape of God"),[42] now becomes a hostile figure, the cosmic adversary. He is conquered by an exemplary figure, the Son of Man, through whom the saints will rule for ever and "the righteous shine like the sun in their Father's kingdom." The Persian dualism now allowed them not to trace all wickedness exclusively back to God. Even the evils which befell the individual were no longer to be regarded entirely as the wages of his or his father's sins (barrenness, says the book of Enoch 98:5, is not in the nature of a woman; if she dies childless it is on account of her deeds). The Persian doctrine accepted that man could himself decide for good; he was judged according to his works and the judge himself was bound by his own law. The Jews and the Church Fathers worked out from this that God had determined the fate of man in advance; likewise that it was not compatible with the majesty of God that the choice between damnation and pardon should be withdrawn from him — such is the paradoxical inhumanity to which the seeker after God can attain in his search for a god made with human attributes to whom he can pray.*

God now no longer simply apportioned good and evil; he was himself engaged in a gigantic battle against evil, and it was decided in every individual's breast whether it would be beaten on the side of the victor. Naturally the ideas of the messianic final days and of the associated period of peace and justice were far from clear. But so much we do know: Satan, the prince of this world, was ruling at that time. The whole condition of a world laid waste by Satan, who had already led so many astray into disobedience of God, was approaching a crisis, and where should it be decided if not in and around Jerusalem?

One thing will always remain a mystery to us: "whence did this tiny and impotent nation derive the audacity to pass themselves off for the favorite child of the Sovereign Lord?" (Freud).[44] Never were the urge for world domination and the rules of a housekeeper more oddly associated. Israel would be redeemed, it was said, if it kept two sabbaths as prescribed. Temple worship and submission to the Law were the two pillars on which the Jewish religion, and thus the existence of the people, rested. In between stood the Sabbath, which God himself celebrated in heaven with his holy angels with the orthodox rites; it was he who gave the Jews their advantage over other peoples.

Six hundred and thirteen commands and prohibitions could be counted at the time of Jesus and Paul. Even the "oral Torah" was entrusted to Moses by God on Mount Sinai. Those who devised new laws, the Pharisee doctors of the law, made a living out of facilitating their circumvention. Herbert Braun, the Mainz biographer of Jesus, gives us the following paragraph about the ritual washing of hands, which Jesus' disciples (actually, no doubt, that means the Christian community) were accused of not observing in Mark's Gospel:

Before every main meal the hands had to be cleaned as far up as the wrists by a ritual pouring on of water. Even here the details are precisely laid down: the precise timing of the meal, the

*Calvin's God, in accordance with an impenetrable decree established since time memorial, has accepted or rejected his creatures purely "for the glorification of his unlimited power over his creation," as it says so matchlessly in the "Westminster Confession."[43] And what about Paul's God, who (Romans 9:22 ff) tolerates "vessels prepared for destruction in his righteous anger" in order to demonstrate to them (i.e. vent upon them) his anger and his power?

225

required amount of water, the proper way to hold the hands. Typical of this painful exactness in the striving after religious purity is the double sprinkling of the hands: the first pouring on takes away the uncleanness of the hands; the second removes the remaining drops of the first pouring out, which have now themselves become unclean.[45]

The washing of hands is not in the law of Moses but in the Pharisees' addition to it, the "oral Torah." Obedience to God's commands should bring about the cosmic intervention of God. Jesus — this much shines through — saw a different means, one that was suspect to many Jews of his time: he demonstrated by miraculous healing that the time was fulfilled, the kingdom of God had come. By his non-observance of the Sabbath he showed that the ruling upper-class of the Jews was getting in the way of redemption. The Sadducees were not even expecting a Messiah; they would not bring about the coming of the kingdom of God. The end of this impertinence could only be measured in months.

Jesus may have believed that in his non-observance of the Sabbath, his nonsubmission to the law, he was fulfilling the "will of the Father," and may even have said so. But it has struck the psychoanalysts, especially Theodor Reik and his pupil Erich Fromm,[46] that Jesus was a rebel against the law of Yahweh, a "revolutionary Son of God" who was putting himself in his Father's place, who wished in a mythical sense to "kill" him as the Jews in their mythical history may perhaps have wished to do to Moses, perhaps to Yahweh himself. (It has certainly been glossed over that Yahweh had wanted to kill Moses in the encampment on the way back to Egypt from Midian; why did Yahweh want to kill Moses, and why did he bury him with his own hand in a place whose whereabouts is still unknown (Deuteronomy 34:6)?)

We are looking at the development too much from a nineteenth-century angle if we accept with Freud[47] that in the development of mankind sensuality is gradually overcome by spirituality. Does that mean that development is always from lower to higher? Even Freud believes that the religious revival associated with the death of Jesus has ended in the dethronement, the elimination of God the Father, the very God to whom it was dedicated. That argument will gain in importance.

Was Jesus then, without knowing it, a rebellious son? Did he unconsciously replace his Father in the minds of his followers?

Was the religious renewal that we call Christianity a Son-religion, as Freud says? Here we should first like to object that the Jews outside Palestine, about four million in the time of Jesus, had of course no such pathological relationship with their God, grounded in compulsory love and unconscious hate, as their co-religionists in the promised land, some half-million. They believed, like many other Hellenists at that time and many Jews today, in a philosophically refined patriarch. (If we look at the theology of the Christian teaching, we must quite properly doubt the development postulated by Freud from sensuality to spirituality, i.e. from lower to higher. If it is correct, as Nietzsche[48] believed, that all religions are at bottom systems of cruelty, then it must also be correct that the cruelty was there before their systemization and would not disappear with the end of the religious systems.)

The old Yahweh, as far as we can make out, was a faithful creation of the unconscious creative psyche of the people, who had not so much chosen them as they him. He is a very bad-tempered and thoughtless Lord, excessively inconsiderate and unjust, vengeful, as he says himself, down to the fourth generation, merciful to the thousandth; obsessed with an almost pathological jealousy, touchy but not sensitive, he lacks wisdom. Though Helmut Gollwitzer may not agree, he is entirely wrapped up in the world: he needs it, he is lonely without it, he must have it as a partner for his love and his anger. He can be treacherous too, and harden the hearts of his people in order to destroy them; he thinks of little but the glorification of his majesty. Yahweh is, one suspects, all that his people would so obviously have liked themselves to be. The weakness, the misery of the individual matched the omnipotence of God. So almighty was he that there was no arbitrary action, no favor, of which he was not capable. He is that God that Nietzsche describes, with whom man makes his deals.[49] Since he knew and recognized no law apart from himself, he was allowed, as every man would like to be allowed, to deal amorally, like a natural catastrophe, a veritable "act of God."

In the Book of Job (thought to date from the time after the exile in Babylon) He lets himself be provoked by Satan, one of his sons, into inflicting the most inhuman tortures and trials on Job, the nonpareil God-fearing man. He does so, says the fallen angel C.G. Jung (fallen from Freud), instead of calling Satan, that practical joker, to order.[50] When Job pleads for justice, Yahweh answers him brutally "out of the tempest," sending him to the struggle:

227

Gird up your loins like a man,
  I will question you, and you shall
  declare to me.
"Where were you when I laid the
  foundation of the earth?
Tell me, if you have
  understanding." (38:3—4)

No wonder Job does not exactly feel encouraged to put his case:

"Behold, I am of small account;
  what shall I answer thee?
I lay my hand on my mouth.
I have spoken once, and I will not
  answer;
Twice, but I will proceed no further." (40:4—5)

When Yahweh reminds him that he has created the hippopotamus and the crocodile, Behemoth and Leviathan (the author evidently knew Egypt), Job reveals that wisdom that Yahweh lacks; he, Job, has gained insight, the insight of the hopelessly inferior:

"I had heard of thee by the hearing of the ear,
  but now my eye sees thee;
therefore I despise myself,
  and repent in dust and ashes." (42:5—6)

Yahweh, far from apologizing for the dirty tricks he has played on Job, gives him double and triple what he has lost, to show what a great king he is. "The superior grants partnership to the inferior," thinks Gollwitzer.[51] "A man outstrips, outshines his God," thinks Ernst Bloch.[52] God and man, thinks Gollwitzer, had called one another to account: "God does so to man in so dominant, so overwhelming a fashion that in the end the complaint of man against God is silenced, the complaint of God against man wins the day." Very smart.

The outcome has been seen by some non-theologians not only as unprofitable for Yahweh but as unsatisfactory for all gods altogether, although Job calls the three daughters he receives from Yahweh in place of those struck down in the whirlwind "Little Dove," "Cassia-Blossom," and "Casket of Rouge." Job perceives that he has been rebuked for his "limited, vulgar shortsightedness" (Bloch); he gives way because he has to. He has been taught a sharp lesson, which he had better not forget (Jung).[53] It is astonishing what people can read into the text of Job; what Albert Görres, the professor of psychology, can find there (in the collection *Jesus und Freud*, 1972): "Thus the freedom of speech, the freedom of protest that the analyst gives the patient, the God of Job gives to his patient."[54] Günter Howe actually believes (*Mensch und Physik,* 1963) that what God wanted to say to Job was that he, God, was in conflict with chaos ("the situation is serious") and was perhaps calling men to follow him.[55]

Yahweh defines himself in the form of the Leviathan, of which he says:

Upon earth there is not his like,
  a creature without fear.
He beholds everything that is high;
  he is king over all the sons of
    pride." (41:33–34)

He only calms down when Job stretches out his neck to him in the classic gesture of submisson. Unconsciousness, thinks Jung, is in the nature of animals, and Job sees in Yahweh "a pre-eminently unconscious being."[56] Yahweh has noticed that he has not had the best of it, that man has "outstripped" him; and now, like the Egyptian and other ancient gods before him, he wants to become human. As Ernst Bloch says, "there is a palace-revolution in God's image of himself."[57] Yahweh, says Jung, is sorry for himself. He has begun to realize that man possesses a light, infinitely small indeed, but more concentrated, than his own. (The comparison between the emotions shown towards their gods by the Germans and the Greeks is not far off the mark.) Man cannot be allowed to have a perception of him that he, Yahweh, does not have himself.

Anyone who recognizes God, says Jung, has an influence on him (or, to put it more profanely, anyone who envisages God thinks of him in human form, creates him; Spinoza says: "If a triangle could talk, it would undoubtedly say that God was eminently triangular").[58] God now wants to become man, and to that end makes use of his Son. But the son whom God wants must, in accordance with the will of the Father, be unswervingly just, rather better, in fact, than the Father. The unconscious will flow into consciousness, yet at the same time would rather remain unconscious; and that, says Jung, means that "God wishes to become man, but not completely."[59]

God, in Jung's view, is a psychical fact, on the one hand, only to be identified psychically; but on the other hand, "it cannot be determined whether the Godhead and the unconscious are two different dimensions." One could not think more charmingly, nor, to Freud's mind—and he is not so inferior to Jung as a writer—more frivolously. He had seen in the Swiss, nineteen years younger than himself, the Moses who should lead the little group of Jewish Freudians out of a Vienna hostile to the Jews into the promised land of general recognition. In 1909 he had actually called him "Joshua" ("Jehoschua der Sohn"): "They (i.e., Jung), playing Joshua to my Moses, will take possession of the promised land of psychiatry which I may only behold from afar."[60] But to his horror, he had to observe that Jung regarded the unconscious not as the breakthrough stage, but as the source of godliness and, at the same time, as something in the nature of the animal. He did not want this revolutionary son's God. He was glad when in 1914 he was free from the "beastly holy Jung" who in 1934 played off the "Aryan unconscious" against the "Jewish categories of this negative psychology" of Sigmund Freud.[61]

The Jews lack the mystic element, Freud once said (which makes psychoanalysis easier for them than, for instance, for the clergyman's son C.G. Jung). But it is now a matter of history that the Jewish myths made an indispensable contribution to the mystic making of the old Yahweh into man. Without the expectation of a Messiah and the myth of a Son of Man, it would hardly have been possible to introduce the human element into the God-man; a son of God more on the lines of Hercules would certainly have come out of the vial.

The mystic trance, meditation with closed eyes, these may not have been the Jewish dowry to Christianity; but how should Christianity have developed otherwise than on the basis of the suffering men of the stories of Abraham and of Jesus, mystically sacrificed by the Father?

The old God of Abraham had only demanded the sacrifice of the son and then not allowed it to be carried out; but now he himself sacrificed his own Son. Obedience to God is converted, even if only in the eyes of heretics, into God's obedience to the higher power embracing God and man. Maybe the Jews are not mystics, but no Jew had ever de-mythified and dismantled the

Jewish myths so humanely as the non-Jew Thomas Mann.[62] When it proved necessary gently to point out to men how they had created God, no one did so with more consideration than the writer of *Joseph and His Brothers,* leading God down from his Father-throne into the fantasy-world of men and whispering to him all the time, as with the sound of flutes, the advantages of the exchange. Mann's Abraham makes for himself a God great enough for him, Abraham, to serve; the creation is intended for the mutual sanctification of God and man: "to what other end, one may ask, should there be a covenant?"

Abraham had "assembled the powers into one power and called it the Lord"; he had founded a collective majesty which raised itself proudly above the thousand meadow and town gods, in spite of the somewhat confusing multiplicity of names that Yahweh unresistingly allowed to be conferred on him. And this god, Abraham's God, had kissed his fingers for joy and cried: "No one ever before called me Lórd and Most Highest; now that is my name!" It is understandable that he no longer liked to be reminded of the intractable goblin he once was, the monster who for no clear motive could lie in wait for Moses by night, the man whom he had every possible reason to wish well. Were there some relapses on the highway to sanctification? "God has not kept in step," thought Abraham's grandson Jacob, the tribal ancestor, when they brought him the coat and the rags of his son Joseph stiff with blood. And "God has not kept in step" might be the judgment of a man of the nineteenth century, looking with amazement on the twentieth. He would simply not believe it possible that God could have left man so far behind that he could shake the horrors of our times from off his shoes, his glory undimmed amid our misery and sham.

God and man—and there is nothing that the seemingly ungodly transmuter of myths from Lübeck would have conceded less willingly—have been going round in circles like Estragon and Vladimir waiting for Godot. They are not unlike Leviathan and Behemoth, the crocodile and the hippopotamus of the book of Job. For two and a half thousand years the shuttle has gone to and fro, weaving the common cloth of God and man; yet God and man seem to have missed one another, wanting in future to have done with mutual self-creation.

9.   Galilean
or liberator?

It can scarcely be doubted that Christ understood the principle of the aim-correcting reaction and applied it to his assessment of the human future. In a time when men thought mechanically and the world was explained mechanically, such a way of thinking must have created a tremendous sensation. We could say that Christ was the first systematic theorist.
—Hans G. Schneider

One symbol of our good case was called, and is called, Jesus.
—Ernst Bloch

A lawless man: one who deliberately sets himself above the law; one, in short, who breaks the law; who does not seem to fear the death penalty and who is in fact executed — such a man always acts as a liberator. He reminds other men of the truth, only dimly perceived, that every law, even though it be proclaimed in the name of the gods, is a kind of oppression barring the way to the realization of our own justifiable desires. In the mind of Søren Kierkegaard, there was "something primitive" about a man who "does not say: one must take the world as it is. . . but who says: whatever the world does, I am bound to an originality that I cannot consider changing, whatever the world may think."[2] Even the satisfaction of seeing such a lawbreaker die on the cross, because the laws must be maintained, has mixed with it the longing to do as he did.

No one else has so good a claim to be considered a man of liberation as the executed lawbreaker. The more one knows about him the less this is so, and vice versa. The breach does not have to be an excessively concrete one; thanks to Plato, it has only too clearly been handed down in the case of Socrates, who told his judges: "I will listen to the god more than to you."[3] The Jew Jesus, on the contrary, against whom all that we can observe is another protest against the leading Jewish lawgivers and, perhaps, also a somewhat extravagant attitude towards the great powers of the time, could be made responsible for all the moves in the direction of evolutionary liberation that shook the ancient world in the seventy years after his death. He died without literate pupils.

The liberating rays of the Graeco-Roman world, between 30 and 100 C.E., were concentrated with a more intensive heat in the person of the risen Christ through the medium of a "Jesuanic image," created with no help from its central figure. The evangelists crystallize in their likenesses that "unique concentration-point of human capabilities" (Peter L. Berger),[4] into which they quite unconsciously injected the conception their own wishes created — the cult-figure from which they drew their inspiration, a man of whom Ernst Bloch says: "One way or another, there is a good deal to be said for him."[5] The man from Galilee (who had never been outside the borders of his Jewish homeland) who, until he appeared in a brief flash, had been without history, became the chance crystallization-point of a timeless conception of man as he ought to be; became, in a way he himself could never have imagined, illuminated as the ideal figure of the historic crossing of frontiers: liberator of the oppressed, of women, liberator of Jewish exclusivity—which he never was.

The heartland of the Jews in the time of Jesus covered a circular area of perhaps twelve hundred square miles. Jerusalem lay somewhat south of its center, in Judea, the true Judea, not the Roman province of that name. Judea is bounded in the east by the Jordan and the northern part of the Dead Sea, into which the Jordan runs; in the south by the province of Idumaea, the old Edom, which stretches from the Dead Sea to the neighborhood of the Gaza strip; in the southwest from the region of the Philistines ("Philistia") and in the north by the province of Samaria.

233

In the heartland of the Jews, which Matthew calls the "Jewish lands," there lived at that time some 150,000 people, (of whom Eduard Lohse[6] reckons that 25,000 lived in Jerusalem). The Jews of the province of Samaria, which in Jesus' time was governed by the same Roman procurator as Judea, were of old not considered orthodox and were excluded from the temple in Jerusalem. The town of Samaria was razed to the ground by the Jewish ethnarch John Hyrcanos I in 107 B.C.E., and in 63 B.C.E. the province was joined to Roman Syria and later fell to Herod the Great, who built up the capital, Samaria (Sebastia), into a kind of fortified garrison.

Perea, east of the Jordan, and Galilee, to the north of Samaria, were provinces of the tetrarch Herod Antipas, who had inherited perhaps a quarter of the kingdom of his great father Herod. Galilee, subdued by King Aristobul I in 104–103 and in the eyes of the Jerusalem temple, rather less suspect than the Samaritans, was bounded in the west not by the sea but by a Phoenician strip belonging to the Roman province of Syria; in the east by the all too well-known Golan Heights, which lay in the tetrarchy of Herod's son Philip, and by the lake which the Bible calls the Lake of Gennesaret or Sea of Galilee, now called the Sea of Chinneret. Half-enclosed by the tetrarchy of Philip, the lake of Gennesaret, a part of Galilee, a part of Samaria and a part of Perea lies the Decapolis, a Greek-oriented free union of ten towns (from which it gets its name) whose civic status is not strictly definable.

Apart from Galilee, let us now have a look at where, Jesus is said to have been according to the synoptics. According to Mark: in Tyre and Sidon, far away on the heathen coasts of Phoenicia; in the region of Caesarea Philippi, that city built by the tetrarch Philip to the honour of Tiberius Caesar almost on the border of Syria; in Bethsaida, east of the Galilean border; in the region of Gerasa (Decapolis); "in the region of the Ten Towns" (Decapolis); then in the area east of the Jordan (Perea) and, finally, in and around Jerusalem.

The routes may not be taken too literally. The missionary endeavors of the evangelists and their communities have probably been mixed up with them. But they do give us valuable indications. First of all, it strikes us that Jesus, according to Mark and Matthew, never touched Samaria, although a large bulk of it lies immediately between Galilee and Judea. It is impossible to bypass Samaria without crossing the Ten Towns.

The instruction that Jesus gave when he sent out his disciples, according to Matthew (10:5—6): "Go nowhere among the Gentiles, and enter no town of the Samaritans, but go rather to the lost sheep of the house of Israel" looks as if it ought to be taken to some extent seriously, although it does not occur in Mark, which is always suspicious. Jesus' missionary area seems to have been, not the whole of Galilee, but for preference the part around the Lake of Gennesaret ("the sea"): Capernaum ("his town"); Bethsaida, in Philip's country, where Jesus heals a blind man and which, according to Matthew and Luke, he curses; Nain, where he wakes a child from the dead, and Cana, where he changes water into wine (both these places in Galilee are found, not in Mark, but in later Gospels).

The excursion in the area of Caesarea Philippi (not to be confused with Pilate's residence at Caesarea on the Mediterranean), where he reveals himself to the disciples as the Messiah, and to Gerasa in the Decapolis, where he sends the evil spirits out of the possessed man into a herd of two thousand swine, are dubious (Rudolf Bultmann: "Jesus' 'northern journey' must therefore be erased from history as a fantasy").[7] Matthew transfers the story of the swine to Gadara, a walk from the Lake of Gennesaret but nearly forty miles from Gerasa as the crow flies. It is only in John, who makes Jesus go to Jerusalem several times, and in Luke that he passes through Samaria, but we must still examine the context.

Apparently he never visits Tiberias, the biggest town in Galilee. But we must be very suspicious about the visit to Tyre and Sidon described in Mark ("Then he left that place and went into the territory of Tyre"). Tyre lies in the middle of the heathen country on the Mediterranean, nearly forty miles from the extreme tip of the Lake of Gennesaret, and we do not really know what Jesus would have been doing among the heathen. There follows immediately the too descriptive episode in which it states concisely: "On his return journey from Tyrian territory, he went by way of Sidon (forty miles to the north of Tyre) to the Sea of Galilee through the territory of the Ten Towns" (more than sixty miles south of Sidon. We must be very suspicious of the geography and no less so of what he does in Tyre (he does nothing in Sidon):

And from there he arose and went away to the region of Tyre and Sidon. And he entered a house, and would not have any one know it; yet he could not be hid. But immediately a woman, whose little daughter was possessed by an unclean spirit, heard of him, and came and fell down at his feet. Now the woman was a Greek, a Syrophoenician by birth. And she begged him to cast the demon out of her daughter. And he said to her, "Let the children first be fed, for it is not right to take the children's bread and throw it to the dogs." But she answered him, "Yes, Lord; yet even the dogs under the table eat the children's crumbs." And he said to her, "For this saying you may go your way; the demon has left your daughter." And she went home, and found the child lying in bed, and the demon gone. (7:24–30)

The Gentile woman (Mark says "Greek," Matthew, "Canaanite") means a heathen woman. What we seem to have here is a "pericope"—the theologians' technical term for a sequence of verses—that is not genuine and certainly does not go back to Jesus, however charming and memorable it may be.[8] In the so-called "Original Mark" (Ur-Mark), a philological invention, there is not thought to be any mention of it; certainly it does not form part of the oldest material.[9] Here again we see that creative urge, that "poetic force" at work, which Martin Dibelius denies to the first writers on Jesus. The argument in the early community, whether or not to send missions to the heathen, is pointed here by means of a legend which leaves the dispute unsettled. Over all stands the test of faith.

But Jesus does not drive any evil spirits out of heathen women's daughters. "According to the Gospel tradition," says the Franciscan, Dautzenberg, "he only very seldom, if ever, had any contact with the heathen."[10] "He never found it necessary to get mixed up with the heathen in any way," says Gustaf Dalman.[11] It is not he who is the author of formative utterances, of striking parables, in the way we think of him. "The whole personality of our Lord" does not, as Martin Kähler believes, come out to meet us in the smallest detail of the tradition, in the shortest scene, "in every little story," "as the sun's light is reflected from every drop in the dewy meadow."[12] That is how he likes to see the preacher, but it is not how he was.

What we might call the liberating trends in the Gospel are to be found in the parables. "We, and we only," says Ernst Bloch, "are addressed, and strangely illumined, by the Christian parables."[13] Whatever position the members of the community might take with regard to Samaritans and women, Greeks and heathen, the unjust and the just, masters and slaves, is to be found in the parables, even if they are not in those in Mark's Gospel or those of an even older level of the tradition. Did Jesus emancipate himself and others, did he break out of a relatively narrow and limited horizon to one more open, more free? Did he "lay rails between the races and the classes" (Hans Jürgen Schultz)? Was he really the "first cybernetic thinker" (Hans G. Schneider), carrying out with scientific strictness continual corrections of aim at the target of "love"?[14]

The parables give us some information. "Therefore every scribe who has been trained for the kingdom of heaven is like a house-holder who brings out of his treasure what is new and what is old" (Matthew 13:52). There were many such householders among the Jews. Even Jesus, like the other rabbinical preachers of parables ("Moshel"), may have combined the old with the new. But who among us older people who still had a religious education would have known by heart a parable which turns out by hindsight to have been already included in Mark's Gospel?

If anyone finds the thought inconceivable that Jesus might not have been the author of even the best-known of his parables, he should realize that parables enjoyed a national and significant tradition in the Palestine rabbinate. As a king who has lost a piece of gold or a pearl can find both with the aid of a candle, so man can arrive at an understanding of Torah, the Law, through a parable.[15] Certainly the meaning of the parables in the Gospels is sometimes far from clear; often they are incomprehensible, often ambiguous, often banal; many have been passed on mutilated or inverted. Only it seems that they are clearer to children and simple people than to the despised intellect.

One would like to know what criteria moved Joachim Jeremias to the statement that anyone who concerns himself with the parables of the first three Gospels is standing on "particularly strong historical ground"; they belong to the "bedrock of the tradition."[16] In fact, this bedrock lies before us in such a way that we could very well trace the images and parables in their development.

We can assign to this bedrock a part of the 114 sayings ascribed to Jesus ("Logia") which were discovered in South Egypt in 1946 and have since been published under the name of the *Gospel of Thomas*.[17] They were written later than the canonical Gospels; but the form of many of the sayings in Thomas corresponds exactly with that which critical research has established as the original form of many of the parables. Thus for instance Logia 31–36 of Thomas's Gospel reads as follows:

31. Jesus said: No prophet is accepted in his own village. No doctor usually heals those who know him.*
32. Jesus said: A city built and fortified upon a high mountain cannot fall and will not be hidden.
33. Jesus said: What you will hear with your ear, preach with your other ear over the rooftops.
   For no one lights a lamp and places it under a bushel, or puts it in a hidden place, but sets it on the lamp-stand so that all who come in and go out see its light.
34. Jesus said: If a blind man leads a blind man, they will both fall into a ditch.
35. Jesus said: It is not possible for anyone to break into the house of the strong man and take it by force, unless he binds his hands. Then he will overthrow his house.
36. Jesus said: Do not be anxious about what you put on from morning to evening and from evening to morning.

The metaphors found in Thomas's Gospel have no context; for the most part they lack meaning without the generalized practical application. That is how the short parable-like metaphors appear, with the help of which — and not only in Thomas's Gospel — the reverse of salvation was originally preached. The lamp belongs on the lamp-stand. The shepherd gives his life for the sheep. The doctor visits the sick. The messenger calls to the supper of the last times. The fisherman takes fishermen into his service. The king enters and is acclaimed. Death is changed to sleep. The strong man is chained, his booty is seized. No man can ride two horses, bend two bows, serve two masters.

The Father's kingdom is compared to the harvest. The sower is in trouble; only a part of his seed-corn falls on good ground. But, once sown, the seed grows without any action on the part of the sower. If the tares that the wicked had planted had been pulled up, the wheat would have been pulled up with it. When harvest-time comes, they will be pulled up and burnt.

*This is presumably the only basis for the "expulsion from Nazareth" mentioned by Mark and spun out at length by Luke.

A rich man plans to sow, to reap, to plant and to fill his barns with fruit. But he dies the following night. One does not harvest grapes from thorns nor pluck figs from cactus. We must seek treasure that is imperishable and lasting and a storehouse where moth and worm do not enter. Man should be like the wise fisherman who throws all the little fish back into the water and keeps only the one good, big fish. Or the merchant who sells the whole of his property to acquire one costly pearl.

We can see it at once: a collection of such little parables or metaphors could be made whether they came from Jesus or from any one of the "Moshel." They would be passed on by word of mouth, and not necessarily letter-perfect, in contrast to the long parable-tales of the later Gospels where all the i's are dotted and all the t's crossed. No one took down what Jesus said. Another thing: these sayings do not rise above the general rabbinical level; their central point is not God, only Jesus.*

The material of the sayings of Jesus in Thomas's Gospel is also used in part in the official Gospels, some only in Mark, some only in Matthew; Thomas's Gospel often makes use of the earlier, older version. Logion 57 of Thomas about the tares among the wheat is drawn out to three times its length in Matthew (13:20−30) with no kind of new theme added. The evangelist gives a very unhappy twist to Logion 8 of Thomas, about the big fish which it is profitable to keep (Matthew 13:47−50): the good fish are collected into pails and the bad ones thrown away, or—and here the iconoclast really comes to grief—the wicked are sorted out from the righteous at the end of the world and thrown into the fire.

---

*Here are some examples of Jewish sayings: "My humiliation is my exaltation and my exaltation is my humiliation," Rabbi Hillel, about 20 B.C.E. From the Proverbs of Solomon (25:6−7):

Do not put yourself forward in the
   king's presence
   or stand in the place of the great;
for it is better to be told, 'Come up here,'
   than to be put lower in the
   presence of the prince."

From the Talmud: "Take no thought for the care of tomorrow." God's words to Israel: "My children, if you have given food to the poor, I count it to you as if you had given food to me."

The theologians Grant and Freedman have objected that Thomas's Logia distorted the image of Christianity because they did not include the most important of the parables — the laborers in the vineyard, the good Samaritan, the progidal son, the rich man and Lazarus, the Pharisee and the tax-gatherer.[19] But this is just the point. These parables are also missing from Mark; they do not belong in the oldest tradition. An allegorical meaning, one of personification through images, was already widespread by Mark's time. Take the parable of the man who handed over the management of a vineyard to wine-growers, as we have it in Thomas's Logion 65. The wine-growers refuse to hand over the due share of the harvest to the man's servant, and "would almost have killed him." He sends another servant who is treated in the same way. The master now sends his son. When the wine-growers realize that this is the heir to the vineyard, they kill him (evidently in the hope that they will then be able to take possession of the vineyard themselves). End of parable.

Of course, it is impossible that Jesus should have told this parable in his lifetime, despite Jeremias': "Jesus was thinking of himself as the son, the last messenger of God." Conzelmann on the other hand agrees with Bultmann and Kümmel in thinking that this is certainly an invention of the community.[20] Never mind that now. Mark (12:1−12) takes further the conclusion only hinted at in the *Gospel of Thomas*. The owner has planted a vineyard and built a wall round it, hewed out a winepress and built a watchtower, just as it says in the book of the prophet Isaiah that the Lord of Hosts does for Israel. Many servants were sent to the tenants, of whom some were beaten and some murdered (the prophets). Finally the owner sends his "beloved son," the same phrase that we came across at the baptism of Jesus. The tenants murder him and throw his dead body out of the vineyard. Now the owner will put the tenants to death and give the vineyard to others, not necessarily to the heathen. The opponents of Jesus, according to Mark and both the other synoptics, understand that this refers to them, and try to arrest him but are afraid of popular feeling. (In Matthew 21:43, Jesus says: "The kingdom of God will be taken away from you and given to a nation producing the fruits of it." The allegory is taken too far and breaks down.)

Parables are just a matter of luck. Thus, in the canonical Gospels, we find the heavenly Father compared to an idle judge, who granted rights to a widow demanding justice only because her persistence would finally wear him out (Luke 18:1–8); to a master who cuts his unprofitable servant "in pieces" (or "in four") (Matthew 24:45–51); to another master who wants to reap where he has not sown and gather where he has not scattered (Matthew 25:14–30). In the parable of the "dishonest bailiff" (Luke 16:1-9) a man fiddles himself into the kingdom of Heaven because he is "unscrupulously fraudulent" (Jeremias).[21]

The socially-minded Luke compares God with a master who not only sends his only servant out to work in the fields all day but also makes him do the housework in the evening (17:7–10). Is the master at all grateful to the servant? He does not even think of it. The servants of God must know — this is the meaning of the story — that they are "miserable servants," that they have only done their duty and have no right to thanks. The idea of the bond-servant, belonging unconditionally to his master, occurs "frequently" (Bornkamm)[22] in the New Testament, and with no negative undertones.

The master rewards (and punishes) as seems good to him. The man who worked all day in the vineyard (Matthew 20:1–16) has no right to more than the agreed wage, even though the one who came to work much later is allowed by his master's favor to get the same pay. Latecomers to the kingdom of God are never too late, and the firstcome cannot rely on the proverb, "First come, first served." That is the ancient Jewish logic of the master and servant: for thus spoke the Lord in Exodus 33:19: "I will be gracious to whom I will be gracious, and will show mercy on whom I will show mercy."

Matthew is particularly awkward with his parables. In the parable of the five wise and five foolish virgins (25:1–13), Jesus likens the congregation to wedding guests (at any rate, Jeremias still thought so in 1970); he wants "to arouse the crowd in face of the coming eschatological crisis."[23] We on the contrary believe — in line with Günther Bornkamm, admittedly no lover of new ideas — that what is at issue is training the congregation in face of the deferment of the *parousia* (the Second Coming).[24] That conclusion is not far from the one Shalom ben-Chorin also draws, that we have here, not ten female wedding guests going to meet the bridegroom, but ten brides.[25] How could the lives of five girls be irrevocably affected just because they run out of oil for their lamps and are not allowed in to the wedding feast of another bride? Where is this bride? Where is her father who would have presided over the whole feast? Matthew, as we have already seen in Chapter 4, has no time for monogamy.

Often enough the pitiless meaning, and indeed the illogicality, of the parables does not get home to churchgoers, as in the case of Matthew's "royal wedding," where the king sends out invitations to his son's wedding; the guests beg to be excused; some of them sneer, some actually kill the messengers. That makes the king angry; he kills the murders and burns their city. Since those actually invited have refused, the servants have to go out into the streets and bring in to the wedding anyone they can find, good and bad alike. Even so, one of them who is not dressed for a wedding is bound hand and foot and cast into outer darkness, where there shall be weeping and wailing and gnashing of teeth. The allegory has a notably unhappy effect. Where should people brought in off the streets get a wedding garment (a "cloth washed clean," as Jeremias tells us[26]) from? It might be identical with the "white cloth" of the saints (Revelation 3:4). It is originally a Persian conception.*

We find the oldest known version in the *Gospel of Thomas,* Logion 64. Those invited, not by a king but by a man, refuse for a number of different reasons, some of them made up. Then the man orders that all those met on the way shall be brought in. No one is killed, neither servant nor guest; no one is beaten. There follows an allegorical, possibly gnostic, interpretation: "Merchants and businessmen will not find their way into my Father's places." The parable is fairly long in comparison with most of those in Thomas's Gospel, and the interpretation sounds rather sceptical. Luke, the well-adjusted social critic, has stereotypes of the poor, the crippled, the lame and the blind invited to the feast (14:15−24). To the second invitation within the city, he adds a third for the "highways and hedgerows" outside the city: an allegorical reference to the missions to the heathen world. It is not Luke but Mark who introduces bias against Israel; Israel has refused God's invitation to accept Jesus. (Actually, the Jewish war has already

---

*Schlüssinger has traced the parable to Jewish literature. A rabbi, a contemporary of the evangelists, said: "Do penance one day before you die!" His pupils asked him: "How is a man to know the day when he will die?" He answered: "Let him do penance all the more today; he might die tomorrow." Rabbi Johanan ben Zakkai, about the same period, speaks of a king who sent out invitations to a feast without naming the time. Those who were wise put on their festival clothes, but the foolish went off to work. Suddenly there came the summons to the meal, and those with dirty clothes were not allowed to take their places at the table.[27]

taken place and Jerusalem has been burnt.) Now the heathen, good and bad, are invited, but woe to those who do not have the garment of life and glory!

In Luke (19:11−27) a nobleman goes on a journey abroad in order to be appointed king (three guesses as to which city) and then returns. He gives one pound each to ten quasi-governors to trade with in his absence. His fellow-citizens send a delegation after him to say: "We do not want this man to reign over us." When he comes back as king, he not only rewards the servant who has gained most, who has made most profit on his pound; he also punishes those who did not want him as king: "bring them here and slay them before me."

The cruelty of this command cannot be attributed to Jesus. Luke, who preaches compassion, was also fond of violent contrast. The story would have been acceptable. Archelaus, of whom our sainted Joseph was so frightened according to Matthew (2:22), went on a journey to Rome after the death of his father Herod in 4 B.C.E. to press his claim to inheritance with Augustus. He was successful, in spite of a fifty-strong delegation of his opponents who followed him; only he did not get the title of king, and in 6 C.E, Judea became the province of a procurator, and he himself was banished to Gaul. "The bloody revenge which Archelaus took after his return from Rome," writes Jeremias, "never forgotten among the people, seems to have been used by Jesus to warn his hearers against false security in a crisis-parable."[28]

However, we are not as innocent as all that. It is unlikely enough that Jesus would have preached about his own going to heaven in terms of such a plot of princes or high priests, and even less likely that anyone would have recollected and written down such a complex parable; so the allegorical references must banish it completely to the realms of the Christian community's fancy.

If it is to make any sense at all, then Jesus must be the "nobleman" who journeyed to a distant land, i.e. to his Father, and who would return as a king. Those who had profited from his message would then be rewarded, while those who had refused to recognize him would be damned.

While Joachim Jeremias believes that the early church changed the meaning of Jesus' parables, making them refer to the non-appearance of the parousia and to their mission, it is quite possible that the early church made up parables for itself. Not every parable was spoken "in a specific situation of Jesus' life"

243

(Jeremias),[29] but rather in a specific situation of a primitive Christian community. When a parable begins: "Which of you . . .", mostly spoken in self defense against opponents, then it does not lead us straight back to the *ipsissima verba Domini*, an area where Jeremias is silent, but to the storehouse of sayings of the evangelists Mark and Luke or of their precursors. The telling of parables is a weapon of the community. "Where the subject turns to Jewish morality and devoutness and the particular eschatological atmosphere that is a characteristic of Jesus' preaching," says Bultmann wisely, "and when on the other hand there are no specifically Christian features, then one can most readily reckon to have a genuine parable of Jesus."[30]

Luke, author of the Acts of the Apostles, is the great teller of parables; he made the Lord Jesus popular, even unrecognizable, in his effort to get women interested in him. It is only in Luke (10:25--37) that we find the most famous and the most touching of all the parable stories, that of the good Samaritan on the road from Jerusalem to Jericho, about seventeen miles long and dropping nearly 3,600 feet into the Jordan valley. When Prior Grüber was asked about Adolf Eichmann in Berlin, why he was so concerned about the Jews, the Prior replied: "You know the road that goes from Jerusalem to Jericho?" (Eichmann was said, perhaps falsely, to have been born in a Templar community on Palestinian soil.)

Note that Luke is reckoned to be a Gentile Christian; he is not writing for the Jews. It is not the Jew who does a kindness to the Samaritan; it is not even the other way round. It is simply that the Samaritan helps a man, any man, who has been robbed and beaten half to death.

The priest obviously thinks the man is dead (this not inessential point is not revealed to us; the Gospel is not very strong on Jewish customs). Obviously he is afraid of being defiled, and prefers his formal, legal godliness to humanity towards his fellow-men, an attitude earning the harshest censure from Jesus. Or else he is afraid that the half-dead man will die in his, the priest's, arms. The Levite does the same; he certainly must have been worried only if he was

244

going up to Jerusalem to serve in the temple, not if he was going home after performing his service.*

There has been endless argument over these questions. There were even rabbis who taught that if a high priest on his way to service in the temple saw a dead man, he must stop and bury him himself, even though that disqualified him for immediate temple service. "Even today," explains Shalom Ben-Chorin, "an orthodox jew of priestly descent, one called Cohn, Cohen, Kagan, Kohnstamm, Kahn etc., will instantly leave a house in which there is a corpse, and he never takes part in a burial except that of his next of kin."[31]

The Samaritan, however, is free from ritual scruples. He does whatever lies to hand. If the question at the beginning was "Who is my neighbor ($\pi\lambda\eta\sigma\acute{\iota}ov$)?" the story makes a striking twist and gives the answer to the question: "Whose neighbor am I?"; in this case, the neighbor of the man who had fallen among thieves. The Samaritan does good not only to *his* neighbor; he is neighbor to anyone else. He sees his brother and comrade not only in his own kind, not only in the members of his own group, but in anyone at all. He is everyone's friend. Herbert Braun sees here an openness to intimate relationships with non-Jews. . . not yet entirely achieved"; it is really too soon to talk in Joachim Jeremias' glowing phrase of a "love without frontiers." Braun believes however that this "relative openness" "no doubt goes back to Jesus." But this "no doubt" makes us stop and think.[32]

For why, after all, is the parable not in Mark and not in Matthew, when it really would have meant something if a half-heathen Samaritan had been held up as a model to a teacher of the law? (The parable was told to a lawyer.) The answer cannot be that those evangelists thought Jesus' parables intolerably daring. It must rather be that in the oldest periods of the tradition, the parable does not appear. Jesus does not find Samaritans ex-

---

*Many people have wondered why the priest and the Levite were not going up to Jerusalem from Jericho, to do their temple service, instead of from Jerusalem to Jericho. It makes no difference to readers of Luke. But it could derive from a rather remarkable root. In 2 Chronicles 28:5–15 the story is told of how Ahaz, the king of Judea, is defeated by Pekah, the king of Israel, and a band of 200,000 prisoners taken to Samaria (they always exaggerated numbers). At the Lord's command, the victor released the prisoners and returned the booty. "And the men who have been mentioned by name rose and took the captives, and with the spoil they clothed all that were naked among them; they clothed them, gave them sandals, provided them with food and drink, and anointed them; and carrying all the feeble among them on asses, they brought them to their kinsfolk at Jericho, the city of palm trees. Then they returned to Samaria" (28:15).

emplary. Marriage with them was forbidden and there was a ban on trade with them because people were afraid they might desecrate religious objects. The disciples were not allowed to go into the cities of the Samaritans.

The Samaritans were despised as "Kuthim." After the destruction of the northern kingdom in 722 B.C.E. the indigenous upper class was deported by the Assyrian kings and a ruling class was imported from other parts of the kingdom, among them from the Babylonian town of Kutha. When a part of the Jewish people returned from captivity in Babylon in 538, the Samaritans were denied membership in the Jewish community, and, be it noted, were not allowed to take part in the rebuilding of the temple in Jerusalem. They were compelled to build a temple sanctuary of their own, on Mount Gerizim above Slechem. They were reputed to keep secretly carved heathen gods there. Between 6 and 9 C.E., Samaritans were said to have defiled the temple court in Jerusalem during a feast of the Passover by strewing human bones there.[33] "Implacable hate reigned on both sides," writes Joachim Jeremias. David Flusser, however, contrary to all feeling in the Bible, states that relations between Jews and Samaritans at that time were excellent.[34]

In Luke and John, both Hellenists, Jesus travels through Samaria; Luke (who may not have been very sure of the geography) says he was snubbed there, but that is not in John. It seems as if the first Christians wanted to break down the ancient hostility to the "Kuthim," though not perhaps until after the destruction of the temple in Jerusalem. The story of Jesus and the Samaritan woman, which only John reports, bears that out:

> So he came to a city of Samaria, called Sychar, near the field that Jacob gave to his son Joseph. Jacob's well was there, and so Jesus, wearied as he was with his journey, sat down beside the well. It was about the sixth hour.
>   There came a woman of Samaria to draw water. Jesus said to her, "Give me a drink." For his disciples had gone away into the city to buy food. (4:5–8)

In the ordinary way, Jews were not allowed to take food and drink from Samaritans, though that may not have applied to water. Jacob's well is filled to overflowing with symbolism.

The Samaritan woman said to him, "How is it that you, a Jew, ask a drink of me, a woman of Samaria?" For Jews have no dealings with Samaritans. Jesus answered her, "If you knew the gift of God, and who it is that is saying to you, 'Give me a drink,' you would have asked him, and he would have given you living water." The woman said to him, "Sir, you have nothing to draw with, and the well is deep; where do you get that living water? Are you greater than our father Jacob, who gave us the well, and drank from it himself, and his sons, and his cattle?" Jesus said to her, "Every one who drinks of this water will thirst again, but whoever drinks of the water that I shall give him will never thirst; the water that I shall give him will become in him a spring of water welling up to eternal life." (4:9—14)

"Living water" is the language of Qumran. Jesus now goes on to tell her that she has had five husbands, but the man she lives with now is not her husband. Why five husbands? The Jews used to say that the "Kuthim," the Samaritans, had come into the country from five different peoples, each with their own god; so their present God (Yahweh) is "not their own": they have remained a half-heathen mongrel people. The woman perceives from Jesus' clairvoyance that he is a prophet, and begins a religious discussion with him:

Our fathers worshiped on this mountain; and you say that in Jerusalem is the place where men ought to worship." Jesus said to her, "Woman, believe me, the hour is coming when neither on this mountain nor in Jerusalem will you worship the Father. You worship what you do not know; we worship what we know, for salvation is from the Jews. (4:20—22)

The different schools of thought can be seen at work here. The splinter-group of Jewish Christians have managed to get in their sentence that the Samaritans worship what they do not know. "Salvation is from the Jews." Jesus now explains to the woman that he is the Messiah, and she makes propaganda for him in the area of Sychar (possibly Shechem at the foot of Mount Gerizim, now called Nablus). And now comes the sentence referring to missionary work among the Samaritans:

I sent you to reap that for which you did not labor; others have labored, and you have entered into their labor. (4:38)

The other one who comes in for the harvest (Acts of the Apostles 8:5) is the Christian Hellenist Philip; he reaps where he had not toiled. To bring the story of the Samaritan woman and Jacob's well to a happy ending, "many" and "many more" Samaritans say that Jesus is "truly the savior of the world." The whole story, shaped with poetic force, is mission history.

So we do not know of any significant parable related by Jesus. He may have used only short parables dealing with the coming of the kingdom of God then and there and of the danger of missing it. He sets free the poetic force of the community, not by his oratorical and literary example as a "Moshel," but by his death and the reports, true and imagined, of the circumstances of his death. Whatever was conceived in the womb of time was able to be fetched out and used in reference to him, and all added to this as it were self-creating appearance of Jesus. Thus with the most beautiful of the stories attributed to Jesus, we may take sides with T.W. Manson, who liked to say that a reported happening showed features of such striking originality that it was hard to credit them to anyone other than the Lord himself.[35]

During the short period of his work in public, Jesus has no time for the heathen and the Samritans. But we should be underestimating the theologians if we assumed they had no evidence tot he contrary. For instance, in Matthew (8:5—13) and Luke (7:1—10) Jesus heals the servant of a captian, evidently a Roman captain, in Capernaum. The captain seems to assume that his servant, suffering from gout, is possessed of an evil spirit, for according to Matthew 8:9, he says:

"For I am a man under authority, with soldiers under me; and I say to one 'Go', and he goes, and to another, 'Come,' and he comes, and to my slave, 'do this,' and he does it."

This obviously does not mean that Jesus is to give the servant orders to stand up and walk about with his gout cured, for the servant, subject to the authorities, is the captain's servant and not Jesus'. What is intended is that Jesus shall tell the spirit of the sickness to yield. Jesus does so and the servant recovers at that moment, the second time in the synoptics that Jesus has healed from a distance.

Now we must be clear that the story of the captain in Matthew 8:11–12, though not in Luke, has the following Christian application:

"I tell you, many will come from east and west and sit at table with Abraham, Isaac, and Jacob in the kingdom of heaven, while the sons of the kingdom will be thrown into the outer darkness; there men will weep and gnash their teeth."

And here is the same application in Luke 13:28–30 in quite a different context, nothing to do with the captain:

"There you will weep and gnash your teeth, when you see Abraham and Isaac and Jacob and all the prophets in the kingdom of God and you yourselves thrust out. And men will come from east and west, and from north and south, and sit at table in the kingdom of God. And behold, some are last who will be first, and some are first who will be last."

Clearly, both of the evangelists are fitting in a saying ascribed to Jesus, but each fits it in in a different place and with a different emphasis. Matthew, who is always waging war against the synagogue in his Gospel, manages to turn a saying already accepted as Jesus' into an attack on Israel (so says the Leipzig theologian Wolfgang Trilling).[36]

Even the details of the story of the captain are presented in characteristically different ways. In Luke, the elders of the synagogue intercede for the captain, for he has built the synagogue for them (!). Matthew, however, cannot find a use for this intervention by the elders of the synagogue; and the help of the Roman occupying power in building the synagogue, if indeed it is not an invention of Luke, must have struck him as all too improbable.

So he makes the captain go to Jesus himself. Bultmann, never at a loss for the right word, cannot "support" the "historicality of the healings at a distance."[37] He sees here, and it is amazing that anyone should think otherwise, "ideal scenes" invented by the community. The captain's words simply refer to the original Jesus, the driver-out of devils. They can only be understood if we assume that Jesus has commanded an evil spirit to go away somewhere else, and so to leave the servant's body.

We recognize that this heathen Jesus is a creation of the evangelists, enthusiasts themselves for a mission to the heathen and writing at the earliest forty to seventy years after the activity and death of Jesus. But Jesus lives on in the tradition of the Jewish benediction: "Praise to thee, eternal, our God, king of the world, who hast not created me a heathen."[38] If we do not accept the heathen Jesus, then should we believe in the Jesus who sat at table with sinners? "The legends describe him eating with such people," writes Herbert Braun.[39]

If we read the holy scriptures of the lawful religions, we come to the inevitable conclusion that it is better, according to the admittedly somewhat professionally biased interpretation of all the priests, to sin and repent, than never to sin at all. "The wholly righteous do not stand in the place where the penitents stand," the rabbis were actually teaching.[40]

But the righteous did not sit at table with sinners, either before or after their conversion. Nonetheless, Jesus seems to have eaten with them, with the tax-gatherers and tax-farmers as well as with sinners in general, not just with the poor and certainly not with slaves (Martin Hengel, the Erlanger New Testament scholar, observes: "He certainly liked feasting, eating and drinking").[41] But one thing is always overlooked because we read with the evangelists' spectacles: Jesus was himself a sinner as defined by his contemporaries. The great bulk of the countrymen, the Am-Haaretz, were sinners, too poor even to know the law, let alone observe it. Those who lived in continual contact with with the heathen, and gained profits unjustly—the tax-gatherers—were sinners; the word is often used as a synonym for "sinners." Anyone who went about, not actually with the Am-Haaretz, but with tax-gatherers, as Jesus did, was also reckoned a sinner. Then, there were also the notorious breakers of the law, and Jesus, the Sabbath-breaker, was counted among them too. He did not merely consort with sinners, he was one of them himself; he was himself charged with "permanent impurity" (Blank).[42] No one who kept to the prescriptions for purity could sit down with people like Jesus, and anyone who spoke up for them was himself defiled, a sinner. (David Flusser insisted on supporting the proposition that Jesus was a "law-abiding Jew."[43] Well, he may have been, but in that case we should have to regard the whole text of the Gospels as no more than *belles lettres*.)

Jesus, as Adolf Holl has pointed out, "accepted the written and oral Torah as and when it seemed right to him, and overstepped them as and when it seemed right to him."[44] That God wanted to deal "only" with sinners, and that Jesus' sinners were above all the poor, the uneducated, the Am-Haaretz: Joachim Jeremias teaches us that in the year 1971, calling Jesus "an original."[45] On the other hand, Bultmann, the smasher of myths, already saw "unconscious coloring of the Christian outlook" in the passage in Mark (2:17), which says that Jesus had come to call sinners and not the righteous.[46]

He might honestly have hated the self-righteous; we certainly get that impression in retrospect, but he would not have been alone in that. John the Baptist had already refused the self-righteous and baptized the tax-gatherers without hesitation, as we can read in Luke (3:12—13). As the Baptist saw it, the tax-collectors must not merely return anything they had collected unfairly, as the rabbis demanded, but must in future take no more than was assessed. Luke makes that quite clear. It is of John the Baptist, not of Jesus, that it says in Matthew (21:32): "the tax-gatherers and prostitutes believed him." Of course we cannot know now what John really preached. But a charismatic announcing the last times—and that applies to Jesus too— would naturally have to take up a position opposed to the religiously orthodox. And where should he look for support if not to the great mass of those who infringed the law?

We cannot say often enough and loud enough (though we read nothing about it in the biographies of Jesus) that slavery is accepted in the Gospels as a matter of course, not subject to criticism. Strack-Billerbeck teach us in forty-seven closely printed pages all about the fate of the so-called "Canaanites" who were forcibly circumcised, and of the so-called "Hebrew" slaves.[47] These last had to be released after six years regardless of whether they had sold themselves or had been sold. In John's Gospel, the evangelist actually draws a comparison between the son who dwells in his father's house for ever and the slave who will have to leave it (8:35). When it comes to money, kindness comes to an end, say Karl Marx (1818—1883) and David Hansemann (1790—1864).[48]

Jesus does not seem to have been entirely infected by the prejudices of the orthodox Jews of his time. But was he wholly free from prejudices? Did a "sinful" Jew perhaps automatically have no prejudices? Did Jesus not think of the non-Jewish nations and members of other faiths as ungodly? What did he think about homosexuality, the "vilest of heathen abominations" (Conzelmann)[49] in Jewish eyes? If we are to believe the text in Matthew (7:6), tailored for Jewish Christians, Jesus thought of homosexuals as "dogs" and so described them.[50] Did he himself have a preference for men? What sort of relations did he have with women, with sinful women? Here if anywhere it should have been possible to see his capacity to take up and press on with a campaign for emancipation.

True, the Jews were not in the vanguard of progress here, so we can hardly be surprised to find little or nothing on the subject in the oldest and earliest of the Gospels. Women did follow Jesus, who seems to have been endowed with supernatural powers. They waited on him, and when he was dead they wanted to anoint and embalm him, which may well have been a task for women. The *Mustard Seed Bible* does have a note, "women followers of Jesus," but that is as far as the good intentions of the editors go — for the women who looked after Jesus' domestic needs were not his followers.

Bultmann believes that a rabbi had no women in his entourage.[51] But we are not talking about a rabbi, not even a learned man, but a charismatic, a miracle-worker. Not until Luke (8:1−3) do we get some more details:

> Soon afterward he went on through cities and villages,
> preaching and bringing the good news of the kingdom of God.
> And the twelve were with him, and also some women who had
> been healed of evil spirits and infirmities: Mary, called
> Magdalene, from whom seven demons had gone out, and
> Joanna, the wife of Chuza, Herod's steward, and Susanna, and
> many others, who provided for them out of their means.

Luke, later in time than Mark and Matthew, and writing for the Hellenistic world, stresses the women's role; and we remember that monogamy was preached to the first Gentile Christians but not to the Jewish Christians in Jerusalem. Jesus, says Professor Hengel, "allowed himself to be supported by rich ladies." Jeremias thinks the references must be to widows.[52] The rabbis certainly do not seem to have been entirely immune to feminine attractions. It says in the Talmud: "When Ula came home from the school he used to kiss his sisters on the breast; some say, on the hands."[53]

Rabbi Gamaliel, who according to the Acts of the Apostles was Paul's teacher, actually wrote a prayer of blessing to the creator for a beautiful heathen girl.* This member of the Council, a descendant of Rabbi Hillel who had defended the man's privilege in divorce, was undoubtedly fairly permissive in sexual matters. To test the virginity of a bride whom her husband suspected, he made her squat over a bunghole and then smelt her breath to see if it smelt of wine.[55] One can only wish that Paul had listened more attentively to this teacher, though it would be quite understandable too if he had conceived some horror of him. All the same, it was this same Rabbi Gamaliel who included the heathen poor, sick and dead in the Jews' social services. And Rabbi Johanan ben Zakkai was teaching in Paul's time that charity absolved the heathen.[56]

Was Jesus susceptible to feminine beauty? Did he ever love women — or a woman? Had he, as Matthew (19:12) seems to hint, emasculated himself like Origen[57] for the sake of the kingdom of God? We know nothing about all this; but we do assume that the aseptic, asexual Jesus is an invention of the community. We hear little of his love for individuals. Lazarus, the brother of Mary and Martha at Bethany, he is reported not only to have brought back to life but to have loved ("How dearly he must have loved him"); he had been lying in the grave not three, but four days. But this story is a late invention of the community, only reproduced by John (11:1−45), who also of course invented that disciple whom Jesus loved. It says of the "rich man" in Mark (10:21) — a "rich young man" in Matthew —: "And Jesus, looking upon him loved him." (Another possible translation is "caressed him.") No further explanation is given. Was Jesus married, as Ben-Chorin suggests, because as a rule a rabbi was married?[58] Perhaps, but we should be no better off if we knew. Was he well-known for hatred of his family? Not at all. Actually, Herbert Braun goes so far as to depict Jesus as a support of his family.[59]

In his relationship to his mother, Jesus seems rather to have modelled himself after the Jewish benediction in the liturgy of the Morning Prayer: "Praise to thee, eternal, our God, king of the

*The orthodox said in excuse for the rabbi that he spoke his praises, not in praise of the pretty girl but in praise of God, just as one might give thanks for a beautiful camel or donkey. "Also it was not his habit to look at women, but this happened at a street-corner, so that he could not help looking at the woman."[54]

world, who hast not created me as a woman."[60] The form of address, "woman," used in John's Gospel, would have sounded very strange to Jewish ears, but then this Gospel was not really intended for Jews. Thus, if Jesus shows a tendency towards emancipation, it can be put down to his "lack of family feeling."[61]

Ben-Chorin indeed writes about the mother Mary: "Unquestionably the mother of Jesus joined the band of disciples in some way or other";[62] but it is not unquestionable at all. It is only in John's Gospel, the last of all and furthest in time from Jesus and his activities, that she is with him in Cana, where he turned the water into wine, and goes on with him afterwards. Jesus treats her in a strictly Messianic way. His exhortation recorded by Luke (14:26) to his hearers to hate their mothers as well as all their other relatives, and their own lives as well, can be taken as a bit of exaggeration on the part of the evangelist. (Herbert Braun quotes this "very probably genuine old word of Jesus" and thinks that Jesus' disciples direct such hate against themselves, "the essential, disobedient I").[63]

Actually, this presumably very awkwardly translated speech means that anyone who wanted to be Jesus' disciple must not be too greatly attached to father, mother, wife and child, or even to his own life. But this "genuine old word of Jesus" could really refer to that popular, contradictory oracle that we know as Logion 101 in the *Gospel of Thomas*. There Jesus says: "No one who does not hate his father and mother as I do can be my disciple; and no one who does not love his father and mother as I do can be my disciple."

Jesus does not have an emancipated attitude towards woman, an attitude as between equals, in the two earliest Gospels, least of all in Mark, but only in the two latest, written for the Hellenized, for Greeks and Romans. Luke says that Jesus is anointed by a sinful woman, not in fact called Mary Magdalene though artists and theologians have given her that exciting name, in the house of the Pharisee, Simon. She wets his feet with tears (washes the dust off his feet), dries them with her hair, kisses his feet and anoints him. The Pharisee speaks to himself, though it must have been audible: "If this fellow were a real priest he would know who this woman is who touches him, and what sort of woman she is, a sinner." Jesus gives him this parable:

A certain creditor had two debtors; one owed five hundred denarii, and the other fifty. When they could not pay, he forgave them both. Now which of them will love him more?" Simon answered, "The one, I suppose, to whom he forgave more." And he said to him, "You have judged rightly." (7:41–43)

In this version, Jesus draws the well-known conclusion: her great love proves that her many sins have been forgiven. A platitude, so rendered in the *Luther Bible* of 1964 and taken over in this form by Braun.[64] But what Luke's Jesus really says — and this is how it appears in the *Mustard Seed Bible* — is: "Many sins have been forgiven her, and therefore she has shown me great love; he to whom little is forgiven shows little love." That way the parable makes sense: the incomparable value of the conversion is revealed. He who has not sinned greatly has little for which to be forgiven, so he cannot love God or Jesus or the church as another does, to whom many sins have been forgiven.

In Luke's "sinful woman" we are faced with a woman recognizable as either a prostitute, or the wife of a man who earns his living in some dishonorable way. George Bernard Shaw sees the woman as a "Dame aux Camellias".[65] But it is not as Ben-Chorin thinks: "Jesus recognizes the germ of love even in the distorted form of commercial love";[66] it is rather: whoever has sinned greatly is the more grateful to him who forgives the sins, i.e. the church, than one who sins little.

Luke writes as a ladies' man. His little romance is aimed at women. Even in the figure of Mary, who listens to the words of the Master instead of preparing the food (10:38–42), there are ideas which no Jew of Jesus' time could have had. It is rather the role of the attentive hetaira, enlivening the talk with clever interruptions, that is clearly being played here; conversation with a woman struck the Jewish scribes as indecent.

Mary from Magdala on the Lake of Gennesaret, alias Miriam from Migdal on Lake Chinnereth, the "penitent" Magdalene, seems to have been a faithful follower. She is early seen as the woman unhappily in love with the Master and trying to divert him from his mission.* (Rilke's Magdalene sings:

---

*See the *Gospel of Thomas*, where Peter (Logion 114) demands that Mary Magdalene should "go away from us," for the women do not deserve to live. Jesus answers: "See, I will lead her and make her manly, so that she too will become a manly spirit, like you men. For every woman who will make herself manly will enter into the kingdom of heaven" — an obscure passage, but also emancipatory?

Those limbs, from every lover so withholding,
for the first time in this love-night I view.
We've never felt each other's arms enfolding,
and now I only weep and watch for you.[67] *

Jesus had driven seven evil spirits out of her. She watched the crucifixion from a distance, and wished to anoint the dead Jesus the day after the Sabbath. But, according to Mark (16:1—8), she does not find him, but finds an angel in his place. He gives her a message to deliver to the disciples, that the Lord is going before them into Galilee. But she says nothing to anyone, because she is beside herself with terror.

In John (20:11—18), on the contrary, the risen Jesus says to her: "Do not hold me, for I have not yet ascended to the Father." Here she takes a message to the disciples that she has seen the Lord. Celsus, the enemy of the Christians, laughs at the hallucinations of the "half-crazy" Mary Magdalene.[68] It is remarkable that it should have been women who were the first to see the risen Christ; they do not occur in the evidence of the oldest and first witness, Paul, though there are of course prophetesses in the Old Testament. Did the followers not trust themselves, and so take for their first witnesses persons whose utterances would not be acceptable in court? Did they unconsciously want to put the blame on women's hysteria? Or did women's hysteria start it all? Ethelbert Stauffer has a quite revolutionary explanation;[69] in the fact that Jesus appeared first to the despised and frightened (!) girl from Magdala there is manifested "the kingly chivalry of Jesus Christ, which is without parallel, not only in ancient Palestine." A *very* early Minnesinger?

It is hard to see how Mary Magdalene has earned such a reputation for sinfulness. Magdala is said to have been "a city known for its permissive ways" (Adolf Holl), a "notorious love-nest" (Stauffer).[70] But it seems to have picked up this reputation from its best-known citizen, just as the city of Nazareth, or an-Nasira, has — perhaps undeservedly — earned its reputation through the refusal of the prophets to be particularly consistent. It may be that the anonymous professional in the house of Simon the Pharisee, who regardless of Jewish custom lets down her hair in

*Rainer Maria Rilke: *Selected Works* Vol II trans. J.B. Leishman ©The Hogarth Press Ltd 1960. By permission of New Directions, New York.

the presence of men, needed a name; the spirit of unchastity could always have been among the seven spirits that were driven out of Mary Magdalene.

Which is all very well; and then we are astonished to read in Strack-Billerbeck, the standard work on the parallels between the rabbinical writings and the New Testament, that the Magdala of our Magdalene is "not our Magdala," not Migdal Nunaija, the seaside town not far from Tiberias on the Sea of Galilee, but Migdal on the Jarmuk, the city of the dyers. The rabbinical literature, written at the earliest during the second century C.E, tells us about Magdala of the dyers: "Three cities used to send their produce up to Jerusalem, Kabul, Sichin and Magdala. And why was Kabul destroyed? Because of its disunity, Sichin because of sorcery and Magdala because of unchastity."[71] So it was just an intentional unintentional name-switch, that's all. Acquittal for Migdal Nunaija, acquittal for Mary Magdalene. And for that matter, nothing might have happened to the dyers' city on the Jarmuk.

We can certainly believe that Jesus had women among his followers. But the tender and touching stories about women in Luke and John have nothing to do with Jesus. Did Jesus have a sense of humor? Could he laugh at himself? Did he ever laugh? Did he make other people laugh? Was he, as our precious Thielicke supposes, fond of playing jokes at weddings?[72] Once more, we know nothing about it, and need to be very careful even with our assumptions. There is another thrilling story-cum-lesson in John (8:2−11), similar to that of the good Samaritan, about a woman taken in adultery. "Go and do likewise" in the parable of the Samaritan, and "Let him cast the first stone," are the Bible's two practical commandments of love:

> Early in the morning he came again to the temple; all the people came to him, and he sat down and taught them. The scribes and the Pharisees brought a woman who had been caught in adultery, and placing her in the midst they said to him, "Teacher, this woman has been caught in the act of adultery. Now in the law Moses commanded us to stone such. What do you say about her?" This they said to test him, that they might have some charge to bring against him. Jesus bent down and wrote with his finger on the ground. And as they continued to ask him, he stood up and said to them, "Let him who is without

sin among you be the first to throw a stone at her." And once more he bent down and wrote with his finger on the ground. But when they heard it, they went away, one by one, beginning with the eldest, and Jesus was left alone with the woman standing before him. Jesus looked up and said to her, "Woman, where are they? Has no one condemned you?" She said, "No one, Lord." And Jesus said, "Neither do I condemn you; go, and do not sin again."

This incident is often quoted by the champions of the theory that the Jews at the time of Jesus' death possessed criminal jurisdiction and so could have stoned him at any time. But it does not prove what still has to be proved, certainly not for Jesus' times. Shalom Ben-Chorin believes that Jesus did not write on the ground but drew a magic circle round the woman to protect her from her accusers, as "Choni the circle-drawer" is said to have prayed for rain in the middle of a circle he had drawn, Choni of whom it says in the Jerusalem Talmud: "When he entered the hall of the temple it grew light." Joachim Jeremias thinks Jesus fulfilled the scripture (Jeremiah 17:13): "They that depart from me shall be written in the earth," but even he admits some doubt as to whether the story relies on the old tradition. The *Wilckens Bible* has the conclusive comment: "It was not in the original text of John."[73]

"Judge not, that ye be not judged," it says in Matthew. "He who has drowned shall be drowned," taught the gentle Rabbi Hillel.[74] Or, we might add, "he who takes the sword shall perish by the sword." We have no idea how the real Jesus reacted to commercial love and to adultery, and what his views on marriage were, just as we do not know what he thought about war and peace. It is nonsense to want to cram seventy years of the civilizing development of the Greek-speaking world, and the growth of the evangelists' faith in their dead hero, into the one single year of his public appearance; even if we are content to read that he was the "first systematic theoretician," who fully evaluated the alternative course of communal development through the employment of cybernetic methods of observation, and who "understood the principle of the aim-correcting reaction" (Hans G. Schneider, born 1945).[75]

When we think of Jesus, we think of Luke's good Samaritan, of John's half-sentence " . . . let him cast the first stone," the emancipating supranational Jesus who first tells the Syrian-

Phoenician woman, "It is not right to take the children's bread and throw it to the dogs" but who is then persuaded otherwise; Jesus talking to the Samaritan woman, whose prejudices are broken down by women on two occasions and who breaks down prejudices himself. The Jesus who impresses himself on us is the one that will also be there for the Samaritans, the one who, as Josef Blank writes, "through his teaching and his works gave the decisive thrust whereby the Biblical faith overflowed its national limitations and took on a new form which all men might receive."[76] Jesus, the man of evolutionary self-realization; Jesus, an "anthropological mutation."[77]

But the Jesus of reality never had time to emerge from within his narrow Jewish horizons, whatever other opportunities of development he may have lacked. He sat at table with sinners, a sinner among sinners; and perhaps he loved the sinners the more because he had more chance of interesting them in the dawning kingdom of God than he had with the righteous. But: "Do not take the road to gentile lands, and do not enter any Samaritan town."

Jesus stayed within his own four walls, and it is by no means certain that he wanted to make his house more comfortable. For who thinks of comfort if he has come to cast fire on earth (Luke 12:49), and wishes it were already kindled?

10. Mark, a disappointing witness

If one took a poll among Christians about which of the ethical commandments represented the quintessence of the Gospels, the commandment to love one's enemies would come out easily top. Yet in the earliest and oldest of the Gospels, that named after one "Mark" (written no earlier than 67 and probably later than that), this commandment surprisingly enough does not appear. Nor does the so-called Sermon on the Mount in which it is contained, nor the Lord's prayer, an abbreviation of Jewish forms of prayer. We do not even find "faith, hope and love," Paul's trinity (1 Corinthians 13:13).

Since we know nothing more reliable about the life of Jesus than what is reported in Mark, it will not do for us to confine ourselves to an examination of what Mark writes; we must also take into account as no less important what Mark does not write.

Forty years after the death of Jesus, Mark represents a Jesus who systematically preaches the love for one's neighbor found in the Old Testament: "You shall love your neighbor as a man like yourself." Rabbi Hillel had taught twenty years before the Christian era: "Do not do to your neighbor what you do not like yourself. That is the whole of Torah, and everything else is just interpretation of it; go and learn it."[3] This so-called "golden rule" flowed from the command to love one's neighbor, but couched in a negative form. In the course of translation into Greek, the sense of Moses' commandment has been changed back into the active voice. Hillel's "golden rule," already to be found in earlier Greek cultural circles, really means: Make your ideal demands on others in accordance with your real relationship with them.[4] Mark's Jesus does not seem to know this, nor does he know the Qumran maxim: "To no man will I repay evil; I will repay men with good, for judgment over all that lives belongs with God."

A very important principle is enshrined in this verse from Qumran, which we also find in Paul: only God will judge, only God will requite good and evil. Man must not avenge himself on his personal enemy, he must repay evil with good. The Qumran community may have recorded that in writing in the first century B.C.E. In the Book of the Proverbs of Solomon, written centuries before the Christian era, we find those verses which Paul—but not Mark — quotes (Romans 12:20):

"If your enemy is hungry, feed him; if he is thirsty, give him drink; for by so doing you will heap burning coals upon his head."

We may consequently affirm that Mark's Jesus had nothing of his own to say about love for one's neighbor, let alone love for one's enemy: there is not a sentence in Mark's Gospel on the lines of the Qumran pattern or the Proverbs of Solomon. In Matthew's Gospel, on the other hand, which is reckoned to have been written towards the end of the eighties, Jesus says:

261

"You have heard that it was said, 'An eye for an eye and a tooth for a tooth.' But I say to you, Do not resist one who is evil. But if any one strikes you on the right cheek, turn to him the other also; and if any one would sue you and take your coat, let him have your cloak as well; and if any one forces you to go one mile, go with him two miles. Give to him who begs from you, and do not refuse him who would borrow from you. You have heard that it was said, 'You shall love your neighbor and hate your enemy.' But I say to you, Love your enemies and pray for those who persecute you, so that you may be sons of your Father who is in heaven; for he makes his sun rise on the evil and on the good, and sends rain on the just and on the unjust."

We must not be friendly only to our brothers; we must not love only those who love us. Two things strike us here: first, the idea that only God forgives is here watered down—God is a liberal who makes it rain on the honest and on the dishonest. Secondly, a straw man has been set up simply to be knocked down. Moses did not in fact command the people to love their neighbor and hate their enemy; in fact, it says in Leviticus (19:18):

You shall not take vengeance or bear any grudge against the sons of your own people, but you shall love your neighbor as yourself: I am the LORD.

If we are going to go the whole way and credit Jesus with the sentences in Matthew, as Gollwitzer, for instance, does ("historically, truly a genuine utterance of Jesus" and "actually one of the most revolutionary"),[5] then we must help ourselves out like Joachim Jeremias,[6] who declares that in verse 43 Jesus was not quoting the Law of Moses at all, but a popular saying. Rabbi Hillel's "golden rule" has now been changed into the positive, following the lines of Qumran and the collector of the Proverbs of Solomon: we must love our enemies too. But that still does not apply in Matthew to national or religious enemies, as even Jeremias recognizes. That step is not taken until we come to Luke, who is not writing for Jews. However, in both Gospels we hear something new, something not known to Mark.

We must once more make it clear that Matthew, and even more so Luke, are writing after the destruction of Jerusalem and the temple — neither of them on Palestinian soil and Luke not even for the early Jews. To get the environment of these two quite clear it must be remembered that the old Jerusalem differentiation—Jew good, non-Jew bad—was all over, just as the complete Jewish theocracy had been all over since the destruction of Jerusalem. The commandment of unlimited love for one's enemies as we find it in Luke could only be formulated in a community open to the world, cosmopolitan, "rootless," spiritual. It is significant that even Paul, who had had his ear to the ground in Rome more than once, had never heard of it. But he is a missionary among the heathen, and so he gives us the maxim: "Bless those who persecute you; bless and do not curse them" (Romans 12:14). Paul quite rightly points out how the brothers bring actions against one another (1 Corinthians 6:1–8), "and before unbelievers" (6:6)* and that on account of "mere matters of business" (6:3–4). He never asks them to love the unbelievers. Bloch, in search of a revolutionary Jesus, tries to prove that Jesus had his own commandment of love for the enemy, apparently not taken so seriously.[7] But it is easier to believe that he knew nothing of his own commandment.

The great mutation, the qualitative leap forward said to have come into the world with Jesus if we listen, not to Bultmann[8] but to the latest innovators; when would all that have taken place? Jesus did not want to inspire mankind continually to the life to come, "in close companionship, despite all wrong and all wretchedness" (Herbert Braun);[9] his message actually contains no "virtual universality, as he fulfilled the deepest designs of the biblical faith" (Josef Blank); the special quality of Jesus does not lie in his having called the outcast classes to the salvation of the kingdom of God with no repentance, no good works, no conversion (Blank);[10] on the contrary, anyone who did not acknowledge him and his vain expectation was in danger of judgment. Nor was he "a reformer of mankind and of the community of men" (Peter P. Kahane in *The Man from Galilee*).[11] It was not Jesus who extended love for one's neighbor to include all the non-Jews; it was the first Gentile Christians, and as "underdogs" they had good reason to preach that men should love their enemies. It is only those who have the upper hand who can

---

*How can people have the face to bring their quarrels "before unbelievers," before the Roman judges, instead of "to the community of God's people"? Why not rather suffer injury, asks Paul? Why not rather let yourself be robbed? If the whole world is to come before you for judgment, how can you think yourselves incompetent to deal with these trifling cases? (The idea of love gets a bit the worse for wear in the light of the fantasy of everlasting judgment.) Yes, are you not aware, asks Paul, that we are to judge angels?

gratify their need to hate legitimately, to murder legitimately, to annihilate legitimately. (Until then, one cursed the unrepentant cities of Chorazin and Bethsaida and wished on them the fate of Sodom and Gomorrha. See that same Matthew of "Love your enemies," 11:20−24).

The maxims of the old Jews were reasonable; they hung so high above mankind that man could never hope to attain to them, but he was nonetheless stimulated to extend himself to the uttermost, or at the very least to fashion a conscience for himself. Quite different was the excessive, extravagant ethic of Matthew's and Luke's Gospels, based on no practicable system of values and without any foundation (though they have their models in Greek philosophy). "It is always possible," writes Freud, "to bind a fairly large number of people together in love for one another, so long as there are others left for them on whom to practice their aggression."[12] To love your neighbor in your own group is a sufficiently demanding commandment which only a select few could follow, if indeed any could. The missionary in a foreign land, confronted by other groups in overwhelming strength, can proclaim universal love of man for man with no fear of damage to his aggressive potential.

Even the command to give away your coat if someone wants your shirt, to turn your left cheek if someone slaps you on the right, to go two miles if you are made to go one, grows out of a situation of collapse, a refined atmosphere; modern public relations psychology is at work. A spiritual community, intent on expansion and held together by a high self-regard and determination to advance, is speaking here; a community that has nothing to gain from confrontation and everything from a show of affection, from submission to the aggressiveness of the enemy. If we want to be as cutting as Nietzsche, we might say that the Christians first enervated and then conquered their enemies.[13]

Did the problem dawn on the writers of the Gospels? It seems not. Their texts are not all testimonies of love. There is a great deal in them about weeping and gnashing of teeth, directed at the unbelievers: "judge not," they say, yet every third line is about judgment. As we have seen, it never even occurred to Matthew in his self-righteousness that he was recommending that all who disputed the verdict of the Council should be treated "as tax-gatherers and Gentiles". (He even makes Jesus say this.) The Gospels are full of contradictions of all kinds, but they also contain a lot of straight-forward statements, rather like: "And if thou'lt not a Christian be, I'll break thy silly head for thee."

It may be worth looking again at the way the love-ethic of Jesus works in Mark's Gospel, in what is recognizably an "ideal scene" (Bultmann)[14], written with obvious difficulty to fill an embarrassing gap:

And one of the scribes came up and heard them disputing with one another, and seeing that he answered them well, asked him, "Which commandment is the first of all?" Jesus answered, "The first is, 'Hear, O Israel: The Lord our God, the Lord is one; and you shall love the Lord your God with all your heart, and with all your soul, and with all your mind, and with all your strength.' The second is this, 'You shall love your neighbor as yourself.' There is no other commandment greater than these." And the scribe said to him, "You are right, Teacher; you have truly said that he is one, and there is no other but he; and to love him with all the heart, and with all the understanding, and with all the strength, and to love one's neighbor as oneself, is much more than all whole burnt offerings and sacrifices." And when Jesus saw that he answered wisely, he said to him, "You are not far from the kingdom of God." And after that no one dared to ask him any question.*

No one who sees the kingdom of God coming down to earth with power speaks like that. And the gap in the maxims on the love-ethic is not the only one in Mark. "Some, or all, the New Testament writers believed that Christ had a pre-existence before his life on earth, a previous existence with the Father in heaven," writes Millar Burrows.[15] That can be expressed more exactly. The writer of Mark's Gospel, and he alone, never suggests that he believes in a pre-existent Jesus. No angel appears to the Mother or the shepherds; instead, the adult Jesus is baptized by John in the Jordan, and that is the moment when he is chosen. The Spirit descends on him from an opened heaven "like a dove", for Jesus announces the new creation, and a voice rings out: "Thou art my beloved son; with thee I am well pleased." (In the *Apocalypse of*

*The questioner praised by Mark, a γραμματεύς, one learned in the scriptures, is turned by Matthew and Luke into a νομικός, a teacher of the Law, who "tempts" Jesus (πειράζων in Matthew) and "tries to catch him out" (ἐκπειράζων in Luke). Could it be that, in the face of all scientific research, Luke did after all know the text of Matthew?

Enoch 71:14, God speaks to the chosen Enoch: "Thou art the man's son, born to righteousness").

He is the son of Mary, like his brothers; he is a carpenter, or even, in other manuscripts, the son of a carpenter, presumably because no one knows his father. He is already surrounded by disciples, but not all the time; often only by several or "many" people. Mark's Jesus sighs and rages, is astonished and distressed; he feels mortal terror; he has doubts on the cross. He gets angry when called on to heal, as they do in the Hellenistic miracle stories (1:41 *Codex Bezae*; 8:5).[16] If anyone believes in him as a miracle-worker, even only from hearsay, his superstition is promptly rewarded with the expected miracle.

Mark's Jesus is also not completely omniscient. He asks the father of a sick child: "How long has he been like this?"; and an evil spirit: "What is your name?" He not only questions, he is also questioned, without the evangelist's immediately assuming that behind every questioner there is a tempter, an *agent provocateur*. He heals involuntarily simply because there is a magic power in him. In the case of a woman suffering from hemorrhages (5:30) who had touched his clothes from behind, he notices only that "power has gone out of him." Käsemann sees this as a "vulgar Hellenistic conception,"[17] unthinkable it seems in a Jew. According to Mark, all those who touched him were healed, which would indeed be unthinkable in Matthew. Luke, on the contrary, in his Acts of the Apostles, swallows the "vulgar Hellenistic" hocus-pocus whole and records miraculous cures by the touching of handkerchieves and scarves (19:12), through Peter's shadow (5:15), etc.

In Matthew, he heals by the laying on of hands if necessary, otherwise by the word. But Mark makes him spit in the eyes of a blind man (8:23). Also, he heals in two stages, as if he had not been able to manage it in one go: first, the blind man sees "men as trees, walking" (8:24–25), which suggests a remarkably ready gift of association; then Jesus lays his hands on his eyes "again," and now the cured man can see clearly. Jesus allows a devil—obviously an outstandingly manifold devil— to go at its own request into a two-thousand-strong herd of swine, which then rushes into the sea and is drowned.* The evil spirits talk with him; the old belief in devils shows up in Mark as strong as ever.

Mark's Jesus is as intolerant as may be, but he has not yet acquired that inhuman range of the later Gospels that enables him to declare at one moment that his yoke is good to bear, his burden light (Matthew 11:30), and at another that he has not come to bring peace, but a sword, that he has come to set a man against his father, a daughter against her mother, a young wife against her mother-in-law (10:34—35). In Mark, Jesus is first and foremost a "rabbi." He does not yet presume to curse to the depth of hell those cities, including "his own city" of Capernaum, which have not been converted despite his miracles. (He must really have cursed Chorazin, thinks Joachim Jeremias; the reference is historic, for it is not mentioned anywhere else that he was in Chorazin).[19] In Mark, Jesus must not yet be forced into human standards and human psychology, a reproof that Albert Schweitzer levels at his generation of theologians. There are none of the "great imperious sayings of the Lord" to be found in him, hardly any of the "imperative, world-condemning demands" (Schweitzer).[20]

No, it cannot yet be said of Mark's Jesus, as Daniélou claims for him, that "by all his conduct he claims the right to heavenly privileges"; he is not even yet the "immeasurably great man" of Albert Schweitzer.[21] "Why do you call me good?" he says to someone who addresses him as "good master"; "no one is good except God alone" (10:18). The passage is missing from Luke and John, which last makes Jesus speak of "my kingdom"; the risen Jesus is hailed (John 20:28) as "my Lord and my God!" Mark's Gospel is also less developed theologically than the other three. Its starting-point is still the reconciliation of the people of Israel with God. The cross is not a step to salvation but an encouragement to "follow" Jesus. To follow him where?

For this Jesus of Mark did not champion a morality that was in any way remarkable, let alone a new morality. He damns the rules of the Jewish law (7:9—13) by which a son may cut off support

*Matthew cuts down this fable of the betrayer betrayed considerably; knowing the geography better, perhaps, he transfers the story from Gerasa, in the middle of driest Transjordan, to Gadara, near the lake of Gennesaret. Ernst Haenchen will not accept the idea of a "Rumpelstiltskin motif", as if Jesus could only gain power over the devils if he had first found out their name; he thinks that "nonsense." And the *Wilckens Bible* rejoices intolerably naively: "Jesus Christ overcomes even the assembled forces of evil."[18]

from his parents if he makes over his property to the temple; the son enjoys the usufruct up to the time of his death, and then the priests inherit.[22] This inhumane prescription was attacked by the Qumran community as well as by some of the rabbis; it was a plum for all the charismatic prophets, or even just for journalists. Anyone who wanted to have a go at the priests found a handy pretext in this screaming injustice.

Actually, we doubt whether Jesus ever concerned himself with that kind of specific point in the law, but we will stretch a point and book this really very obvious argument to the credit of the ethical account because we would like to give Jesus credit for the pregnant saying: "You have a fine way of rejecting the commandment of God, in order to keep your tradition!" (7:9) — though it was said more expressively, and more angrily, by the prophets Amos and Micah.

And then there is the "rich young man," whom Mark says Jesus "loved" (or "took a fancy to" or "caressed"), and to whom he suggested that he should give all his goods to the poor and follow him, Jesus (10:21). The young man does not want to, and Jesus comments: "It is easier for a camel to go through the eye of a needle than for a rich man to enter the kingdom of God" (10:25). A glance at the Greek text shows that it does not say "a rich young man" but "a rich man" — Matthew invented the young man (19:20) because a rich young man is more appealing than any man, no matter who, who happens to have "great wealth." Luke (18:18) goes so far as to make him "a man of the ruling class."

The rich man is told to follow Jesus. But the talk of following, we learn from Ernst Fuchs, must be "looked at with care."[23] The saying about the camel and the needle's eye is recognizably not traceable back to Jesus; moreover, men did not enter the kingdom of heaven, the kingdom of God was to come from heaven to earth, to break here over mankind.[24] So why are the disciples shocked, frightened; why do they ask, "Then who can be saved?" After all, they were not rich men, and rich men must surely have been, then as now, in the minority? Wellhausen indeed considers that the reference must be, not to "a rich man," but to any man, and Ben-Chorin thinks it is not a camel ($\kappa\acute{\alpha}\mu\eta\lambda o\varsigma$) that will go more easily through the needle's eye, but a rope ($\kappa\acute{\alpha}\mu\iota\lambda o\varsigma$).[25] Thus the most beautiful story can be made to vanish with the pale cast of thought; and then, with the help of Ernst Bloch, it can be freshened up again: "Jesus gives the true chiliastic advice, "to withdraw in this way personally as object of Caesar's vested interests."[26]

Qumran teaches us that property is spiritually evil.[27] Apart from the similarly Qumranic rules about marriage, Mark's Gospel contains no other outstanding ethical point.* Mark's Jesus does not forgive Judas, who betrays him to his enemies, but says: "It would be better for that man if he had not been born"(14:21). Nor does he pray for his executioners. For anyone who corrupts a single one of those little ones who believe in him, "it would be better for him to be thrown into the sea with a millstone round his neck" (9:42); again clearly an apostolic, not a Jesuanic, utterance.

We should have to hold it against him, in the interests of this innocent plant, that he had cursed a fig-tree (11:12–22), if we did not know for certain that this ill-conceived allegory had been foisted upon him. We might find it attractive, if hardly historical, that he allowed himself to be anointed instead of giving the money to the poor ("For you always have the poor with you, and whenever you will, you can do good to them; but you will not always have me," 14:7.) How does that fit in with the "rich young man?" It need not fit in, unless every individual passage is to be regarded as valid.

So our conclusion is that Jesus acquires no ethical or moral outline in Mark's Gospel, any more than he does in Paul's writings. He is under no circumstances, as Jaspers makes him out to be, "a prophetic figure that unlike any other sheds his revolutionary light into the measureless greatness of evil, into the depths of love, into the radicalness of the needed conversion;"[28] he is also far from being, as Burrows says, "the highest religious teacher of mankind."[29] What can be credited to him in the way of ethical maxims is without character; he might well have said it but it would make no difference to our estimation of him. Matthew and Luke are the first to add anything to it.

To preserve at least his uniqueness as a "highest religious teacher of mankind" the whole armament of modern philology has been deployed, words counted, hairs split, with a result that might well have been foreseen: it is not the genuineness of the words ascribed to Jesus by the synoptics that must be established,

*Anyway, the edifying story of the "widow's mite" (12:41–44) was circulating in quite similar form in Hellenistic and Jewish literature of the time. The *Luther Bible* of 1964 testifies to the interpretation of such tract-religiosity: "How much interest might these widow's mites have earned in all the centuries of the Christian era!"

as the Bultmann school thought,[30] but their ungenuineness.[31] A retrograde movement can be established, with Joachim Jeremias at the head of the cavalcade. During a public debate between Catholic and Protestant theologians in Düsseldorf in January 1972, Willi Marxsen of Münster was able to declare[32] "that we are amazingly united in our opposition to Bultmann."

No doubt. We know a bit more about Jesus today. Joachim Jeremias praises his "unique relationship with God,"[33] and in the broadcast "Jesus — a heretic?" on the Second German Network on 28 November 1971 it was actually said: "The God to whom Jesus prays is a different God."[34] He actually calls on God — once also in Mark — as *Abba* (Jeremias: "the very heart of Jesus' relationship with God"),[35] when he prays in the garden of Gethsemane that the cup may be taken away from him, a prayer incidentally that no one can have overheard and to which he received no answer. *Abba* is Aramaic and means Father. *Abba* is not only what children say to their father, it is also what the Jewish man says to his rabbi. It does not mean only "Daddy." If, as is supposed, Jesus spoke only Aramaic,[36] then he could not have addressed the Father in any way but just *Abba*.

Did no one in Jerusalem really dare to address God as *Abba*, as German television with all its authority declares?[37] That does not seem to have been so at all. But if it is true that this form of address was not customary in the orthodox land of Judea, and we know little enough about it, then Jesus too would not have used it. "The individual," says Strack-Billerbeck, "was afraid of being too familiar if he addressed God as 'my Father.' "[38] That may well have been so. But the speech is rendered in Hebrew, the religious language, and was translated into Greek, so that *Abba* was by now recognizable only as a religious word. The Hellenists, the Jews of the Diaspora, the Jews outside the Aramaic speech-area, spoke Greek; many of them did not understand Hebrew at all.

In the book of the wisdom of Jesus son of Sirach, written in the second century B.C.E. and forming part of the Greek Bible — we know it better as Ecclesiasticus — faithful Jews could read: "O Lord, Father and God of my life, do not give me haughty eyes" (23:4); and "O Lord, Father and Ruler of my life, do not abandon me to their (my enemies') counsel" (23:1). The book of the *Wisdom of Solomon*, written in Greek before the birth of Christ, contains the verse (14:3): "But it is thy providence, O Father, that steers its course, because thou hast given it a path in the sea, and a safe way through the waves." So is this mode of address to God, *Abba*, really "without analogy in the whole of Jewish literature" (Joachim Jeremias)?[39] It certainly does not seem so. It was in fact Hellenists, Greek-writing Jews, who first formulated Jesus' mode of addressing God. They inferred from the Alexandrian Book of Wisdom ("... calls himself a son of the Lord ... boastingly calls God his Father") that Jesus had made himself known as the Son of God.

Paul, who certainly never tried to find out from Peter and James how the Lord addressed his God in prayer, and who moreover took nothing over from his enemies in Jerusalem, writes quite calmly and as a matter of course in his letter to the Galatians (4:6): "And because you are sons, God has sent the Spirit of his Son into our hearts, crying, 'Abba! Father!' " Paul is sure that the Aramaic *Abba* sounds more loving than the Greek πάτερ. That was written in 55 or 56 C.E. But even the Gospel according to Mark has a Hellenistically-educated author, who for instance divides the night into four watches in line with the usage in the Roman army (6:48; 13:35), and not into three as was usual in Palestine (as in Luke 12:38). We may doubt whether Jesus addressed God as *Abba*. What we may not doubt is that Hellenistic Jewish Christians attributed this form of address to him. It bore out that special relationship that they assumed to exist between God and the Son of God.*

If we count up the number of places in which God is spoken of as "my, thy, our, your Father," we find that they tend to increase with the passage of time:

- ° Mark 4 times
- ° Matthew 44 times
- ° Luke 17 times
- ° John 109 times.

When Jesus says "your Father," according to the oldest traditions he is speaking only to the disciples, that is, to a very small although open circle, and not to all faithful Jews or to all the Jews, least of

*At about this period, the Hellenistic mode of thought seems to have rubbed off on rabbinical literature. About the year 70, for instance, Rabbi Zadok entered the sanctuary of the ruined temple and said: "My Father, who art in heaven, thou hast destroyed thy city and burnt down thy temple, and still thou art silent and uncaring!" (God tells Rabbi Zadok: "Have trust, Jerusalem!") Rabbi Eleazar ben Azariah, about the year 100, is reported as saying: I should like to eat pigs' flesh, I should like to live with a forbidden woman; but what am I to do, since my Father that is in heaven has determined for me that I shall not do it?[40]

271

all to all men. The address "our Father" is found in many Jewish prayers of the period. But this collective address was changed by the Hellenistically thinking Jewish Christians into a personal "father." The man they write of was not a child of God in the sense generally handed down, but God's personal son, clearly distinguished as such.

Our Father in heaven, in the heavens, our Father who art in heaven, this was the current language of rabbinical prayer, also, and indeed especially, in Aramaic. Matthew, the most Jewish-Christian-oriented of the evangelists, adopts this usage. The Lord's prayer, probably composed some fifty years after the death of Jesus, evidently existed as "our Father," and as a Gentile Christian prayer using the form found in Luke, "Father." In Matthew, we find "Our Father in the heavens," a form of address which, says Ulrich Wilckens, the evangelist has assimilated from the "current liturgical forms of address to God in the Jewish tradition."[41] "It has often been stated," writes Millar Burrows, "that every word of this prayer is typically Jewish."[42] So we find in the pre-Christian Kaddish: "Honored and hallowed be his great name in the world, which he created according to his will. May he bring his kingdom to power . . . in your lifetime and in your days." Mark, forty years after the death of Jesus, tells us nothing about the Lord's prayer; nor does Paul. But Joachim Jeremias, with the magic formula that amounts almost to a fetish with him, reckons the Lord's prayer, not even a Christian prayer, to be on linguistic and on material grounds the "bedrock of the tradition."[43]

What is likely to happen when a new doctrine is first of all outlined which conflicts with its familiar surroundings, and almost at once spreads out into a world with a different language? Over a period of time—here not less than forty years and more likely seventy years— a great number of new ideas and conceptions are impressed on it. In the present case, the more speculative the attribution to Jesus himself, the less he can be claimed as originator of the doctrine. Those who, according to the latest research, first made him out to be the Son of God, the Son of Man, the Messiah, the Son of David— the evangelists—naturally endowed him with a voice of authority, full of "Amen, amen" and "Verily I say unto you" and "If you have ears to hear, then hear." The further we get from the year of Jesus' death, the further from Palestinian soil, the more we find authority in material and form, the more fancy and fantasy. So we are left with Bultmann's fifty-year-old discovery that there are few cases in which we can have "any sort of confidence" in ascribing a single one of the sayings to Jesus.[44] Whether the words of Jesus contained in the ascertainably oldest period of the tradition were really spoken by Jesus is something about which we can have "really no certainty."[45] Jeremias the philologist is the blind man who leads Jeremias the lame logician into the ditch, though neither of them seems to have noticed it.

As another piece of bedrock, he gives us the New Testament word "amen," a form of confirmation sometimes rendered as "verily." It occurs commonly in rabbinical literature and in the Qumran writings, but, to quote Jeremias again,[46] Jesus did not use the word simply to strengthen other people's utterances but exclusively to strengthen his own words. We have here, undoubtedly, to use another of our friend Jeremias' favorite expressions, the *ipsissima vox* of our Lord, the very highest.

Joachim Jeremias particularly claims the "cryptic sayings" of Jesus as *ipsissima vox*.[47] Now it has to be admitted that the Gospel according to Mark, like the rest, contains much uncorroborated evidence, much that is tendentious (and much of that not properly worked out), much clumsy editing. But it does not contain Jeremias' boasted cryptic sayings. Instead, there are a great many passages that are simply incomprehensible. There is the obscure piece about slandering the Holy Spirit:

"Truly, I say to you, all sins will be forgiven the sons of men, and whatever blasphemies they utter; but whoever blasphemes against the Holy Spirit never has forgiveness, but is guilty of an eternal sin." (3:28−29)

The context shows that some people had accused Jesus of being possessed by Beezebul (corrupted from Baal-Zebul to Baal-Zebub = Lord of the Flies, later Beelzebub) and that he drove out evil spirits with the help of this superior evil spirit. Mark may have thought this a slander of the Holy Spirit active in Jesus, and that something should be done to counter it. "For they said," so the interpolation reads, "that he had an unclean spirit." Both times, once used with the epithet holy and once with the epithet unclean, the Greek word for spirit is $\pi\nu\epsilon\tilde{\upsilon}\mu\alpha$. Why should man be allowed to slander God but not the Holy Spirit? Science can look forward to a treat here, and gives us a generous helping, but still remains guilty of an only half-complete explanation.* Meanwhile the "sin against the Holy Ghost" has worked its way irresistibly into our vocabulary. In the same way, every cheapjack nowadays can "cast out devils through Beelzebub."

It is not Jesus who speaks in riddles, but the evangelist who finds so much of his material puzzling, so that he has to guess at its meaning. How can the Messiah be David's Son if David himself calls him Lord? How can the Son of Man rise from the dead, since it says in the scriptures that Elijah must come first? To whom will a woman belong at the resurrection if she has married seven brothers one after another and been seven times widowed? Jesus always has the answer. This kind of thing is called *pilpul*, over-subtle disputation between rabbis. But of course Jesus "towers above" his adversaries (Stauffer).[49]

Many talks with children have been fathered on him. The dispute about whether children ought to be baptized is reflected in one of Jesus' sayings ("Let the children come to me"). "Whoever does not receive the kingdom of God like a child," Jesus is reported as saying Mark (10:15), "shall not enter it." But according to Jesus' conception men did not enter the kingdom of God; the kingdom of God came to the Jews on earth. This is the community speaking again. Children believe in miracles, as many a bishop has been glad to discover. Much that was hidden from the wise and clever was clear to the young.

The kingdom of God, comments Wilckens, is open "only to men who are small themselves, and accept it innocently as children accept presents."[50] But children are not so innocent about taking presents, and they do not even believe in miracles any more. Anyone who believes will be blessed, says the ordinary man, like the extraordinary man; and in so saying, significantly corrupts the meaning of the Gospel: only one who believes like a child will be blessed. Perhaps we should do well never to lose sight entirely of Jesus the eschatological crank, to whom such edifying sermons are never unconditionally apt.

---

*The lack of logic has disappeared in Matthew and Luke; perhaps they were drawing on the ominous source Q. Luke changes the meaning round (12:10): one who slanders the Son of Man will be forgiven, but not one who slanders the Holy Spirit. Matthew puts in both variants one after the other (12:31–32). Eduard Schweizer discerns a "missionary principle" here.[4x]

The Lord Jesus cannot have known about all the Jewish proverbs that have been put into his mouth, but perhaps he did use them himself without embarrassment. When the fig-tree that he cursed is withered, Jesus has to say: "Have faith in God" (Wellhausen: "an odd way to demonstrate his faith");[51] he then has to add the not strictly true assurance: "Whatever you ask in prayer, believe that you receive it, and you will" (Mark 11:24, where the meaning must really be the contrary: "If you only believe, you will pray for nothing more than what you will receive", i.e. for faith). When the writer comes across the threat of judgment "everyone will be salted with fire", he hangs a saying on to it:

> "Salt is good; but if the salt has lost its saltness, how will you season it? Have salt in yourselves, and be at peace with one another." (9:50)

Who cannot hear the nightingale, the community, warbling when Jesus has to reassure the disciples (10:29−30) that there is no one who has given up home, brothers or sisters, mother, father or children, or land for his sake or the Gospel's, who will not receive in this age a hundred times as much—houses, brothers and sisters, mothers and children, and land—"with persecutions"; and in the age to come eternal life. There is a guarantee a bit wide of the mark. He who will lose his life for Jesus' sake shall save it (9:35): that much is clear. But what does the next sentence mean, that it shall not profit a man if he gain the whole world but forfeit his life? The editor has simply hung a proverb on without thinking. Wealth is no use to you when you are dead, or "There's no pocket in your shroud," as my barber used to say so nicely in his vernacular.

The most fertile and perhaps the most momentous of the sayings of Jesus in Mark—"Render to Caesar the things that are Caesar's, and to God the things that are God's" to which Logion 100 in the *Gospel of Thomas* adds "And what is mine, give to me")—so exactly corresponds with the interests of the community that we can only be astonished that there are still theologians, including even Bultmann,[52] who ascribe it to Jesus. There is also another saying in Mark which must have been equally significant for the first Christians but about whose meaning theologians have never reached agreement. It refers to the Jewish "purification laws":

275

"There is nothing outside a man which by going into him can defile him; but the things which come out of a man are what defile him." (7:15−19)

Note that this reputed word of Jesus was not taken over by Luke. Käsemann sees here the smashing of the foundations of late Judaism; he sees the *Weltanschauung* of the ancients, with their contrast of sacred and profane and their demonology, let off the hook. Braun hears "unheard-of tones." Joachim Jeremias, on the other hand, and it is hard this time not to agree with him, declares firmly that what is meant here is not a lifting of all the rules in Torah about clean and unclean food, clean and unclean animals; a word of such far-reaching significance could not have appeared in such complete isolation in Mark's text.[53] Paul, again, is "absolutely convinced, as a Christian, that nothing is impure in itself" (Romans 14:14); "only, if a man considers a particular thing impure, then to him it is impure." Thus speaks the lapsed Jew, but all of them rely on the authority of Jesus.

Is the "Old Testament legislation, with its distinction between clean and unclean animals and foods, withdrawn from circulation," as Herbert Braun (1972) believes? On the contrary, says David Flusser (1971), the observation is quite correct even from the Jewish point of view: "Even the foods forbidden in the Bible do not make anyone who eats them ritually unclean, and digestion lifts the distinction between clean and unclean even for the foods themselves." Flusser sees a Jewish saying here, Braun, on account of the extreme un-Jewish attitude, a certainly genuine saying of Jesus.[54] It is hard to understand the dispute. The evangelist (or the community supporting him) was forced to intervene, and so Mark gives the Lord a resounding pronouncement which agrees with both sides.

No, the Gospel according to Mark contains no significant ethical impulses. From that point of view we could well do without it, since we cannot go beyond the act of Jesus' sacrifice described in it. (Zahrnt: "The Son is sacrificed by the Father, and then a sort of compensation deal is made out of it"). In Braun's words, the Gospel is "a book strange to us," with its far-reaching legendary pronouncements, its ancient belief in devils. Why has it made so great an effect, even up to the present day? What is the source of its effectiveness?[55]

In the combination, it would seem, of supernatural miracles with a superman who only reluctantly reveals himself, keeping hidden the true supernatural secret. During the first half of the Gospel, only the devils recognize Jesus (1:34;3:12), then the disciples (8:30;9:9), and finally the Romans, who execute him (15:39−41).

"You are the Holy One of God," cries a man possessed of an unclean spirit (1:24). "Have you come to destroy us?" All the evil spirits recognize him, and Jesus does his best not to let them speak so that they shall not make him known. All the people with unclean spirits rush to meet him and cry: "You are the Son of God!" The spirit called "Legion" ("for we are many"), which later goes into the herd of swine, calls him "Jesus, Son of the Most High God."

At essential points of his narrative, Mark hits on the stylistic device of making Jesus ask his disciples questions. Right on the Syrian border, oddly enough, near Caesarea Philippi, he puts the question to them, who they think he is (8:27). Peter answers in the name of all of them: "You are the Messiah" (". . . to be designated as legend," says Bultmann).[56] Then he gives them strict instructions "not to tell anyone about him." The writer's editorial work follows the line that in spite of all his works, Jesus does not wish his true nature and identity to be made known for the time being. That is why he will not let the devils speak. That is why he tells the lepers he has healed to say nothing to anyone (1:44); likewise the relatives of the twelve-year-old girl he raised from the dead (5:43); likewise the crowd of people (!) who saw how he cured a deaf and dumb man (7:36); likewise that blind man who first saw men as trees, walking, and then saw quite clearly (8:26). This device of the evangelist makes its effect, although the prohibitions seem at first sight to be senseless, because no one observes them (". . . the more he forbade them, the more they published it", 7:36). It is only in the land of the Gentiles that Jesus tells the man whose evil spirits he has sent into the herd of pigs that he should go home and tell his own people what the Lord in his mercy has done for him (5:19).

After Jesus' disciples, through Peter, have recognized Jesus as the Messiah, (8:29), they too share the secret. He lets them know that the Son of Man must suffer and rise again after three days (8:31;9:31;10:33−34). The three disciples who beheld the transfigured Jesus talking with Moses and Elijah are not to tell anyone what they have seen (9:9). No one was to know that they were all going through Galilee together (9:30). No demand to keep silence is laid on the blind beggar Bartimaeus, "son of Timaeus," whom Jesus heals on the roadside at Jericho. Jesus is now approaching Jerusalem, where he will do no more miracles but will declare to Caiphas and his other adversaries what they will not accept: that he is the Messiah, the son of the All Highest, the coming Son of Man. Only the heathen Pilate regards him as king of the Jews, and only the heathen captain under the cross as the Son of God.

Mark has given the disciples the thankless role, as it were, of professionally misunderstanding the Lord. The duller they are, the more irresistibly the hidden majesty of the Lord unfolds. The editor makes the disciples so narrow-minded that, if the story was handed down by them, every misunderstanding in the text could be explained by their denseness ("You do not understand this parable? How then are you to understand any parable?" 4:13).

They learn nothing from the miracles that are continually taking place before their eyes, for their hearts are "hardened." If the disciples ask the meaning of an obscure lesson, he replies (7:18): "Are you as dull as the rest?" And when they continue to think about food although he can multiply bread and fishes at will, he goes on (8:17): "Have you no inkling yet? Do you still not understand?"

"Relentlessly," as Wilckens says,[57] Mark exposes the disciples' weaknesses. They declare they will die with him, but they leave him alone in death. They cannot stay awake for their Master's sake for a single hour. "It is only the active, secret Messianic self-awareness of Jesus (that shapes) the events and their interconnection," writes Albert Schweitzer.[58] Jesus speaks to the disciples in parables; but it is only to them that he reveals the parables' "solution." That is what Mark says, and as his only evidence, he immediately expounds the all too clear meaning of the parable of the sower (4:1–20). And now we penetrate to the very heart of the whole arrangement, and it is as dark as ever. What is Jesus' object? Does he want to save as many as possible, all if possible, or just a certain number? Of course, we cannot know what he really wanted. We can see only what the evangelist imagines, and one result of that is that he attributes to Jesus a deliberately obscure manner of speaking (Wilckens):

And he said to them, "To you has been given the secret of the kingdom of God, but for those outside everything is in parables; so that they may indeed see but not perceive, and may indeed hear but not understand; lest they should turn again, and be forgiven." 4:11–12)

There are of course a lot of theologians who are quite sure that Jesus intended to abandon a number of his hearers, quite possibly the majority of them, to their obduracy or impenitence. That would mean that the parables were not meant to make something clear, but to keep something hidden. Others only find it possible to maintain the authenticity of these ostensible words of Jesus by postulating a false translation; others again blame the evangelist for a misunderstanding.[59]

But there is also a quite simple and credible explanation. We do not have to assume that Jesus deliberately wanted to leave men trapped in their own hardheartedness. Actually, the text of Mark relies here on the prophet Isaiah, where it says:

And he said, "Go and say to this people:
'Hear and hear, but do not
    understand;
see and see, but do not perceive.'
Make the heart of this people fat,
    and their ears heavy,
    and shut their eyes;
lest they see with their eyes,
    and hear with their ears,
and understand with their hearts,
    and turn and be healed." (6:9–10)

Either the author of Mark, or an earlier writer, found material for his elitist theory in Isaiah and worked it into the text; certainly Jesus himself did not. Matthew and Luke break through Mark's policy of secrecy occasionally; also they reduce the slow-wittedness with which Mark endows the disciples. Where Matthew takes over some fault on the part of a disciple from his Marcan model, "he makes a practice of toning it down" (Joachim Gnilka).[60] But both of them accept Mark's theory of the parables and of impenitence: Jesus speaks in parables in order that his hearers shall not understand; only the disciples are to know the secrets of the kingdom of heaven (Matthew) or the kingdom of God (Luke).

279

The texts of all the Synoptics present Jesus' message as a secret message, intended for the gathering together of the chosen, although it is by no means certain that Jesus himself had such an elite in mind. Certainly, ideas which to modern eyes look so misguided were to be found in the apocalyptic thinking of the sects of that period. At Qumran, certain manuscripts of the "men of error" were not allowed to be circulated.[61] And the early Christian community, too, used to strengthen themselves inwardly with the consciousness of having been chosen. The New Testament authors never asked themselves what Jesus might have thought, but what they themselves thought about him. Thus, God appears in the joyful tidings as one who has hardened the hearts of mankind and condemned them as a proof of his own majesty, and even Jesus as one who, for the majority, did not open up the way to salvation but withheld it from them.

We cannot of course assert that Jesus himself did not hold such misguided ideas; once again, we simply know nothing about it. We can only ask what value we are to accord to the earliest and least inauthentic account of Jesus* as a source of enlightenment, when it contains essentially the story of a man who drove out devils and worked miracles and who, for reasons we can no longer discern, deliberately sought to be put to death by an earthly jurisdiction; the story of a man said to have worked miracles in which, as such, we cannot believe; who, commanding belief because of those miracles, foretold events which never happened, and whose credibility after death can only be maintained by the further miracle of resurrection.

It is set out in Mark almost without any grounds that the High Priests, Pharisees and lawyers wanted to kill Jesus. Their convictions are hostile to his and vice versa. He challenges their authority with his miracles, even on the Sabbath; he insults them, and they are envious of him. That is all we get out of it. How can that satisfy us? The real reasons can remain hidden, since Jesus has

---

*The end of Mark gives the impression of having been broken off; he leaves out the climax of his story, the description of the disciples' amazement after their eyes were opened through the resurrection. In the ending of Mark generally held to be authentic (16:1−8), the Galilean women are commanded by an angel to tell the disciples that the Lord will go before them into Galilee and that they will see him there. In the version of the ending not thought to be genuine (16:9-20), the disciples are given special powers and Jesus is then "taken up into heaven" and takes his seat at the right hand of God. It is never reported where it was he last saw his disciples, in Jerusalem or in Galilee. Thus, the missionary command, the only international passage in the whole of Mark, is found in this unauthentic ending.

to die to fulfil God's holy will. The other three evangelists, twenty or thirty years after Mark, were as weak on historical truth as he. But for their own reassurance they put in more motivation, and this requirement culminates in the Gospel according to John.

Here Jesus must die because, on the one hand, he breaks the Law, Torah, above all because he breaks the Sabbath; and on the other hand, because he has made himself the equal of God (5:18). His opponents achieve their object because, as Luke also says, he might have been a nuisance to the Romans. Even his opponents were but the tools of a higher will, although in all humility. The Jesus who, rejoicing over his expulsion of the devils, declares that the kingdom of God is here, is not to be found in Mark and no more indeed in John; he is the offspring of a great deal of thought.

As for Jesus in the flesh, all we can find in Mark is the "Galilean wandering preacher and miracle-doctor" (Rudolf Otto),[62] who will always reward blind faith with a miracle, and will do as much for a clever answer ("Even the dogs under the table eat the children's scraps"). The charge of Sabbath-breaking is brought against him by "false witnesses," not even by the high priest in the Council chamber. His talk of the coming end of the world, of the false Christs and of the appearance of the Son of Man at the Last Judgment (13:1−32), seems almost to have been stuck on. The Sabbath-breaker and the prophet of the last times: they recede in a remarkable way and never fit together to form a unity, so that we are at once back in the same confusion about the figure we had first outlined.

Jesus only says once in Mark's Gospel, and that in a passage (1:15) that theologians do not even consider authentic,[63] that the time is fulfilled and the kingdom of God is come. He speaks of the coming of the Son of Man and the Kingdom of God a second time (". . . some of those standing here will not taste death") immediately after Peter's acknowledgement that he is the Messiah at Caesarea Philippi, i.e., at the turning-point of Mark's story. This, like everything said about the Son of Man, is suspected of being an invention of the Christian community. Then he speaks again about the coming of the Son of Man two days before his last Passover (13:26−27), in a sermon about the Last Judgment which is quite obviously distilled from Jewish apocalyptic and Christian ideas. "Brother will betray brother to death, and the father his child; children will turn against their parents and send them to their death."

The entire account of the Passion by Mark, to which no kind of credible motives have been added by other evangelists, must be read not only side by side with the Jewish apocalypse but also against the background of the war which the Jews launched against the Romans in 66. Jesus prophesies about the temple that not one stone will remain upon another, that all will be thrown down: either the evangelist foresees the catastrophe of the year 70, or else he has already seen it:

> And as he came out of the temple, one of his disciples said to him, "Look, Teacher, what wonderful stones and what wonderful buildings!" And Jesus said to him, "Do you see these great buildings? There will not be left here one stone upon another, that will not be thrown down."

There will be wars and rumors of wars; nation will make war against nation; there will be earthquakes; there will be famines. All this is the beginning of the so-called "Messianic woes" out of which the new age will arise. But the end has therefore not yet come.

The troubles of the Christian community are described in detail. The followers of Jesus will be handed over to the courts. They will be flogged in synagogues. But they are not to worry, for they will be able to defend themselves. The Holy Spirit will inspire them. Joachim Jeremias, we have read, gives the Lord God credit that he will not allow these times of suffering — the symbolic three days — to run their full course, but will shorten them for the sake of his chosen people. [64]

The dreadful time cannot last too long, as the evangelists see it, because Jesus tells his hearers that they should pray that all this will not happen "in winter." False Messiahs will arise ("it is I") and will do signs and wonders. Even the chosen, the holy ones, the righteous would be misled, "if such a thing were possible." There is only a holy remnant that, in accordance with God's will, cannot be led astray. The sun and moon will lose their light, the stars will fall from the sky, the powers that hold heaven and earth together will be shaken — and the Son of Man will appear.

It is thought today to be very unlikely that Jesus prophesied all this. "There is at least the possibility," thinks Bultmann with unwonted caution, that the verses were simply put into Jesus' mouth. Leaving Jesus out of it altogether, what we have is obviously a "Jewish apocalypse in a Christian adaptation."[65] Hölscher even thinks that these apocalyptic passages were taken from a kind of leaflet that is reckoned to have appeared about the years 39 to 41, when the emperor Caligula had his statue put in the temple in Jerusalem.[66] Pesch too (who, though a Catholic, collaborated on the Protestant *Wilckens Bible*) puts the writing of the leaflet at about the year 40, i.e., some time after the death of Jesus, but he thinks it was misused thirty years later in view of the destruction of the temple to stimulate an early expectation of the last times; at the same time a counter-operation to circulate verses warning against such misuse was mounted.[67]

The more the scholars, the more the opinions. Did Mark, as Marxsen supposes,[68] expecting an imminent parousia, wish to exhort the readers of his scripture "to set off at once" away from Jerusalem?* Was Mark the spokesman for a popular missionary movement in Palestine which knew itself to be in opposition to the Christian community in Jerusalem (Etienne Trocmé)?[69] None of that can ever be ascertained. Up to now, we have said nothing at all about who the evangelist was, where, and for whom, he wrote, whether is was on Palestinian soil or in the broad Roman empire, whether it was for Jews *and* Gentiles or exclusively for Gentiles. Mark seems to know the Graeco-Roman routine better than he does the Jewish festival customs; but why did he so persistently put in references to the obscure province of Galilee? Could "Galilee" have been the codeword for some kind of armed insurrection?

The evangelist has found it possible to mention a number of the details of contemporary events, although otherwise he knew no details and probably only had fragments to work from. Enormous influence was exercised on the Jews of that period by a self-

---

*The discovery published in March 1972 that Chapter 6:52−53 of Mark's Gospel had been reconstructed from a papyrus fragment, written in Greek, which could be dated not later than the year 50 C.E. deserves no sort of credit (" . . . for they did not understand about the loaves, but their hearts were hardened. And when they had crossed over,they came to land at Gennesaret, and moored to the shore"). The originator of this new theory, the Catalan professor Jose O'Callaghan, was not even working from the original document but was using a reproduction. On it two letters are legible in each of three lines and four letters in one line, i.e., altogether ten letters from a presumed reconstructed text of a total of one hundred and twelve letters. Papyrus experts have placed the fragments very roughly between 50 B.C.E. and 50 C.E., because they are written in an ornate style, which could just as well mean, without any other indications, that the writing was completed between 100 B.C.E. and 100 C.E. The only other writings found in the cave near Qumran in which the fragment was discovered were Old Testament scriptures. Pater Benoit, head of the *Ecole Biblique et Archéologique* in the Old City of Jerusalem, comments: "It may well be psychologically difficult to recognize the authorship of such a discovery as doubtful."[70]

appointed leader called Menachem, whose name — it means "comforter" — was used in later times instead of the description "Messiah." He is said to have been the son, or the grandson, either of "Judas of the Galileans," founder of the Zealots (a kind of resistance party) or else of Judas' reputed father, the Galilean "robber chieftain" Hezekiah, whom the young king Herod had had executed, according to Josephus. (The precise relationship is confused, but the spirit of resistance is clearly in the family.)[71]

Let us remember that the Zealots were sometimes called simply "the Galileans." Theologians believe that Messianic claims were imputed to all three, to the "robber chieftain" Hezekiah, to "Judas of the Galileans" and to Menachem, though we have no idea whether the people expected any apocalyptic or eschatological manifestations from such figures; the lawyers and the Qumran monks were not the whole of the people. The upper class (Sadducees) and the lowest class (Am-Haaretz) might at least have expected the Messiah. But even the Pharisees, who set the tone in religious questions, may well have been divided into Messianic and non-Messianic wings.

Rabbinical prophecies proliferated about the Zealot Messiah Menachem after his violent death in 66 C.E. His rapid end — he was killed by other insurgents in Jerusalem — clearly made a great impression: the legend has him born at the time when in fact he died, and puts the event in a royal palace in Bethlehem. As a child he was ripped from his mother's womb by winds and storms. Cow and ox (not ox and ass) have a part to play. It was said to his mother about him: "We are quite sure that the temple was destroyed on his account, but that it will be built up on his account."[72]

Mark cannot possibly have known the legend, but he could have had the historical figure in mind. Menachem on his own authority gave the signal for the start of the rising against the Romans which ended with the destruction of the temple. He plundered the armory in the fortress of Masada, armed his followers, and (we are indebted to Josephus for this account)[73] advanced on Jerusalem "like a king" at the head of an armed host. He led the siege of the Roman garrison which had taken up position in the fortress of Antonia.

He held out for four weeks in Jerusalem and in that short time, as his enemies at any rate found out, he became an "intolerable tyrant" (Josephus). He set fire to the city archives "in order to destroy the record of debts owing to the money-lenders and to make the collection of debts impossible." A priestly group around a man called Eleazar installed Menachem in the temple,* "to which he proceeded to say his prayers in a splendid robe, decked in royal garments and followed by a crowd of armed supporters." Menachem, who is described as one learned in the scriptures, escaped from the massacre but was caught before the city gates and "put to death with frightful tortures." (The Roman soldiers then offered a safe passage to Eleazar's men, but cut them down as soon as they had laid down their arms, and that on a Sabbath.)

Every word about the temple which Mark says Jesus was falsely accused of having spoken, but which John says he really spoke — that he would throw the temple down and build another in three days — might perhaps "have first found its way into the Gospel tradition after the destruction of Jerusalem," in the view of the theologian Hugo Gressmann. This is by no means impossible. Gressman also thinks that Menachem's ceremonial entry into Jerusalem as a king might have served the author of Mark's Gospel as model for his description of "a similar event in the life of Jesus Christ."[74]

Christian and Jewish myths can often not be kept apart. In the Revelation of John a child is born to a woman, a son "destined to rule all nations with an iron rod." This child was snatched up to God and his throne, so that nothing happened to him; but the rabbinical legend says of Menachem: " . . . ripped from his mother as a child by winds and storms."[75] Like Jesus, Menachem lives on after his death in the timelessness of a misplaced myth; the name and the family-conception become all one. As the first and last great triumph against the Romans is connected with Menachem, so events after the catastrophe are reinterpreted. The Messiah has indeed come, but only as a little, unknown child, immediately taken back to God's throne; the man who gave the impetus for the destruction of the temple is now not born until the day the temple is destroyed.

---

*According to Matthew (23:35) and Luke (11:51), Jesus inveighs against Jerusalem as the murderer of prophets, and the innocent blood spilt on the ground from Abel to Zechariah son of Berachiah, "whom you murdered between the sanctuary and the altar." Both murder and man are unknown — and in Jerusalem, with the possible exception of Jesus himself, we know of no prophet being killed, though one could say figuratively of Menachem that he was killed "between the sanctuary and the altar."

Menachem, for the benefit of Mark's narration, goes up to Jerusalem "like a king" at the head of a great crowd, occupies the temple, is learned in the scriptures, is chased out by the priestly party, tortured and killed, all within four weeks. Mark could have heard of it, he could have seen it, could even have been an eyewitness. If we start with the Menachem uprising, and then add the "woe-to-Jerusalem" Jesus who was flogged to the bone under the procurator Albinus in the year 62, and also the mocking of the Jewish king Agrippa in Alexandria in 38 with the help of the "Carabas" caricature-figure, we cannot help wondering whether the description of the last days and weeks of Jesus was not modelled far more on events after his death than on the actual facts (which may well have been unknown to the evangelist and only transmitted in scraps of poetry). There were already historians well before Jesus' time who took care with facts; but the four evangelists (or, if they knew nothing, the writers of the sources on which they drew) were not among them, not even Mark. As Karl Ludwig Schmidt so rightly says, the oldest tradition of Jesus is "outside history."[76]

We are quite exhausted by our effort to establish a concrete Jesus in his most credible witness, Mark. As William Wrede has already recognized, "we have to say quite clearly that Mark no longer has any genuine perception of the historical life of Jesus."[77] The man remains unrevealed in the tangled thicket of old verses. No analytical path, no recognizable connection leads from some "historical" preacher called Jesus to the Christ preached by the faith.

Mark's Jesus has no sensible explanation to offer us either for his own suffering or for suffering in general. Unless we believe that Jesus himself intended to give up his life "as a ransom for many" (10:45), then all that is left to us is a religious legend of the first Christians. That is the "holy remnant" that remains under the line after we have done the "critical subtraction sum" (Martin Kähler). Jesus has vanished into the incomprehensible.

11.   What has been made of him

The world cannot be ruled according to the Gospel, for the Word is too small and too limited; it has little effect; the ordinary man does not accept it; and so no outward authority can be founded on it.[1]
—Luther

Europe can thank the Gospel of Jesus Christ for the position it has achieved in the world in the past.
—Heinemann

Luke, the story-teller, is not only the *homme à femmes*; he alone among the four evangelists represents a completely political attitude of social criticism. Anyone who in Roman times ever rebelled against his fate of exploitation and oppression can appeal to him. If we examine the historical effect that Christian teaching is claimed to have had on countries and people throughout the world; and if, on the other hand, we investigate why the communities calling themselves Christian have achieved no social impulse, why "Jesus, the great blessing for all mankind" (Gollwitzer)[3] has not really achieved anything at all; the challenge that faces us from the start is not Jesus the Jew but Luke the Hellenist.

The word "poor" ($\pi\tau\omega\chi\acute{o}\varsigma$) is found ten times in Luke, five times each in Mark and Matthew. The word "rich" ($\pi\lambda o\acute{u}\sigma\iota o\varsigma$) is used by Luke eleven times, by Mark twice and by Matthew three times. The contrast "poor-rich" is retained and worked upon only by

287

Luke. He is the one who makes Jesus the child of poor people; the sacrifice brought by Mary and Joseph for Mary's purification after the birth of her child is that prescribed for poor people, two doves.

In the parable of the great feast, it is only Luke who has the poor and the maimed, the blind and the lame invited — and he really does mean poor and maimed, blind and lame. Only Luke's Gospel has the story of the anonymous rich man and the poor Lazarus (whose name means "whom God helps"). The two characters have no connection with one another; the moral of the story is simply that the rich man must suffer torture in Hades merely because he was rich, whereas the poor man Lazarus, because he enjoyed no good times while he was alive, is comforted and compensated after death. Perhaps the rich man's failing lies in his never having taken any notice of Lazarus who lay before the rich man's gate; that he never treated his sores nor assuaged his hunger. But why did the two of them never exchange a word? Because the parable refers to no more than the simple reversal of social conditions; there is a settlement — after death.

In the *Magnificat* of the Virgin Mary, too, Luke assumes an attitude of class warfare: the Lord, cries Mary exultantly:

He has put down the mighty from
   their thrones,
and exalted those of low degree;
he has filled the hungry with good
   things,
and the rich he has sent empty away.

There is nothing new in that: the *Apocalypse of Enoch*, which lies behind the New Testament scriptures in more than one connection, already contains the verdict: "Woe to you who are rich, for you have given yourselves over to your wealth; you must leave your treasures, for you did not think of the Most High in the days of your wealth . . . Woe to you who deal badly with your neighbor, for as you do shall you be requited . . . Woe to you, lying tongues . . . But you who suffer, fear not, for salvation shall be your portion: bright light will shine upon you and you will hear the voice of the Prince of Heaven . . . Woe to you fools, for you will be destroyed by your folly."

Compared with his model, Mark, Luke finds a voice of his own. It is picked up from the old scriptures. Certainly the poor, uneducated Jews of Palestine, the Am-haaretz, hated the middle and upper classes more than they ever hated a foreign army, or, as Rabbi Hija said, more than Israel hated the Gentiles. Rabbi Akiba's saying has been handed down: "When I was still an Am-Haaretz, I said, Ah, would I could meet a lawgiver, I would bite him like an ass." Rabbi Jonahan said: "One may tear an Am-Haaretz to pieces like a fish." Anyone who wanted to marry the daughter of an Am-Haaretz ran foul of the sentence in the Talmud: "Cursed is he who sleeps with an animal."[4]

The so-called Sermon on the Mount in Matthew is a made-up affair; laws always have to be proclaimed on a mountain, like those proclaimed on Sinai. But Luke, in contrast, spoke to his disciples "on level ground" in a somewhat politically colored sermon. In his *Wintermärchen* (XIII), Heinrich Heine sympathizes with his "poor cousin" Jesus in the view of the town of Paderborn:

"With a different text, when you preached on the mount,
Your words might have sounded oddly,
But your wit, your talent would have sufficed
And you might have redeemed the godly!"

Now Matthew redeems them, provided of course they are rich and godly. His sermon refers to all men without discrimination, rich and poor, high and low alike. Even the rich can be sorrowful and be meek, even the mighty hunger and thirst after righteousness, after conversion to the will of God.

Those of whom Matthew speaks suffer hunger and thirst not literally but in a symbolic sense; they want to follow God's ways:

"Blessed are those who mourn,
for they shall be comforted.
Blessed are the meek, for they
shall inherit the earth.
Blessed are those who hunger
and thirst for righteousness, for they
shall be satisfied."(5:4−6)

When Matthew speaks of the poor, he means, as his Qumranic model means, the humble, the poor before God who stand before God with empty hands in the knowledge of their spiritual poverty. But the one who preaches this sermon cannot also be the author of the sermon "on level ground" in Luke, which only superficially resembles it. Luke really means the poor, the hungry, the weeping:

And he lifted up his eyes on his
  disciples, and said:
"Blessed are you poor, for yours is
  the kingdom of God.
Blessed are you that hunger
  now, for you shall be satisfied.
Blessed are you that weep now, for
  you shall laugh."

As in the parable of the rich man and the poor Lazarus, he
distinguishes rigorously between rich and poor, full and hungry,
between people who are well off ("who laugh now") and people
who are in want ("who weep now"). Everything will be all right for
the poor, the hungry and the weeping after Day X; the rich, the full
and the laughing will be completely rejected. They haven't a
chance, because they had all they wanted in this life:

"But woe to you that are rich,
for you have received your consolation.
Woe to you that are full now,
for you shall hunger.
Woe to you that laugh now, for
you shall mourn and weep." (6:24−25)

Once more he is preaching a radical reversal of social conditions:
down shall be up and up, down. Let us remind ourselves again that
Mark and Paul had never heard either of Mark's Sermon on the
Mount or of the corresponding address in Luke. Both are
inventions and further developments of the community.

This protest against social conditions is only expressed in Luke,
who knew the Graeco-Roman world and seems not to have been
particularly interested in theology. Even the so-called "proto-
Communism" of the first Christians in Jerusalem seems to go back
to Luke. There is no evidence for it except in the Acts of the
Apostles, which Luke wrote:

Now the company of those who believed were of one heart and
soul, and no one said that any of the things which he possessed
was his own, but they had everything in common. And with
great power the apostles gave their testimony to the resurrection
of the Lord Jesus, and great grace was upon them all. There was
not a needy person among them, for as many as were possessors

of lands or houses sold them, and brought the proceeds of what was sold and laid it at the apostles' feet; and distribution was made to each as any had need. (4:32—35)

Actually we only hear of one man, Joseph called Barnabas, a Cypriot, who sold his field and laid the money at the feet of the apostles. His action is represented as something rather special, as an exception. And in contrast we hear of one Ananias who brought the apostles only part of the money realized from the sale of his field. (He dies on the spot.) "We can clearly see," writes Ulrich Wilckens, "that the tradition on which Luke draws told only of rumored acts of individual Christians. Luke has taken these to be examples of the conduct of the community and has thus described an ideal picture of the early apostolic community."[5] A community on Communist lines, Conzelmann points out, could only exist if, first of all, production was organized. In Jewish groups such as that at Qumran, he says, that was the case, but not among the first Christians.[6]

So it is rather touching to read what Hans Kilian believes he has discovered: that the naked force of the Roman emperors was broken by the attempt to repress those early Christian communes, which, he says, not only preached an end to social divisions and the oppression of slave-owning as a theoretical doctrine, but also practiced it among the followers of Jesus of Nazareth.[7]

We read nothing of any such social achievements. So is the sociologist Eugen Lemberg going too far when he assumes that Christianity was conceived as a movement of the "left"?[8] Luke is "left", that is clear enough; his Gospel inspires a spirit of rebellion, though even he has to defer his revolution to a time after the death of the individual, or to Day X. So is the Bible, as Ernst Bloch says, "the most revolutionary religious book of them all"?[9] We should like to know what effect it has actually had, and where the Marxist theoretician Karl Kautsky gets his idea that the class-hatred of the modern proletariat has scarcely attained such fanatical forms as that of the Christians.[10]

There is little evidence of such a rebellious spirit. Of course, the enemies of the Christians blamed them for all the evils of the time, as in the passage by that opponent of Christianity, Celsus, which is so well fitted to give comfort to all those who see a world-shaking novelty in the rebelliousness of present-day students, teachers and pupils. (Of course we only have the—quite fair—refutation of

Celsus on the part of the worthy Origen, and have to reconstruct Celsus from that. The burning of books, as of men, was not Hitler's own invention.) "In private houses also," says Celsus,

> we see wool-workers, cobblers, laundry-workers, and the most illiterate and bucolic yokels, who would not dare to say anything at all in front of their elders and more intelligent masters. But whenever they get hold of children in private and some stupid women with them, they let out some astounding statements as, for example, that they must not pay any attention to their fathers and schoolteachers, but must obey them; they say that these talk nonsense and have no understanding, and that in reality they neither know nor are able to do anything good, but are taken up with mere empty chatter. But they alone, they say, know the right way to live, and if the children would believe them, they would become happy and make their home happy as well. And if just as they are speaking they see one of the schoolteachers coming, or some intelligent person, or even the father himself, the more cautious of them flee in all directions, but the more reckless urge the children on to rebel. They whisper to them that in the presence of their fathers and their schoolmasters they do not feel able to explain anything to the children, since they do not want to have anything to do with the silly and obtuse teachers who are totally corrupted and far gone in wickedness and who inflict punishment on the children. But, if they like, they should leave father and their schoolmasters, and go along with the women and little children who are their playfellows to the wool-dresser's shop, or to the cobbler's or the washerwoman's shop, that they may learn perfection. And by saying this they persuade them.[11]

Celsus may have recorded this complaint about the year 180. So even then the patriarchal system of authority of the Roman Empire seems to have been broken down, presumably, not only (perhaps not at all) by the Christians. The emperor's order was no longer enforced. Of what was the Christian following in the first two centuries composed? We read of beautiful women who, according to the Acts of the Apostles, thronged around Paul and his companion Silas in Thessalonica, present-day Salonika; Luke, the ladies' man, tells it so. But for the rest, we can presumably take

292

it that Paul's following might more or less have corresponded to that opinion that the missionary expresses about the Corinthian congregation in the First Letter to the Corinthians:

> For consider your call, brethren; not many of you were wise according to worldly standards, not many were powerful, not many were of noble birth; but God chose what is foolish in the world to shame the wise, God chose what is weak in the world to shame the strong, God chose what is low and despised in the world, even things that are not, to bring to nothing things that are. (1:26−28)

This must refer to people of the lowest classes, small handworkers, slaves, freedmen, their wives. But the question is, what is this new movement doing for its members? They are referred to the other world, to the cosmic revolution, to the end of the world, to an hour whose coming they cannot influence, to the time after death for which they should prepare themselves. The "differences between freemen and slaves, noble and base" had already ceased to mean anything in the mystery religions, says Bornkamm,[12] but were they any better off in their daily lives as a result? It seems that oppression and poverty remained unaffected by the religious arrangements.

True, the mouth of that unequalled man of sorrows, the Biblical "Job," was stopped by "heavenly decree" (Kant).[13] "But is that an answer?" wrote Heine on his bed of suffering.[14] Paul, in his second Letter to the Corinthians (4:17), found another, one in which Heine at any rate might again not have believed:

> "For this slight momentary affliction is preparing for us an eternal weight of glory beyond all comparison. . . "

(This is what the early Christians gave out. No discovery has ever done more to make things easier for men than that of a heaven, thought Lichtenberg.)[15]

Slaves were expressly admonished by Paul to stay with their masters. Even those who had a chance of becoming free were to remain in their station of slavery. For the slave is a freedman of Christ, and the free man a slave of Christ. All Christians are sold for a high price to become God's servants. "So brethren, in whatever state each was called, there let him remain with God" (1 Corinthians 7:24). And not only before God.

The slave should be obedient to his earthly master in every way, with a pure heart, in fear of the Lord (Letter to the Colossians, ascribed to Paul 3:22 in Wilckens' translation). The master is to be just and fair to his slave. This teaching differs in no way from that of the contemporary Seneca, whom Engels calls the "uncle of Christianity":[16] the slave is to be a "co-slave," a fellow-creature.[17] "In Paul's opinion, as in that of all the first Christians," comments Wilckens, "faith in Christ brings all inequality among men to an end, but at the same time it does not demand its elimination."[18] This was no revolutionary religion, but rather one which promised compensation to men when Christ should appear, and which also offered them an outlet for their fantasies of revenge. If Paul could already think that it was no longer worth reorganizing this run-down time of the world, the new teaching soon finds its way back to the everyday paths, not to be changed again right up to Luther's exhortation to the poor, "Suffering, suffering, cross, cross — that is the Christians' right."[19] So we find in the First Letter of Peter 2:18−21 (which Professor Joachim Jeremias has recently reclaimed for the right Peter):[20]

> Servants, be submissive to your masters with all respect, not only to the kind and gentle but also to the overbearing. For one is approved if, mindful of God, he endures pain while suffering unjustly. For what credit is it, if when you do wrong and are beaten for it you take it patiently? But if when you do right and suffer for it you take it patiently, you have God's approval. For to this you have been called, because Christ also suffered for you, leaving you an example, that you should follow in his steps.

Submission to the will of authority is everywhere demanded. For the early expectation of the return of the Lord had proved false, as the so-called second Letter of Peter complained:

> First of all you must understand this, that scoffers will come in the last days with scoffing, following their own passions and saying, "Where is the promise of his coming? For ever since the fathers fell asleep, all things have continued as they were from the beginning of creation."

The scoffers do not want to hear about the Day of Judgment and of the damnation of ungodly men. But one day before God is like a thousand years, and the Day of Judgment, with a new heaven and a new earth, will come:

> The Lord is not slow about his promise as some count slowness, but is forbearing toward you, not wishing that any should perish, but that all should reach repentance. (3:9)

This second Letter of Peter, in which it significantly mentions "Paul, our friend and brother," no more comes from the apostle Peter than does the first, it is hardly necessary to point out. There is no evidence of its use before the beginning of the third century. To arrive at a proper assessment of this change in the expectation of the end we need, as Conzelmann, with presumably unintentional irony, put it so exactly, "not knowlege of the facts, but knowledge of the time."[21]

But what was it that changed in the Christian content of the new movement during the first two centuries? For we shall be continually coming up against a statement first briefly formulated by Martin Hengel, professor at Erlangen: "Jesus is the man from whom the greatest effects in the generality of world history flowed."[22] But world history does not mean saving souls for eternal life, but material changes, material effects on existing conditions with lasting and developing consequences. That would mean that primitive Christianity must, in the first place, have been unthinkable without Jesus, and that secondly it must have given an impetus that changed wide areas of the world and made whole ages pass otherwise than they would have done without the Christian impulse. Is that really so?

Obviously this great, this all too great theme would be unacceptably limited if we were prepared to acquiesce in the statement that Christianity has gambled away the revolutionary impulse that we find, for instance, in Luke. Even Gollwitzer's pretty formula that the "victory *of* Christianity" has been a victory of the upper classes *over* Christianity[23] does not really get us much further. Siegfried Kracauer writes of the "well-worn experience that the community, as if on their own initiative, adapts for its own purposes everything that is caught in its net. They gulp down all the ideas with which they are fed, and in so far as they meet their own unexpressed requirements they often completely distort them from their original meaning."[24]

More correct, or at any rate more sound, than Gollwitzer's are the conclusions of the Marxist critics. Engels and Lenin agree that in those days there was no real way out for the enslaved, the oppressed and the impoverished. Every organized revolt would have been suppressed. There was a way out, of course, but not in this world. Engels writes: "As things lay, there could only be a religious way out."[25] Lenin puts it rather more sarcastically: "Religion teaches humility and patience here below to him who works and suffers need all his life, and comforts him with the hope of a heavenly reward. But to him who lives by the work of others religion teaches charity here below, with which he can offer them a nice, cheap vindication of his whole life of exploitation and can buy himself tickets for heavenly bliss at a bargain price." Münzer, long before Lenin, called that "chalking up drinks on Christ's account."[26]

Lenin regards a belief in a better land to come as "irresistible" in such circumstances, which must mean that in his presumably expert view, Christianity or no Christianity, a revolutionary situation did not exist. The teaching of the Christians was "the ideal accommodation in a world in need of comfort" (Martin Robbe).[27] Belief in the reason of the Greeks had dried up; belief in another world on the "other side" was common to all classes. The Christians, with the expectation of the last times that they had taken on from the Jews, were able to overtrump the wishful mood and give it a goal. Only from the Jewish hope of a Messiah could this physically perceptible man have emerged, in whom God had come down to men and who would draw them up to God. Mithras,* for instance, who for a time during the second and third centuries was the best-seller in the competition among the religious systems, had been born of a virgin rock and had never been a tangible man.

The Christians had an advantage over the cult of Mithras in the canon of their holy scriptures that they had taken over from the Jews, as also in the intensity of their consciousness of sin, both inherited from the Old Testament. Like the Old Testament, Jesus' stories of God's love and God's judgment were tailored for a childlike understanding. We know of no Paul, Luke, John among the followers of Mithras, though that is not the whole reason why

---

*He had come down to earth from heaven in order, amid heavy labors, to kill a bull ("horn of salvation"), whose marrow and blood he changed into the heavenly foods bread and wine. The faithful were strengthened in this way for their ascent to the most high god Ormuzd (Ahura-Mazdah). Mithras was the mediator between Ormuzd, the god of light in heaven and Ahriman, alias Satan, alias Belial, alias Beelzebub, in the depth of the earth. His birthday was celebrated on 25 December.

the Christians destroyed all the scriptures of competing sects. We have no evidence either that heretics were sniffed out and expelled among the Mithraists; they clearly lacked the scholarly and organizational infrastructure.

Mithras was strong among the Roman legions; in contrast to Christianity, he excluded women completely. The emperor Aurelian (270–275), finding that the emperor-worship that held the empire together was exhausted, made Mithraism the state religion. But Mithraism did not contain what had been expected of it. The emperor Constantine, who ruled 306–337, recognized basically the power of integration that lay within the Christian faith, the system built up from the Jewish ethic of obedience. "In complete inner independence from all Christian perceptions" (as Jacob Burckhardt writes) this non-Christian commissar of God lent his support to the Christian bishops at the council held at Nicea in the year 325 fot the purpose of formulating their religious dogmas.

His court theologian Eusebius saw in this unbaptized Caesar, who called himself "Pontifex maximus" and had himself described as Helios, i.e., as the sun-god (a Mithraic figure), "a kind of common bishop" of the Christian church; Constantine himself called himself "bishop of external affairs."[28] He had the new capital of the empire, Constantinople, dedicated in the year 330 not by a Christian but by a Neo-Platonist.

No religious movement could have been reoriented in a more unprincipled way than was the Christian church under Constantine, who is said to have had himself hastily baptized on his deathbed in 337. Not ten percent of the people of the empire followed the Christian teachings when he came to power in 306. But the emperor, who chained small farmers to the ground of their holdings in 332, knew how to bind what had hitherto been the Christian opposition to his government bandwagon. At the council of Arles (314), the church laid a curse on every deserter from the emperor's army. There was no more about voluntary poverty, no more about pacifism, about scorn for the things of this world. Observance of the Christian teachings was driven out of the world into the monastary and the almshouse. Church and state announced their engagement. The state church, to which the man Jesus had fallen victim, sat at the right hand of God, and for that now God had become man.[29]

Forty years after the death of Constantine, the church had already acquired a tenth of the whole of the landed property in Rome's western empire, a figure that in western Europe rose to a third during the Middle Ages. After 416, only Christians were recruited into the army. The kingdom not of this world built up its earthly power.

Towards the end of the fourth century, the first heretic was executed with the sword in Trier. The persecuted had become persecutors. The famous woman philosopher Hypatia, compared by Ernst Bloch with Angela Davis,[30] was pulled from her coach by a Christian mob in Alexandria in 415, dragged into a church, stripped naked and torn to pieces. It could not be permitted in God's state, surmised the great Augustine (354—430), as the Roman state permitted it, to consent without discrimination to the expression by philosophers of different and opposing views. Further, such freethinkers should be suffered in God's state "not without discrimination and not without correction."[31]

This greatest spirit of the old church, the discoverer of "original sin," summarized the disruptive opportunism of his church once again in a brilliant theology. Rome he called the second, the western Babylon. He saw in the Roman empire the last world state. The first had been founded by the fratricide Cain. God's state on the other hand finds itself on a pilgrimage with its earthly part as it were imprisoned by the world state. The world state, so long as it exists, is to bring peace and guarantee it, and Christ therefore, owes the world state all support.[32]

This last, the Roman world state, falling apart into a western and an eastern half, showed signs of breaking up. Augustine was not an opportunist like Eusebius. But it can at least be said of him that — unconsciously, perhaps? — he glossed over the question of power in a masterly way (Frederich Heer).[33] He both feared and longed for the imminent fall of the Roman empire, not yet foreseeing that his church would simply inherit it. The church would scarcely have been able to declare itself an independent power if it had not succeeded in keeping central Italy, including Rome, free from domination by "earthly" powers.

Rome had two things to offer the nomads who were preparing to conquer Europe: a government religion and superimposed state administration, both already inseparable under Charlemagne; and, later, the monasteries, centers of education and of industry. To bring light to the heathen and at the same time to make them familiar with the advantages of Roman law were one and the same thing. Christianity would have had no historical effect at all without the change of course under Constantine, that we can safely say. It is just that which strikes many as a betrayal of many of the early Christian lessons which lay the foundations of the historical effect. Clearly history does not move exclusively in steps of violent revolution. What moves in men's subconscious and in the history of their traditions often comes to pass without revolutionary shock, without the overthrow of a class-constructed society.

The church since the time of Constantine affords proof that it is not spiritual truth that has triumphed with the spread of Christianity but human power. It took with both hands what it gave with its mouth. Modern theology is probing laboriously into the question whether the Biblical faith did not have in it from the beginning a tendency to forms of adaptation "which today we have to arrange in a system of politically reactionary style" (Hubertus Halbfas);[34] whether a blockade of rational research processes was not already being applied in the New Testament in, for instance, the insistence on blind obedience, the rule of fear, in narrow-mindedness and self-righteousness and the hatred of other groups. "In the service of God and of herself," said the chronicler and royal secretary Hernando del Pulgar, the Catholic Isabella had more than seven hundred people burnt in Seville alone between 1480−1488.[35]

We who are not theologians find it easier to turn to Marx. The ethic of the Christian communities — leaving aside the saints — was not decided by the New Testament appeals, only justified. Authority based on religion can only be blind, rule without fear must be ineffectual. Only where religion set free productive forces was the relationship between man and man settled by it. Against the superstructure of the luxuriant ethic, the common ethic arising mechanically from technique and economics and common interests declares itself unaffected and untouched. Jaspers sees the New Testament Christ and the development of a material culture as a "union of the incompatible."[36]

But how are we to explain the unprecedented, and in practice unique, ability of the communities professing Christianity to organize the world? If Marx gives us no more help, should we perhaps try Freud? We saw that Theodor Reik had worked out a theory for the old Israelites, a theory unpopular in Zionist circles but one which does explain what otherwise remained incomprehensible. What theory has psychoanalysis to offer us?

Erich Fromm, another biographer of the great Sigmund Freud, can claim credit for having brought the relevant soul-searching down from the heavens of figures and abstractions to the ground of Palestine and the Roman empire. Fromm leaves the historical Jesus entirely on one side. Of Jesus as an object of faith, however, he states that he was originally a son's god of the little people rising up against the authority of God the Father, a god of the powerless and enslaved; that the Christian faith was originally "a religion of rebels and revolutionaries."[37]

Meanwhile we have all learned too much to accept this striking interpretation without further investigation. Certainly the Christ believed in consciously and subconsciously by his direct adherents may have died as a son revolting against the law of his father. Not for nothing did his brother James go to such pains to fulfil the Law of Moses so fanatically, and to make it seem that Jesus was just such another follower of the Law. But did the ancient world outside Palestine ever get to know this Jesus who rebelled against the law? And was early Christianity, as Fromm believes, opposed to authority and to the state? Did it fulfil in that way the revolutionary, anti-father wishes of the lowest, oppressed classes? It was opposed rather to the world, to reality, and always neutralized its hostility to the earthly state the more readily, the further God's state disappeared below the horizon. Adolf von Harnack writes: "The escapist fanatics, waiting for the heavenly state of the future, became revisionists of the existing order."[38] Exactly so. Or rather, not *exactly* so. Heaven and earth are here intolerably confused. It was not the urge to change the earthly society that appeared first. True, the rich and powerful of this earth could unburden their conscience with regard to those they ruled with the help of a Christian religion which, in consequence of the continued non-appearance of all prophesied eschatological events, had become an institution of those who held power in this world; Jesus had suffered too, and if the hungry suffered now, well, suffering was the reward of their sins. They were being punished because they had killed the Son of God, and were killing him anew every day by their sins.

The risen Christ, enthroned, translated, other-worldly, exactly met the requirement for the stabilization of authority, thinks Adolf Holl.[39] But was it not the rulers of this world who made a reigning Son of God out of him in the first place? The Graeco-Roman world scarcely regarded the deification of a man as a "son's putsch." It was a mankind steeped in gnosis who first imagined him, not as a man who only became a god after his death, but as a constituent part of the Father, proceeding from the Father and returning to the Father, bone of his bone.

There is certainly more than one motivation behind the fact that the upper class of the Roman empire, especially the women, embraced the new teaching between 150 and 350. It was clear that the rich and powerful, the "fathers," had nothing to fear from this "son's religion"; not, however, because a conservative religion might have been made out of a revolutionary one, but because the cult of the other world did not provide for communal practice. The idea that this was a man who had offended against the laws of his father, who had wished to protest against the institution of the temple which alone could confer blessing, was never at first brought home to the heathen world, and was suppressed in Jerusalem.

But the Christian teaching had other requirements "not of this world": those of the unconscious, more properly fulfilled than any others. They drew on the unique reservoir of Judaism, but, unlike the Jewish mentality, they did not exist by an exclusive self-assertion, but retained an enormous power of accommodation, coupled with a determination to prevail. Of course we can see the obvious advantages that Christianity had to offer the emperor Constantine, but the simple rule that "power attracts power" will not explain everything.

How Christian teaching acquiesced in the urgent requirements of the unconscious can be illustrated by the case, so important to the psychoanalysts, of the defense and the deification of Mary. Here rather than in the revolt of the son there appears a decisive conflict, the significance of which is clear from, for instance, Ernest Jones' statement that the enormous civilizing influence of Christianity can be explained by "sublimated homosexuality throughout the Christian religion," of which we shall have more to say.[40]

Even the author of John's Gospel must have recognized the need for a mother's mediation: one can often persuade a mother of things that one would hardly dare to expect of a father. At the wedding in Cana, when Jesus miraculously turns the water into wine, he gives Mary the role of a mediator: "Do whatever he tells you." Although we cannot extract a "historical" Mary out of his theology, he does present her as a figure that we can visualize, especially impressive as she stands under the cross — though admittedly he does so in order to confirm his own credibility as writer of the Gospel and as eyewitness.* It was this evangelist who started her off on her way to heaven as an historical figure.

The people needed a queen of heaven, as the Israelites needed one in Jeremiah's time, one for whom they could bake cakes, a great mother, a fertility-prostitute; but she was half shown to them, half withheld, and Freud only gives us half the truth when he says that the Christian religion recreated the mother-god.[42] The same evangelist who sketches the mother of God also introduces the Holy Spirit, a sort of sub-deity of the Father-Son divinity, always presented as a double personality. The Son, identical with the Word, is presented as "in his Father's bosom" or "nearest to his Father's heart." The "wisdom of God," regarded among the Jews as female, has disappeared, and in her place we have, partly the Word, partly the Holy Spirit; he already has a Field-Marshal's baton in his knapsack.

He is the divine origin, comprehending male and female. Neither man nor woman, he "overshadows" (Luke) the Virgin Mary, as Saint Augustine[43] among others believes, "through the ears." (It must be admitted that Augustine also believed in the Cappadocian mares who were impregnated by the wind.)[44] The Holy Spirit dispenses "word" and "blessing" where the reader might expect phallus and semen, and appears in the form of a dove, "one of the most female phallic symbols," so Ernest Jones tells us, a bird of love and of procreation; let us remember that in Babylon it brooded over the abyss as a mother-goddess.[45] The Holy Spirit was announced by an angel whose name, Gabri-El, actually means "husband of God."

The God who started as one and indivisible could not assert himself against these pressing needs, and became a group of gods, at first two, then three, and in fact really four persons; once again Freud is too subtle when he says that Christ "actually became God in place of his Father."[46] It is true enough that the universal God was not able to maintain his sole authority. But Yahweh, the old

---

*Bultmann has "no doubt" that this scene has a symbolic meaning. The mother of Jesus represents Jewish Christianity, the beloved disciple Gentile Christianity. Jewish Christianity is to know itself raised up in future into the house of the great religious society. The scene must also have another meaning besides this symbolic one, and even then the (anonymous) Mother of Jesus still plays the part of a mediator.[41]

302

thunderer, was still strong enough to keep the woman off the official list of royalty, though at the price of himself having to take on female attributes in the form of his Holy Spirit and to sleep with a human woman. What other meaning could the Trinity have than that of warding off a trinity of father, mother and son, with all the Oedipal complications involved in that? The attempt to establish a three-in-one comprising father, mother and Messiah-son was finally rejected at the Council of Constantinople as long ago as 381.

If the father-god could only be saved by "dissection," the "dissection" of the woman Mary turns out in the same way to be the *ultima ratio* to prevent a break-in by the incalculable oriental mother- and fertility-goddess; the West here overcame a danger overshadowing all that the Turks ever achieved in their advance to Vienna. Mary, we must say again, is never mentioned by name by Paul, the earliest witness, who knew the Lord's brother James by name. In Mark, the oldest of the Gospels, Jesus appears as a "son of Mary," with no father: a bastard. That is where the rise of the unknown woman starts, a rise paralleled in mirror-image by a fall in rabbinical literature ("hairdresser," "mistress of a Roman legionary called Panthera," "Panther-cat," all mixed up with menstruation-spells etc.). The writer of John's Gospel gives her a role in Jesus' public life and at his death; legend has it that this evangelist took her in as he was commanded and that she lived with him until her death in, significantly, Ephesus. This was the home of the cult of the Great Mother, the worship of Artemis, very similar to that of Astarte or Ishtar. In Ephesus — and this may have been no accident — the Council met which in the year 431 gave the title of honor "Mother of God" to the mother Mary.

Four hundred years after the death of her son, it was adequately confirmed that no penis ever penetrated her, that she had borne the fruit of her womb neither through her vagina nor by Caesarean section, that the brothers of Jesus were either "cousins" or stepbrothers from an earlier marriage of the luckless Joseph. She had conceived "immaculately."*

About the middle of the second century an "infancy gospel" of one "James" explained that Joseph had Jesus' brothers by an earlier marriage and brought them with him into his new

---

*This is not, as it may seem, a slip on Augstein's part, as the next paragraph will make clear. — Editor's note.

household. The great Origen agreed. Tertullian, about the year 200, commented on Paul's statement that Jesus was born of woman with the assertion that Jesus was born of a virgin,* and here too Origen agrees — myths (and that is what he calls this) never caused him any difficulties.[47]

It was not until the sixth century that it was agreed that Mary had also ascended into heaven, but the dogma of her bodily assumption was first proclaimed in 1950. Thomas Aquinas (12-25−1274) attacked the theory that Mary's birth by her mother, "Saint Anne," was also attributable to an immaculate conception, to an announcement from above.[48] In 1854, the dogma was confirmed that the Virgin Mary was born by her mother "immaculately." Mary was then called "supreme intercessor" and by several Popes "co-redeemer of the human race." Indeed, at the conclusion of the Second Vatican Council in 1964, she was called by Pope Paul "Mother of the Church," and if Pope Pius XII had lived longer, she would by now have been credited with giving birth to the church.

The West had its "queen of heaven"; like the goddess Ishtar, she stood upon the crescent; like Aphrodite, she was *stella maris*; Star of the Sea, I greet thee. But she had to pay a price, that of sexlessness. Dante speaks of her as "virgin and mother, daughter of her son"; the Son again, in the crypt of the church of Dormitio Sanctae Mariae (of Mary's going home) in Jerusalem, greets the soul of his Mother with the words: "Rise up quickly, my beloved, my dove, my fair one, and come!" No one can have God as father unless he recognizes the church as mother: sexual suppression and confusion without end. The Catholic young man swears a love "pure as lilies" to Christ the King in his song, the young girls love the "sweet light" of the heavenly bridegroom with "an eternal longing."

---

*Thomas Aquinas, the great theologian of the Middle Ages, also found the virginity of Mary confirmed in Old Testament scripture. The prophet Ezekiel prophesies of the future temple:

> And he said to me, "This gate shall remain shut; it shall not be opened, and no one shall enter by it; for the LORD, the God of Israel, has entered by it; therefore it shall remain shut" (44:2).

One verse later it says: "Only the prince may sit in it to eat bread before the LORD . . . "; an exception is made of him, but it is prescribed that he shall come in and go out "by the vestibule of the gate." The Church Fathers, including Origen and some other distinguished gentlemen, did not express themselves on such contradictions.

The nursing Mother of Jesus reconciles forgiveness and sins. Jesus, the crucified, becomes a "bridegroom of the soul", becomes an infant, a little child, beside his Mother. Rilke's*nun prays:

"Lord Jesus, you have all
the wives you ever want."[49]

The downtrodden man could suffer with the suffering Jesus, hope with the risen Christ, flirt with the soul-bridegroom, be soothed and quieted with the infant Jesus; there is a figuration for every need.

Freud explains the religious images as "illusions, fulfilments of the oldest, strongest, most compelling wishes of mankind"[50]; the fulfilment takes place in the imagination. Are these illusory images only superstructure, as Marx says?

Did the Christian religions really provide only compensations and an ideology of justification. Did they influence the historical course of things differently, or not at all? Was the Christianity of the moment never more than the unreal superimposed clothing of real wishes and interests? The mechanics of it looks too simple. Freud himself speaks of the "sacrilege against the great diversity of man's life" committed by those who will only recognize motives arising from material needs.[51]

But when, where and how did Christian ideas ever determine the course of history? Ernest Jones believes that Christianity offered the world an hermaphroditic ideal, that by the renunciation of elements of masculinity it supplied to a culture having that form the advantages of both sexes. The womanly clothing of the priests, the enforced celibacy (which Freud sees as a continuation of the prohibition of the early fathers to approach females), the tonsure, all that avoidance of male attributes, it is all equivalent to symbolical self-castration; we remember that Freud put the Jewish custom of circumcision into the same category. Jones sees the monstrous significance of Christianity — and, for the sake of completeness, also of Judaism — to mankind in submission to the will of the father, in the struggle for his love by taking up feminine attitudes towards him.[52]

*Rainer Maria Rilke: Selected Works Vol II trans. J.B. Leishman © The Hogarth Press Ltd 1960. By permission of New Directions, New York.

Jones does not hesitate to transfer the Oedipus complex, that rivalry of the two- to five-year-old boy with his father in the battle for his mother (and, conversely, of the daughter for the love and possession of the father), to all the societies professing Christianity, societies quite differently composed in respect of people, economy, geography, climatic conditions and *Zeitgeist* and influenced by the most various external forces.

If it matures without complications, the Oedipus complex goes "under" in the child; psychoanalysis assumes that the sublimated homosexuality thereby liberated has a culturally and socially educative effect. But if, as we well may, we take it as correct that the attitude of a child to its father is reproduced in the attitude of an adult to God: is it then permissable to draw the same conclusion from the relationship of a religious or cultural group with the father-god? Are religious phenomena, as Freud says, (only) to be understood in accordance with the pattern of individuals' neurotic symptoms, as a return of long-forgotten, significant events of the past in the primal history of the "human family"?[53] Does a content of historical truth accordingly survive within them? Is there, as there is a spiritual life of the child and of the adult, also a "spiritual life of the people"? We do not presume to answer, but we do doubt whether it is permissible to see Christianity as a unity, even if it sees itself so in its ideology. We must not draw conclusions from a homogeneous theme as being the basis of this religion. Can "Christianity" be analyzed like an individual? May we, for instance, assess the victory of a religious dogma at a Council as we do the outcome of an intra-psychic conflict?

The questions posed here can also be answered from the psychoanalytical standpoint in quite the opposite sense, as we shall see. But Ernest Jones gives us yet another hint. He believes that the greatest psychological effects were always achieved through extreme contrasts.[54] Christianity could give shape in flesh and blood to the contrasting wishes of the unconscious. The conception of the virgin corresponded to the boy's wish to exclude the father from everything connected with the birth. At the same time, the mother was excluded from the Trinity, the Father was subdued into the Son, the erotic connection of the Son with the Father was strengthened, the humble submission of the son was accomplished;* and he now raises the Mother to himself like a bride, which once more reduces the Holy Spirit to the status of a kind of house-tutor. "In the fashioning of religious myths," says Freud, "no one can claim that they take much trouble about logical coherence."[55]

On the one hand, the crucifixion is an act of submission to the Father's will (however much the real Jesus may have rebelled against the super-ego of Yahweh). On the other hand, all men have killed Jesus, who is now raised up to be Father, identified with the Father; and in the Communion, to escape the Father's wrath, they experience a repentant piety, they experience union and identification. Jeshua, who rebelled against the law of Yahweh, has become, first, Jesus, obedient unto death, and then the slain God whose killing is repeated and pardoned in the ritual of the Communion. Extreme contrasts: in the combination of virgin and mother, the man finds his ideal woman, the woman her model. The man's wish to be a child, the woman's child; the mother's wish to be a young girl; the girl's wish, to be a mother; the father's wish, to have a perfect and obedient son; that of the young man, to replace his father and to grow like him; the wish of the homosexual for the love of his own sex; that of the girl, for a man's love; no wish, no illusion that fancy cannot fulfil. The uniquely expansive, world-shaking power of Christian civilization seems to be explicable by its enormous range between diametrically opposed principles, such as is not found, for instance, in Islam, another otherwise successful subjugation-ideology: between the supernatural and the real, the sacred and the profane, spiritual and worldly, church and state, emperor and Pope; tension too between sexual austerity and sexual desire, love for one's enemies and military conquest, monastic and at the same time active life, between soul and body, the spirit and the flesh. Culture, says Freud, can only shape itself in the continual struggle between the suppression of desire and the revolt against this suppression, "between the Scylla of repression and the Charybdis of regression" (Dieter Wyss).[56]

"Ever since Jesus, it has been impossible to play off God and man against one another," writes the progressive Catholic Josef

---

*Freud does not differentiate sufficiently, in my view, in calling Christianity a "son-religion." Precisely this ambivalence, now a father-religion, now a son-religion, constitutes a part of its great effectiveness. But this at least must be right, that the needs of mankind might not be satisfied with a strong father alone.

Blank.[57] But that — playing off God and man against one another in the name of Jesus — was just the business of the church(es). No one knew as well as the Christian church how to subject a man to the tension of a sense of guilt, to pass a current through him. When the voltage rose to an unbearably high level, there was the church with the means of grace, the forgiveness of sins, ready to switch off and bring relief. How could a man acquire enormous wealth and still be poor and chaste, still love his enemies? The church in Rome, with its worldly hand, pointed a way of not following the Christian teaching and still being freed from the consequences of not following it, of being "redeemed."

Tension which is not discharged soon leads to conquest and creates culture. The childlike thinking of C.G. Jung has worked it out that the more Christian the conscious appears, the more heathenishly the unconscious behaves;[58] the devil, merely pushed aside, is all the more active in the back room, even in the back rooms of the churches. The unconscious, then, never accepted the ethic laid down by Matthew and Luke of love for one's enemies; it ran counter to essential values. Resentment and thoughts of revenge, which according to Matthew and Luke are to be expelled from our consciousness, go on rumbling under cover and break out when they get the chance, as in the Revelation of John, which, following after Enoch, "gives a slap in the face to all ideas of Christian humility, patience, love for one's neighbor and for one's enemy, of a loving Father in heaven and a Son and Savior who redeems mankind".* (There is so little that is Christian in the book that ever since Luther, who does not find "Christ bright and clear" in it, its Christian inspiration has been continually denied.)[59]

It is from the impossibility of fulfilling its spiritual and ethical demands that Christian culture — whatever that phrase may comprise — has derived its drive. But we must remember that authority over men was made easy in ancient Israel through the religion of Yahweh, but that authority over men actually became harder through prophetic agitation. A comparable antagonism is to be found in the Christian societies, which now, of course, unlike Israel, cannot be destroyed by foreign conquerors. The opposition

*Where did John get this orgy from? In the seeker after perfection both positive and negative desires are stored up. Thus the "new Jerusalem" that came down from heaven — a cube, incidentally, with sides of about 1,400 miles — was sealed by the suppressed wishes of the saints. Its walls are of jasper, the city itself of pure gold like pure glass, the foundation stones of the city walls set with precious stones of all kinds, jasper, sapphire, emerald, topaz, and the city gates of pearl. The builder of St. Peter's in Rome must have just helped himself.

between priest and king, between spiritual and temporal authorities, was uniquely sharp in the Christian Middle Ages. The barefoot emperor before the castle at Canossa, begging his militarily powerless enemy to lift the sentence of excommunication: this dualism between the two empires, comprehended by Augustine in a brilliant formula while the Roman empire was falling and the heavenly kingdom was still awaited, left room for maneuver, room for the growth of every independent movement which we have to thank (?) for our present times. Every party, spiritual as well as temporal, had to pay with licenses for the support of feudal lords, cities, guilds and theologians. The distinction between sacred and profane enabled science first to secularize itself and then to take the place of the sacred.

Unlike the beneficiaries of the Mohammedan religion ("Reclaiming of the single great ancestor," in Freud's words),[60] the Popes had entered history as rulers of a kingdom not of this world. The kingdoms that were of this world, authority over which the popes wanted to appropriate to themselves, consequently became hostile to them. This rivalry did not destroy the nominally Christian societies; it made them stronger. So it cannot have been the powers of the unconscious alone that, behind the economic interests, and not with equal weight on every step of historical development, helped to shape Christian history.

Can religion hinder the development of appropriate and necessary and feasible requirements of production? It certainly seems so in India. But the religion of the mythical ages differs in its social potential from that of the sixteenth century, and that in turn from that of the nineteenth century. Erich Fromm, whose theory of a "son's putsch" we have looked at, has asserted (contrary to the theories on Christianity of his teacher Reik, as well as those of his colleague Jones and of his master Freud) that "Christianity" could not be made the subject of psychoanalytical research because one was dealing with several Christian ideologies. Fromm sees in the Christian faith an original attitude of hostility to the father, which — and this he finds conclusive — he believes to have changed in the first two Christian centuries into one of passive masochistic docility.[61]

What Ernest Jones regards as significant in the positive sense, the feminine attitude of pre-Reformation Christianity, the reunciation of elements of masculinity,[62] Fromm takes to be a passive-infantile attitude. A more active attitude on the part of the masses was not made possible until the Reformation's return to God the Father. But a return to God the Father means a return to humble submission to the will of the father, as in the Judaism of the Israelites, or in Reik's words, "an ever-intensifying feminine-homosexual attitude towards the heavenly Father."[63] They cannot all three be right, Jones, Reik and Fromm: the psychoanalysis of the historical process still awaits further research.

Did the return to God the Father during the Reformation really make possible for the first time a more active attitude on the part of wider strata of society? I should have thought just the opposite. Active behavior (not only by the masses) was not so much suggested by a new unconscious, it was rather made possible and necessary by social and scientific-technical advances. First the Catholic Portuguese discovered a new world. The new possibilities of production and exploitation that came into existence at the same time, the newly created structures of a craftsmen's and townsmen's culture led to liberation from the parasitic immobility of Roman Catholicism.It was no accident that the Reformation began with quarrels about pay and ended with redistribution of land. The spirit of the times cunningly made use of an old Catholic reactionary called Martin Luther (not forgetting the craft of printing, with the aid of which the holy scriptures were made available to the many, and so desecrated).

But the spirit of the times is far from cunning. It is just that a return to the sources often looks like a bold breakthrough, and the restorer is hailed as an innovator. If the reformers wanted to break the domination of Rome, did they have to govern themselves according to the whispering of their unconscious, or did they have, perhaps no less unconsciously, to extract full political value from theological disputes? It seems to me that anyone who took the field against the church of Rome must have had to cast doubts on everything that had made it rich and powerful: celibacy, the monasteries, infallibility, the forgiveness of sins, the flagship *Queen of Heaven*,* the art of painting, transubstantiation in the Mass, and a lot more.

*Precise balances are not often struck in history. As Italy, the land of the Popes, has remained essentially free from witch-hunts, it was left to Luther to write about the Virgin Mary: "It would have been right to order a golden coach for her, drawn by four thousand horses, and to have trumpeted and shouted before the coach: Here comes the woman above all women, the princess among the whole of the human race."[64]

The reformer had to reach back to the true faith as it was before the Roman church had (ostensibly) corrupted it, which means that the Holy Spirit stayed in the doctrine but not the Virgin Mary. But it can hardly be denied that the Reformation fixed, or at least sketched out, new conditions not only for the areas which it itself embraced but also for those that remained Catholic. Max Weber, important also as a religio-sociologist, has therefore investigated the influence, especially that of the Calvinistic persuasion, on the economy of the new urban culture, and the origin of the capital economy ("capitalism"). He sees a connection between the commercial expansion that emanated from the centers of Puritanism (Holland, West Switzerland, London, New England) and the teaching of John Calvin, who suggested that financial success should be looked on as a sign of heavenly selection.[65]

Certainly Calvin himself had described the choice as being God's affair and not to be undertaken by living people; but his successors, above all the business community, knitted up the connection, which Calvin never proclaimed, between membership of the elect and commercial success. Money-making became a religious duty. It was the commandment of God not to spend money but to make more profit from it. This "inner asceticism," as Max Weber describes it, had a double effect: it checked indiscriminate spending on private consumption, which it clawed back into an increasingly comfortable pile, and it freed the struggle for profit, thenceforth regarded as fulfilling the will of God, from the curb imposed by traditional ethics as expressed in the sentence: *Homo mercator vix aut numquam potest Deo placere*, the merchant can hardly or never please God — the stress being on "hardly." Now it is clear that the axis of world domination moved away northwards between 1500—1700 into the countries now Protestant, and there are factors explaining this which have a lot to do with the Roman church as a politico-social institution and only a little with religious content. It remains a question whether Calvinism was more than a doctrine of ideological vindication, whether it had any decisive influence or simply dressed up a process having its own rules in ideological costume.

Specialization had gone far enough by the beginning of the sixteenth century; society had slipped over from its former "Catholic" unity into semi-autonomous spheres of religious, political and economic institutions. The structure of society no longer appeared as cosmically all-embracing in the Idea; state and

311

industry were set free from the religious cosmos and the platform was prepared for capitalism, the nation-state, technology and science. Religion was never again what it had been when it embraced all fields, all institutions in its all-pervasive authority — not even in the countries of the Counter-Reformation, no matter what astonishing feats the unconscious peformed by means of splendid-sounding formulae to conceal from men the new forms of authority.

Weber did not claim to replace a one-sided materialistic causality of culture and historical interpretation with a spiritual causality equally one-sided. But he explains (subject to further research, as he himself specifies) both causalities as "equally possible."[66] In another connection, he praises Judaism for having set Christianity on its way as "a religion essentially foreign to magic," and points to India, where superstition about caste, and China, where superstition about natural spirits, had held up technical and economic advance.[67]

Yet it looks as if the tradition of the Roman empire was more free from magic than that of the Jews; and Christianity did not become free from magic until the Reformation. Dealing in money had become suspect to the church (and to Luther), as Weber recognizes. Money dealings created impersonal relationships which led away from the church and its ethical influence. The contrast with the Calvinist profit-ethic is striking. It was the abolition of magic which ensured an advantage in respect of economy and education to the Protestant half of the world to this day. And although even the Counter-Reformation could not get back to the status quo ante, much intelligence and enterprise wa driven out of its sphere into the reformed countries.

Weber himself was not prepared to say that capitalism as an economic system was a "product of the Reformation"; he himself saw that capitalism had developed anti-traditionally and rationalistically, both in contradiction to the essence of the Roman church, but he considered religious influences to be "in partnership." The trends of his "Protestant Ethic" proved to be challengeable on uncommonly many points; they did not always stand up to detailed examination. Specifically, it is an objection not easy to get over that, in the countries where capitalism was able to develop its decisive power, Calvinism appeared later than capitalism. But Weber's "wrong idea" has stood firmer than many of his correct ones, and has still not had the shine completely rubbed off.[68]

Max Weber saw in the ascetic activities of the Puritans a revival of the heritage of the ancient Jewish prophecy; he occupied himself all his life with the contrast between the world-renouncing contemplation and mysticism of Buddhism and the world-molding asceticism of what he called the *Abendland*, the Occident. But if it is right that the prophets preached the simple life in accordance with the law of Yahweh, then it must be just as right that their actions were not determined by authority gained by worldly success. On the contrary, political and military destruction only strengthened the belief in the prophets; Yahweh's reputation was enhanced, not diminished, by the destruction of the temple. I cannot see this ethic of inner-worldly activity, free from an irrational search for salvation, that Max Weber sees in the Jewish prophets.[69] Other religions, indeed, have very similar requirements in their everyday ethics; there is nothing exceptional here about ancient Judaism.

To have submitted the daily life of men to the commandments of an ethical system determined by heaven seems to Weber to be the great merit of the ancient Jews, the turning-point indeed of western culture. But that was the very tradition that was lost by Christianity under Constantine; otherwise there would not have seemed to be any point in any reforming return to the early teaching. Moreover,the everyday Christian ethic in the technical, scientific, rational sphere would have worked both ways: it would also have imposed limitations. The Puritans of the sixteenth and seventeenth centuries went back to the Old Testament because they wanted to return to the original sources of the Fathers, just as the French Revolution was hypnotized by the virtues of ancient Rome. But the Puritans, their old Jewish names notwithstanding, no more became old Jews than the French, until Napoleon's time, became Romans. Money, profit, was their God. They were indeed secularistic without knowing it. They, the classic shippers of slaves and exterminators of Indians, are the perfect example of a religion's characteristic of self-justification. Christ had now literally died for the rich, the chosen people from eternity to eternity.

It would seem that Weber was in search of those developments which have saved the West from the fate of the Indians, which, no doubt with some foreboding, must have seemed exceptionally terrible to him. True, the West was essentially free from mysticism, from interior meditation, free from Buddhism, that religion of far greater intellectual purity which gave no thought at all to the organization of everyday life — a religion spiritually so outstanding and so useless, if not actually damaging, in the morasses of this world. If we accept Weber's historical perspective, we cannot simply call the Christians' sexual morality a "wrong development" (as the healthy mind is inclined to do, most recently in the person of the church specialist of the *Süddeutsche Zeitung*, Gisela Uellenberg).[70] How else could the heavenly discipline be kept more keyed-up, more demanding of culture, more eager for gain, than by this very Christian sexual morality? It is the drive enforced by fear that begets aggression.

Are we then to say that only a religion of guilt, and indeed only one developed from the Jewish material, could have prevented an Indian-style renunciation of the world? Would there have been no "one God" (although in three persons) without the Jewish prophets, no personal God, no one to whom man could have entrusted himself in the expectation of reward and punishment? Would a "shame-culture" such as used to exist in old Japan have hindered expansion, crippled the inventive spirit, strangled the imagination? Would a kind of Buddhism have spread over Europe if it had not been for the Jewish prophecies? And can we seriously say, in view of the old pre-Christian evidence, that the doctrine of each man's individual worth was brought into the world by Christianity (Emil Erwin Hölscher),[71] or that the European man's awareness of personaity is a result of Christian teaching (Gollwitzer)?[72]*

Freud, Max Weber, Arnold Gehlen and state-organized Communism are all agreed that, without asceticism, there is no culture. (Freud writes: "It seems moreover that every culture must be built up on coercion and self-restraint.")[74] But a human community has hardly ever grown up without enforced asceticism. The decision to become an ascetic "voluntarily" on the basis of one's own chosen motives has always been a luxury of the few, while it was not open to the majority of men to live however they wished. Werner

---

*How seriously should we then underrate the Stoics, whose obedience to God was more cheerful and more practical and clearer and more constructive than that of the tormented Christians and Jews? Here is the wise man speaking in a piece written by the freed slave Epictetus (50−138): "I have never been prevented when I wished, nor compelled when I did not wish. But how is that possible? I have submitted the running of my life to God. He wants me to have fever. So do I. He wants me to desire something. So do I. He wants me to achieve something. So do I. He does not want it. Nor do I . . . "[73]

Heisenberg has not yet given us a world-formula for the explanation of culture.

"The greatest of all periods in the history of mankind," is how Hölscher describes the development of Christianity, "the only really fundamental inversion of the general structure of humanity" — he said that in 1931, and it may be he would not say it now. We who know so little do know that the religion of guilt not only relieves tensions but also creates them, partly, indeed, creates them in order to relieve them. We believe that we can observe particularly intensive tensions during the Christian Middle Ages. But while we think we know why the Christian religion has "succeeded" in this or that shape or form, we cannot show what spiritual energies, what figurations of the unconscious spurred on the annexation of territory, technology, art and science, and it is small comfort to us that Karl Marx cannot explain it either.

Marx, like Freud one of the great uplifters of and contributors to the intellect (Hans Kilian calls him "a thinker with the unconscious Utopian identity-structure of the Jewish cultural tradition"),[75] did not avoid the temptation to make an unconditional law out of his discovery of a material-economic principle and to foist upon history a law of motion which eventually becomes a definite, and definitely positive, terminal stage. It was left to Engels, who survived him — not such an original thinker but of a more practical turn of mind — to explain that what could be, if indeed it did not have to be, deduced from the writing of his honored friend was an erroneous interpretation. In 1890, six years after Marx's death, he wrote in a letter to Joseph Bloch, then 19 years old, later for many years editor of the *Socialist Monthly*, that the production and reproduction of "real life" were certainly "in the last instance the decisive impulse in the history of production," but that the economic impulse was not "the only decisive one." The various impulses of the superstructure, says Engels, affect the course of the historical struggles and in many cases determine their form. Thus, history results from the conflict of a great number of individual wills, each one of which has been made what it is by a great number of particular living conditions. Engels sees "every man for himself" as a parallelogram of forces; the infinite group of these parallelograms can be seen as the product of a force "working on the whole unconsciously and with no firm intention." "For what any one individual wants is baulked by every other individual, and the result is something that none of them wanted."[76]

So history unfolds as a sort of natural process. The will of every individual wants what his bodily constitution and his external — in the last instance, his economic — circumstances, both his own and those of society, impel him to: "Men who are developing their material production and material trade also change their thinking and the product of their thinking together with their actuality."[77]

One can see a considerable number of back doors being opened here, or perhaps they are shutters like those on the windows of an Advent calendar. The "external" circumstances which determine the will of the individual are only in the last instance economic; before that, they can be obstructed both in the individual and in the social process, and for a time can be overlaid by a superimposed consciousness, by religion, or, if that has disappeared, by ideology.

Now, if we take men's new productive powers, science and technology, into account in their "material production" and "material trade," as we presumably must, we find that we get an amazingly simple Marx, who says only that economic stimulus, technology and science make their effect in the last instance, and in the light of that reality men change their thinking and the product of their thinking: who is there, from Heidegger to Wittgenstein, who would argue with that?

Only, the role of the unconscious remains unfilled in this interpretation of Marx, and that may be why we can accept Freud's rather than Marx's interpretation the farther we go back into the mythical darkness of the history of man (although we are always in danger of transferring the unconscious of the child of today to the unconscious of the primal society of man without the necessary adjustment).

But as soon as we come to modern times, the Marxist assessment works wonders in stripping the magic from the artificial superstructure. As the examples of Dante or Thomas Aquinas, Luther or John Calvin show, wherever a religious ideal came up against an economic interest, that interest remained untouched. Christianity became the ideology of a superimposed technology. The "guilt-culture" turned itself inside out and, renouncing its inward part, penetrated into all the nations of the world.

12.   What happens without him?

We ourselves shall be the seventh day of the Creation.
—Augustine

When I ask myself why I have always sincerely tried to be considerate, perhaps even indulgent, to others, and why I did not give it up when I saw that people were injured by it, that they became as it were an anvil because others are brutal and untrustworthy, I simply do not know the answer.
—Freud[1]

It is not the intention of this book to dispute the existence of a man called Jesus who was put to death during the governship of Pontius Pilate on account of his eccentric, perhaps even anti-social, behavior. We have been concerned with something different. We wanted to find out what happens when a religious idea is transformed into another, almost contrary idea. We wanted to make the process visible, like the developing of a photograph.

What, we have asked ourselves, are the driving forces that have fashioned a symbolic figure of the order of magnitude of Jesus Christ? Are they exhausted yet, have they run dry, or have they been diverted into other productive fields? What sides of our nature are lying in torment if there is no longer any mythical fantasy that makes us tick, if all mystery, magic and all that is holy have entirely disappeared from our lives? If there is no longer any "ultimate," no absolute moral value? What needs did the Christian churches meet, institutions, in the words of Gustav Heinemann,* "not of this world"?[2]

Modern theology has drawn conclusions from an event which it transcribes as the death of God or absence of God. One of its most tireless champions, the Protestant theologian Dorothee Sölle,[3] born 1929, has worked out the consequences that follow "where God has become unnecessary as a moral, political and scientific working hypothesis."

It has not escaped her that "by means of its rationalization and its living technique, in the widest sense of the words, society has taken over certain outstanding functions that used to be God's," that it "is completely in a position to fulfil those functions for which God was once responsible." The manifestations of God in the past, which she calls "objectivations," objectivations "in miracles, historical dispensations and continuing revelations, however understood," are washed out and leached away by critical science, and Sölle finds no fault in critical science for that: "There is no longer anything that obliges us to attribute those objectivations to God, to see his hand where historical, sociological and psychological laws are in control or where blind chance is in charge." The "childlike relationship with the Father up above the tent of stars" has become impossible; "impossible, too, is direct religious certainty."

There remains of course man's desires to find himself, to be identified with himself. He seeks the kingdom "where identity and joy laugh" (Sölle), he wants to recognize himself, to learn the meaning of his existence and his nature ("To know God and the soul," says Augustine, "That is my desire. Nothing more? No, nothing else.");[4] he wants, says Paul, to be known and in the last instance to be held dear. A need that it would be hasty to describe as "religious" longs for meaning and truth in the future, for a fulfilled and pleasant life.

How does modern theology answer this need? With a challenge. Since God is "dead" or (still) absent, and since society leaves gaps in its replacement of him, a Someone must take his place, a someone the need for whom can be derived only from the no-longer-present, or not-yet-present, God — as Sölle says, a substitute.

*President of the Federal Republic of Germany.

318

Modern Christian theology does not take much trouble to trace this substitute back to an actual man, such as a Jesus of Nazareth. Little more than lip service is paid to him. No, it quite consciously recalls the privilege of theology discovered by Paul, of designing the figure of a redeemer in the abstract according to the needs of man himself — needs presumed or admitted or simply felt within oneself. The former Jesus-Jeshua is now completely unimportant, not because there is no more that we can know about him but because he could not in any way meet man's requirements. A new Christ is designed by modern theology, not the same that the original community believed in.

Frau Sölle's Christ "replaces the absent God for as long as he does not show himself among us"; he "takes over the role of God in the world, he plays the part which would be unfilled without him." He assists the absent God; he is God's forerunner. He is the teacher, the true pedagogue; he punishes us, of course, but himself suffers under the punishment he inflicts. Only because we find out that he identifies himself with our own offense can we learn to accept the punishment. He identifies himself with the other man's offense too, and so becomes a servant who takes over and suffers for us. Christ replaces us before the (absent) God and replaces the (absent) God before us.

These are just the slogans of modern theology; one cannot base any valid argument on them. But they do make it abundantly clear that deliberate postulation and thought are at work here. A mediator — Sölle calls him a substitute — is still needed even when the occasion for mediation has dropped out of sight. Frau Sölle quotes Dietrich Bonhoeffer with approval: "Man is called upon to share the suffering of God on the godless earth."[5] The church, for whose reform Frau Sölle hopes, "encourages God in his world not to cease to wait for this world" — he, who never shows himself among us.

We cannot help having serious doubts about such earnest playing with ideas: is there really any call for this kind of comfort and this kind of hope except in the minds of the reforming theologians themselves? We are impressed by the honesty with which our old faith in Jesus is declared to be finished, but the artificial Christ offered in its place is quite unnecessary. It gives no comfort, if offers no hope: it seems that theology must follow the thorny path of self-promotion to the end.

Everyone, not only the theologians, finds himself face to face with the simple fact that, even where it still brings comfort, religion no longer offers any future. Even Israel, the visible home of the Jewish community, seems to have ceased to believe in what Gershom Scholem calls a "life in suspension,"[6] in a Messianic fulfilment some day, however bravely they may pray there. Men's problems leave no room for a "life in suspension," and in the interim they leave no room for a substitute life. Now as in the time of King Hezekiah, there is just the one, undivided life, no new heaven and no new earth; though there is a new theology.

God himself is in a crisis, God is suffering from his world and his creatures; he wants to free it from its chains side by side with them, say the new theologians. It is "the We," says Ernst Bloch, "that assumes the Messiah and presses for his coming." But the Messiah never happens; the return of the "missing" nature, as Bloch says, of the nature till now misused by man, never shows up at all. No longer is the past conceived as a promise of the future.

We can well believe that the theologians are in a crisis: God, or his Messiah, has waited too long in the wings. The "changing of the world through his hope against all hope" which Karl Rahner offers us in his Easter message of 1972, the "new creation of all things through the God of Christ's resurrection" (Moltmann), is a placebo. To be able to do what is possible, to hope for what is reasonable, it is best to put aside such false comfort, such false hope. Can there really be "the certain awaiting of an absolute and realized future, the inexhaustible well of social fantasy and of just and politic imagination in the name of freedom," as Jürgen Moltmann declares? It certainly does not appear so.[7]

True, the churchmen and churchwomen go on talking to each other, but even among the most liberal, "Some Day" eventually reaches the point at which they cannot go on, at which, as at the trial of Captain Dreyfus, the "bordereau" has to be brought to the notice, not of the accused, but only of the judges. "Their whole trade," wrote Nietzsche of the dogmatists, "involves them in only admitting certain truths." Thus, theology only proves that all talking and thinking about God is a sin, a sin against the Holy Spirit (at any rate, thank God, we need have nothing more to do with the God of Helmut Thielicke, who makes "summit conferences break up" and Stalin die of a stroke, at whose sign "racial conflicts . . . occur," to whom the "earthquakes in Chile" are "servants," and who, "if everything was swallowed up in the destruction of the earth ... " goes on "ruling over the graveyards"; in this *bon bourgeois* chatterbox of the church of Saint Michael in Hamburg, the last deadly frivolity of theology reaches its height).[8]

Are we then to think of God as man *and* wife, as the fashionable theologian Harvey Cox suggests? Are we to read yet another meaning into the message, "that God becomes man continually and eternally" (as suggested by Hubertus Halbfas, who was called to order by his Catholic superiors)? Does Christianity stand or fall, as Jürgen Moltmann declares, "by the reality of the awakening of Jesus from the dead by God"? Are there, when the theologians talk about God, "scars on the body of Christ"?

They go on talking, the theologians, because so far "there is no sign that God has told us to keep silent about him" (Heinz Zahrnt).[10] That *their* God does not exist they can learn from him themselves; they can never manage without making a picture of him. But we can no longer accept that a god acted once and never again, once for all. That is myth and magic grown up from the childhood of man, to be hunted down and caught in the unconscious. There is no god who acts now for Israel, now against Israel, who first accepts the sons of men as burnt offerings and then "sacrifices his own son" for us, who does not desire evil and at the same time permits it (the most vicious blackguard would be ashamed to resemble him, sneers the French Dominican Jean Cardonnel).[11] The search for truth and the struggle for certainty cancel one another out. There is no god whom we can know or whom we can discuss. The fundamental philosophical question, "Why does anything at all exist; why is there not just nothing?" will not lie down; it cuts away the grounds on which we could ask more. What was before the beginning of everything, and will be at the end everything if indeed we can talk of a beginning and an end. That goes beyond our concepts, silenced indeed in two verses of the Indian Veda, written long before the first text of the Bible was written (and translated into German by Paul Deussen,[12] he who declared that anyone who doubted the earthly existence of Jesus was "a fool"):

What man has ever had the wit
To learn creation's origin?
The gods themselves came after it,
So who knows where it could begin?

He who the universe begot,
Who looks down on it, here below,
Who made it — or who made it not,
He knows! or does he too not know?

But the theologians still "know" in the way old Enoch knew. Was Jesus really the one for whom Moses (!) and the prophets were hoping (Millar Burrows)? Is the nation of Israel the place where God chose to give his consent to the world (the Gottingen Old Testament scholar Walter Zimmerli), and what about the other nations? Was king Ahaz given a unique chance, one that never occurred again in the history of the world, by the prophet Isaiah in 733 B.C.E. — "If ye will not believe, surely ye shall not be established," and did something "unique and decisive" happen at that time (the Bonn Old Testament scholar Martin Noth)? Does God use the nations "as his axe and his scourge against his own people" (Günther Bornkamm)? Did Judaism have to pay for its decision in favor of the robber Barabbas and against Jesus with the destruction of Jerusalem (Ethelbert Stauffer)? Are the Old and New Testaments, in contrast to other religious and philosophical prophecies, "revelation from heaven" (the Hamburg Old Testament scholar Klaus Koch)?[13]

If Jesus really is the central point of history, what conclusions do the theologians manage to reach? Wolfhart Pannenberg still believed in 1970 that the completion of history had already begun in Jesus Christ, that with the rising of Jesus from the dead, the end of history had already happened *to him*, though *for us* the end of history was still awaited. Anyone who, like our kind of people, will not see the "patently obvious," the "simple, in no way supernatural" truth that God revealed himself in the fate of Jesus Christ is one of those "extraordinarily deluded" people who "have to be brought to reason so that they can see straight." Pannenberg very decently concedes that the continuity of the faith of Christ is smashed for anyone who finds that the apocalyptic expectation of the Last Judgment and the resurrection of the dead is "quite impossible of fulfilment."[14]

Even Bultmann says that it is not for any particular moral error that God forgives us, but rather the fundamental sin of our existence, the one sin "which consists in our having broken away from God, in our having as it were left him in order to be something for ourselves, by our own efforts";[15] the one sin, one

322

might add, that we have become men. There remains the old claim that man offends absolutely against the absolute God, and not against men and beasts according to relative, variable norms. "No slave has become, nor will become, like a mountain," it says in the book of *Enoch* (98:4), and "no woman's handmaid like a hill, even so sin was not sent down upon the earth, but men have created it out of themselves."

But we are firmly against the theologians when they tell us who has offended, when, in what way, against whom. Gollwitzer[16] states (1970) that anyone who thinks that the religious and the scientific attitudes cannot be combined is "not on top of the spiritual situation of our times." But what does he exhort us to believe? That, until Jesus, man "destroyed the meaning of his existence," that he "gambled away his meaning," "forfeited his right to meaning through his offenses." Why is that so? We must look back at this from the objective at which "reconciliation takes place," at which the "lost man" can be "brought home." Why until Jesus? Why in Jesus?

In Gollwitzer's view we must be sinners because we do not want to receive the meaning of life from an outside source from which we get the "comand" — literally — the "command for the hope of meaning." "Jesus alone is my commander-in-chief" — Gollwitzer quotes the Harvard professor, Harvey Cox, with evident approval. We cannot help being astonished to find this military vocabulary still being used by a theologian endowed with a contemporary sensorium. Theology ought to shy away from appearing on "that front which we call the present" (Jürgen Moltmann),* or more correctly, perhaps, on that present which he calls a front. We are (and we must be), in Augustine's terminology, *nihilisti*, "people who no longer believe in anything, only in nothing, and who are hardened in that belief" (Bornkamm). Yes, that is how they would like it.[18]

Bultmann, the last of the great inconsistents among theologians, has told us that it is always a sin to talk about God, and we suddenly realize what that could mean when we hear Gollwitzer: God does not desire evil, he is the negation of it, but he is the Lord

---

*Certainly these metaphors from the commonplaces of war read more comfortably than those taken from road traffic. The theologian Thielicke tells me that God wants me to love him more and more, but that to reach this destination I must sit at the steering-wheel, switch on the headlamps and stare ahead through the windshield so that I may arrive at the crossroads in the right lane. So that's what God is like![17]

of History and all that is real comes from him. He is the eternal friend, the final basis of existence; he will make the finality of the world that he created intolerable for us, will bring it to "the goal of a peaceful communion of love between the creator and his creatures." But God's hope (and after all, he is the creator!) is in himself alone, not in us, his creatures; his world-creation is compassionate love. Let us get our breath back for a moment with the amateur theologian Kafka: "It cannot be said that we lack faith. The simple fact of our life alone is inexhaustible as a source of faith."[19]

"But there is a God!" cry the theologians with one voice, and science does not contradict them. "The universe does not know that men live in it," quotes Gollwitzer from Thornton Wilder's Caesar, and answers: "The universe is not alone." Both of them, Wilder's Caesar and Gollwitzer, might strain themselves with such statements.[20]

Theology has borrowed arguments from the logician Wittgenstein, but even he is going to disappoint us. That which we are dependent on, says Wittgenstein, we could call God.[21] But he also says that to believe in a God means to see that all is not yet over with the facts of this world. Are we dependent on facts other than those of this world? Should humanity, through a series of catastrophes, move towards one final catastrophe, would hope then wave to us from outside?

What we cannot speak about we must keep quiet about; that is what we have learned from Wittgenstein. It is no good attacking the speech if we lack the comprehension; there is nothing to be gained from that. Even the meaning of life, Wittgenstein tells us, we might call God; why not? Believing in God means seeing that life has a meaning; understanding the question of the meaning of life; again, why not? But why should the individual stop asking about the meaning of life just because God has stopped giving him prophecies? That, as Kant recognizes, would be like stopping breathing altogether in order not to go on creating tainted air.[22] Is a man godless if he ends his life because it seems to have no more meaning for him? And is everyone who does not commit suicide a believer?

The logician fails us when it comes to the logic of salvation, but even the so-called precise Wittgenstein cannot help us. Paul Dirac, winner of the Nobel Prize for physics in 1933, led a discussion in 1971 in Lindau "from the standpoint of a physicist" on the question: "Is there a God?" (a question which Heisenberg puts this way: Can one get face to face with the central ordering of things as directly as one can with the soul of another man? Heisenberg answers "Yes."). Dirac draws the conclusion that there would certainly be no God if the causality and determination of physical and biological occurrences were established completely and consistently. But now there are the so-called "quantum-breaks" which occur within the atom when the electrons surrounding the nucleus alter course. Quantum-breaks influence, for instance, the form of crystals and of molecules, possibly even of genes, the carriers of hereditary programming. They are not at present calculable. "It could be," says Dirac, "that there is a God who influences these quantum-breaks."[23]

In 1927, when Dirac was twenty-five years old and already beginning to grow famous, he expressed himself very much more sloppily and disrespectfully in the presence of Werner Heisenberg, (then twenty-six years old and already famous) and the twenty-seven year-old Wolfgang Pauli, who became famous later. "Yes, yes," said Pauli, "our friend Dirac has a religion, and its creed runs: 'There is no God, and Dirac is his prophet.' "[24] In any case, even the older and wiser Dirac still insists that there is at present no prospect "of finding a direct way to determine whether there is any heavenly influence on quantum-breaks"; it is clear, though, that all the Christian academies will have a foot in the door.

To find another answer, however, Dirac takes up the question of how life began. Most scientists believe that life could come into existence anywhere where the appropriate physical conditions prevailed, temperature and atmosphere and also thunderstorms to supply energy, in short, "biosphere." Life could thus have grown up on very many of the planets in the universe. Dirac, on the other hand, discussed in the abstract another possibility: he assumed for the moment that the start of life was so extremely difficult that there was no life, and never had been, outside the earth. In that case, thinks Dirac, it seems necessary to him to assume the existence of a God.

Dirac reckons that it will be two hundred years before science can definitely establish whether there is life on other planets (too long to hold back publication of this book). But it seems to me, also, that his reasoning on this one point is not logical. If life on the earth were as yet unique (which there is not the least reason to assume), then the assumption of a God standing above the laws of nature would still not in any way be in any way essential. Jacques Monod, who won the Nobel Prize in 1965 for his work on molecular biology, in his book *Chance and Necessity*,[25] considers the rarity or even uniqueness of life discussed by Dirac and comes to exactly the opposite conclusion: life on the earch came into existence only by chance, on the grounds of an "accidental" coincidence of extremely rare constellations. It could not have been inferred from the basic pattern of the world. So man must make up his mind that he is alone in the uncaring immeasurability of the universe, from which he emerged only by accident: "a gipsy on the edge of the universe . . . which is deaf to his music and indifferent to his hopes, his suffering or his wrongdoing."

All round the world, all the highest circles trembled, shaken by this shocking theory. But Monod's theory is based on such a well-known illusion that it is hard to attribute it simply to the scientist's intellect. Monod says that it is "probable," using the word with a truly theological firmness, that the *a priori* probability of the phenomenon "life" before it actually appeared was "practically nil," and the *a priori* probability of the phenomenon "man" before his appearance was "equally unlikely," i.e., "practically nil."

"Practically nil," a magical conception like the Holy Trinity. But now, suppose there were after all life on about a million stars? In the galaxy of "our" Milky Way alone, according to the calculations of the Soviet astro-physicist G.A. Tichow, there could be as many as five million planets resembling earth on which life could have originated or expired.[26]

But the best-selling author cannot use more than one inhabited world. Evolution is therefore an "absolute creation," and so the physicist can believe in a God, and the smart theologian can stick his boot in the doorway again. Buy why should it be an "absolute creation"? Because evolution grows out of errors and disruptions, imperfections in its conservation mechanism, errors in the reproduction of the program of heredity, the so-called mutation, which are as incalculable as the "quantum-breaks"; Monod sees a "quantum-phenomenon," an accidental reminder, in every single mutation.

But suppose these milliards of accidents, these errors, these disruptions were part of a system of which selection made up the other part? Is it permissible to go on regarding as blind errors what has happened milliards of times, what first made the development of species possible? Suppose the production of mutations grew up,

326

not from blind failure, but from a change-inducing force — a force which for the time being we may describe as the blind producer of errors and disruptions, but which would none the less be defined and added to, as if it were formulated, by the preference and prejudice of an existing and, seen as a whole, constantly changing environment? Man would then not be "foreseen" in the universe only because we had wisely ceased to envisage any foresight, any design for creation, or even any creation, all that goes beyond our comprehension.*

God, the causer of quantum-breaks and mutations — let us call him that — would certainly not have the least thing to contribute either to the Christian faith or to the Christian ethic: all those Christian academies can take all their thousand feet out of those thousand doorways. Do we have to be reminded that it is the fittest that survive, not the people who give away their shirts as well as their coats? Manfred Mezger, professor of practical theology at Mainz, has shown all those academies and conferences working for reconciliation between Christians and non-Christians the bill of divorce. "As though," he writes, "it did any good when the physicists — by one means today, by another tomorrow — explain that there are irregularities or interruptions in the strict causality! How much honey will the theologians or defenders of the faith be able to suck from that? Has the Christian faith anything of its own to say, or must it look elsewhere to see if it is eligible for partnership?"[27]

If man no longer believes in a life after death — and in a poll held in West Germany in 1967, only forty-eight percent believed in it — if the spirit is not "a living thing that cannot be destroyed,"[28] then our values and norms are related only to men, to the group, the economic community (the state, as we used to say), and to humanity. The "vulgar," simple, banal ethical systems like those of the ancient Greeks and of Rabbi Hillel, if they could be followed, would be enough for the maintenance of mankind. But perhaps they will be followed too late: the principle of mutual solidarity and help is no longer thought of as a principle but only as a bonus to ward off its importance the more certainly. Ethics is

*Monod's book, evolution, Christianity — they all live by their errors and deviations. It is often enough in Monod just to stand all his pompous statements on their head. No, evolution is indicated in the basic pattern of the world. Yes, the universe bears the seeds of life, the biosphere the seeds of man. The creation of man was no more accidental than a win at roulette.

not possible, but necessary. We have to live with such modest caretaker's principles, worthy of the absurdity of religious systems. No logical system is in a position to describe fully its own structure, so man does not "know" why he needs to act in accordance with a system of values and norms which he then ignores or changes as necessary. Does it help him to hear from the theologians of Mainz that God is "the whence of our 'I must' and 'I may' " (Herbert Braun)?[29] Does that really help him?

Many, and not the worst Christians, tell us that Christianity has been on the wrong track for sixteen hundred years, ever since Constantine, that it has had a wrong conception of God all that time and is only now in a position to disclose its social mores — in short, that it must start all over again. But when religion was powerful, it never wielded any positive influence on social mores, so why should it do so today, when it is a survival sinking out of sight? The appeal to the "widow's mite" gives the individual an easier conscience, but it is water dripping on a stone; it makes no difference to social customs. The "good feeling" too often attested to is still no more than a feeling; it is still the exception, it does nothing to determine the usages of the social groups.

Of course, there is a lady therapist who affirms that the Christian faith is directly and existentially important to her, that the driving force of Christian force and the attraction of Christian hope together made the motivation of her psychotherapeutic profession.[30] There are priests who defend the persecuted at the risk of their lives. And why should we not believe it possible that the "Jesus trip" frees certain drug addicts for a while, or even forever, from the former link with the drug-users' group by linking them with a new (sensational) group-consciousness? Freud was afraid, and recognized in himself, that he had "turned religion into a human neurosis."[31]

However useful, however important to society, perhaps to keeping drug usage under control, it would still be basically a self-deception to want to attribute to the Christian faith any power to solve the problems of human society. The author Alfons Rosenberg thought that the Christian would be distinguished from his companions in the future society only by his knowledge about the greater relationships, his liberalness and his calm, and his gift of doing enough to fill every moment. That reminds us of the basic thought urged on us in the Gospels, in the view of the Dominican Oivier Rabut: to accept responsibility, to live, not to weaken, to

328

seize the initiative demanded by each situation. Or, as the Protestant Manfred Mezger quite un-solemnly exhorts us: "This service today, ye people, and tomorrow there will be new services!"[32]

Is there any need for the Gospel? We see only that the nominal Christians are just as reluctant as those they call non-Christians (quite apart from the professedly Christian political parties, who are even less ready than all the others) to undertake those social changes — slowing down the birthrate, exorcising the fetishes from the growth of the economy, drastic reduction in the use of raw materials — which are so essential if disasters of undreamed-of magnitude are to be avoided; the Roman church even bans abortion and birth control.* According to a poll taken in North America, Quakers and agnostics display more awareness of their responsibilities, more social engagement than Christian churchmen of the traditional faiths, less narrow-mindedness and hostility.[33] Perusing the Bible is of no help to a humanity which arranges its destiny with about as much imagination as did the dinosaurs, antedeluvian monsters too deep in debt to Mother Nature, so much so that they lost the faculty of adjustment and died therewith. But extinction when fully conscious would be something quite new, a challenge without precedent. Maybe it will be then, and only then, that man will find an answer.

Spiritual appeal must always be ineffective simply because of the material responsibilities. Thus, a church which wants to assert its own power is only passing the time by appealing to the conscience of politics. The will not to yield is a basic characteristic of all institutions, even the ecclesiastical. The theology of revolution never leads to revolution: the revolutionary priest must choose between his church and his gun.

If it was true, as Pope Paul VI states, that man "is collapsing under his own weight," then there is no God to help him, no church, no faith. It is just the same: man is slithering into an open, unprotected future and no one knows whether or when he will be "overtaxed" by it (Gehlen). The foreboding says Theodor Adorno, is general: "as the control of nature progresses it moves

---

*The good or harm done by the Christian churches in the world cannot be seriously assessed without knowledge of the actual communities involved. Where money is poured out for Olympic Games, concert halls and opera houses, the consolation is worth the money in itself. Only one must ask whether the consolation of the churches in West Germany reaches those who stand most in need of it, and from that point of view, there is a lot to be said for the argument that the money would be better spent on establishing special schools for the underprivileged than on paying theologians.

inexorably towards the very disaster it wanted to guard itself against." The "real liberation in the sense of Jesus of Nazareth," which the Marxist-oriented anthropologist Hans Kilian thinks possible from the state of the forces of production, already no longer exists; the actual survival of many, perhaps even of all, is debatable.[34]

Man is centered on himself alone, thinks Eugen Lemberg, an ideological sociologist favorably inclined to religions; but he is able to cope with this solitude, and so there is no longer any need for an anchorage in the transcendental. With no partners and no opponents, says Werner Heisenberg, he stands on this earth facing no one but himself. Every historical appearance, every human or social condition is final, every kind of faith is relative. The perception is there — it even found its way into Jacques Monod's book — but it is not yet widespread. Philosophy and social science, like theology before them, shut themselves off from this new and necessarily banal ethic, which "seems to reduce the capacity for longing" (Adolf Holl). The dethronement of metaphysics does indeed look like "a triumphal procession of banality" (Peter L. Berger). Don Quixote has come home to a humdrum world as if into a captivity where he is tortured by "the cruellest of all torturers: by sound commonsense" (Alfred Schütz).[35]

Max Horkheimer has said that philosophy, too, has come to an end with theology, together with "all that we call 'meaning.'"[36] But that seems to be rather an optical illusion, a bit exaggerated. Transcendental meaning is finished, like secularized theology, secularized doctrine of salvation, philosophy as a substitute for religion. This historic philosophy will keep going as successor to the good God: the good primitive man (Rousseau), the development of freedom (Kant), the necessary progress (Hegel), the rebuilding of the true reality of man (Marx), the new overman (Nietzsche), absolute time (Bloch), mankind as evolving God (Teilhard de Chardin). It is not only theology that has had to pay up. Even its successor, teleology, a very German lady, looks a pretty poor performer. That man is programmed for a process of higher development and his better part destined for the marking-out of such a positive happening, every commentator a peak in the world of eternal reason — that has not proved possible to maintain.

Two world wars have shattered Europe's philosophy of the "intelligent causes" of the world (Dilthey). But even the edifice

330

built up on the ruins contains a purely negative system with still too much of Jewish-Christian theology. Once again, the world has been weighed in the balance and found wanting. Once again, as in the time of the Jewish apocalypse, the requirements laid down by the prophets have been presented as real, the opposition facing their realization as only apparent. Once again, says Theodor W. Adorno, world history, with Auschwitz as its temporary climax, is utterly destroyed and this age is ruled by Belial: "Theory sets the excessive burden of historical necessity in motion only when what is recognized as illusion becomes real, when historical determination is seen as metaphysically inessential." If we call Belial by his name, if we describe the system of evil, we have already almost driven the devil out, we have broken the totality "in the claim of its absoluteness."[37]

Hate for a world in which there is suffering makes the frustrated metaphysician creative. Disregarding history, he imagines another, more valuable world. Like Adorno, Herbert Marcuse sees a society of "advancing negativity"; redress is only possible through a revolution that will completely change everything "on the attainable level of liberation."[38] Who are the revolutionaries to be? In place of the proletariat — a group certainly idealized by Marx, but historically always exclusive — Marcuse envisages a bringer of revolution who will develop only out of his own participation in revolutionary processes, in every way a new, a second Adam; only the kind of man who has been himself liberated from the conditions of society can bring about revolution within that society. Thus, Marcuse's Messiah, like that of Israel of old, emerges from the very conditions that he is to create, like Munchhausen pulling himself out of the swamp by his own hair. The telos, the ultimate end, of this urgent need is the transformation of "society to the artifact," to the work of art. In fact, the esthetic is to become the "social productive force," a "new Jerusalem" indeed. It seems to us as if every effort since Marx to bring about the Christian Utopia on earth has become powerless; according to Mao, the doer, and Marcuse, the esthete, there are no Utopias any more. "In the fully administratively organized world," says Max Horkheimer, "ideas lose their significance."[39]

Marcuse's retreat into the esthetic explains a retreat into the simplicity of the nursery on the part of his teacher Martin Heidegger, Rudolf Bultmann's philosophical dynamo, as it were the terminus of philosophy for the time being. Man, says Heidegger, should direct his thought into the dimension of the holy. Thought gives to man "an indication of the original dimension of his place in history"; it must descend "into the poverty of his present existence." Thought must no longer yield power to (this world's) logic, to (this world's) reason, Paul's λογισμοί "reason, glorified for centuries, (is) the most implacable opponent of thought."[40]

Heidegger, who has buried the Christian, the moral, the metaphysical God, awaits the coming, "more godly" God, hopes for the Whole and the dimension of the Holy, which last is apparently identical with Being as a dimension; the dimensional, the essence of the dimension, is Being itself, It itself. We learn further about Heidegger's more godly God: " . . . even God is, if he is, a being, stands as a being in Being and its essence"; he exists as a being and stands out in Being, the essence of which "comes to pass out of the worlds of the world."[41]

Heidegger also interprets world history according to a negative system; he too is aware of a conflict between Ormuzd and Ahriman: the distinction — if indeed it is a distinction — between the "supremacy of the entity" (read western metaphysics) and the "dominance of Being" (read the philosophy of Heidegger). Man can deny himself the consolation of Being. For it is not really so, as Martin Heidegger presumably knows, "that sooner or later only a new God, or the old one over again, breaks in out of the trap." Although men cannot land him, by prayer or by any other means, yet they must get an abode "suitable for a God" ready for him, or "where should he turn at his coming again"? The truth of Being must be brought to mind following the unthinking abandonment of Being by the entity. Thought is Advent-thought, "based on being as what is to come (l'avenant)"; it is the reminder, the prayer; shepherds stand ready with the song of praise, glory be to the truth of Being in the highest.[42]

But the entity, says Heidegger, is not only isolated from Being; Being has been forgotten, so that the need of the needlessness of the age (the "world-night," the "un-world") is dominant. We recognize this kind of needlessness as something dreadful. Let us then for the moment leave aside the difference between the "basic question" of the being of the entity and that other "basic question" of the truth of Being: are we to take over from Heidegger the conception of questioning as a "godliness of thought"? Very well, so long as this godly questioning concerns itself with disagreeable practices and the conditions of this world, and does not seek, and find, satisfaction in the thought-decor of sheer wilful hair-splitting and nit-picking.[43]

Bloch, the atheist hoping for a Messiah, Wittgenstein, the religious *rentier*-logician, Heidegger, who looks forward to a non-Christian, a more godly God: Christian theology lives by their pillage.

The most valuable result of all this brain-cudgelling is the realization that this entity, man, boxed in on all sides in his perception of being, has to live with no "final understanding," "final reason for being," "final friend," with no answer to the ultimate in general and to the question of the "being of the entity" or of the "truth of Being"; no one can digest old leaven. Why are we here on earth? The German Catholic catechism told us the answer as long ago as 1955: "To do the will of God and so to go to heaven." But only a battle-scarred professional cleric could proclaim, as the Archbishop of Freiburg, Hermann Schäufele, did in 1971: "So this very day Christianity, the church, is not moving towards a pathetic twilight but striding through the night towards a glorious morning." The Jesuit Domenico Grasso, professor of the Papal Gregorian University, sees "with certainty" the coming of the religious revival because more and more people are interesting themselves in astrology.[44]

To be a Christian is a demand we make of the Christians; the demand we make of ourselves is no different. We shall never believe what Max Horkheimer said in a memorial address for the theologian Paul Tillich, that the idea of respect, even of love, for one's neighbor loses the logical basis of the last trace of theology.[45] One might have supposed that the idea existed before the elements of logic and before all theology.

Can we live without religion? We will have to. Religion as the Christians understand it, religion which embraces the vicarious sacrifice, the revelation of another world and a mystic union with the transcendental principle, religion which embraces judgment and mercy and a hereafter, cannot be replaced by another, least of all by a non-Christian, religion. If that is all believed symbolically, then the images must still make sense, and today they have no power to do so. The symbols are like "flags representing a country of which no one knows the name" (Horkheimer). "In truth, I would not believe the Gospel," says Augustine, "if the authority of the Catholic church did not move me to it." Religion can no longer, as it is used, save men from "hanging on to the void"

(Gehlen). Only a painted umbrella can be hung on a hook that is only painted on the wall.

It is common experience that substitutes for lost religions are being invented on all sides as if with a magic wand; that the concept of religion is being broadened beyond any expectation (even the Christian Catholic *Rheinische Merkur* thinks nothing of writing about "the religion of pop and the underground" without even using quotation marks). Psychedelics go on trips to heaven with the new wonder drugs; God comes out of the amplifier. Unction and loving humility are found in the type of the "groupie," the new Magdalen.

It is no accident that the new "religions," pop and the underground and the Jesus people, are not concerned with the problems of society. This is the field of circus ringmasters like Billy Graham, though even staid bishops are known to snatch at the coat-tails of the anti-hash Jesus people. A popular preacher, already quoted here quite often, not only wants to bring the Jesus people to critical rationality but will even betray some of the mysteries to them in exchange, which brings us one lap further on. "The glory of Jesus is close to *The Threepenny Opera* and to a chorale."[48] But the Jesus people, it goes without saying, will in the last analysis have cured about as many people of drug-addiction as the television stations will have cured ladies of tippling, and the ecclesiastical adepts will preserve their new mysteries no better than the old. Since religion can no longer meet the requirements of men for change, men are turning change into a religion.

There must be ethics; the will to survive will impose an ethical norm tailored for survival. The ethic of the groups has not fallen from heaven; it is biologically and socio-economically determined. Each individual's ethic varies from those of other men like his finger prints. In the box of Tinker Toys from which, on this as on any other star, human ethics are taken out, there is room even for the behavior of a man (let us say a Polish Franciscan) who in a death camp (say of the National Socialists) voluntarily takes on himself the "punishment" of a fellow prisoner "condemned" to death by starvation, though himself sick and in pain, but still not without some prospect of dying less painfully, perhaps even, who knows, of surviving his time in prison.[49] Deliberately to sacrifice one's life, deliberately to accept death in place of one's neighbor as the Bible story says that Jesus did — even this is included as a motivating possibility among all the forms of behavior of all human creatures, and is found even in the instinctive behavior of animals.

Have we advanced a bit since the days of Pilate, do we have a "higher"ethic as a result of the legend of the Nazarene? Surely not. What is ethics but "a kind of rule of the road for traffic among men" (Freud)?[50] Cicero, quite certainly not a Christian, long ago described that single, eternal and immutable law, of which God is the one common master and ruler:

> But the true law is honest judgment, in tune with nature,
> extended over all things, constant, sempiternal, which summons
> to duty by its commands and by its restraints deters from fraud,
> yet which does not command or forbid just men for no reason
> nor move the unjust by command or by prohibition. Nor is it
> right for this law to be repealed, nor lawful for it to be amended,
> nor can it be wholly annulled; indeed, we cannot be freed from
> this law either by the Senate or by the people . . . nor can there
> be any other law in Rome, any other in Athens.[51]

Conscience, we have perceived, is one thing in Washington, another in Peking.

We are "alone," alone in the universe, as long as we have no communication with any other human species. We cannot believe it possible that, far away on other stars, sentient beings have been killed because, like Jesus, like Jan Hus or the Superintendent of Ladenberg, they were not prepared to follow the established religion, or even because they maintained the existence of other worlds like Giordano Bruno, or even only because they belonged to a different group from their killers. The "postulate of a moral world order" which Freud could not see on the planet earth will no doubt also remain in the dark beyond the Milky Way.

> The stars stain
> the vault of heaven
> with the blood of the butchered and beheaded.[52]
>   Mayakovsky

Man as a species goes on producing himself in a continually changing environment, as part of which he too changes. He is adapted, and adapts himself, for the future, in part consciously but in far greater part unconsciously, regardless of the limitations of himself and his species. Hope for the future is innate in him, hope for change and/or improvement.

How then shall we escape anonymity and tedium, the fear of anonymity and tedium? Identity and stimulation — how shall we find them? How, if not in meaningful work, meaningful joy and meaningful hate, if not in heartfelt and sympathetic openness to the needs and the interests of our fellow men? How shall we fulfil our lives, if even existence for others holds out no more hope? Since all human absoluteness is unrealizable, we are driven back on a stoic calm. All philosophy goes back to a rational, utterly banal life-control. The meaning of life, according to our grandiose philosophical judgment, is its meaning for us, the living. True, the gods, and God, as Heidegger wrote in 1946, have "passed away," "the splendor of their godhead vanished in world history."[53] But the dream and the longing remain, to be seen in every face. As in the Jewish-Christian religion, the master wanted to have his game with mankind although he already knew from the beginning of time what the result of the game would be, so we must act as if we were free, as if proceeding actively and deliberately were the same as making progress. Since we do not know the rules of the game nor the object of the game, we must from our own drive for existence believe it to be "true," that it is worth it for ourselves and for others to accept the game. "The point is," says the other, the practical, Gollwitzer, "to fight for progress, but without believing in it."[54]

If Pascal in suggesting his "wager" had recommended man to concern himself with God, either to prevail over him or at worst to finish up no worse than before,[55] then there is nothing left for us to do but accept ourselves, our life and the society we live in. We can make the better, the relative best, out of ourselves, our life and society. If we do not improve anything, if we fail, then at least we are no worse off than before. We put in nothing but what comes out of us in the first place, if we do not first venture to make the effort.

Jesus-Joshua, a son of two human beings, is no more than a transfer as a religious figure. We have dreamed him up out of our imagination. What concerned me in my childhood and my youth, because I was concerned with it, still concerns society today in a stage-world either with no ground at all or with a double or treble false bottom. Forms of life from which all life has long leaked out must collapse. We should like to know what percentage of clerics and theologians believe what they say. The answer can only be guessed, but fairly accurately: about the same as the percentage of all professing Christians by and large who believe that Jesus is God and that there is an eternal life. About half, perhaps?

Suppression is a good thing, to bring into consciousness a better. As a wise man once said, everyone is always atoning for his youth.[56] A rational work-out has been good for me, and society needs it. It is just when we are least aware of it that we are unconsciously controlled by our own past. There was no "Fall" in human history that has to be atoned for. Man will die as little by chance, and as little burdened by sin, as he was created. "Thou shalt not make any image of God" means in our language: thou shalt not be able to know who thou art, nor what thou shalt become.

Afterword by
David Noel Freedman

The appearance of Rudolf Augstein's *Jesus Menschensohn*, in English dress, is an important publishing event, not only because the subject matter is of perennial interest and the treatment is iconoclastic and provocative, but also because the author, who is notable if not notorious in his own right, is the flamboyant Editor of *Der Spiegel*, the very popular and widely influential journal of West Germany these many years. Like the otherwise very different volume by Werner Keller, *Und die Bibel hat doch recht* (*The Bible as History*), Augstein's book has created a sensation in Germany and a storm of controversy. Keller's book became a runaway best-seller in the United States, partly at least because it told millions what they wanted to hear, but it remains to be seen whether Augstein's vastly more sophisticated opus can have a comparable success telling what most people probably do not want to hear. While the books arrive at opposite conclusions about the reliability and historical accuracy of the biblical records and data, together they reveal that even or especially in this supposedly irreligious age, literary treatments of the Bible (and the more opinionated the better) find a ready, willing and often combative audience. While the present volume has many intriguing qualities, at the least it deserves to be read by the American public to discover what is stirring the minds and hearts of fellow human beings in Germany and Europe, with whom we share this common religious tradition.

It should be said at the outset that the book is a personal statement by Augstein, although the material on which it is based appeared in a series of articles in *Der Spiegel* some years ago. The author says little or nothing about himself and his own history of faith or lack of it, but it is clear from hints dropped broadly throughout the book that he has had a long and embattled relationship with biblical religion in the form dispensed by the institutional church. He is under compulsion, intellectual and emotional, to make his case against that institution and its official representatives. He asserts passionately the right to and need for individual freedom of mind and conscience to pursue the truth, wherever the trail of serious scholarship leads, and to proclaim it without fear or favor, especially if it challenges the confident claims of historic Christianity.

Augstein writes as an angry man who is still in rebellion against Mother Church (having been spoon-fed as a child, one gathers, and now repudiating what was forced upon him). He is determined to expose the hypocrisy of the church, that is, the huge credibility gap between what its best minds have known for decades and what it nevertheless continues to teach and preach to the masses. He also attacks its magisterial claims to authority in the areas of faith and morals, especially where its rulings and decisions are enforced by coercive means and pressures. Considering the generally depressed and weakened condition of the churches in this country today, the charges seem curiously archaic and misdirected. Americans must remember, however, that the churches of Europe, in particular the Roman Catholic communion, have played a large, often dominant, role in the governing party of countries like Germany and Italy, to mention only the most striking examples. While his intentions toward the church are hardly altruistic, the effects of his advice, if taken seriously, would doubtless be beneficial. Experience in America and elsewhere has shown that the strength and influence of the churches have tended to increase as their political visibility has diminished, and that obvious grabs for power tend to backfire. Efforts to extend authoritarian rulings to those outside the church through the political process produce resentment and reaction. Even within the membership, crude assertions of authority in sensitive areas result in resistance and ultimately rebellion. People of all faiths and persuasions — and of none — are inclined to listen respectfully when the church speaks out of principle and for the common good, but *not* when it does so for its own advantage and in disregard of the well-being of others. The citizenry generally look to it as the keeper of the conscience of the nation, but do not wish to see it as part of the power structure, still less as its controlling force.

That the church would exert coercion in matters of faith and morals, of conscience and conviction, is at once unthinkable and undeniable. While one would take for granted the church's

339

acknowledgement of the principle that God alone is Lord of the conscience, the facts are otherwise: the church when given the opportunity has encroached repeatedly in this area. While the tendency has been observed more easily in Western Europe, where since the Second World War the governments of the major countries have been dominated or strongly influenced by conservative Christian Democratic parties, backed vigorously and openly by the Roman Catholic church (often with substantial Protestant support), it is not unknown in this country for churches to use political pressure when and where they were able to do so. Some Protestant churches have functioned effectively at the local and state levels, notably in the South, while the Catholic church has had a dominant political voice in many of the larger cities, and has also exerted notable pressure on state and national governments.

Augstein contends that the church imposes even more constraints internally, but in a paradoxical fashion. In its pronouncements and from its pulpits, the church affirms the classic claims of Christianity concerning the Godhead (in its threefold character, or as Augstein maintains, its quadrilateral composition including the Virgin *Mater Dei*), the Church, and as a point of special interest, the Bible. Church and Book go together, each supporting and finding support in the other. Depending upon the point of view, whether Protestant or Catholic, the Bible is the ground upon which the Church is built, or the Church is the matrix from which the Bible emerges. Historically, the Church has been the preserver and protector of the Bible, its champion and exclusive interpreter. While for the church the Bible has remained fixed and its interpretation unchanged over the centuries, biblical scholars and research have also been sponsored and supported by the church. These men, over several generations, have analyzed the text and reached conclusions which often contrast startlingly with the traditional position of the church. While the church can hardly be said to have welcomed these developments, and from time to time has endeavored to discipline and even suppress the more dissident and dissonant voices (with tragic results in individual cases), the work of critical scholarship has not diminished in any respect, but has increased in vigor and volume in the course of time. The author delights in pointing out that the findings of critical New Testament scholars over the past 100 years have consistently been in flat contradiction with what the church continues to teach in its official documents and pronouncements.

The contradiction is most obvious in the case of Jesus, concerning whom the church has promulgated a series of doctrinal statements regarding his person and status, while modern scholars have reached radically different conclusions on the basis of the same biblical data. Augstein's primary objective, therefore, is to set the record straight on the figure of Jesus. He emphasizes that from a scientific historical point of view based on a critical examination of the available source material, there is very little that is known or can be said about Jesus: where he lived and when, in general terms, and how he died. Virtually all of the available information about Jesus comes from the New Testament, mostly from the four gospels, and it cannot be considered a reliable source from an *historical* point of view. The purpose of the Gospels is not to provide objective data about Jesus, but to present him as the Risen Lord, the unique Son of God, the fulfiller and fulfillment of Old Testament prophecy. He is authoritative teacher, divine healer, wonder-worker without equal, prophet like Moses, king like David and priest, not like Aaron, but that greater, more mysterious figure, Melchizedek. Everything told about him and predicated of him in the New Testament is permeated by the convictions of the church, which preserved his memory and produced these works.

Sorting out the original authentic tradition from the later accretions is dangerous, difficult and delicate work. Augstein, without being a scholar, has nevertheless threaded his way successfully through the labyrinth of modern critical scholarship. He is conservative and cautious in his conclusions in the sense that he goes with the great names and mainstream figures of the most radical German scholarship. He finds Bultmann and the Marburgers most to his liking, while unreconstructed traditionalists and mavericks like J. Jeremias and D. Flusser are treated brusquely, their contrary options dismissed with some scorn. When all the layers are peeled away, there is precious little left beyond the bare assertion that Jesus existed. One can only wonder why the church would bother to create such an elaborate multi-dimensional divine-human figure out of such a nondescript nonenity. The logic of the method is inescapable, and the validity of its premise cannot be questioned: the original figure of Jesus has been reworked and shaped by the community in the light of its needs and opportunities, and the result is a composite which reflects the history of the experience of the church and only in a secondary way the life and experience of Jesus. While it is impossible ever to return to an older uncritical and harmonistic position, a fresh approach and a new assessment of the current state of affairs would seem to be in order. Thus, Augstein acepts too meekly the now traditional two-source hypothesis (i.e., Mark and Q, the common sayings-source of Matthew and Luke) as a basic solution to the Synoptic Problem, although it is being challenged by scholars from different quarters and for different reasons, and a reconsideration is surely in order. Similarly, Augstein considers fixed beyond doubt an evolutionary sequence among the four gospels, so that development can be traced rigorously from Mark, the oldest, to John, the latest. Certain assumptions underlie these rather neat and simple arrangements, which beg to be questioned, however. Is evolution always uni-directional: do things develop from short to long, and simple to complex, and never go the other way? Is it clear that John is late, the latest of the gospels, or is this a matter of bias built into tradition (or the other way around)? Must Luke be a Gentile for Augstein (or the scholars upon whom he depends) to make his points about the gospel attributed to him: the universal sweep of Christianity and the concern for the enemy as well as the friend? Must Matthew be a Jew so that other points can be made? Or are these stereotypes imposed by mechanical reasoning or unreflective adherence to established positions? Augstein, the inveterate iconoclast, should have been more critical of the critics and treated less reverently their "assured findings" and other speculations.

For a scholar in the field of biblical studies, there is a shock in seeing how an interested, intelligent and articulate layman has absorbed and organized scholarly data and opinions, and then restated them in his own brash journalistic way. The carefully wrought shadings and nuances, the modifications and strictures, the exceptions and caveats necessary to a balanced scholarly picture are ignored or swept aside in a simplified presentation which distorts as much as it affirms. No doubt this is the source of much of the excitement generated by the book, along with uninhibited judgments expressed about churches and churchmen, theologians and biblical scholars by the irrepressible Editor. In the end, however, Augstein justifies his position: The Gospels must be read as highly differentiated compositions by those who served the interests of the church or Christian community to which they belonged. The figure of Jesus that emerges is theirs, not his. The church might have decided for one or another among them, but for various reasons, and in typical fashion, chose to preserve and make use of all four, separately, not together (for which we may be grateful). The real Jesus remains a shadowy figure (not because he was like that, but because there is no way to recover him) behind the Gospels, a mystery forever. It would appear that Augstein's real quarrel with the Church is not that it opted for the Gospels (what else could have been done?), but that it insists on equating these stylized portraits with the real Jesus. It would suffice if the package were labelled properly, as a tendentious reworking of older materials, not to be confused with the Jesus of history who has been lost in it. There are not any workable alternatives, since scholarly and literary portraits are notoriously inadequate, but so are those pictures derived from sociological and psychological models.

While Augstein does remarkably well with the intricacies of New Testament scholarship, and his work of analysis and classification is a tour de force (the same is true of his survey of the major features of the Old Testament by way of preparation for the appearance of the Gospel, and of developments in Christian dogma in the centuries after its appearance), he cannot control the primary materials or the scholarly results and is ultimately the victim of the people on whom he relies. He is at his lively best when sparring with churchmen and theologians on home turf, debating the great issues of survival on the planet today. He tilts cheerfully at the *berühmte* heros of modern faith who have made a name for themselves on both sides of the Atlantic, men like Thielicke, Pannenberg and Moltmann, all of whom he criticizes as inadequate physicians for the sickness of mankind, men who prescribe poultices and nostrums when surgery is required. In their earnest sententiousness, they merely restate old formulas in catchy phrases, which the church repeats for its comfort, but which long ago lost pertinence and even meaning. They are like the fatuous optimists of a biblical age who announced peace with honor where there was neither peace nor honor. Augstein is especially critical of Moltmann who insists on speaking of the resurrection of Jesus as an historical event within the framework of definable and determinable human experience. Even the New Testament writers found this a difficult assignment, in fact, beyond them, and they did not have to face up to structural linguists and scientific positivists. What is needed, according to Augstein, is not a reversion to the simplicities of an earlier age, but serious confrontation of the new age of atomic energy, rock music, ecology, population explosion, pollution and all the other problems and ills to which man is heir.

Augstein's examination of the gospels is a springboard for discussion not only of the historical Jesus, but the Jesus figure constructed and reconstructed by the church, whereby the Jewish carpenter of Galilee was transmuted into a divine-human savior of the world. The author is intrigued by the possibilities of further transformation and mutations, in the continuing fascination with the person of Jesus, and the ways in which the church and the world have adapted and adjusted this figure to changing circumstances. From this base, he asks about the place and role of religion in our age, which is so different from earlier periods. The names of Marx and Freud loom large in his thinking, as their contributions have penetrated to every level and unit of society. He also discusses a short list of scientific thinkers who have contributed to the notion of religion in the new world of the interior of the atom, and the configuration of the macrocosm. (Curiously, Augstein never mentions Einstein, who, like Freud and Marx in their fields, intentionally or not, opened the way to a new understanding of the universe.) In spite of all, or perhaps because of all, the public remains steadfast in its acknowledgement of God, whom it neither knows nor serves, but whom it seeks. The certainty of his existence, and the necessity of the quest, which is nevertheless doomed to frustration and failure, constitute the human predicament. If we may paraphrase the second commandment (with which Augstein concludes his book), man must forever make images, and construct models of the God whom he seeks, but these can only be crude caricatures of the reality they reflect and must be destroyed as desecrations of the divine. Worse than a prohibition, the word from Sinai is a statement of fact: there can be no adequate portrayal or image of God.

The Albright Institute
Jerusalem, Israel
20 December 1976

List of works
frequently cited

Antijudaismus. Antijudaismus im Neuen Testament? Exegetische und systematische Beiträge. Ed. W.P. Eckert et al. Munich, 1967

Ben-Chorin: Jesus Ben Chorin, Schalom: *Bruder Jesus. Der Nazarener in jüdischer Sicht.* 3rd. ed. Munich, 1970

Ben-Chorin: Paulus Ben-Chorin, Schalom: *Paulus. Der Völkerapostel in jüdischer Sicht.* Munich, 1970

Ben-Chorin: Mirjam Ben-Chorin, Schalom: *Mutter Mirjam. Maria in jüdischer Sicht.* Munich, 1971

Blank: Christus Blank, Josef: *Der Christus des Glaubens und der historische Jesus.* (In) *Der Mann aus Galiläa.* Freiburg, 1971

Blinzler: Prozess Blinzler, Josef: *Der Prozess Jesu.* 4th ed. Regensburg, 1969

Bloch: Atheismus Bloch, Ernst: *Atheismus im Christentum. Zur Religion des Exodus und des Reichs.* Frankfurt, 1968

Bloch, Münzer Bloch, Ernst: *Thomas Münzer als Theologe der Revolution.* Frankfurt, 1962

Bornkamm: Studien Bornkamm, Günther: *Studien zu Antike und Urchristentum.* Gesammelte Aufsätze. Vol. 2. 3rd. ed. Munich, 1970

Bornkamm: Jesus Bornkamm, Günther: *Jesus von Nazareth.* 9th ed. Stuttgart, 1971

Braun: Gesammelte Studien Braun, Herbert: *Gesammelte Studien zum Neuen Testament und seiner Umwelt.* 3rd ed. Tübingen, 1972

Braun: Jesus Braun, Herbert: *Jesus. Der Mann aus Nazareth und seine Zeit.* 3rd ed. Stuttgart, 1972

Braun, Qumran Braun, Herbert: *Qumran und das Neue Testament.* Vols. 1, 2. Tübingen, 1966

Braun: Radikalismus Braun, Herbert: *Spätjüdisch-häretischer und frühchristlicher Radikalismus.* 2nd ed. Vols. 1,2. Tübingen, 1969

Bultmann: Glauben und Verstehen I Bultmann, Rudolf: *Glauben und Verstehen.* Gesammelte Aufsätze. Vol. 1. 6th ed. Tübingen, 1966

Bultmann: Glauben und Verstehen II Bultmann, Rudolf: *Glauben und Verstehen.* Gesammelte Aufsätze. Vol. 2. 5th ed. Tübingen, 1968

Bultmann: Jesus Bultmann, Rudolf: *Jesus.* Tübingen, 1926 (1961)

Bultmann: Johannesevangelium Bultmann, Rudolf: *Das Evangelium nach Johannes.* 19th ed. Göttingen, 1968

Bultmann: Synopt. Trad. Bultmann, Rudolf: *Die Geschichte der synoptischen Tradition.* 8th ed. Göttingen, 1970

Bultmann: Synopt. Trad. Ergänzungsheft Bultmann, Rudolf: *Die Geschichte der synoptischen Tradition. Ergänzungsheft.* Rev. Gerd Theissen and Philip Vielhauer. 4th ed. Göttingen, 1971

Bultmann: Theologie d. NT Bultmann, Rudolf: *Theologie des Neuen Testaments.* 6th ed. Tübingen, 1968

Burrows: Mehr Klarheit Burrows, Millar: *Mehr Klarheit über die Schriftrollen.* Munich, 1958

Burrows: Schriftrollen Burrows, Millar: *Die Schriftrollen vom Toten Meer.* 3rd ed. Munich, 1960

Conzelmann: Grundriss Conzelmann, Hans: *Grundriss der Theologie des Neuen Testaments.* 2nd ed. Munich, 1968

Conzelmann: Jesus Conzelmann, Hans: article, "Jesus Christus" (in) RGG III

Daniélou: Qumran Daniélou, Jean:*Qumran und der Ursprung des Christentums.* 2nd ed. Mainz, 1959

Dautzenberg: Jesus-Report Dautzenberg, Gerhard: *Der Jesus-Report und die neutestamentliche Forschung.* (in) *Rabbi J. Eine Auseinandersetzung mit Johannes Lehmanns Jesus-Report.* Ed. Karlheinz Müller. 2nd ed. Würzburg, 1970

Dibelius: Formgeschichte Dibelius, Martin: *Die Formgeschichte des Evangeliums.* 3rd ed. Tübingen, 1959

Dibelius: Jesus Dibelius, Martin: *Jesus.* 4th ed. with postscript by Werner Georg Kummel. Berlin, 1966

Dupont-Somer: Schriften Dupont-Sommer, André: *Die essenischen Schriften vom Toten Meer.* Tübingen, 1960

Eisler: Ἰησοῦς βασιλεύς Eisler, Robert:Ἰησοῦς βασιλεὺς οὐ βασιλεύσας. Vols. 1, 2. Heidelberg, 1929-1930

Flusser: Jesus Flusser, David: *Jesus in Selbstzeugnizzen und Bilddokumenten.* Reinbek, 1968

Flusser: Jesus Flusser, David: *Jesus und die Synagoge.* (1n) *Der Mann aus Galiläa.* Freiburg, 1971

Freud: Mann Moses Freud, Sigmund: *Der Mann Moses und die monotheistische Religion.* (in) *Gesammelte Werke.* Vol. 16. 3rd ed. Frankfurt, 1968

Freud: Zukunft Freud, Sigmund: *Die Zukunft einer Illusion.* (in) *Gesammelte Werke.* Vol 14. 4th ed. Frankfurt, 1968

Fuchs: Hist. Jesus II Fuchs, Ernst: *Zur Frage nach dem historischen Jesus.* Vol. 2. 2nd ed. Tübingen, 1965

Hennecke-Schneemelcher: Apokryphen Hennecke, Edgar and Wilhelm Schneemelcher: *Neutestamentliche Apokryphen in deutschen Übersetzung.* 3rd ed. Vols. 1, 2. Tübingen, 1959, 1964

Holl: Jesus Holl, Adolf: *Jesus in schlechter Gesellschaft.* Stuttgart, 1971

Goguel: Leben Jesu Goguel, Maurice: *Des Leben Jesu.* Zurich 1934 (French ed., *La Vie de Jésus.* Paris, 1932)

Gollwitzer: Krummes Holz Gollwitzer, Helmut. *Krummes Holz — auf rechter Gang. Zur Frage nach dem Sinn des Lebens.* 3rd ed. Munich, 1971

Haenchen: Weg Jesu Haenchen, Ernst: *Der Weg Jesu. Eine Erklärung des Markus-Evangeliums und der kanonischen Parallelen.* 2nd ed. Berlin, 1968

Hengel: Zeloten Hengel, Martin: *Die Zeloten.* Leiden, 1961

Jeremias: Lehrer Jeremias, Gert: *Der Lehrer der Gerechtigkeit.* Gottingen, 1963

346

Jeremias: Abba Jeremias, Joachim: *Abba. Studien zur neutestamentlichen Theologie und Zeitgeschichte.* Göttingen, 1966

Jeremias: Gleichnisse Jeremias, Joachim: *Die Gleichnisse Jesu* 8th ed. Göttingen, 1970

Jeremias: Theologie I Jeremias, Joachim: *Neutestamentliche Theologie. Part I. Die Verkündigung Jesu.* Gütersloh, 1971

Jerusalem Bible.Die Bibel. Die Heilige Schrift des Alten und Neuen Bundes. Mit den Erläuterungen der Jerusalemer Bibel. Ed. Diego Arenhoevel, Alfons Deissler and Anton Võgtle. 2nd ed. Freiburg, 1969

Jesus oder Christus (report of debate) *Jesus oder Christus. Der Mann aus Nazareth und unsere Zeit.* Debate of 11.1.1972, organized by the Bildumgsforum Düsseldorf. Those taking part: Martin Hengel, Adolf Holl, Willi Marxsen, Rudolf Schnackenburg

Jones: Studie ü.d. Hl. Geist Jones, Ernest: *Eine psychoanalytische Studie über den Heiligen Geist.* (In) *Zur Psychoanalyse der christliche Religion.* Frankfurt, 1970

Jubiläumsbibel.Die Bibel oder die ganze Heileige Schrift des Alten und Neuen Testaments nach der deutschen Übersetzung M. Luthers mit erklärenden Anmerkungen. Stuttgart, 1964

Jung: Antwort Jung, Carl Gustav: *Antwort auf Hiob.* 4th ed. Zurich, 1967

Kähler: Jesus Kahler, Martin: *Der sogenannte historische Jesus und der geshichtliche, biblische Christus.* Ed. E. Wolf. 4th ed. Munich, 1969

Käsemann: Hist. Jesus Käsemann, Ernst: *Das Problem des historischen Jesus.* (In) *Exegetische Versuche und Besinnungen.* Vol 1. Göttingen, 1960

Kautzsch: Apokryphen Kautzsch, Emil: *Die Apokryphen und Pseudepigraphen des Alten Testaments.* Vols. 1, 2. Tübingen, 1900 (reprinted 1921)

Kerygma I.Kerygma und Mythos. Ein theologisches Gespräch. Ed. Hans-Werner Bartsch. 5th ed. Vol. 1. Hamburg, 1967

Kerygma II.Kerygma und Mythos. Diskussionen und Stimmen zum Problem der Entmythologisierung. Ed. Hans Werner Bartsch. Vol. 2. Hamburg, 1952

Kümmel: Einleitung Feine, Paul and Johannes Behm: *Einleitung in das Neue Testament.* Newly revised by Werner Georg Kummel. 16th ed. Heidelberg, 1970

Lauenstein: Messias Lauenstein, Diether: *Der Messias. Eine biblische Untersuchung.* Stuttgart, 1971

Lehmann: Jesus-Report Lehmann, Johannes: *Jesus-Report. Protokoll einer Verfalschung.* Düsseldorf, 1970

Lohse: Texte Lohse, Eduard: *Die Texte aus Qumran.* Hebrew and German. 2nd ed. Munich, 1971

Luther: Werke Luther, Martin: *Sämtliche Werke.* Vols. 1-67 Erlangen, 1826-1857

Luther Bible.Die Bibel oder die ganze Heilige Schrift des Alten und Neuen Testaments. Stuttgart, 1966

Maier: Texte Maier, Johann: *Die Texte vom Toten Meer.* Vols. 1, 2. Munich, 1960

Marxsen: Einleitung Marxsen, Willi: *Einleitung in das Neue Testament.* 3rd ed. Gütersloh, 1964

Müntzer: Schriften Müntzer, Thomas: *Schriften und Briefe. Kritische Gesamtausgabe.* Ed. Günther Franz and Paul Kirn. Gütersloh, 1968

Otto: Reich Gottes Otto, Rudolf: *Reich Gottes und Menschensohn.* 2nd ed. Munich, 1940

Pannenberg: Christologie Pannenberg, Wolfhard: *Grundzüge der Christologie.* Gütersloh, 1964

RE.Paulys Realencyclopädie der classischen Altertumswissenschaft. New revised ed. Ed. Georg Wissowa et al., Stuttgart, 1893-

Reik: Gott Reik, Theodor: *Der eigene und der fremde Gott.* Wien, 1923

RGG. Die Religion in Geschichte und Gegenwart. Handwörterbuch f. Theol. und Religionswiss. 3rd ed. Vols. 1-6. Tübingen, 1957-1965

Schürer: Gesch. d. jüd. Volkes Schürer, Emil: *Geschichte des jüdischen Volkes im Zeitalter Jesu Christi.* 3rd and 4th ed. Vols. 1-3. Leipzig, 1901-1909

Schweitzer: Leben-Jesu-Forschung Schweitzer, Albert: *Geschichte der Leben-Jesu-Forschung.* 6th ed. Tübingen, 1951

Senfkornbibel (Mustard Seed Bible) Die Bibel oder die ganze Heilige Schrift des Alten und Neuen Testaments. 2nd ed. Stuttgart 1971

Shaw: Aussichten Shaw, George Bernard: *Die Aussichten des Christentums.* Frankfurt, 1971. (From the preface to his play *Androcles and the Lion*)

Stauffer: Jerusalem Stauffer, Ethelbert: *Jerusalem und Rom im Zeitalter Jesu Christi.* Berne, 1957

Stauffer: Jesus Stauffer, Ethelbert: *Jesus, Gestalt und Geschichte.* Berne, 1957

Strack-Billerbeck Strack, Hermann L. and Paul Billerbeck: *Kommentar zum Neuen Testament aus Talmud und Midrasch.* 5th ed. Vols. 1-5/6. Munich, 1969

Strauss: Leben Jesu Strauss, David Friedrich: *Das Leben Jesu, kritisch bearbeitet.* Vols. 1, 2. 3rd ed. Tübingen, 1838-1839

Strauss: Leben Jesu f. d. dt. Volk Strauss, David Friedric: *Das Leben Jesu für das deutsche Volk bearbeitet.* 2nd ed. Leipzig, 1864

Thomas-Evangelium Quotations and numbering from *The Gospel of Thomas* (in) E. Hennecke: *New Testament Apocrypha,* Vol. I. London, 1963. (Translated from Hennecke-Schneemelcher: *Apokryphen,* q.v.)

ThWB. Theologisches Wörterbuch zum Neuen Testament. Ed. Gerhard Kittel. (Vols. 5-8 ed. Gerhard Friedrich.) Vols. 1-8. Stuttgart, 1953-1969

Weber: Aufsatze Weber, Max: *Gesammelte Aufsätze zur Religionssoziologie.* Vol. 1, 4th ed. Tübingen 1947. Vol. 3, 2nd ed. Tübingen, 1923

Wilckens Bible. Das Neue Testament. Translated with commentary by Ulrich Wilckens. 2nd ed. Hamburg, 1971

Zahrnt: Jesus Zahrnt, Heinz: *Es begann mit Jesus von Nazareth.* 3rd ed. Gütersloh, 1969

Notes

Foreword

1. Augustine: *De praedestinatione sanctorum* II, 5: "Nullus quippe credit aliquid, nisi prius cogitaverit esse credendum."
2. Cadbury, Joel Henry: *Dunkelheit um den historischen Jesus.* (In) *Wer war Jesus von Nazareth? Die Erforschung einer historischen Gestalt.* Ed. by Gerhard Strube. Munich 1972, p. 182
3. Knopf, Rudolf, Hans Leitzmann and Heinrich Weinel: *Einführung in das Neue Testament.* 5th edition, Berlin 1960, p. 1
4. Paul VI: "Sedula Cura". (Quoted from:) *L'Osservatore Romano* July 1971: " ... Deum non privato doctorum iudicio, sed Ecclesiae suae Sacras commisisse Scripturas."
5. Trost, Franz Josef: *Wahlverwandtschaft auf katholisch.* (In) Deutsches *Allgemeine Sonntagsblatt,* 5 March 1972
6. Zahrnt: *Jesus,* p. 126
7. Fuchs, Ernst: *Programm der Entmythologisierung.* (In) *Glauben heute.* Ed. by Gert Otto, Hamburg, 1968, p. 185
8. Letter of 19 July from Franz, Cardinal König to Dr. Adolf Holl; cf. Chapter 2, Note 82
9. Schmaus, Michael: *Katholische Dogmatik.* Vol. 1, 6th edition, Munich, 1960, p. 118
10. Thielicke, Helmut (Quoted from) *Welt am Sonntag,* 11 July 1971
11. Otto, Gert: *Zur Einführung* (In) *Glauben heute.* Ed. by Gert Otto. Hamburg, 1968, p. 11
12. Zahrnt: *Jesus,* p. 67 ff.
13. Rabut, Olivier: *In Ungewissheit glauben.* Munich 1970, pp. 29, 26, 27, 47
14. Zahrnt: *Jesus,* p. 67 ff.
15. Montaigne, Michel de: *Essais*

Chapter 1

1. Conzelmann, Hans: *Zur Methode der Leben-Jesu-Forschung.* (In) *Die Frage nach dem historischen Jesus. Zeitschrift für Theologie und Kirche,* Year 56, 1959, first supplement, p. 8
2. Non-Christian source material apart from the works of Josephus adds nothing to our concrete knowledge of Jesus.
   The Roman governor Pliny the Younger, in a letter to the emperor Trajan (111-113), mentions the name of a Christus who was honored as a god in Bithynia, in Asia Minor. (*Epistulae X,* 96: "quasi deo carmina dicunt.") The Roman historian Tacitus reports in the year 117 that Nero has persecuted a group of so-called Christians. The originator of the name,

Christus, is said to have been executed by the governor Pontius Pilate under the emperor Tiberius. (*Annales XV,* 44: "ergo abolendo rumori Nero subdidit reos et quaesitissimis poenis adfecit, quos per flagitia invisos vulgus Christianos appellabat. Auctor nominis eius Christus Tiberio imperitante per procuratorem Pontium Pilatum supplicio adfectus erat; repressaque in praesens exitiabilis superstitio rursum erumpebat, non modo per Judaeam, originem eius mali, sed per urbem etiam, quo cuncta undique atrocia aut pudenda confluunt celebranturque.")

The Roman historian Suetonius in the year 120 names one "Chrestus," said to have been responsible for messianic riots in Rome under Claudius. (*Vita Claudii* 25, 4: " . . . Iudaeos impulsore Chresto assidue tumultuantes Roma expulit.") It must be doubtful whether Jesus is meant here. It is not likely that any Christians were living in Rome under Claudius (41-54). The accounts of the Roman historians do not suggest that they had any direct knowledge of Jesus. At best they are evidence that the church believed in Jesus at the beginning of the second century.

The few references to Jesus in the early Talmudic writings are scarcely to be regarded as historical evidence on account of their polemical character. Jesus is described in them as a sorcerer and a deceiver of the people who had five disciples and was hanged on the day of preparation for the Passover. The only useful fact emerging is that no doubt is cast on the existence of Jesus. (*Babyl. Talmud, Tract. Sanhedrin* 43a, Baraitha: "On the eve of the Passover Jesus (the Nazarene) was hanged. For forty days the herald had gone before him and proclaimed: 'Jesus of Nazareth should be stoned because he has practised sorcery, has led Israel astray and has behaved as a rebel. If any man will speak on his behalf, let him come and bear witness for him.' But no one was found to speak for him and he was hanged on the eve of the Passover.") (Quoted from) Klausner, Joseph: *Jesus von Nazareth.* Berlin, 1930, p. 39

The Catholic theologian Josef Blinzler believes that the earliest non-Christian account of Jesus is in "an ancient private letter". "The Syrian Mara bar Sarapion, a Stoic of whom nothing else is known, wrote to his son studying in Edessa shortly after 73 C.E. In his letter he recounted among other things that the Jews had executed their wise king, who had given them new laws, and had been deprived of their kingdom as a punishment for it, some having been put to death and the rest scattered through the whole world." (Quoted from) *Zum Prozess Jesu* (in) *Aus der Welt und Umwelt des Neuen Testaments.* Collected essays 1, Stuttgart 1969, p. 127.

3.   In the rabbinical scriptures the name Jeshua is mostly rendered as Jeshu. Since the abbreviation is found only in the name of Jesus, it has been suggested that the name is deliberately garbled from anti-Christian motives. (Cf. Strack-Billerbeck I, p. 64)
      David Flusser, however, maintains: "That is almost certainly the Aramaic pronunciation of the name." (*Jesus,* p. 13)

4.   In this passage Paul compares himself with a ἔκτρωμα (too early, premature miscarriage).
      Conzelmann, Hans, comments (*Der erste Brief an die Korinther.* Göttingen, 1969, p. 305 ff. on 1 Cor. XV:8): "It cannot be discerned whether Paul is

here describing himself as a miscarriage or as an abortion. We may never be able to decide on these alternatives. Possibly he had passages in the Old Testament in mind."

5. Bornkamm: *Jesus*, p. 14

6. The Jewish historian Justus of Tiberias, a contemporary of Josephus, says nothing about Jesus in his chronicle of the Jewish kings, which goes as far as Agrippa II. The patriarch Photius of Constantinople, who in the ninth century was able to read the work, or parts of it, though it is now lost, has written: "(Justus) does not say a word about Jesus, nor about the events connected with him nor the miracles that he performed." (*Myriobiblion, sive Bibliotheca librorum quos Photius.. legit et censuit.* Edidit David Hoeschelius et Andreas Schottus, 1611, col. 19 - c. 33)
   In the works of the Jewish philosopher Philo of Alexandria (20 B.C.E.-45 C.E.) there is also no mention of Jesus.

7. Josephus (Ant. XVIII, 5, 2 trans. Wm. Whiston, 1737): "Now some of the Jews thought that the destruction of Herod's army came from God, and that very justly as a punishment of what he did against John, that was called *The Baptist*; for Herod slew him, who was a good man, and commanded the Jews to exercise virtue, both as to righteousness towards one another and piety towards God, and so to come to baptism; for that the washing (with water) would be acceptable to him, if they made use of it, not in order to the remission of some sins (only), but for the purification of the body; supposing still that the soul was thoroughly purified beforehand by righteousness. Now, when (many) others came in crowds about him, for they were greatly moved by hearing his words, Herod, who feared lest the great influence John had over the people might put it into his power and inclination to raise rebellion (for they seemed to do anything he should advise), thought it best by putting him to death, to prevent any mischief he might cause, and not bring himself into difficulties by sparing a man who might make him repent of it when it should be too late. Accordingly he was sent a prisoner, out of Herod's suspicious temper, to Macherus, the castle I before mentioned, and was there put to death. Now, the Jews had an opinion that the destruction of this army was sent as a punishment upon Herod, as a mark of God's displeasure against him."

8. John's disciples preached of him as "prophetic Messiah and forerunner of God" (Luke 1:14-17 and 1:76 ff.), as heavenly light (Luke 1:78 ff.; cf. John 1:8; 3:30; 5:35) and perhaps as Logos (John 1:1 ff.); his honoring as Messiah (*Clem. Rec. I*, 54.60), the actual expectation of his return (Syr. Clem. 54,8), are declared later. Vielhauer, Philipp: article, John the Baptist (in) RGG III, col. 807.
   Thus, the Mandaean sect, which followed the Baptist (manda = gnosis = knowledge), recognized John the Baptist as a redeeming figure and argued against Jesus in his name. It is clear from their writings that the Mandaeans were linked with a tradition that looked on the followers of John and of Jesus as opponents of one another.
   In the *Ginza (Ginza: The Treasure, or the Great Book of the Mandaeans,* translated into German with a contemporary by Mark Lidzbarski, Göttingen, 1925) Jesus is described as a "false prophet" and the "third angel

of deceit," "the forger who falsifies the first lesson" (p. 46). "Do not believe him (Jesus) for he deals in sorcery and deception . . . the hidden things are not revealed to the false Messiah" (p. 29).

9. Hölscher, Gustav: *Geschichte der israelitischen und jüdischen Religion.* Giessen, 1922, p. 227.

10. There is nothing in the synoptic Gospels about any baptizing by Jesus. The references to baptism in John's Gospel (3:22 ff. and 4:1) are explicitly corrected in 4:2 — though there is a suspicion that the gloss is interpolated: "although in fact it was only the disciples who were baptizing and not Jesus himself."
Cf. Dinkler, Erich: article, *Baptism in early Christianity* (in) RGG VI, col. 628: "Nothing is said about the practice of baptism at the time of the historical Jesus or in the area in which he moved." Cf. also Bultmann: *Jesus,* p. 129: "The later tradition that he himself baptized is probably unreliable."

11. Cf. *Damascus Document*: "And they take each the daughter of his brother or the daughter of his sister. But Moses has said: Thou shalt not approach the sister of thy mother, for she is a blood relation of thy mother. And the law concerning incest is recorded for men, but is (applicable) likewise for women. And if the daughter of the brother uncovers the nakedness of the brother of her father, then she is (still) a blood relation." (CD V, 7–11; Lohse; *Texts,* p. 75)

12. The Passover, most important of the great Jewish feasts, was in Jesus' time a pilgrim-feast. According to the prescription of the law, every male Israelite from the age of 13 must "look on the face of Yahweh in the place that he chooses" every year at the three main feasts, of the Passover, of Weeks and of Tabernacles (Deuteronomy 16:16; see also Exodus 23:17 and 34:23). That means he must make a pilgrimage to Jerusalem.
There are figures given in Josephus for the numbers taking part in a Passover celebration between 63 and 66 C.E. (trans. H. St. J. Thackeray, 1928) (Bell. Iud. VI 9, 3): "Accordingly, on the occasion of the feast called Passover, at which they sacrifice from the ninth to the eleventh hour, and a little fraternity, as it were, gathers round each sacrifice, of not fewer than ten persons (feasting alone not being permitted), while the companies often include as many as 20, the victims were counted and amounted to 255,600; allowing an average of ten diners to each victim, we obtain a total of 2,700,000, all pure and holy. For those afflicted with leprosy or gonorroea, or menstruous women, or persons otherwise defiled were not permitted to take part in the sacrifice, nor yet any foreigners present for worship, and a large number of these assemble from abroad." Joachim Jeremias reckons that the actual number of pilgrims must have been considerably less. According to his calculations, we get "about 125,000 pilgrims. We should not be justified in increasing or decreasing this figure by more than about half." (*Jerusalem zur Zeit Jesu,* 3rd edition, Göttingen, 1962, p. 96)

13. Bornkamm: *Jesus,* p. 25

14. Josephus calls the empress "a God-fearing woman" (*Ant.* XX. 8:11). From the expression used here, θεοσεβὴς γὰρ ἦν, it was concluded that she was a Jewish convert.
In Hellenistic and Roman times, "this word had become simply a

description of the Jews." "The Jews call themselves 'the God-fearing' in a sense denoting exclusiveness." Thus George Bertram: article, θεοσεβής (in) *ThWB* III, p. 125.

15. In the entire works of Josephus twenty people called Jesus are mentioned, ten of whom are contemporaries of Jesus of Nazareth. Cf. Foerster, Werner: article, Ἰησοῦς (in) *ThWB* III, p. 285.

16. Books XVIII to XX of the *Antiquitates* have only survived in three manuscripts, the oldest of which (the *Codex Ambrosianus* F. 128 sup.) is from the eleventh century. Cf. Schürer: *Gesch. d. jüd. Volkes* I, p. 546.

17. *Hist. eccl.* I, 11, 7 (Quoted from) Friedrich Andreas Stroth: *Eusebii Kirchengeschichte aus dem griehisch übersetzt,* Vol. I. Quedlinburg, 1777, p. 57 ff. The *Testimonium Flavianum* comes to us quoted in two works of Eusebius: "*Historia ecclesiastica*" I: 11,7; "*Demonstratio evangelica*" III: 5 (124)

18. Hubert van Giffen seems to have expressed his opinion about the passages in Josephus only in correspondence or in lectures. Cf. letter from Sebastianus Lepusculus to Severin Ertzberg of 24 Feb. 1559, in which he attacks van Giffen without however naming any of his works: "Hubertus Giphianus ... existimavit hunc locum esse spurium et a Christiano quopiam patre, qui Iudaeis simul et Christianis factum vellit, interpositum." (*Epistolarum Philogicarum Centuriae* IV, p. 250, Frankfurt, 1619; printed by Melchior Goldast)

19. Conzelmann: *Jesus*, col. 622 Cf. also Hölscher, Gustav: article, *Josephus* (in) *RE Halbbd* 18, 1916, col. 1993: The passage XVIII, 3.3 "has long been recognized in its entirety to be a Christian interpolation."

20. Lucas Osiander (the Elder): *Epitomes Historiae Ecclesiasticae.* Cent. I, lib. II, c. 7. Tübingen, 1592, p. 17

21. Origen: *Contra Celsum* I, 47 describes Josephus as a καίτοι γε ἀπιστῶν τῷ Ἰησοῦ ὡς Χριστῷ and *Comm. in Matthaeum* X, 17, where he accuses him: ὅτι τὸν Ἰησοῦν ἡμῶν οὐ καταδεξάμενος εἶναι Χριστόν.

22. This is also Schürer's judgment: *Gesch. d. jüd. Volkes* I, p. 548: "Even the genuineness of these passages is very questionable. In fact one must say the opposite: it is just those references that we have to James that show up the Christian interpolations in Josephus. For in his text of Josephus Origen has read a text about James which without doubt was a singular Christian interpolation which has not survived in the ordinary text." And Hölscher: *Josephus* (in) *RE Halbbd.* 18, col. 1993: The passage is "apparently more firmly anchored in the text," yet "its genuineness is probably quite rightly" doubted.

23. Origen: *Contra Celsum*: 47, trans. Henry Chadwick, Cambridge University Press, 1953: "For Josephus in the eighteenth book of the Jewish antiquities bears witness that John was a baptist and promised purification to people who were baptized. The same author, although he did not believe in Jesus as Christ, sought for the cause of the fall of Jerusalem and the destruction of the temple. He ought to have said that the plot against Jesus was the reason why these catastrophies came upon the people, because they had killed the prophesied Christ; however, although unconscious of it, he is not far from the truth when he says that these disasters befell the Jews to avenge James

353

the Just, who was a brother of 'Jesus the so-called Christ,' since they had killed him who was a very righteous man." Cf. also *Contra Celsum* II:13: The destruction of Jerusalem on the orders of Titus occurred "in the opinion of Josephus, on account of James the just, the brother of Jesus who is called Christ."

24. Pinès, Shlomo: *An Arabic version of the Testimonium Flavianum and Its Implications.* Jerusalem, 1971, p. 14.
Professor Pinès (Jerusalem) is convinced that the *Testimonium Flavianum* in the extant edition is a Christian interpolation. He nevertheless thinks it likely that there could have been a reference to Jesus in the *Antiquitates* and believes he has found the genuine text in an Arabic work of history published in the tenth century. (Agapius Episcopus Mabbugensis: *Historia Universalis.* Ed. by L. Cheiko, 1912.) Agapius wrote his history of the world in 942, as bishop of Hierapolis.

25. Pinès: *Arabic Version,* p. 5: "The so-called *Testimonium Flavianum* . . . contains, if genuine . . . perhaps the earliest evidence concerning Jesus written down by a man who was not a Christian."
Prof. David Flusser (Jerusalem) explained to an American correspondent that Eusebius might have reproduced the original reference to Jesus in the first edition of his *History of the Church,* which was written before the Council of Nicea. "There is a possibility that if Eusebius quotes Josephus' words about Jesus in his earlier edition (or editions) in its original form, that later, because of heavy suspicions about his Christian faith, Eusebius rejected the original text of the passage and began to quote the more orthodox version by way of precaution." (Quoted in) Grose, Peter: "Israeli's Advance Historical Proof that Jesus Lived." (In) *International Herald Tribune* 14 Feb., 1972.

26. Cf. Schmaus, Michael: *Der Glaube der Kirche.* Vol. 2, Munich, 1970, p. 678: "The 'brothers of Jesus' referred to several times in the scriptures (Mark 3:31 and 6:3; John 2:12; Acts 1:14; 1 Corinthians 9:5; Galatians 1:19) could be literally Jesus' own brothers, but according to the biblical Greek they could also be his cousins (Genesis 13:8; 14:4). The Catholic exegesis accepts the latter for reasons of prudence. For, according to Mark 6:3 and 15:40 Mary, the mother of Jesus' brothers, is different from the mother of Jesus herself."

27. Cf. *Gospel according to Thomas,* Logion 12.
Cf. Eusebius: *Hist. eccl. II,* 23.3 et seq. trans. Lawlor and Oulton, S.P.C.K., 1927: "Nevertheless Hegesippus, who belonged to the first succession from the apostles, gives the most accurate record concerning him, in his fifth Memoir. He says as follows: 'Together with the apostles James the Lord's brother succeeded to (the government of) the Church. He received the name of 'the Just' from all men, from the time of the Lord even to our own; for there were many called James. Now he was holy *from his mother's womb.*" Cf. Origen *Contra Celsum I,* 47 and II, 13.

28. *Acts of Paul,* 2:5 ff: "Then Paul turned himself to the East and raised his hands to heaven and prayed for a long time; and after he had joined with the fathers in prayer in the Hebrew tongue, he bowed his head without speaking further. But when the executioner struck off his head, milk spurted

out on to the soldier's clothes. The soldier and all who stood by marvelled when they saw this and praised God who had given such glory to Paul. And they went and told Caesar what had happened. When he heard (it), and marvelled greatly and was in great perplexity, Paul came about the ninth hour, while many wise men and the centurion stood by Caesar, and stood before them all and spoke: 'Caesar, here am I, Paul, the champion of God: I have not died, but I live to my God. But much ill and severe punishment will befall thee, thou wretch, because thou hast unjustly shed the blood of the just, not long after these days.' And after Paul had said this, he went away. But when Nero had heard (that), he was greatly troubled and ordered the prisoners to be released, Patroclus as well as the companions of Barsabas." (Quoted in) Bartsch, Hans-Werner: *Anklage: Brandstiftung. Lebe und Tod von Paulus von Tarsus.* Wuppertal, 1969, p. 83.

1st Letter of Clement, 5:6 ff: "Seven times in chains, banished, herald in the East as in the West, he received the true glory of his faith: he taught the whole world justice, came to the very boundary of the West and bore witness before the rulers; then he departed from the world and went to the holy place, the greatest example of patience." (Quoted in) *Die apostolischen Väter.* Ed. J.A. Fischer. 5th ed., Darmstadt, 1966, p. 33.

29. *Gospel according to the Hebrews,* 7: "But when the Lord had given the linen cloth to the servant of the priest, he went to James and appeared to him. James had sworn that he would not eat bread from that hour in which he had drunk the cup of the Lord, until he saw him risen from the dead. But soon thereafter the Lord said to him: bring a table, and bread. And at once they were fetched; he took the bread, blessed it and broke it and gave it to James the just and said to him: My brother, eat thy bread, for the Son of Man is risen from the dead." (Hennecke-Schneemelcher, *Apokryphen* I, p. 108) This account from the apocryphal Gospel contradicts the New Testament tradition. According to the old "kerygmatic formula" (1 Corinthians 15:3 ff.) and the Easter message on which it is based (Luke 24:34: "It is true: the Lord has risen: he has appeared to Simon"), the first appearance was allotted to Peter; thus Joachim Jeremias. The downgrading of Peter goes back to the "radical circle of Palestinian Jewish Christendom," which "objected to the universality of Peter and so pushed him out of his role as recipient of the first appearance" (*Theologie I,* p. 291).

30. Galatians 5:12: "Would God they were rooted out that trouble you." (From the Bible 1522) (Quoted in) Luther, Martin: Critical Complete Edition, *The German Bible,* Vol. 7. Weimar, 1931, p. 187.

31. Wrede, William: *Paulus.* Halle, 1904, p. 86.

32. Deussen, Paul: *Allegemeine Geschichte der Philosophie mit bes. Ber. der Religionen.* Vol. 2:2.2 Leipzig, 1919, p. 189: "Only a fool can doubt the authenticity of the person of Jesus. The facts recorded in the New Testament, like the first genesis of Christianity, remain wholly inexplicable if we do not accept an historical Jesus, whatever kind of person he may have been, as originator of the whole movement."

33. Troeltsch, Ernst: *Die Bedeutung der Geschichtlichkeit Jesu für den Glauben.* Tübingen 1911, p. 32 ff. Zahrnt: *Jesus,* p. 50, 55

34. The neo-Platonist Sallust in his work: Περὶ θεῶν καὶ κόσμου: "ταῦτα δὲ ἐγένετο μὲν οὐδέποτε, ἔστι δὲ ἀεί." (Quoted in) Sallustius: *Concerning the Gods and the Universe*. Ed Arthur D. Nock. Cambridge, 1926, p. 9

35. Bultmann: *Jesus*, p. 11

36. Cf. Blinzler: *Prozess*, p. 101 ff, *Exkurs: Das Datum des Prozesses Jesu*, p. 107: According to the 'Neulichttafeln' of the Berlin Institute of Astronomical Calculation, checked by Karl Schoch, 14 Nisan fell on a Friday twice during the years 28−34, i.e. in 30 (7 April) and 33 (3 April). On the question of whether 15 Nisan fell on a Friday in one of those years: "It appears from Schoch's tables that that was the case only once between 28 and 34, i.e. in the year 34 (23 April). However, this year is no longer to be considered, since it falls much too late. Astronomical research therefore seems to verify John's dating of Good Friday rather than that of the synoptics."

37. Stauffer: *Jesus*, p. 18

38. In the last section of his work *"De stella nova"* (entitled *"De Iesu Christi servatoris vero anno natalitio"*), in 1606, Kepler tried to show that the great conjunction of Jupiter and Saturn in the constellation of the Fish took place in the year 39 of the Julian era (i.e. 747 ab urbe condita or 7 B.C.E.). This conjunction introduced the 800-year period of a "fiery triangle." (Cf. Kepler, Johannes: *De stella nove in pede serpentarii et de trigono igneo*. Prague, 1606, pp. 134−5: chap. xxvi, iv)
Kepler, Johannes: *Discurs von der grossen Conjunktion und allerlei Weissagungen über das 1623. Jahr*. (In) *Die Astrologie des Johannes Kepler. Eine Auswahl aus seinen Schriften*. Munich, 1926, p. 67 ff.
Stern der Weisen. (In) *Lexikon für Theologie und Kirche*. 2nd .edition, vol. 9. Freiburg, 1964, col. 1058.

39. Macrobius: *Saturnalia II*, 4.11: "Cum audisset inter pueros quos in Syria Herodes rex Iudaeorum intra bimatim iussit interfici, filium quoque eius occisum, ait (Augustus): melius est Herodis porcum esse quam filium."

40. *Wilckens Bible*, p. 210.

41. Bloch, Ernst: *Das Prinzip Hoffnung*. Vol. 3. Frankfurt, 1959, p. 1482: "Prayer is made to a child born in a manger. A gaze into the heights cannot be broken off more closely, more lowly, more secretly. At the same time, the manger is true; so humble an origin for the founder cannot be invented. Legend does not make us pictures of wretchedness, certainly not wretchedness continued through a whole life. The manger, the carpenter's son, the fanatic among little people, the gallows at the end — all this is of the stuff of history, not the golden stuff beloved of legend."

42. Kusenberg, Kurt: "Ochs und Esel sind dabei." (In) *Süddeutsche Zeitung* of 24-26 Dec. 1971.

43. Cf. Kierkegaard, Søren: *Einübung im Christentum*. (In) *Ges. Werke*. Düsseldorf, 1951. 26th section, p. 122 et seq. ("The slave-concept is the undiscernible — the incognito") and Kierkegaard, Søren: *Abschliessende unwissenschaftliche Nachschrift zu den philosophischen Brocken* (in) *Ges. Werke*, 16th section T. 1, p. 191 et seq ("The infinite sympathy of warmheartedness").

44. Strauss: *Leben Jesu* I, p. 265

45. Stauffer, *Jesus,* p. 25
46. Stauffer, Ethelbert: *Jesus war ganz anders.* Hamburg, 1967, p. 51. And in another place: "We learn in the Old Testament that David's family received an allocation of land in the area of David's former town of Bethlehem after the return from the exile in Babylon. Hence Bethlehem is the appropriate reporting center for the tax-return of Joseph, being of the family of David." (p. 48)
47. Cf. Käsemann: *Hist. Jesu,* p. 196: "We can confirm from historical tradition that the legend of Moses established the distinctive features of the tradition of Jesus, and we can add from religious tradition that such a transfer of features can be abundantly demonstrated and represents a typical case of legendary over-painting and the creation of myth."
48. Bauer, Walter: *Griechisch-deutsch Wörterbuch zu den Schriften des Neuen Testaments und der übrigen urchristlichen Literatur.* 5th edition (reprint), Berlin 1963, col. 1053.
49. In the Gospels and in the Acts of the Apostles we find as surnames for Jesus the forms Ναζαρηνός and Ναζωραῖος. Mark uses the form Ναζαρηνός throughout (1:12; 10:47 (v.1. Ναζωραῖος); 14:67; 16:6). Matthew has exclusively the form Ναζωραῖος (2:23; 26:69 (v.1. Γαλιλαῖος); 26:71). In Luke we find both forms, Ναζαρηνός (4:34; 24:19 (v.1.Ναζωραῖος) and Ναζωραῖος (18:37 (v.1. Ναζαρηνός); both words seem to be used in the same sense. In John, Jesus is called Ναζωραῖος three times (18:5 (v.1. Ναζαρηνός); 18:7; 19:19) The author of the Acts of the Apostles uses the term Ναζωραῖος six times to describe the person of Jesus (2:22; 3:6; 4:10; 6:14; 22:8; 26:9) and the Christians are once called by the same name (24:5). Paul and the other New Testament authors do not use either name. Cf. Schaeder, Hans Heinrich: article, Ναζαρηνός , Ναζωραῖος (in) ThWB IV, pp. 879—884.
50. Bultmann: *Synopt. Trad.,* p. 30: "This seems to me to be a typical example of how an idealized scene is composed from an independent saying."
51. Brückner, Martin: *Nazaret als Heimat Jesu.* (In) *Palästinajahrbuch,* year 7, Berlin, 1911, p. 81.
52. Robertson, John Mackinnon: *The Gospel Myths.* Jena, 1910, p. 51 ff seq.
53. (4 Q patr 3-4) Blessings of the patriarchs: "(The thousands of) the people of Israel are the feet, until the coming of the anointed of righteousness, the shoot of David; for to him and to his seed is given the covenant of the kingdom over his people for eternal generations . . . " (Quoted from) Lohse: *Texts,* p. 247.
54. Ben-Chorin: *Mirjam,* p. 34: Jesus "will be a Nazarene, because he shall fulfil the prophecy of the neser," and p. 35: "also we have to be careful about Nazareth, for here too the statements are so few that we must regard the fulfilment as the primary motif." Of course, in 1970 Ben-Chorin had already written in the 3rd edition of his book on Jesus: "Everyone knows from this that Jesus comes from Nazareth . . . There is an almost precise fact given here: 'Can anything good come from Nazareth?' (John 1:46)" (*Jesus,* p. 37 ff)
55. Hieronymi liber interpretationis hebraicorum nominum: "Nazareth flos aut virgultum eius vel munditiae aut separata vel custodita. Scribitur autem non z litteram, sed per hebraeum sade, quod nec s nec z littera sonat."

357

(Quoted from) Lagarde, Paul de: *Onomastica sacra*. Hildesheim, 1966 (reprint), p. 95

56. Stauffer, *Jesus*, p. 25
57. Bornkamm: *Jesus*, p. 48
58. To Mark 6:3: "Is not this the carpenter, the son of Mary . . ." Other manuscripts offer the version: "Is not this the son of the carpenter and Mary?" Lauenstein regards this text as nearer the original and puts forward the view that the alternative text, that Jesus himself was the carpenter, came into being through the faith of one of the copyists in the immaculate conception of Jesus. (*Messiahs*, p. 208)
59. Cf. Flusser: *Jesus*, p. 22: "Carpenters were regarded in those days as specially learned. When a difficult question was being discussed, people used to say: 'Is there a carpenter here, a carpenter's son, who can solve this question for us?' Jesus was either a carpenter or a carpenter's son; probably he was both."
60. Cf. Barth, Karl: *Die kirchliche Dogmatik*. 3rd edition, vol. 1, 2, Zollikon, 1945, p. 192: "Jesus is of course not the actual son of Joseph, and thus of David; but he is his legitimate son, not the natural son but the son lawfully entered on the register of the tribe in consequence of his adoption."
61. Matthew 1:16: "Jacob (was the father) of Joseph, the husband of Mary, who gave birth to Jesus called Messiah." Some manuscripts give the version: "Joseph was the father of Jesus." It stands thus in the ancient Syrian palimpsest manuscript (sy^s), discovered in St. Catherine's Monastery in the Sinai peninsula in 1892, which goes back to a translation made in the second century: "Ja'qob begat Josef, Josef, to whom Miriam the virgin was betrothed, begat Jesu, who is called Messiah." (Quoted from) Merx, Adalbert: *Die vier kanonische Evangelien nach ihrem ältesten bekannten Texte*. Berlin, 1897, p. 2
62. Stauffer: *Jesus*, p. 2
63. Steiner, Rudolf: *Die geistige Führung des Menschen und der Menschheit*. Freiburg, 1946, p. 62 ff.
64. Cf. Stauffer: *Jesus*, p. 23: "Jesus is Mary's son and the son of Mary only, not of Joseph. That is here of course meant in a defamatory sense." Against which we have Bultmann: *Synopt. Trad. Ergänzungsheft*, p. 26: The references to the mother is not intended to be contemptuous. For "at that time . . . Mary must have been known as a woman specially chosen. It is more likely that she was already honored as the Lord's mother."
65. In Luke 2:4: "He (Joseph) was of the house of David by descent." In place of αὐτόν = he, some miniscule manuscripts have αὐτούς = she; a Syrian source (sy^s) has ἀμφοτέρους = both. (Nestle-Aland: *Das Neue Testament griechisch und deutsch*. 16th edition, Stuttgart, 1957, p. 144.)
66. Stauffer: *Jesus*, p. 44
67. Stauffer: *Jesus*, p. 21: "When men in the New Testament talk about Davidic descent, they do so in the sense of an historical statement which can be historically verified."
68. In Luke 2:24: Strack-Billerbeck II, p. 123: "Two turtle doves or two young pigeons were prescribed by the law only in case the mother could not afford the sacrifice otherwise prescribed (Leviticus 12:6) of a year-old lamb

(Leviticus 12:8) . . . The sacrifice of pigeons (Leviticus 5:8; 12:8) was vulgarly called the 'poor man's sacrifice' ".

69. Cf. *Jerusalem Bible*, p. 1040: "In the opinion of many students of the Bible, including Catholics, the 'sign' shown here consists in the imminent birth of the future king Hezekiah, the son of Achas."

70. Cf. Dibelius, Martin: *Jungfrauensohn und Krippenkind*. (In) *Botschaft und Geschichte*, Vol. I. Tübingen, 1953, p. 40: "We cannot entirely exclude the possibility that the Septuagint, or at any rate its first readers, took the text about the pregnancy of the παρθένος (Isaiah 7:14) to refer to a virginal conception."

71. Matthew 1:24 ff. " . . . he took Mary home to be his wife, but had no intercourse with her until she bore a son." In certain Codices we have, instead of "a son," the readings "her son," "him a son" and "the firstborn son." The line " . . . but had no intercourse with her" is omitted from three manuscripts. (Nestle-Aland: *Das Neue Testament griechisch und deutsch*. 16th edition. Stuttgart, 1957, p. 3)
Stauffer: *Jesus, p.* 24
Barth, Karl: *Die kirchliche Dogmatik*, 3rd edition 1, 2, Zollikon, 1945, p. 198: "The church presumably knows well what it did when it placed this dogma as it were like a seal on the door to the secret of Christmas . . . It will preach as an ordinance of the church that acceptance of the teaching of the virgin birth is essential to the true Christian faith."

72. Bornkamm: *Jesus*, p. 48

73. Cf. Marxsen: *Einleitung*, p. 124: " . . . it can be stated firmly that (with the exception of 6:21) all passages about Galilee (1:9; 14:28, 39; 3:7; 7:31; 9:30; 14:28; 16:7) are editorial. The pre-Marcan traditions name occasional places that belong to Galilee, but do not stress them particularly."

74. Marxsen: *Einleitung*, p. 124

75. Cf. *Traktat Schabbath* 16, 15d, 50 (Jerusalem Talmud): "Rabbi Ula (about 280) has said: (Rabban Jochanan ben Zakkai, about 80 C.E.) lived in Arab (in Galilee) for 18 years and only two cases were brought before him (for judgment). Then said Rabban Jochanan ben Zakkai: 'Galilee, Galilee, thou hatest learning; in the end thou wilt belong to the robbers!' " (Quoted from) Strack-Billerbeck I, p. 157.

76. Cf. Hengel: *Zealots*, p. 57 ff - p. 61: "Even if accounts of the zealots being described as Galileans are scarce and relatively unusual, we may assume with a certain degree of probability that they were so called to some extent. They had after all set up an independent 'sect' side by side with the other Jewish religious groups, and their origin was to be sought (as their name implies) in the activities of the Galilean Judas." Cf. also Bousset, Wilhelm and Hugo Gressman: *Die Religion des Judentums im späthellenistischen Zeitalter*. 3rd edition. Tübingen, 1926, p. 87, note 3: "In the list of heretics, certainly Jewish and/or Jewish-Christian, prepared by Justin in *Dial. 80* and Hegesipp in *Eusebiuks H.E* IV, 22, 7, the zealots appeared as Galileans."

77. The earliest tradition of the death of the Messiah ben Joseph appears in *Traktat Sukkah* 52a, 52b. Cf. the *Babylonian Talmud* with the insertion of the complete *Misnah*, edited by Lazarus Goldschmidt, Vol. 3. Berlin 1925,

p. 146 ff. - (Hereafter the *Babylonian Talmud* will be quoted in Lazarus Goldschmidt's edition unless indicated otherwise.)
Cf. Strack-Billerbeck II, p. 292: "The figure of a Messiah ben Joseph or ben Ephraim, not met with in any form in older traditions, suddenly crops up in rabbinical literature about 150 A.D." Wilhelm Bousset considers the theory of the dying and defeated Messiah to be an "artificial speculation of the scribes" from the post-Christian era. (*Kyrios Christos*. 2nd edition. Gottingen 1921, p. 23)
Joachim Jeremias on the contrary assumes a pre-Christian expectation of the Messiah ben Joseph and refers to the so-called *Testament of Benjamin*, which he dates about the second or first century B.C.E. Jeremias quotes an Armenian version of the passage *Test. B*. 3:8, said to be free from Christian interpolations: "To thee (Joseph) will the prophecy of heaven be fulfilled, which foretells that the guiltless shall be defiled for the lawless and the innocent shall die for the Godless." In *Test. B*. 3:8 we have probably the oldest example of the expectation of a Messiah of the tribe of Joseph . . . "
— "The fact that the passage mentioned in the rabbinical literature on the Messiah ben Joseph, Zechariah 12:10 ff., 10 et seq, is already interpreted messianically in the New Testament makes it very probable that the expectation of a Messiah ben Joseph goes back to pre-Christian times." (Further literature in J. making the case for the pre-Christian origin of this tradition.) Article (in) *ThWB* V, p. 685; 685 note 243
78. Cf. Eisenmenger, Johann Andreas: *Endecktes Judenthum*. Frankfurt, 1700 Part 2, p. 720 ff.: "It is thus written in the book *Sechené luchóth habberíth*, folio 242 column I: 'First will come the Messiah, the son of Joseph, and after him the Messiah, the son of David; and then shall the house of Joseph restore that which has been wasted through the division of the kingdom of the house of David. For the Messiah, the son of Joseph, will not come for his own ends, but shall appear on behalf of the Messiah, the son of David; for he will sacrifice himself and give up his soul in death and his blood will redeem God's people."
79. Bloch, Ernst: *Symbol: Die Juden*. (In) *Geist der Utopie*. Munich 1918 (reprinted 1971), p. 320 ff.: "The Jews as we first saw them were an agricultural people, simple and vigorous and shaken by religious impulses. Then that strange blinding occurred to them, that happened in the midst of them. There followed the foretold dispersion into all lands and, if you like, the terrible price of punishment paid for the blood of Josua of Nazareth."
80. Mann, Thomas: *Joseph und seine Brüder*. Frankfurt, 1960, p. 96
81. *The Sibylline Oracle* V, 258 (quoted from) Kautzsch: *Apokryphen* II, p. 211
82. *Damascus Document*, CD VII, 20 and CD I, 7; *Blessings*, I QS b V, 20 (quoted from) Lohse: *Texte*, p. 81, 67, 59
83. *Manual of Discipline* 1 QS IX, 11
84. *The Testament of Simon* (II, 7: "And now, my children, hear Levi, and you will be redeemed through Judah. And stand not against these two tribes, for out of them will spring up to you the salvation of God. For the Lord will raise up a high priest out of Levi and a king out of Judah.") The *Testament of Levi* (III,2: "And through thee and Judah will the Lord appear among men, saving among them every tribe of men"). The *Testament of Judah*

360

(IV,21: "For the Lord gave the kingdom to me and the priesthood to him (Levi) and he made the kingdom subordinate to the priesthood"). (Quoted from) Kautzsch: *Apokryphen* II, pp. 465, 466, 476

85. Burrows: *Mehr Klarheit*, p. 157: "The author (of the *Testament of the XII Patriarchs*), from the references he makes to a Messiah from the tribe of Levi and from the tribe of Judah, is clearly thinking of fulfillment through a single person."

86. Schweitzer, Albert: *Geschichte der Leben-Jesu-Forschung*. 2nd edition. Tubingen, 1913, p. 512

87. Kähler, Martin: *Der sogenannte historische Jesus und der geschichtliche, biblische Christus*. 2nd edition. Leipzig, 1896, p. 187

Chapter 2

1. Nietzsche, Friedrich: *Zur Genealogie der Moral*. Second Essay, 6.

3. Cf. Strack-Billerbeck II, p. 542: (in John 10:33): "The riotous conduct of trial and punishment adopted against Jesus was regarded as justifiable in certain cases. (*Traktat*) *Sanhedrin* 9:6 . . . if any man blaspheme the name of God . . . it is lawful for zealots to attack him."

3. Käsemann: Hist Jesus, p. 188

4. (Quoted from) Reumann, Kurt: "Ist die Mainzer Theologie auch christlich?" (In) *Frankfurter Allgemeine Zeitung*, 18 Sept. 1971

5. Braun: *Jesus*, p. 30
   Braun, Herbert: *Vom Verstehen des Neuen Testaments* (In) Braun: *Gesammelte Studien*, p. 295

6. Luther, Martin: *Welches die rechten edlisten Bücher des Neuen Testaments sind:* "Since now John writes very little about the works of Christ but very much about his teaching, whereas the other three Gospels describe much of his work and little of his word: the Gospel of John is the one tender, true, chief Gospel and far, far to be preferred to the other three, and to be exalted higher." (In) Luther: *Works*, Vol. 63, p. 115

7. Bultmann: *Theologie d. NT*, p. 418. Cf. also p. 419: "Thus John in his Gospel presents only the That of the revelation without making clear its What." Heidegger, Martin: *Über den Humanismus* . Frankfurt, 1968, p. 19

8. Bultmann: *Jesus,* p. 15

9. Shaw: *Prospects*, p. 55

10. Bultmann: *Synopt. Trad.*, p. 103

11. Cf. Jaspers, Karl: *Philosophie*, 3rd edition, Berlin 1956. (Vol. 1, p. 319: "In its positive declarations, philosophy expresses thoughts which have the character of possibility. Its positivity is true only as a separation, a roll-call, confirmation." Cf. also Vol. 2, p. 432 ff. and Vol. 3, p. 157 ff.)

12. The Papias documents have not survived. For what we know of them we have to thank Eusebius, though he himself had none too high an opinion of his chief witness: "For he (Papias) was clearly very narrow-minded, as we can well deduce from his writings." (Eusebius: *Hist. eccl.* III, 39, 15)
    Cf. Eusebius: *Hist. eccl.* III, 39, 15 et seq.
    Cf. also Irenaeus: *Adversus haereses* III, 1,1: "After their death (i.e. of Peter and Paul) Mark, Peter's pupil and interpreter, recorded their preaching for us."

13. Cf. Eusebius: *Hist. eccl.* III, 39, 16, trans. Lawlor and Oulton, SPCK, 1927: "Such then is Papias' account of Mark. But the following is the statement concerning Matthew: So then, Matthew compiled the oracles in the Hebrew language; but everyone interpreted them as he was able."
    Cf. Irenaeus: *Adversus haereses* III, 1,1: "Matthew wrote his Gospel among the Hebrews in the Hebrew tongue, when Peter and Paul were preaching the Gospel to Rome and founding the church."

14. *Jubiläumsbibel*, *NT*, p. 20

15. Cf. Irenaeus: *Adversus haereses* III, 1,1: "Similarly Luke, the companion of Paul, has put down the Gospel that he preached in a book."

16. Irenaeus: *Adversus haereses* III, 1,1: "Lastly John, the Lord's pupil, he who leaned upon his breast, issued his Gospel during his stay at Ephesus in Asia."

17. The earliest New Testament manuscripts include:
    1. Ryland's Papyrus 457 (p^{52}) = a fragment of John (18:21−34:37−38), dated about 125.
    2. Ryland's Papyrus 5 (p^{32}) = a piece of the Letter to Titus (1:11−15; 2:2−8) and
    3. Magdalen Papyrus (p^{64}) = some verses of Matthew (26:7, 10, 14−15, 22−23, 31−33).
    Both these manuscripts were put at the second half of the second century.

18. The so-called Aristaeus letter gives us a legendary account of the coming into being of the Septuagint. He tells of the translation of the Torah into Greek by "six elderly men skilled in its law" (32) from each of the twelve tribes of Israel, on the orders of king Ptolemy II (285−246 B.C.E.) in Alexandria. "And they (the seventy-two) carried out (the translation), reaching agreement on a version by comparisons with one another." (302) "It so happened that the translation was completed in 72, as if it had been done so on purpose" (307). (Quoted from) Kautzsch: *Apokryphen* II, p. 8, 30

19. The concept was coined by Johann Jakob Griesbach in 1776, when he printed the parallel texts of the first three Gospels side by side in his Synopsis of the Gospels of Matthew, Mark and Luke, in order to make possible a simultaneous consideration and critical comparison.

20. Stauffer: *Jesus*, p. 121

21. Bultmann: *Synopt. Trad.*, p. 354

22. Jeremias: *Theologie* I, p. 46

23. Marxsen: *Einleitung*, p. 129, 136, 143, 219

24. *Wilckens Bible*, p. 14, 199, 309, 127

25. Marxsen: *Einleitung*, p. 219, 143, 136

26. Cf. Eusebius: *Hist. eccl.* II, 15
    Cf. Clemens Alexandrinus, quoted by Eusebius: *Hist. eccl.* VI, 14, 6, trans. Lawlor and Oulton, SPCK, 1927: " . . . but that the Gospel according to Mark came into being in this manner: When Peter had publicly preached the word at Rome, and by the Spirit had proclaimed the Gospel, that those present, who were many, exhorted Mark, as one who had followed him for a long time and remembered what had been spoken, to make a record of what was said; and that he did this, and distributed the Gospel among those that

asked him. And that when the matter came to Peter's knowledge he neither strongly forbade it nor urged it forward."

27. Cf. the numerous loan-words, e.g. Mark 4:21 μόδιος = Latin *modius* = bushel; 5:9 λεγιών = Latin *legio* = legion; 6:27 σπεκουλάτωρ = Latin *speculator* = executioner; 6:37 δηνάριον = Latin *denarius* = penny; 7:4 ξέστης = Latin sextarius = jar; 12:14 κῆνσος = Latin *census* = poll-tax; 12:42 κοδράντης = Latin *quadrans* = mite; 15:15 φραγελλοῦν = Latin *flagellare* = scourge; 15:16 πραιτώριον = Latin *practorium* = courtyard; 15:39 κεντυρίων = Latin *centurio* = centurion.

28. Marxsen: *Einleitung*, p. 128
29. Trilling, Wolfgang: *Das wahre Israel*. 3rd edition, Munich, 1964, p. 223 ff.
30. Conzelmann: *Grundriss*, p. 27
31. *Jubiläumsbibel*, *NT*, p. 5, 136
32. *Lutherbibel* 1966, Supplement p. 35
33. *Jerusalem Bible*, p. 1357
34. *Jubiläumsbibel*, *NT*, p. 62, 84
35. Dautzenberg: *Jesus-Report*, p. 63
36. *Jubiläumsbibel*, *NT*, p. 32
37. *Jerusalem Bible*, p. 1361 ff.: "If the Holy Ghost does not let his interpreters arrive at a perfect conformity in detail, that is because he does not attach special significance to such material preciseness, nay more, because he wishes there to be these differences in the witness ... The Holy Ghost, whom we believe to have inspired the writers of the Gospels, guided this whole process in advance and used it for the development of faith; he guaranteed to the results of this work that true infallibility that is fashioned not so much from the actuality of the facts as from the message of faith that will be carried by it. Thus, the Holy Ghost prepared a feast of faith, which the faithful would be able to receive; he it is who especially endowed the three evangelists with the gift that each might present the common message in his own way."
38. Bloch, Ernst: *Zerstörung, Rettung des Mythos durch Licht*. (In) *Verfremdungen* I, Frankfurt, 1963, p. 156
39. Bultmann, Rudolf: *Neues Testament und Mythologie*. (In) *Kerygma* I, p. 46. Cf. Bultmann, Rudolf: *Die Bedeutung des geschichtlichen Jesus für die Theologie des Paulus*. (In) Bultmann: *Glauben und Verstehen* I, p. 208
40. Bultmann: *Jesus*, p. 11
    Bultmann, Rudolf: *Zur Frage der Christologie*. (In) Bultmann, *Glauben und Verstehen* I, p. 101
41. Bultmann: *Jesus*, p. 12: " ... so that means that we know virtually nothing about his personality. I am personally of the opinion that Jesus did not believe himself to be the Messiah, but I do not conceive that I have any clearer picture of his personality on that account."
42. Bultmann: *Jesus*, p. 12: "I have not ... taken this question into consideration, not for the basic reason that there is nothing more certain to be said on it but because I hold the question to be immaterial."
    Bultmann, Rudolf: *Die Christologie des Neuen Testaments*. (In) Bultmann: *Glauben und Verstehen* I, p. 265
43. Bultmann: *Jesus*, pp. 7-14, esp. p. 9 ff.

44. Bultmann: *Jesus*, p. 13 ff.
45. Bultmann: *Jesus*, pp. 14-16: "What the sources have to offer us is fairly certainly the teaching of the community, which they do indeed for the most part trace back to Jesus. But of course that does not prove that the words they put in his mouth were really spoken by him. In many of his words the evidence is rather that they originated in the community, in others that they have been adapted by the community . . . Thus we arrive by critical analysis at the earliest period, though even this we can only pick out with relative certainty. Of course we have no certainty at all that these words from the oldest period were really spoken by Jesus . . . how far the community has preserved an objectively true picture of him and of his preaching is another question . . . As the bearer of these ideas (those we find in the earliest period of the tradition), the tradition names Jesus; it is overwhelmingly probable that it really was he. But had it been otherwise, it would still make no difference at all to what is said in this tradition."
46. Bultmann, Rudolf: *Zu J. Schniewinds Thesen das Problem der Entmythologisierung betreffend.* (In) *Kerygma* I, p. 132
47. Bultmann, Rudolf: *Neues Testament und Mythologie.* (In) *Kerygma* I, p. 47. Cf. Danner, Helmut: *Das Göttliche und der Gott bei Heidegger.* Meisenheim am Glan, 1971, p. 70 — Cf. also Heidegger, Martin: " . . . *dichterisch wohnet der Mensch . . .* " (In) *Vorträge und Aufsätze.* Pfullingen, 1954, p. 190: "Man speaks only insofar as he conforms with the speech . . . "
48. Bultmann, Rudolf: *Welchen Sinn hat es, von Gott zu reden?* (In) Bultmann: *Glauben und Verstehen* I, p. 37
49. Barth, Karl: *Die neue Welt in der Bibel.* (In) *Das Wort Gottes und die Theologie.* Gesammelte Vorträge 1, Munich, 1926, p. 28
50. Barth, Karl: *Die Lehre von den Sakramenten.* (In) *Zwischen den Zeiten*, Year 7, 1929, p. 449
51. Gunther, Joachim: *Theologie im Zeitgeist.* Karl Barth — Rudolf Bultmann: "Briefwechsel 1922—1966", (In) *Frankfurter Allgemeine Zeitung* of 12 Oct. 1971.
52. Barth, Karl: *Die neue Welt in der Bibel.* (In) *Das Wort Gottes und die Theologie.* Gesammelte Vorträge 1. Munich, 1925, p. 28
53. Bultmann: *Jesus*, p. 16
54. Cf. *Ist Jesus auferstanden wie Goethe?* Extended version of the *Spiegel* interview with Professor Rudolf Bultmann. (In) Harenberg, Werner: *Jesus und die Kirchen.* Stuttgart, 1966, p. 206 ff.
55. Cf. Bultmann: *Jesus*, p. 78: "It is excessively clear that there is actually no 'new' ethical commandment of Jesus, that the directions he actually gave are plentifully paralleled in the Jewish tradition." P. 96: "There is also a second thing to be said, that neither Jesus nor his congregation thought that the message of love was a new commandment which no one had ever heard of before."
56. Bultmann: *Jesus*, p. 95
57. Bultmann: *Jesus*, pp. 78, 96, 74
58. Bultmann: *Jesus*, p. 73 ff.
59. Bultmann: *Jesus*, p. 74

60. Bloch, Ernst: *Zerstörung, Rettung des Mythos durch Licht.* (In) *Verfremdungen* I. Frankfurt, 1963, p. 156
61. Bultmann, *Jesus*, p. 12
62. Bultmann: *Jesus*, p. 11
63. Bultmann, Rudolf: *Marburger Predigten.* Tübingen 1956, 71–78; sermon of 24 July 1938: "The Lord's word which we hear is one of the most intimate in the New Testament. In it we can descry the figure of the Lord Jesus Christ, his arms outstretched in invitation, crying: 'Come here to me!' "
64. Holl: *Jesus*, p. 191, 185, 182, 170, 166
65. Braun, Herbert: *Vom Verstehen des Neuen Testaments.* (In) Braun: *Gesammelte Studien*, p. 287
66. Holl: *Jesus*, p. 164, 139
67. Bloch, Ernst: *Das Prinzip Hoffnung.* Vol. 3. Frankfort, 1959 p. 1487
68. Gollwitzer: *Krummes Holz*, p. 264
69. Vidal, Gore: *Julian.* Cologne, 1970, p. 182
70. Bloch: *Münzer*, p. 110
71. (In) *Ausslegung des andern unterschyds Danielis, dess prophetes, gepredigt auffm schlos zu Alstet vor den tetigen, thewren herzcogen und vorstenern zu Sachssen durch Thomam Müntzer, diener des wordt gottes.* Alstedt MDXXIIII.
   (Quoted in) Müntzer: *Schriften*, p. 241 ff.
   (p. 247) "that poor, simple men are thus led astray by the wicked scholars . . . who teach and say, that God no longer reveals his holy secrets through true visions."
   (p. 254) "Yes, it is a true apostolic, patriarchal and prophetic spirit to expect visions and to receive them with sore distress. Therefore it is no wonder that Brother Fatpig and Brother Softlife disapprove."
72. Cf. Münzer's letter to Frederick the Wise. Allstedt, 4 October 1523. (Quoted in) Müntzer: *Schriften*, p. 395
73. (In) *Aussgetrückte emplössung des falschen glaubens, der ungetrewen welt durchs gezeugnus des evangelions Luce vorgetragen, der elenden, erbermlichen christenheyt zur innerung jres irsals. Ezechie am 8. cap. Lieben gesellen, last uns auch das loch weytter machen, auff das alle welt sehen und greyffen müg, wer unser grosse hansen sind, die Got also lesterlich zum gemalten mendleyn gemacht haben. Jere. am 23. cap.* Thomas Müntzer, *mit dem hammer.* Mühlhausen, MDXXIIII. (Quoted in) Müntzer: *Schriften*, p. 310 ff., 267
74. Cf. *The Prague Manifesto.* 1521. (Quoted in) Müntzer: *Schriften* p. 496 et seq
75. (In) *Ausslegung der andern unterschyds Danielis . . .* (Quoted in) Müntzer, *Schriften*, p. 263
76. Cf. *Hochverursachte schutzrede und antwort wider das gaistlose, sanfftlebende fleysch zu Wittenberg, welches mit verkärter weysse durch den diepstal der heiligen schrift die erbermdliche christenheit also gantz jämerlichen besudelt hat.* Thomas Müntzer. Alstedter. 1524 (Quoted in) Müntzer: *Schriften*, p. 322
77. Cf. Luther, Martin: *Tischreden . . . vom jüngsten Tage.* (In) Luther: *Werke*, Vol. 62, p. 19: "I do indeed hope that the day is not far distant and that we shall experience it."

     An den Rath und die Gemeinde von Mühlhausen of 14 Aug. 1524. (In) Luther: *Werke*, Vol. 53, p. 255

78. Bloch: *Münzer*, p. 51

79. Bornkamm: *Jesus*, p. 163

80. Hengel, Martin: *War Jesus Revolutionär?* 2nd ed. Stuttgart, 1970, p. 20

81. Conzelmann: *Grundriss*, p. 149

82. To the "troubled" inquiry of Franz Cardinal König of 19 July 1971: "For you, Jesus is an outstanding human being who was made into a god after his death. Others have said that before you. But you are the first priest to do so. As a priest you must know that the whole of Christianity stands and falls by the belief that Jesus was the son of God. You live from the church, but do you still live in the church? I ask you in deep distress, and your brethren, the members of congregation and our diocese, ask with me, do you believe in Jesus Christ as the Son of God? If you no longer believe in Jesus Christ as the Son of God, in the church founded by him — despite all its errors, shortcomings and weaknesses — then this is your personal decision. This decision may sound sad to us, but we will not deny our esteem to the man if he draws the conclusions from it. I beg you for a clear answer . . . " Holl replied: "In your letter of the 19th inst. you put the question to me whether I believe in Jesus Christ as the Son of God. To this question I answer Yes." Holl: *Jesus*, p. 159: "Nonetheless, various views are maintained, often enough with some animosity. Books are filled with arguments and counterarguments about forms of words. Whether Jesus was the Son of God. Whether he walked on the water. Whether he rose from the dead. Whether Joseph was his real father."

83. Conzelmann: *Jesus*, col. 629 ff: the three passages in Mark whose authenticity is in question: Mark (8:27 ff.); (12:35-37); (14:61)

84. In Jesus' time the expressions *'enosch, 'enoscha, bar nasch* and *bar 'enosch* were current in Aramaic. All four could mean "the man" or "a man," and also "someone"; *bar nasch* and *bar 'enosch* also meant "every man" and *'enosch* and *enoscha* the collective "mankind." The expression ὁ υἰὸς τοῦ ἀυθρώπου represents a verbal reflection of the Aramaic *bar 'enosch* or *bar nasch*; it can be misunderstood in Greek because it is only to be understood genealogically. It remains uncertain whether "man" is to be taken in its everyday sense or in its eschatological—Messianic sense; only the context decides.

85. Bloch: *Atheismus*, p. 191, 207

86. *Gospel according to Thomas*, Logion 86

87. Conzelmann: *Jesus*, col. 631: "If we take the whole conception of the Son of Man as folk-theology, then we have to explain the fact that it is only found in the mouth of Jesus. However, that ought to be possible."

88. *Wilckens Bible*, p. 43

89. Cf. Jeremias: *Theologie* I, p. 261

90. *Jerusalem Bible*, p. 1024

91. Jeremias: *Theologie*, p. 263

92. Bultmann: *Theologie d. NT*, p. 30 ff.

93. Heinemann, Gustav: "Im Reiche dieses Konigs hat man das Recht lieb" (Lecture on church day in Leipzig on 9 July, 1954) (In) *Seid Fröhlich*

in Hoffnung (Stuttgart, undated). *Reports, working-group III*, p. 315: "God has concentrated his anger and his judgment for all our disobedience in the sentence of death on a single man. This one man was the only one without sin, the only one who did God's will — God's own son. The gallows on Golgotha is the sign that God's kingdom is a kingdom of justice. Here right and justice are practiced towards him who submitted to this judgment for us."

94. Cf. Otto: *Kingdom of God*, p. 1: "Without prejudice to his special, unique character, we can place the figure of Jesus in the frame of a common type, of which we have other examples. He was a 'wandering preacher,' and in fact he was a Galilean."

95. *The Apocalypse of Enoch* - between 170 and 30 B.C.E. and originally written in Hebrew or Aramaic — has not survived in an original text. There exist Hebrew and Aramaic fragments from Qumran, some Greek papyrus and, as a coherent text, the Ethiopian translation of a Greek edition of the book (dated about 500 C.E.). The scripture was accepted into the early Old Testament canon of the Ethiopian church. The so-called Slavic Enoch — which we can date before the second destruction of the temple in 70 C.E. — is available in two Old Slav translations from the Greek.
The Book of Enoch is quoted here from Kautsch: *Apokryphen* II.

96. Cf. Jeremias, Joachim: *Zwischen Karfreitag und Ostern*. (In) Jeremias: *Abba*, p. 325: "The thought-world (of the *Book of Enoch*) had great influence in New Testament times, which is actually reflected in the New Testament."

97. Otto: *Reich Gottes*, p. 196. Cf. David Friedrich Strauss: *Leben Jesu f.d. deutschen Volk*, p. 233 ff.: Jesus "had reason to take from the Messianic prophecies in Isaiah 50, 52, 53 even the actual events of his passion . . . Even the point of view . . . that regarded his death as a sacrifice for sin he could have adopted from Isaiah 53."

98. Holl: *Jesus*, p. 193: "Jesus was no tortured intellectual, that much is certain."

99. Bultmann, Rudolf: *Das Verhältnis der urchristlichen Christusbotschaft zum historischen Jesus*. Heidelberg, 1960, p. 11

100. Burrows: *Mehr Klarheit*, p. 63

101. Cf. Strack-Billerbeck I, p. 481, 485: "An interpretation . . . became accepted comparatively late by which the 'servant of Yahweh' was taken to mean the people of Israel. This interpretation, now generally accepted among the Jews, . . . had its advocates as early as the time of Origen."

102. Otto: *Reich Gottes*, p. 314

103. Otto: *Reich Gottes*, p. 186: "What he saw before him was not a bodily resuscitation and resurrection after death but a translation and exaltation like those of Enoch, and, from the time that he realized that the Son of Man must suffer, he saw death itself as the direct path to exaltation."

104. Baldensperger, Wilhelm: *Das Selbstbewusstsein Jesu im Lichte der messianischen Hoffnung seiner Zeit*. 2nd ed., Strasbourg, 1892, p. 9

105. Beer, Georg: *Das Buch Henoch*. (In) Kautsch: *Apokryphen* II, p. 234

106. Burrows: *Mehr Klarheit*, p. 63

107. Jeremias, Joachim: *Zwischen Karfreitag und Ostern*. (In) Jeremias: *Abba*, p. 325

108. Bultmann, Rudolf: *Neues Testament und Mythologie.* (In) *Kerygma* I, p. 21
109. Cf. Fuglister, Notker: *Die Heilsbedeutung des Pascha.* Munich, 1963, p. 93 ff.: "The blood of the passover and of the circumcision are together the blood of the Covenant whereby Yahweh delivered Israel. That explains how it was that Jesus on the actual occasion of a Passover meal was able to describe his blood as the 'blood of the New Covenant.' " (Matthew 26:28).
110. *Jerusalem Talmud, Traktat Sanhedrin,* 6,3 (Quoted in) *Le Talmud de Jérusalem,* Traduit par Moïse Schwab. Vol. 6, Paris, 1969, p. 279 ff. (Unless otherwise indicated, the *Jerusalem Talmud* will hereafter be quoted from the Moise Schwab version.)
111. Schott, Anselm: *Das Messbuch der heiligen Kirche.* Freiburg, 1956, p. 60
112. Bultmann: *Synopt Trad.,* p. 163
113. *Wilckens Bible,* p. 113
114. Cf. Stauffer: *Jerusalem,* p. 75, in which he places the Oracle text in the time of the Maccabees (Chap. 8–10 in the *Assumptio Mosis*).
115. *Assumptio Mosis* Chap. 9, 6–10, 1 (Quoted in) Kautsch: *Apokryphen* II, p. 326 et seq
116. Jeremias: *Theologie* I, p. 128: "The attempt to sketch a Jesus looking to the future is based on the fact that he was convinced that his mission was the signal for the coming of the eschatological time of distress. No one should imagine he has come to bring peace — no, he brings a sword (Matt. 10:34), he will set fire to the world (Luke 12:49), he foretells the cosmic baptism of suffering (v. 50). The murder of God's last messenger by the prophet-murderers of Jerusalem will make the measure of guilt set by God overflow (Matt. 23:32), will exhaust his patience (Mark 12:9), and will bring the hour of darkness (Luke 22:53). Jesus knew that his own suffering was inseparably bound up with that of his disciples; he saw a collective suffering breaking over his people, starting with his own passion. That this expectation was not fulfilled in this form is the subject of reproach in the word dealing with it in the time before Easter."
117. Hartmann, Walter: *Wundergeschichten der Bibel in der Grundschule,* III (In) *Evangelische Unterweisung,* Year 21, 1966, p. 44: "We must say quite clearly that Jesus was 'man' and not 'as man.' And what the ancients thought when they said 'true God' we can only express thus: In what Jesus is and does we are enabled to see what God has done on earth, wishes to do and will do through men who, as men, are nothing."
118. Schweitzer, Albert: *Von Reimarus bis Wrede. Eine Geschichte der Lebens-Jesu-Forschung.* Tübingen, 1906, p. 367: "Silence all round. Then the Baptist appears and cries: Repent! For the kingdom of heaven is at hand! Shortly thereafter Jesus comprehends, as if he, who knows himself to be the coming Son of Man, were giving the last turn to the spokes of the wheel of the world to set it in motion, and were bringing the natural history of the world to an end. As it does not move, he hangs himself upon it. It turns and crushes him. Instead of bringing eschatology, he has destroyed himself. The wheel of the world keeps turning, and the tatters of the body of the one immeasurably great man, who had the power to conceive himself as the spiritual ruler of all mankind and to violate history, still hang upon it. Thus he conquers and rules."

This passage is missing in the 2nd (1913) edition and the later editions of the *Lebens-Jesu-Forschung*. It is also missing in the English translation known as *The Quest of the Historical Jesus.*

119. *Was glauben die Deutschen?* Pub. by Werner Harenberg. 2nd ed. Munich, 1969, p. 84 ff.
120. Bultmann: *Jesus*, p. 12
121. Braun: *Jesus*, p. 40
122. Conzelmann: *Grundriss*, p. 159; see also p. 149 ff.
123. Blank: *Christus*, p. 236
124. *Wilckens Bible*, p. 76
125. Blank: *Christus*, p. 235
126. Stauffer: *Jesus*, p. 118
127. Tyrrell, George: *Christianity at the Cross-Roads,* London, 1963, p. 123.
128. Zahrnt: *Jesus*, p. 107

Chapter 3

1. The Rector of the University of Prague, Jan Hus, shortly before he was burnt at the stake on 6 July 1415, in a letter of (?) 25 June 1415 to friends in Konstanz, from his prison cell in the Barfüsserkloster in Konstanz. Latin text of the letter in: M. Jana Husi: *Korespondence a dokumenty*. Spisuv M. Jana Husi č. 9, vydal Václav Novotný. Praze, 1920, pp. 312–314; quotation p. 313
2. Schmiedel, Paul Wilhelm: *Die Person Jesu im Streite der Meinungen der Gegenwart*. Lecture given at the 17th conference of the Swiss Verein für freies Christentum at Chur on 11 June 1906. Leipzig, 1906, p. 29
3. Kant, Immanuel: *Die Religion innerhalb der Grenzen der blossen Vernunft.* (In) *Works*, pub. by Wilhelm Weischedel, Vol. 4. Wiesbaden, 1956, p. 773 Schweitzer: *Leben-Jesu-Forschung*, p. 633
4. Braun, Herbert: *Vom Verstehen des Neuen Testaments.* (In) Braun: *Gesammelte Studien*, p. 294
5. Kähler: *Jesus*, p. 44, 42, 84, 37, 38
6. Jeremias: *Theologie* I. Cf. particularly pp. 102, 128–141, 167, 177, 192, 228 ff., 257, 263
7. Wilckens, Ulrich: *Das Offenbarungsverständnis in der Geschichte des Urchristentums.* (In) *Offenbarung als Geschichte.* Ed. by Wolfhard Pannenberg. 4th ed., Göttingen, 1970, p. 62, 64, 88
8. Dautzenberg: *Jesus-Report*, p. 89
9. Blank: *Christus*, p. 218, 235, 241, 216
10. Gollwitzer: *Krummes Holz*, p. 363 ff., 199
11. Braun: *Jesus*, p. 61, 15, 154, 157, 162
12. Dautzenberg: *Jesus-Report*, p. 90
13. Blank: *Christus*, p. 239, 210
14. "Jesus oder Christus" (Debate, report) pp. 33, 41
15. Rahner, Karl: "Was Hoffnung vermag." (In) *Süddeutsche Zeitung* of 1–3 April 1972
16. Conzelmann: *Grundriss*, p. 50
17. Pannenberg: *Christologie*, p. 280
18. Conzelmann: *Grundriss*, p. 228

19. Dautzenberg: *Jesus-Report*, p. 90
20. Bultmann: *Synopt. Trad.*, p. 286
21. Bultmann: *Jesus*, p. 144
22. Jaspers, Karl: *Der philosophische Glaube angesichts der Offenbarung.* Munich, 1963, p. 483
23. Conzelmann: *Grundriss*, p. 366
24. Conzelmann: *Grundriss*, p. 365
    On Jewish wisdom, of. Ecclesiasticus 24 and Proverbs 8:22–31:
    22. The Lord created me the beginning of his works,
        before all else that he made, long ago.
    29. when he prescribed its limits for the sea
        and knit together earth's foundations.
    30. Then was I at his side each day,
        his darling and delight,
        playing in his presence continually,
    31. playing on the earth, when he had finished it,
        while my delight was in mankind.
25. Dautzenberg: *Jesus-Report*, p. 92
26. Zahrnt: *Jesus*, p. 54 ff.
27. Conzelmann: *Grundriss*, p. 372
28. Romans, 1 Corinthians, 2 Corinthians, Galatians, Philippians, 1 Thessalonians, Philemon. Cf. Bornkamm, Günther: article, *Paulus* (in) *RGG* V, co. 166
29. Freud: *Mann Moses*, p. 192
30. Cf. Bornkamm, Günther: *Paulus*, 2nd ed., Stuttgart, 1970, p. 122: "Paul shows himself in no way bothered to carry on the preaching of the earthly Jesus. Nowhere does he speak of the rabbi of Nazareth, the prophet and miracle-worker who ate with tax-gatherers and sinners, of his sermon on the mount, his metaphors of the kingdom of God and his battle against the Pharisees and lawyers. We do not even find the Lord's Prayer in his letters. He quotes only four very different and far from characteristic words of the Lord (1 Cor. 7:10; 9:14; 11:23; 1 Thess. 4:15). Just a few of his admonitions to the congregations are clearly formulated with some recollection of Jesus' words and show that as a result of his meetings with Christians, before or after his conversion, he must have possessed a limited acquaintance with the tradition of Jesus. But this little, casual knowledge alters nothing in the picture as a whole. The earthly Jesus seems to have been shelved."
31. Conzelmann: *Grundriss*, p. 111, 31
32. Shaw: *Prospects*, p. 108
33. *Wilckens Bible*, p. 591
34. *Wilckens Bible*, p. 608
35. 2 Corinthians 12:7 is reckoned to describe an illness from which Paul suffered, about the diagnosis of which there is no certainty. It has often been thought to refer to epilepsy. Cf. Wendland, Heinz-Dietrich in *Die Briefe an die Korinther*, Göttingen, 1971, p. 249 ff., who comments: "However, it is impossible to attribute Paul's ecstatic experiences to his illness . . . On the other hand, it should not be disregarded that a deep connection must have

existed between the attacks which Paul suffered and his tendency to visionary experiences, that is, between his bodily and his 'religious' constitution."

36. Cf. Bornkamm, Günther: *Paulus*. 2nd ed., Stuttgart, 1970, p. 111–120, with the resume: "Thus the destinies of the last years of his life up to the end of it lose themselves in darkness."

37. According to Josephus, *Ant.* XX, 9.1, he was stoned on the orders of the high priest Ananias. According to the legendary account of Hegesipp (in Eusebius: *Hist. eccl.* II, 23.4–18), scribes and Pharisees hurled him from the pinnacle of the temple and then stoned him, since he had not died from his fall. Finally, as he still knelt on the ground praying, "one of them, a fuller, took the club with which he beat out the clothes and brought it down on the just one's head. Thus he was martyred." (Trans. Lawlor and Oulton SPCK, 1927.)

38. *Wilckens Bible*, p. 505

39. *Wilckens Bible*, p. 727 ff.: "The furious passion in these sentences reads strangely; there are even motifs that remind one of contemporary anti-Semitism . . . Paul, who wrote Romans 1:9 et seq, is not one we can readily believe capable of such an attack. But undoubtedly it comes from a Christian hand. If we look today at the history of suffering of the Jewish people in the Christian countries of the West, we must deeply regret that such sentences in the Bible have justified Christian anti-Semitism over the centuries."

40. Jeremias: *Theologie* I, p. 291

41. Cf. Freud: *Mann Moses*, p. 193: "I have already mentioned that the Christian ceremony of the Holy Communion, in which the believer incorporates the flesh and blood of the Redeemer, repeats the content of the old Totem feast; it does so, it is true, only in its tender and adoring sense, not in its aggressive sense."

42. Burrows: *Mehr Klarheit*, p. 44

43. Bultmann, Rudolf: *Die Christologie des Neuen Testaments.* (In) Bultmann: *Glauben und Verstehen* I, p. 247

44. In 186 B.C.E. the mysteries of Dionysus were forbidden in Rome by a decision of the Senate. Cf. Leopoldt, Johannes: article, *Mysteries* (in) *RGG* IV, col. 1234

45. Bornkamm, Günther: *Glaube und Vernunft bei Paulus.* (In) Bornkamm: *Studien*, p. 123 ff.

46. Bornkamm, Günther: *Gesetz und Natur.* (In) Bornkamm: *Studien*, p. 115

47. Seneca: *De Ira* III, 36: "All minds can be weaned from feebleness, they are by nature docile if the inner man does not continually destroy them; only we must call ourselves to account every day. This is what Sextius used to do: When the day was over, he asked himself when he retired to rest: what sickness of the soul have you cured today? To what vices have you offered resistance? From what aspect have you become better? Anger will be relaxed and moderated if it knows that it must appear before its judge every day. What is lovelier than this habit of going through the whole day in detail? What sleep follows this self-examination? How restful, deep and

undisturbed will it be if the soul, praised or warned, confesses its doing and being to its own secret judge?"

48. Philo: *Quod deterius potiori insidiari soleat* 146: "So, when we are convinced of our failings through our conscience, let us entreat God rather to punish us than to let us go. For if he let us go, he makes us no longer his, the merciful one's, but slaves of the pitiless world around us; but if he punish us, in his kindness he will considerately and gently put right our errors, sending his own word into our soul for the correction of our faults even as he berates it for our sins, and rebukes it, and seeks to save it."

49. Bornkamm, Günther: *Der Lohngedanke im Neuen Testament*. (In) Bornkamm: *Studien*, p. 73

50. Plato: *Politeia*, 362a. Plato uses the word ἀνασχινδυλευθήσεται, which can be translated as impale, crucify. Friedrich Schleiermacher translates it as "hanged." "In the theology of the ancient church the forms of Plato were understood as a prophecy of Christ." (Schneider, Johannes: article ἀνασταυρόω (in) *ThWB* VII, p. 584, note 1)

51. In an ecumenical re-translation of the Apostles' Creed by the non-sectarian "working party for a common liturgical text for the churches of the German-speaking countries," it now says:" . . . descended into the kingdom of death." But that does not make interpretation any simpler.

52. Otto: *Reich Gottes*, p. 184

53. Cf. Lohse, Eduard: *Umwelt des Neuen Testaments*. Gottingen, 1971, p. 171

54. *Wilckens Bible*, p. 319

55. Strauss: *Leben Jesu f.d. dt. Volk*, p. 601

56. Jeremias: *Gleichnisse*, p. 218

57. Barth, Karl: *Die neue Welt in der Bibel*. (In) *Das Wort Gottes und die Theologie*. Gesammelte Vorträge 1, Munich, 1925, p. 28

58. Definition of the Trinity after Rahner, Hugo: article, *Dreifaltigkeit* (in) *Lexikon für Theologie und Kirche*. 2nd ed., Vol. 3, Freiburg, 1959, col. 548

59. All quotations from Rahner from *Spiegel* 9/1972, p. 112 ff.: "Jesus would have understood nothing by it." Interview in *Spiegel* with Karl Rahner, SJ, professor of theology, about the controversy about dogma of a papal infallibility.

60. Kung, Hans: *Unfehlbar? Eine Anfrage*. Zürich, 1970, p. 152

61. *Dogmatische Konstitution uber die göttliche Offenbarung*. Third chapter (art. 11). (Quoted in) *Lexikon für Theologie und Kirche. Das Zweite Vatikanische Konzil, Dokumente und Kommentare*, Part II. Freiburg, 1967, p. 549 ff.

62. Nolte, Josef: *Dogma in Geschichte*. Freiburg, 1971, p. 115

Chapter 4

1. Dietrich Bonhoeffer on 21 August 1944, in a letter from the Tegel prison in Berlin to his friend Eberhard Bethge. Cf. Bonhoeffer, Dietrich: *Widerstand und Ergebung. Briefe und Aufzeichnungen aus der Haft*. Pub. by Eberhard Bethge. Munich, 1964, p. 196

2. Burrows: *Mehr Klarheit*, p. 45, 75

3. Thielicke, Helmut: *Und wenn Gott wäre . . .* 2nd ed., Stuttgart, 1971, p. 32

4. Dibelius: *Formgeschichte*, p. 31

5. Braun: *Jesus*, p. 136, 63, 137, 33–37

6. Frederick II on 18 Oct. 1770 in a letter to d'Alembert: "Jesus was actually an Essene; he was soaked in Essenic ethics." (Quoted from) *Briefe Friedrichs des Grossen*, ed. by Max Hein. Vol. 2, Berlin, 1914, p. 192
Voltaire: *Dictionnaire philosophique*. Amsterdam, 1789, p. 274: "Quelques savans ont cru que Jésus Christ . . . était un de ces Esséniens."
Lehmann: *Jesus-Report*, p. 35
7. Josephus: *Bell. Iud.* II, 8.2; Josephus: *Vita*, §2
8. *Songs of Thanksgiving:* 1 QH XVIII, 14. Translated by Jeremias, *Theologie* I, p. 171 and Burrows, *Mehr Klareit*, p. 82; *Gemeinderegel:* 1 QS I, 16−II, 25
9. *Habbakuk Commentary*: 1 Qp Hab IX, 1f. Translation by Burrows: *The Dead Sea Scrolls*, p. 306
Jeremias: *Lehrer*, p. 282 ff. 313 ff.
The name of the Teacher of Righteousness is unknown; only his title is mentioned. The dating of his life is made possible only by his opponent, the so-called priest of sacrilege, about whom the Qumran texts have likewise nothing precise to tell us. Experts on Qumran suppose him to be the high priest officiating in the temple in Jerusalem. André Dupont-Sommer wavers with regard to the person of the high priest between Alexander Jannaeus and Hyrcanos II. "The Teacher of Righteousness probably, so we believe, began his service towards the end of the second century B.C.E.; he carried it out during the whole period of government of Alexander Jannaeus (103−76) — not indeed without suffering some persecution on the part of the high priest; but the main persecution was undertaken by Hyrcanus II, who had the Teacher killed about 65−63." (Writings, p. 130 ff.) But it is more likely, in agreement with Karl Georg Kuhn and his pupil Gert Jeremias *RGG* V, col. 745) that the priest of sacrilege can be identified with the Maccabean Jonathan: "This gives us a secure basis for the dating of the Teacher: his conflict with the priest of sacrilege, Jonathan, took place during the latter's period of office, 153−143 B.C.E." (*Lehrer*, p. 76)
10. Jeremias: *Theologie* I, p. 173
Jeremias: *Lehrer*, p. 334
11. Jeremias: *Lehrer*, p. 351, 327, 325, 263, 146
12. *Habbakuk Commentary*: 1 Qp Hab VII, 1−5
Commentary on Psalm 37:4 Qp Ps 37 III, 15f. Lohse: *Texte,* p. 277; 4Qp Ps 37 III.5. Lohse: *Texte*, p. 275
13. Küng, Hans: *Unfehlbar? Eine Anfrage.* Zurich, 1970, p. 18
14. Daniélou: *Qumran*, p. 106
In this interview with *Spiegel*, Cardinal Daniélou, SJ, in 1970 described the dogma of the virgin birth and the dogma of bodily resurrection as being for him the fundamental dogmas, and, out of his love for Christian people, demanded greater severity towards heretical theologians. Cf. *Spiegel* 31/1970, p. 108 ff.: "Heresy must be condemned."
Burrows: *Mehr Klarheit*, p. 73 ff.
15. Danielou: *Qumran*, p. 108
16. (Quoted from) Schweitzer: *Leben-Jesu-Forschung*, p. 167
17. *Habbakuk Commentary*: 1 Qp Hab VII, 7 et seq
18. Cf. Gaster, Theodor H.:*The Dead Sea Scriptures*. New York, 1956, p. 16−18.

      Against that, *Qumran* I, p. 281
19. Daniélou: *Qumran*, p. 46
20. Conzelmann: *Grundriss*, p. 46
21. *Gemeinderegel*: 1 QS VI, 12.20; VIII, 1
      Gemeinderegel: 1 QS VIII, 7 ff. Translated Maier: *Texte* I, p. 36
22. *Songs of Thanksgiving*: 1QH VII, 8 ff. Translated Maier: *Texte* I, p. 91
23. *Songs of Thanksgiving*: 1 QH VI, 24–26
24. Jeremias: *Theologie* I, p. 198
25. Josephus: *Bell. Iud.* II, 8.4: "They have no certain city, but many of them dwell in every city." (Trans. Wm. Whiston, 1737.) Against that, Philo reports: *Quod omnis probus liber sit* 12,76: "The first thing that strikes one about them is that they live in villages and avoid entering towns on account of the wickedness that becomes habitual among town dwellers."
      Gemeinderegel: 1 QS VI, 18 ff., 24 ff.; Braun: *Jesus*, p. 122 ff.
26. *Manual of Discipline* (*Gemeinderegel*): 1 QS VI, 1
27. Josephus: *Ant.* XVIII, 5.2
28. Blank: *Christus*, p. 228
29. *Gemeinderegel*: 1 QS VI, 5; *Gemeinschaftsregel:* 1 QSa II, 18–21
30. *Gemeinderegel*: 1 QS III, 20–23
      Gemeinderegel: 1 QS I, 9; III, 13, 24 et seq
31. *Manual of Discipline* (*Gemeinderegel*): 1 QS I, 10
32. Cf. John 3:21 and the *Gemeinderegel*: 1 QS I, 5: V, 3; VIII, 2
      John 3:15 and the *Gemeinderegel*: 1 QS IV, 7; John 8:12 and the *Gemeinderegel* 1 QS III, 7
      John 14:7 with the *Gemeinderegel*: 1 QS IV, 21
      John 14:4–6 and the *Damascus Document*: CD I, 16. On this subject see Braun: *Qumran* II, p. 118–144
33. Cf. *Gemeinderegel*: 1 QS III, 24
      Damascus Document: CD XIX, 34
      Gemeinderegel: 1 QS IV, 20–22
34. *Kriegsrolle*: 1 QM XIV, 7; *Habbakuk Commentary*: 1 Qp Hab XII. Cf. Braun: *Qumran* I, p. 13
35. Burrows: *Mehr Klarheit*, p. 82
36. Harder, Günther: *Jesus und das Gesetz.* (In) *Antijudaismus*, p. 105
37. Dibelius, Martin: *Evangelienkritik und Christologie.* (In) *Botschaft und Geschichte*, Vol. 1. Tübingen 1953, p. 306
38. Bultmann: *Synopt. Trad.*, p. 113–115, 134–136
      Fuchs, Ernst: *Das Zeitverständnis Jesu.* (In) Fuchs: *Hist. Jesu* II, p. 346
39. Enoch 58, 2; *Slavic Enoch* (Quoted from) Otto: *Reich Gottes*, p. 311
      Otto: *Reich Gottes*, p. 310
40. *Gemeinderegel*: 1 QS VI, 2
41. *Habbukuk Commentary*: 1 Qp Hab XI, 13–15. Burrows, *Dead Sea Scrolls*, p. 308
42. *Gemeinderegel*: 1 QS X, 17 et seq. Translated by Lohse: *Texte*, p. 39
43. Aramaic Targum Pseudo-Jonathan on *Leviticus* 22:28 (Quoted from) Burrows: *Mehr Klarheit*, p. 43
44. *Damascus Document*: CD VI, 20 ff.
45. Bultmann: *Jesus*, p. 95 ff.

46. *Songs of Thanksgiving*: 1 QH IV, 32 ff.; XI, 9
    Manual of Discipline (Gemeinderegel): 1 QS VIII, 6
    Commentary on Psalm 37:4 Ps 37 II, 4−8
47. *Gemeinderegel*: 1 QS V, 1 ff. Translated Maier: *Texte* I, p. 29
    Kriegsrolle: 1 QM I, 3. Translated Maier: *Texte* I, p. 123
48. Dupont-Sommer: *Writings*, p. 131 dates the exile of the Essenes in the years
    around 65−63, when Hyrcanus II is said to have had the Teacher of
    Righteousness killed; cf. above, note 9. "At that time the sect founded by
    the Teacher must have fled to the region of Damascus to escape the
    persecution of the Jewish high priest."
    Burrows: *Mehr Klarheit*, p. 198 inclines more to the view that "the
    migration to the land of Damascus really stands for the move of the group
    to Qumran itself."
49. Daniélou: *Qumran*, p. 19
    Brownlee, William Hugh: *The Meaning of the Qumran Scrolls for the Bible*,
    New York, 1964, p. 113: "Yet the ideas of John's later preaching have so
    much kinship with Essene thought as to suggest that he lived among the
    Essenes as a boy . . ."
    Josephus: *Bell. Iud.* II, 8.2.
50. Schmidt, Karl Ludwig: *Der Rahmen der Geschichte Jesu*. Berlin, 1919, p.
    18−22
    Bultmann: *Synopt. Trad.*, p. 261
    Damascus Document: CD XII, 14
51. Cf. *Damascus Document*: CD IV, 13; VI, 8; VII, 10
52. Bultmann: *Synopt. Trad.*, p. 320
53. Burrows: *Dead Sea Scrolls*, p. 217
54. Burrows: *Dead Sea Scrolls*, p. 271
55. Jeremias: *Lehrer*, p. 328, note 6
56. Lehmann: *Jesus-Report*, p. 76
    The *Gemeinderegel* mentions a two-year novitiate (1 QS VI, 13−23).
    Josephus (*Bell. Iud.* II, 8.7) speaks of three years.
57. Lehmann: *Jesus-Report*, p. 148
58. Bultmann: *Synopt. Trad.*, p. 54
59. Lehman: *Jesus-Report*, p. 119
60. Braun: *Jesus*, p. 20, 161
61. Dautzenberg: *Jesus-Report*, p. 88
62. Braun: *Jesus*, p. 36
63. *Damascus Document*: CD X, 14 − XII, 22; Strack-Billerbeck, I, p. 615−618
64. Josephus: *Bell. Iud.* II, 8.9
65. Strack-Billerbeck, II, p. 5
    Conzelmann: *Grundriss*, p. 153 ff.
66. Flusser: *Synagoge*, p. 32
67. Jeremias: *Theologie* I, p. 89
68. Käsemann: *Hist. Jesus*, p. 206
    Harder, Günther: *Jesus und das Gesetz*. (In) *Antijudaismus*, p. 115
69. Shaw: *Prospects*, p. 44
70. *Wilckens Bible*, p. 167
71. Cf. Strack-Billerbeck I, p. 312−320, 804 ff.

72. *Damascus Document:* CD II, 16. Translated Maier: *Texte* I, p. 49
    Damascus Document: CD IV, 20 ff. V, 1. Translated Maier: *Texte* I, p. 52
    Jeremias: *Lehrer*, p. 100
    Flusser: *Synagoge*, p. 32
73. *Wilckens Bible*, p. 31
74. *Babylonian Talmud*, Traktat Jabmuth 62b, 63a
75. Jeremias: *Theologie* I, p. 217
76. Bauer, Walter: *Jesus der Galiläer.* (In) *Festgabe für Adolf Jülicher.* Ed. by Rudolf Bultmann and Hans von Soden. Tübingen, 1927, p. 27
77. Bornkamm: *Jesus*, p. 20
78. Cf. Braun: *Qumran* II, p. 111−114
79. Lehmann: *Jesus-Report*, p. 98, ff.
80. *Gemeinderegel:* 1 QS XI, 9. Translated Burrows: *Dead Sea Scrolls*, p. 325
81. Manual of Discipline (*Gemeinderegel*): 1 QS XI, 9−15. Translated Burrows: *Mehr Klarheit*, p. 104; *Habbakuk Commentary:* 1 Qb Hab VIII, 1−3. Translated Burrows: *Dead Sea Scrolls*, p. 306
82. *Songs of Thanksgiving:* 1 QH XI, 3
84. Holl: *Jesus*, p. 122
85. Cf. Strack-Billerbeck I, p. 759
86. Smith, Morton:"The Jewish Elements in the Gospels" (In) *The Journal of Bible and Religion.* Vol. 24 No. 2, 1956, p. 96
    Daniélou: *Qumran*, p. 111
87. Dirks, Walter: "Paragraph 218 — das Feld der Diskussion" (In) *Publik* of 10 Sept. 1971
88. Blank: *Christus*, p. 228
89. Stauffer: *Jerusalem*, p. 6
90. *Gospel according to Thomas*, Logion 6: "His disciples asked him, saying: Is it your will that we fast? And how should we pray and give alms, and what rules should we observe about food? Jesus answered: Lie not, and do not that which you hate, for all is revealed before heaven."
91. Hegel, Georg Friedrich Wilhelm: *Encyklopädie der philosophischen Wissenschaften*, 396 appendix. (In) *Werke*, Vol. 7 Pt. 2. Berlin, 1845
92. Hegel to Goethe on 18 Oct. 1827. (Quoted from) Eckermann, Johann Peter: *Gespräche mit Goethe.* (In) Goethe, Johann Wolfgang von: *Gedenkausgabe der Werke, Briefe und Gespräche.* Vol. 24. Zurich, 1948, p. 670
93. Bultmann: *Theologie d. NT*, p. 27
94. Kasemann: *Hist. Jesus*, p. 211
95. Zahrnt: *Jesus*, p. 103
96. *Damascus Document:* CD VII, 18 ff.

Chapter 5

1. Goethe, Johann Wolfgang von: *Maximen und Reflexionen.* (In) *Gedenkausgabe der Werke, Briefe und Gespräche.* Vol. 9, Zurich, 1949, p. 617
2. Zimmerli, Walther: *Das Alte Testament in der Verkündigung der christlichen Kirche.* (In) *Das Alte Testament als Anrede.* Munich, 1956, p. 81

3. Conzelmann: *Jesus*, col. 630
4. Shaw: *Prospects*, p. 118
5. Cf. Bultmann: *Synopt. Trad.*, p. 282–316, particularly p. 297 ff., 301 ff. Bultmann assumes as the oldest traceable constituent of the Passion story a kerygmatically accepted short account of historical recollection of the arrest, trial and execution, the historical origin of which cannot be ascertained.
6. Dibelius, Martin: *Die alttestamentlichen Motive in der Leidensgeschichte des Petrus - und des Johannes-Evangelium.* (In) *Botschaft und Geschichte.* Vol. 1. Tübingen, 1953, p. 223
7. Pannenberg: *Christologie*, p. 280
8. Tosephta, *Traktat Joma* I 6 (180); cf. Jeremias, Joachim: *Jerusalem zur Zeit Jesu.* Third edition, Gottingen, 1962, p. 223, note 5.
9. Blank: *Christus*, p. 233
10. Tacitus: *Historiae* 4, 81: "And so he (the blind man) begged the prince that he would be so gracious as to smear his cheeks and eyelids with spittle from his mouth. Another, who had an ailment in his hand, prayed . . . the prince to touch him with the sole of his foot . . . So then Vespasian, believing that in his good fortune everything was possible and that nothing in future should be thought impossible for him, with a friendly expression, before the tensely waiting multitude, did as he was asked. The hand was at once made whole, the light of day shone anew for the blind man. Both stories are told to this day by eyewitnesses to whom an untruthful account would bring no profit."
11. Blank: *Christus*, p. 231, 233
12. Bultmann: *Synopt. Trad.*, p. 329, note 3
13. Braun: *Jesus*, p. 71
14. Klausner, Joseph: *The Messianic Idea in Israel*, London 1956, p. 523
15. Dibelius: *Jesus*, p. 112: "If we do not actually know that such an amnesty (Pilate's Passover amnesty) was customary, that is no reason to doubt the scene; to assume that it was invented would be to credit the first reporters with a creativity and a poetic force which is not to be observed elsewhere."
16. Cf. Olrik, Axel: *Epische Gesetze der Volksdichtung.* (In) *Zeitschrift für deutsches Altertum.* Vol. 51, 1909, pp. 1-12; quoted with approval by Dibelius in *Formgeschichte*, p. 1
17. Bultmann: *Synopt. Trad.*, p. 288, 306
18. Origen: *Commentary on John*, X:16: "Let us imagine the Son of God as he takes up the cords and makes himself a whip out of them to drive the dealers out of the temple — if this does not seem thoughtless, presumptuous and rowdy."
19. Schonfield, Hugh J.: *Planziel Golgotha.* Aldingen, 1969, p. 172 ff., 144, 181. (The original English title is *The Passover Plot*.)
20. Burrows: *Mehr Klarheit*, p. 63
21. Cf. Lauenstein: *Messias*, p. 159, 300. All that can be shown is that the Messianic hopes in the Davidic Zerubbabel were associated with the re-establishment of David's kingdom (Haggai 2:20 ff; Zechariah 4:6 ff.)
22. Bultmann: *Synopt. Trad.*, p. 281

23. Goguel: *Leben Jesu*, p. 281
24. Ben-Chorin: *Jesus*, p. 140 ff
25. Dalman, Josef: *Jesus—Jeschua*. Leipzig, 1922, p. 97
26. Cf. Grimm, Jacob and Wilhelm: *Deutsches Wörterbuch*, Vol. 6. Ed. by Moriz Heyne. Leipzig, 1885, col. 294
27. Cf. Schurer: *Gesch. d. jüd. Volkes* II, p. 329, note 57
28. Harnack, Adolf von: *Das Wesen des Christentums*. Leipzig, 1900, p. 88
29. Ben-Chorin: *Jesus*, p. 148
30. Bultmann: *Synopt. Trad.*, p. 59

    Braun: *Jesus*, p. 77

31. Eppstein, Victor: *The Historicity of the Gospel Account of the Cleansing of the Temple*. (In) *Zeitschrift für die neutestamentliche Wissenschaft*. Vol. 55, 1964, p. 42 ff.
32. Stauffer: *Jesus*, p. 59
33. Jeremias: *Theologie* I, p. 145, note 15
34. Karl Kautsky cites as an illustration: "That would be rather as if the Berlin police paid an informer to point out someone called Bebel (the German equivalent of Smith) to them."
35. Blinzler: *Prozess*, p. 87
36. Not counting cases where a warrior kills himself, or has himself killed, to avoid the enemy (Judges 9:54, 1 Samuel 31:4 ff; 1 Kings 16:18)
37. Cf. on this Strack-Billerbeck I, p. 36-43, 678: *Des Leben Jesu nach jüdischen Quellen*. Ed. by Samuel Krauss. Berlin, 1902, p. 88 ff.
    Klausner, Joseph: *Jesus von Nazareth*. Berlin, 1930, p. 23 ff. Ben-Chorin: *Mirjam*, p. 36 ff.
38. Cf. Gerock, C.F.: *Versuch einer Darstellung der Christologie des Koran*. Hamburg, 1839, p. 58 ff.
39. *Das Leben Jesu nach jüdischen Quellen*. Ed. by Samuel Krauss. Berlin, 1902, pp. 53-56
40. Reik: *Gott*, p. 103; cf. generally Reik: *Gott*, p. 75−132
41. See also Wrede, William: *Judas Ischarioth in der urchristlichen Überlieferung*. (In) *Vorträge und Studien*. Tübingen, 1907, p. 140: "A *scholion* attributed to Eusebius says that Judas hanged himself, but the rope broke; he fell to the ground and wounded himself severely in the lower stomach. They laid him on a bed and he lay there for two days half dead and breathing heavily; then he suddenly grew worse and died from a rupture of the bowels. According to the so-called Persian prophet Aphraates (ca. 340) Judas hurled himself into the sea with a millstone round his neck . . .Others say that Judas shut his door and locked it on the inside, and no one opened the door of his house to look inside until he had rotted and the whole contents of his body poured out . . . The detailed account of Papias is older: monstrous swelling of the body so that he could not even get past where a cart could easily drive through, his eyelids so swollen that the doctor could not even see his eyes, pus and worms in his whole body and other loathsome things, till at last he died painfully on his piece of ground. Then a stench came forth from the remains of his body on this ground so that no one could live there; indeed, says Papias, to this day no one could

pass by without holding his nose. It is thus a legend in the harshest of colors. One feels especially here the pleasure with which the story is served up, and, too, the interest that the early Christians took in Judas' end. The more gruesome, the better. Such a monster must naturally receive God's punishment, and in full measure."

42. Gollwitzer: *Krummes Holz*, p. 272
43. *Gospel According to Peter*, 59 (In) Hennecke—Schneemelcher: *Apokryphen* I, p. 124
44. Cf. Bultmann: *Synopt. Trad.*, p. 282 ff., 284 ff., 289 ff., 294
45. *Was glauben die Deutschen?* Ed. by Werner Harenburg. 2nd ed., Munich, 1969, p. 89
46. Ben-Chorin: *Jesus*, p. 173
47. The version "in the treasury" has prevailed over the wording in the Masoretic text (*hajjoser* = potter) and in the Septaugint (χωνευτήριον = furnace) y reason of a conjecture: according to the Syrian translation at the passage in question *ha'osar* = treasury-house is the proper reading.
48. Cf. Exodus 21:32: "If the ox gores a slave or a slave girl, its owner shall pay thirty sheckels of silver to their master, and the ox shall be stoned."
49. Bultmann: *Synopt. Trad.*, p. 290
50. Brandt, Wilhelm: *Die Evangelische Geschichte und der Ursprung des Christenthums auf Grund einer Kritik der Berichte über das Leiden und die Auferstehung Jesu.* Leipzig, 1893, p. 32
Dalman, Gustaf: *Orte und Wege Jesu.* 4th ed., Darmstadt, 1967, p. 299, note 9
Jeremias, Joachim: *Jerusalem zur zeit Jesu.* 3rd ed., Göttingen, 1962, p. 54
Strack-Billerbeck I, p. 992 ff.
51. Fuchs, Ernst: *Glaube und Erfahrung.* Tübingen, 1965, p. 18
52. Haenchen: *Weg Jesu*, p. 499
53. Bultmann: *Synopt. Trad.*, p. 289 ff.
54. Stauffer: *Jerusalem*, p. 82
55. Lehmann: *Jesus-Report*, p. 30 ff.
56. Cullmann, Oscar: *Jesus und die Revolutionären seiner Zeit.* Tübingen, 1970, p. 16, 22 ff., 70
57. Hengel, Martin: *War Jesus Revolutionär?* 2nd ed., Stuttgart, 1970, p. 11
58. Eisler: Ἰησοῦς βασιλεύς II, p. 247, 256, 266 ff. Eisler thinks it unlikely (p. 267) that Luke 22:35—38 belongs with the account of the arrest in Gethsemane: "It is almost unthinkable that, in the moment that he knew himself to be betrayed and lost, Jesus should have told his disciples, not to escape from their persecutors as quickly and secretly as possible, but quite inappropriately to waste time selling the last articles of clothing they could spare and buying a weapon quite useless to a solitary fugitive pursued by the soldiers, and so quite possibly give themselves away . . . These words thus belong to quite a different period, when Jesus was preparing his disciples, some considerable time after their first mission, for a longer period of travel, and wished to see them armed."

59. Mommsen, Theodor: *Römisches Strafrecht.* Leipzig, 1899, pp. 537—594
60. *The Psalms of Solomon.* Translated and edited by Rudolf Kittel. (In) Kautzsch: *Apokryphen* II, p. 127—148
61. Geiselmann, Josef Rupert: *Jesus der Christus.* Part 1. *Die Frage nach dem historischen Jesus.* Munich, 1965, p. 112.
62. Stauffer: *Jesus,* p. 99

Chapter 6

1. Regius, Heinrich (pseudonym of Max Horkheimer): *Dämmerung. Notizen in Deutschland.* Zürich, 1934, p. 14
2. Fuchs, Ernst: *Jesus Christus in Person.* (In) *Hist. Jesus* II, p. 37
3. Blinzler: *Prozess,* p. 332, 316 ff., 293
4. Blinzler: *Prozess,* p. 267, 21
5. *Babylonian Talmud, Traktat Sanhedrin* 52b
6. Braun: *Jesus,* p. 51
7. Stauffer: *Jesus,* p. 108
8. *Gospel acc. to Peter* 3 (In) Hennecke-Schneemelcher: *Apokryphen* I, p. 121
9. (Quoted in) Burrows: *Mehr Klarheit,* p. 132. Burrows translates "with a rich man". The Masoretic text and the Qumran scroll of Isaiah 1 QJs[a] read "among the rich." Cf. Chapter 7, Note 32
10. Conzelmann: *Jesus,* col. 630
    Bultmann: *Synopt. Trad.,* p. 290
11. Bartsch, Hans-Walter: *Wer verurteilte Jesus zum Tode?* (In) *Novum Testamentum.* Vol. VII. Leiden, 1964/65, p. 212
12. Hahn, Ferdinand: *Christologische Hoheitstitel.* 3rd ed. Gottingen, 1966, p. 177
    Schneider, Gerhard: *Verleugnung, Verspottung und Verhör Jesu nach Lukas 22:54—71.* Munich, 1969, p. 32
    Dibelius: *Formgeschichte,* p. 192 ff.; Dibelius, Martin: *Das historische Problem der Leidensgeschichte.* (In) *Botschaft und Geschichte.* Vol. I, Tübingen, 1953, p. 254 ff.
    Holtzmann, Heinrich Julius: *Das messianische Bewusstsein Jesu.* Tübingen, 1907, p. 49
13. Stauffer, Ethelbert: *Geschichte Jesu.* (In) *Historia Mundi.* Vol. 4. Munich, 1956, p. 169
14. Cf. *Jerusalem Talmud, Traktat Sanhedrin* 6,6. Cf. also *Mishna-Traktat Sanhedrin* 6,4 (In) *Mischnajot. Die sechs Ordnungen der Mischna.* 3rd ed., Basle, 1968, p. 169
15. The Jewish code of law rests on the Torah. The idea of the Mishna was originally connected with the oral law: it embraced not only the interpretation of scripture but also the orally transmitted common law. The legal system of the Mishna was codified towards the end of the second century B.C.E. "Zur Frage der Geltung des mischnischen Strafrechts in der Zeit Jesu" s. Exkurs IX (In) Blinzler: *Prozess,* p. 216—229
16. Lohse, Eduard: *Der Prozess Jesu Christi.* (In) *Ecclesia und Res Publica.* Ed. by Georg Kretschmar and Bernhard Lohse. Göttingen, 1961, p. 34
17. Eisler: Ἰησοῦς βασιλεύς II, p. 252

18. Jeremias: *Theologie* I, p. 247
19. Just as Nicodemus, the Jewish doctor of law, on the evidence of the evangelist (John 3:2) did not openly declare himself a follower of Jesus, but came to Jesus in secret, so do underground camps communicate with one another secretly by signs in a secret speech and/or secret literature: "Nicodemism".
20. Cf. *Babylonian Talmud, Traktat Sanhedrin* 93b: Bar Kochba "said to the rabbis: 'I am the Messiah.' They answered him: 'It is written of the Messiah that he smells out and corrects; we wish to see whether you smell out and correct.' When they saw that he did not smell out and correct, they killed him." (Quoted in) Strack-Billerbeck II, p. 439
21. Philo: *In Flaccum* 36—39: "Then the crowd standing around broke out into a mad shouting: 'Marin,' they cried — that was what the ruler was called by the Syrians; for they knew that Agrippa was a Syrian." — Marin corresponds to the Aramaic *maran*. Cf. 1 Corinthians 16:22
22. Thoma, Clemens: *Der Prozess Jesu in Religionsunterricht.* (In) *Judenhass — Schuld der Christen?* Ed. by W.P. Eckert and E.L. Ehrlich. Essen, 1964, p. 129
23. Bloch: *Atheismus,* p. 179
24. Tertullian: *Apologeticum* 21, 24: "Ea omnia super Christo Pilatus, et ipse iam pro sua conscientia Christianus, Caesari tunc Tiberio nuntiavit."
25. Stauffer: *Jesus,* p. 54
26. *Wilckens Bible*, p. 193: "probably . . . intentional avoidance of the question put."
27. Ketter, Peter: *Das Matthäus—Evangelium.* Arranged with commentary by P. Ketter, Stuttgart, 1939, p. 64: "The appalling self-condemnation shows what can happen to a people when they listen to ignorant heretics."
28. Schweizer, Eduard: *Zum Prozess Jesu.* (In) *Neue Zürcher Zeitung* of 4.5.1961
29. Maccoby, Hyan Zoundell: *Jesus and Barabbas.* (In) *New Testament Studies,* Cambridge. Vol. 16, 1969/70, p. 56
    Winter, Paul: *On the Trial of Jesus.* Berlin, 1961, p 99, 95
30. Blinzler: *Prozess*, p. 314
31. Lohse, Eduard: *Der Prozess Jesu Christi.* (In) *Ecclesia und Res Publica.* Ed. by G. Kretschmar and B. Lohse. Göttingen, 1961, p. 36
32. Goguel: *Leben Jesu,* p. 479, note 8
33. Cf. Pinès, Shlomo: *The Jewish Christians of the Early Centuries of Christianity According to a New Source.* (In) *The Israel Academy of Sciences and Humanities.* Vol 2, No. 13. Jerusalem, 1966, p. 53—55
34. Josephus: *Bell. Iud.* VI, 5.3, trans. H. St. J. Thackeray, 1928
35. Ben-Chorin: *Jesus,* p. 203 ff
36. Hengel: *Zeloten,* p. 303
37. Origen: *De Principiis* I, 6.3: "But whether among those orders that live under the chieftainship of the devil and conform to his wickedness there are some who will one day in the ages to come succeed in turning to goodness." (trans. G.W. Butterworth, SPCK, 1936)
38. Blinzler: *Prozess,* p.333

39. *Wilckens Bible*, p. 380
40. Cf. *Neue Zürcher Zeitung* of 15 Sept. 1972.
    As early as 1948, after the establishment of the state of Israel, an application was put before the first president of the Supreme Court, Moshe Smoira, for revision of the trial of Jesus, which was not accepted for lack of any kind of judicial basis. Cf. Blinzler: *Prozess*, p. 15 ff. and Ben-Chorin *Jesus*, p. 191

Chapter 7

1. *Commentary on Nahum*, 4 Qp Nah I, 6ff.: "(. . . And he filled) his cave (with loot) and his camp with booty (2:13). His explanation refers to the Lion of Wrath, . . . Vengeance on those, who seek after sweet things, when he hung up men alive (. . .) in Israel formerly." (Quoted in) Lohse: *Texte*, p. 263 and note, p. 298
2. Josephus: Ant. XIII. 14.2, trans. H. St. J. Thackeray, 1928: "The most powerful of them, however, he shut up and besieged in the city of Bethoma, and after taking the city and getting them into his power, he brought them back to Jerusalem; and then he did a thing that was as cruel as could be: while he feasted with his concubines in a conspicuous place, he ordered some 800 of the Jews to be crucified, and slaughtered their children and wives before the eyes of the still living wretches."
4. Josephus: *Bell. Iud.* II, 14.9, trans. Wm. Whiston, 1737: "Florus ventured to do what no one had done before, that is to have men of the equestrian order whipped, and nailed to the cross before his tribunal who, although they were by birth Jews, yet were they of Roman dignity notwithstanding." Also *Bell. Iud.* V, 11.1: "The (Roman) soldiers in their monstrous fury now amused themselves by nailing up the prisoners in different attitudes, and there were so many of them that soon there was not enough room for the crosses and not enough crosses for the bodies."
5. Cf. also Haas, Nicu: "Anthropological Observations on the Skeletal Remains from Giv'at ha-Mivtar." (In) *Israel Exploration Journal.* Vol. 20, No. 1/2, Jerusalem, 1970, p. 38 ff.
6. Cicero: *In Verrem* II 5, 64 (165): "crudelissimum taeterrimumque supplicium."
7. Brückner, Martin: *Der sterbende und auferstehende Gottheiland in den Orientalischen Religionen und ihr Verhältnis zum Christentum.* 2nd ed. Tübingen, 1920, p. 45
8. Cf. Blinzler: *Prozess*, p. 384
9. Lützeler, Heinrich: *Christliche Kunst — Erkenntnis oder Mythos.* (In) *Mann aus Galiläa*, p. 280
    The oldest known representatives of the crucifixion are an ivory panel (casket with Passion scenes, British Museum, London) of about 425 and a relief on the wooden door of Santa Sabina (Rome), about 450. On both representations only Jesus' hands are pierced, not his feet.
10. Dürer, Albrecht: *Die Kleine Passion*, title-page (1511)
    Christ on the Cross with three Angels. (The picture served to decorate a ticket of indulgence. The page is not believed to be genuine by all art historians.)

The Revelation of John, song of praise of the elect in Heaven (1498)
The Trinity (1511)
The Little Passion, the driving of the dealers out of the temple, and the flogging (1511)

11. *Der Messias.* Eighth song, verses 79–81. (Quoted in) Klopstock, Friedrich Gottlieb: *Der Messias.* Vol. 2, 3rd ed. Carlsruhe, 1822, p. 118

12. Baumgarten, Otto: *Die Johannesbriefe. Der erste Brief des Johannes.* (In) *Die Schriften des NT.* Ed. J. Weiss. 2nd ed., Vol. 2, Göttingen, 1908, p. 895

13. Rist, Johann: *Wach' auf mein Geist erhebe dich.* A Good Friday song. (In) *Himmlische Lieder.* Lüneburg, 1652, p. 36 ff., 39

14. Zinzendorf, Nikolaus Ludwig von: *Twelfth supplement to Gesangbuch der Evangelistischebn Brüdergemein,* ed. of 1743, songs Nos. 2336, 2344. "Ist dieser nicht des Hochsten Sohn," song No. 145. (In) *Gesangbuch zum Gebrauch der evangelistischen Brüdergemein.* Barby, 1802, p. 73 ff

15. Zinzendorf: *Twelfth supplement . . .,* song Nos. 1990, 2098, 2112, 2114

16. Cf. Eisler: ᾽Ιησοῦς βασιλεύς II, p. 321 ff., 361 ff
    In his eagerness to give examples of the ugliness of Jesus from the writings of the Church Fathers, Eisler has sometimes allowed himself to be carried away into untenable interpretations. Thus (᾽Ιησοῦς βασιλεύς II, p. 394) he finds the sentence in Tertullian: "tota oris contumelia mugiret, si posset" (*De pallio,* c. 4) and translates it: "The shocking ugliness of the face (of Jesus) would cry out (as witness against heretics) if it could." The wording and the context of the quotation, however, do not admit a reference to Jesus here; Jesus is not the subject of the text.

17. *Acts of Thomas*: a collection of apocryphal acts of the apostles, especially favored by gnostic circles but sharply condemned by the main Church. In them "the Lord Jesus" appears "in the likeness of the apostle Judas Thomas" (*Acts of Thomas,* 11). Cf. also: *Acts of Thomas,* 38: "That you could not see me, the little one." (Quoted in) Hennecke-Schneemelcher: *Apokryphen* II, p. 313, 324

18. Blinzler: *Prozess,* p. 367, note 43

19. Eisler: ᾽Ιησοῦς βασιλεύς II, p. 361 ff.

20. Origen: *Contra Celsum* VI, 75: Origen opposes Celsus (VI, 77): "It is not remarkable that matter, which is by nature subject to change, alteration and transformation into anything which the Creator desires, and is capable of possessing any quality which the Artificer wishes, at one time possesses a quality of which it is said 'He had not form or beauty,' and at another time a quality so glorious and striking and wonderful that the three apostles who went up with Jesus and saw the exquisite beauty fell on their faces."

21. Tertullian: *Adversus Marcionem* III, 17: "Isaiah helps us again here: We have already been told by him (about his appearance), he said, (He is) like a little boy, like a root in dry earth. He has neither grace nor beauty. We have seen Him and He had not grace, nor charm, but rather was his appearance wretched, despised among all men. In the same way the Father spoke before to the Son: How many will recoil at Thy sight because Thine appearance will be more ugly than that of the children of men. Yet however that little body may be shaped, of what form was it, of what appearance?

However inglorious, however ignoble, however dishonored, He will be my Christ."

22. Schleiermacher, Friedrich: *Der christliche Glaube.* 7th ed., edited by Martin Redeker. Vol, 2, Berlin, 1960, p. 81, note 1
23. Stauffer: *Jesus*, p. 53, 54
24. Tertullian: *De carne Christi*, c. 5. In this passage Tertullian controverts Marcion and his docetic Christology, which declares that Christ was only apparently crucified. "Most accursed of men, why do you excuse the murderers of God? Christ of course suffered nothing from them (God's murderers) if he did not really suffer. Do not offend against the only hope of the whole globe. Why do you destroy the outrage that is essential to the faith?"
25. Blinzler: *Prozess*, p.363 ff.
Wernle, Paul: *Altchristliche Apologetik im Neuen Testament.* (In) *Zeitschrift für die neutestamentliche Wissenschaft.* Year 1, 1900, p. 43, note 1
26. Bultmann: *Synopt. Trad.*, p 296
27. Blinzler: *Prozess*, p.363 ff.
28. Stauffer: *Jesus*, p. 54
29. Strauss: *Leben Jesu für das deutsche Volk*, p. 580
30. Bultmann: *Synopt. Trad.*, p 293, 307
31. Cf. Braun: *Jesus*, p. 50: "The inscription over the cross, formulated in an un-Jewish way, seems to be an unhistoric Christian conception arising from the perception of Jesus as the Messiah."
For the historicity of the inscription, see also Dibelius: *Jesus*, p. 78 ff: "The oldest Christian communities, however, included eyewitnesses of the crucifixion, and we can therefore believe the report that the charge against Jesus was written up."
32. In the Hebrew text, instead of "among the wicked," it says "among the rich." This is quite certainly a change made by the copyist which could happen very easily as a result of the similarity of the words in Hebrew. (Masoretic text: óše raʿ = among the wicked, ʿāšir = among the rich; LXX: πλουσίους, variant: δόλος)
33. Bultmann: *Synopt. Trad.*, p 295
34. *Wilckens Bible*, p. 301
35. Stauffer: *Jesus*, p. 119
36. Ben-Chorin: *Jesus*, p. 224
37. Cf. Otto: *Reich Gottes*, p. 187: "From the day on which he recognized that he must suffer, he naturally took his death for granted. And he realized at the same time that he would be taken down and buried, and would be raised up to God through death; thus, that he would not remain in death but would overcome death."
38. Dibelius: *Jesus*, p. 109: "This is not the cry of a man in despair but the beginning of the 22nd Psalm, and a man who prays thus is not in a state of rebellion against God but is living and dying at peace with God."
Conzelmann: *Jesus*, col. 647: "When this word was understood, then his death was shown to be a fulfillment and the outrage of the cross was overcome. Thus we need not take the words psychologically in order to reconstruct the feelings of the dying man."

39. Cf. Rengstorf, Karl Heinrich: *Das Evangelium nach Lukas*, Göttingen, 1971, p. 275: "In his account Luke follows his own special source and has not taken over what Mark (15:34 ff) reports about the last minutes of Jesus. Psalm 31:6 in the mouth of the dying man gives us a picture of simplicity rather than greatness, for these words were already used by the pious in those days as a prayer before going to sleep."

40. 1 QH IV, 11, *Songs of Thanksgiving*: "And they kept the drink of knowledge from the thirsty, and gave them vinegar to drink to quench their thirst."

41. Jeremias: *Theologie* I, p. 16, note 15

42. (Quoted from) Pinès, Shlomo: *The Jewish Christians of the Early Centuries of Christianity According to a New Source*. (In) *The Israel Academy of Sciences and Humanities*, Vol. 2, No. 13. Jerusalem, 1966, p. 61: (95a) "It is (said) in the Gospels and in their narratives (akhbār) that, when Christ was crucified, his mother Maryam came to him with her sons James (Ya'qūb), Simon (Sham'ūn) and Judah (Yahūdhā), and they stood before him. And he, (while attached) to the piece of wood, said to her: 'Take your sons, and go away (inṣarifi).' "

43. Gollwitzer: *Krummes Holz*, p. 254, 257, 260, note 48

44. Bishop Wölber, reported in *Die Welt* of 29 Feb. 1972 (Dankwart Guratzsch: "Ist die Kirche ein Beat-Schuppen?) He would not expect a winking crucified Christ from the "rather formal German members of the church" (Wolber).

45. Blank: *Christus*, p. 241

46. Vogel, Heinrich: *Die Verantwortung der Christen für die Zukunft des Menschen im technischen Zeitalter*. (In) *Communio Viatorum. A Theological Quarterly*. Vol. 2, Prague, 1959, p. 299

47. Gollwitzer: *Krummes Holz*, p. 256

48. Thielicke, Helmut: *Und wenn Gott wäre . . .* 2nd edition, Stuttgart, 1971, p. 270, 96

49. Bultmann, Rudolf: *Neues Testament und Mythologie*. (In) *Kerygma* I, p. 20

50. Cf. "Ist Jesus auferstanden wie Goethe?" Extended version of the *Spiegel* interview with Dr. Rudolf Bultmann. (In) Harenberg, Werner: *Jesus und die Kirchen*. Stuttgart, 1966, p. 207 ff.

51. Bultmann, Rudolf: *Zur Frage der Christologie*. (In) Bultmann: *Glauben und Verstehen* I, p. 96 ff: "It is not easy to see in what way the historical Jesus, who went his way to death in obedient love, stands higher than all those who went the same way in obedient love for example in the world war, and whose way has much more to say to us, not only because of its greater vividness but also because we were bound to them in a living, intimate relationship. To want to apply such experiences to a person of the past seems to me artificial and leads to sentimentality."

52. Bultmann, Rudolf: *Humanismus und Christentum*. (In) Bultmann: *Glauben und Verstehen* II, p. 141: "That is the meaning of the Christian message: God has revealed himself on the cross of Christ as the God of forgiving grace; Christ is the word of the forgiving grace."

53. Josephus: *Vita*, 75, trans. H. St. J. Thackeray 1928: "... when ... on my return (I) saw many prisoners who had been crucified, and recognized three of my acquaintances among them, I was cut to the heart and came and told Titus with tears what I had seen. He gave orders immediately that they should be taken down and receive the most careful treatment. Two of them died in the physicians' hands; the third survived."
54. Bloch: *Atheismus*, p. 175
55. Bultmann: *Synopt. Trad.*, p. 305
56. Cf. Strack-Billerbeck I, p. 223 (*Babylonian Talmud, Traktat Aboda Zara* 18a)
57. Dibelius, Martin: *Die altestamentlichen Motiven in der Leidensgeschichte des Petrus - und des Johannes-Evangeliums.* (In) *Botschaft und Geschichte.* Vol. I. Tübingen, 1953, p. 236
58. Augustine: *De civitate Dei* XV: 26
59. Wellhausen, Julius: *Einleitung in die drei ersten Evangelien.* Berlin, 1905, p. 115
60. Freud: *Mann Moses*, p. 195
61. Luther, Martin: *Eine andere Predigt am Tage der Himmelfahrt Christi.* (In) Luther: *Werke*, Vol. 12, p. 183
62. Stauffer, Ethelbert: *Jesus, Paulus und wir.* Hamburg 1961, p. 24
63. Bultmann: *Synopt. Trad.*, p. 314
64. Dautzenberg: *Jesus-Report*, p. 72
    Lohse, Eduard: *Umwelt des neuen Testaments.* Göttingen, 1971, p. 162
    Cassius Dio: *Historia Romana* 56:46: "This woman (Livia, Augustus's wife) made a present of two and a half thousand denarii to a certain senator, Numerius Atticus ... because he swore he had seen him (Augustus) rise up into heaven."
65. Zahrnt: Jesus, p. 117
66. Pannenberg, Wolfhart: *Jesu Geschichte und unsere Geschichte.* (In *Radius.* Year 1, 1960, p. 21
67. On the trial of Giordano Bruno by the inquisition: According to the articles of the law in Venice, which have been preserved and published, in addition to other points ("quod dixerit Christum peccasse") special seriousness was attached to the lessons of the plurality of worlds ("plures esse mundos") and of the infinity of the universe ("circa aeternitatem mundi") (Quoted from) Mercati, Angelo: *Il sommario del processo di Giordano Bruno.* Rome, 1942, p. 5 ff.
    Bruno had had formally to retract his theses in Venice. Nevertheless the Roman inquisition demanded that he be handed over. After seven years' imprisonment in Rome, in 1599 he was shown eight heretical lessons from his writings, which he was required to retract. Bruno's refusal let to his condemnation. He was handed over to the temporal authorities with the usual formula, that they should "punish him as gently as possible, and with no bloodshed." A German eyewitness reported about the death of Bruno: "So he was slowly burnt, dying miserably, amd may now be proclaiming in those other worlds which he imagined how the Romans are accustomed to deal with blasphemers and profaners." (Quoted in) Brunnhofer, Hermann: *Giordano Bruno's Weltanschauung und Verhängnis.* Leipzig, 1882, p. 129

Chapter 8

1. Schelling, Friedrich Wilhelm: *Philosophische Briefe über Dogmatismus und Kritizismus.* (In) *Werke,* Vol. 1. Munich, 1927, p. 210
2. Gehlen, Arnold: *Urmensch und Spätkultur.* 2nd. ed., Frankfurt, 1964, p. 153
3. Mitscherlich, Alexander: *Rede zur Entgegennahme des Friedenspreises des Deutschen Buchhandels 1969.* (In) *Börsenblatt für den Deutschen Buchhandel.* 25th year, No. 84, p. 6011
4. Cf. Gressman, Hugo: *Altorientalische Texte und Bilder zum Alten Testamente.* Vol. 1. Tübingen, 1909, p. 195
5. Bloch: *Atheismus,* p. 61
6. Freud, Sigmund: *Neue Folge der Vorlesungen zur Einführung in die Psychoanalyse.* (In) *Gesammelte Werke,* Vol. 15, 5th ed. Frankfurt, 1969, p. 180
   Bloch: *Atheismus,* p. 24
7. Dali, Salvador: *The Secret Life of Salvador Dali.* London, 1948, p. 397
8. Cf. Marx, Karl: *Thesen über Feuerbach.* (In) Marx-Engels: *Studienaugsabe* I. Frankfurt, 1971, p. 139 ff.
9. Freud: *Mann Moses,* p. 136
   Goethe, too, is convinced that Moses was murdered: " . . . and we must be very much mistaken if Joshua and Caleb did not bring to an end the regency they had borne for a limited man, for several years, and did not requite him as seemed best for the countless misfortunes of which he was the author."
   Goethe, Johann Wolfgang von: *Israel in der Wuste.* (In) *Noten und Abhandlungen zu besserem Verständnis des Westöstlichen Divans.* (In) *Gedenkausgabe der Werke, Briefe und Gespräche.* Vol. 3, Zürich, 1948, p. 514
10. Freud: *Mann Moses,* p. 230
11. Cf. Wyss, Dieter: *Marx und Freud. Ihr Verhältnis zur Modernen Anthropologie.* Göttingen, 1969, p. 91 ff.
12. Weber, Max: *Das antike Judentum.* (In) Weber: *Aufsätze.* Vol. 3, 2nd ed., p. 146 ff.
13. Freud: *Mann Moses,* p. 230
14. *Midrash Pesiqtha* 40b (quoted in) Strack-Billerbeck I, p. 719
15. Freud: *Mann Moses,* p. 151 and 103 ff.
    Freud denies to Moses the origin of the Israelites. He believes that Moses was a high-ranking, rebellious Egyptian, who deserted to the children of Israel and enforced on them the "only" god Aton, "beside whom another god is unthinkable," as the God of the chosen people. The theory that monotheism is of Egyptian origin was first published by Freud in 1937 and 1939, so that a part of it appeared after his exile. He was well aware that, only a few years after the Nuremberg Laws, he was depriving his people of "the man whom they extolled as the greatest of their sons." Nonetheless, he believed that "he must not withold the truth on account of any supposed national interests."
16. Bloch, Ernst: *Symbol: Die Juden.* (In) *Geist der Utopie.* Munich, 1918 (reprinted 1971), p. 328
17. Gollwitzer: *Krummes Holz,* p. 264 ff

18. Freud: *Mann Moses*, p. 191
19. Bloch: *Atheismus*, p. 223
20. Bendix, Reinhard: *Max Weber. Das Werk.* Munich, 1964, p. 173
21. Freud: *Mann Moses*, p. 180
22. In the "Law of the Return," one of the statute laws of Israel, a Jew is defined as someone "who has a Jewish mother or who has been converted to the Jewish faith and professes no other religion."
23. Jones: *Studie über den Heiligen Geist*, p. 130 ff.
24. Reik: *Gott*, p. 63 ff.
25. Freud: *Mann Moses*, p. 243
26. Gehlen, Arnold: *Religion und Umweltstabilisierung.* (In) *Hat die Religion Zukunft?* Pub. by Oskar Schatz, Graz, 1971, p. 93
27. Bloch: *Atheismus*, p. 106
    Proust, Marcel: *A la recherche du temps perdu.* Paris, 1921−1924. Vol. 9, p. 18
28. Mann, Thomas: *Joseph und seine Brüder.* Frankfurt, 1964, p. 34
29. Gollwitzer: *Krummes Holz*, pp. 203 and 334
30. Kilian, Hans: *Das enteignete Bewusstsein.* Neuwied, 1971, p. 78
31. Conway, Moncure Daniel: *Demonology and Devil-lore.* London 1879. Vol. 2, p. 59
32. Weber, Max: *Das antike Judentum.* (In) Weber: *Aufsatze*, Vol. 2, 2nd ed., p. 282
33. (Quoted in) Ling, Trevor: *Die Universalität der Religion.* Munich, 1971, p. 233
34. Augustine: *De civitate Dei* XVIII: 44
35. Cf. Hegel, Georg Wilhelm Friedrich: *Die absolute Religion.* (In) *Vorlesungen über die Philosophie der Religion.* Vol. II, 2nd ed., pub. by Georg Lasson, Hamburg, 1968
36. *Jerusalem Bible*, p. 1361
37. Keller, Werner: *Und die Bibel hat doch recht.* Düsseldorf, 1958, p. 199
38. Gressmann, Hugo: *Altorientalische Texte und Bilder zum Alten Testamente.* Vol. 1, Tubingen, 1909, p. 172
39. Bendix, Reinhard: *Max Weber. Das Werk.* Munich, 1964, p. 187
40. Weber, Max: *Das antike Judentum.* (In) Weber: *Aufsätze*, Vol. 3, 2nd ed., p. 287
41. Freud, Sigmund: *Neue Folge der Vorlesungen zur Einführung in die Psychoanalyse.* In *Gesammelte Werke*, Vol. 15, 5th ed., Frankfurt, 1969, p. 181
42. Luther, Martin: *Predigt am fünften Sonntag nach Epiphaniä.* 1528. (In) Luther, *Werke*, Vol. 2, p. 62
43. Weber, Max: *Die protestantische Ethik und der Geist der Kapitalismus.* (In) Weber: *Aufsätze*, Vol. 2, 4th ed., p. 84 ff.
44. Freud: *Mann Moses*, p. 168
45. Braun: *Jesus*, p. 20 ff.
46. Reik: *Gott*, p. 68 ff.
    Fromm, Erich: *Das Christusdogma.* Munich, 1965, p. 49 ff.
47. Freud: *Mann Moses*, pp. 226 and 194
48. Nietzsche, Friedrich: *Zur Genealogie der Moral.* Second Essay, §3

49. Cf. Heidegger, Martin: *Nietzsche*, Vol. 1. Pfullingen, 1961, p. 321
50. Jung: *Antwort*, p. 49
51. Gollwitzer: *Krummes Holz*, p. 225 ff and 265
52. Bloch: *Atheismus*, p. 152, 154
53. Jung: *Antwort*, p. 28
54. Görres, Albert: (quoted in) *Jesus und Freud. Ein Symposium von Psychoanalytikern und Theologen.* Ed. by Heinz Zahrnt. Munich, 1972, p. 61
55. Howe, Günter: *Mensch und Physik.* Berlin, 1963, p. 114
56. Jung: *Antwort*, p. 29
57. Bloch: *Atheismus*, p. 134
58. Spinoza in a letter to Hugo Boxel. (In Spinoza, Baruch de: *Sämtliche Werke.* Vol. 3. Leipzig, 1914, p. 229
59. Jung: *Antwort*, p. 108, 120
60. Freud in a hitherto unpublished letter of 17 January 1909 (quoted in) Grubrich-Simitis, Ilse: "Sigmund Freuds Lebensgeschichte und die Anfänge der Psychoanalyse." (In) *Neue Rundschau.* Year 82, 1971, p. 331
61. Freud, Sigmund, and Karl Abraham: *Briefe 1907–1926.* Frankfurt, 1965. Letters to Abraham of 26 July 1914, 3 May and 23 July 1908
   Jung, Carl Gustav: "Zur gegenwärtigen Lage der Psychiatrie." (In) *Zentralblatt für Psychiatrie und ihre Grenzgebiete.* Vol. 7, 1934, p. 9 ff.
62. Mann, Thomas: *Joseph und seine Brüder.* Frankfurt, 1964, p. 314 ff and 477

Chapter 9

1. Schneider, Hans G.: *Die Zukunft wartet nicht.* Stuttgart, 1971, p. 319
   Bloch: *Atheismus*, p. 169
2. Kierkegaard, Søren: *Tagebücher.Eine Auswahl. Ausgewählt und übersetzt von Elisabeth Feuersenger.* Wiesbaden 1949, p. 200
3. Plato: *Apologia* 29d
4. Berger, Peter L.: *Auf den Spuren der Engel.* Frankfurt, 1971, p. 119
5. Bloch: *Atheismus*, p. 197
6. Lohse, Eduard: *Umwelt des Neuen Testaments.* Göttingen, 1971, p. 112
7. Bultmann: *Synopt. Trad.*, p. 68
8. Luther, Martin: *Kirchenpostille. Predigt über Mattäus* 15, 21–28. (In) Luther: *Werke*, Vol. 2, p. 119
9. Cf. Bultmann, Wilhelm: *Synoptische Studien.* First number. Halle (Saale), 1925, p. 49–52
10. Dautzenberg: *Jesus-Report*, p. 89
11. Dalman, Gustaf: *Jesus—Jeschua.* Leipzig, 1922, p. 4
12. Kähler: *Jesus*, p. 60 ff.
13. Bloch, Ernst: *Geist der Utopie. Bearbeitet Neuauflage der zweiten Fassung von 1923.* Frankfurt 1964, p. 227
14. Schultz, Hans-Jürgen: "Jesus — ein Name für alles?" (In) *Merkur* 286, year 26, 1972, p. 128 ff.
   Schneider, Hans G.: *Die Zukunft wartet nicht.* Stuttgart, 1971, p. 319 ff.
15. *Midrash, Song of Songs* 1:1 (79a); cf. Strack-Billerbeck I, p. 653 ff.
16. Jeremias: *Gleichnisse*, p. 7; Jeremias: *Theologie* I, p. 39

17. *The Gospel of Thomas* survives in a Coptic version from the fourth or fifth century. It is written in the normal Sahidish of southern Egypt. This Coptic version goes back to a Greek copy, now lost, which is thought to have been written in the middle of the second century in Syria or northern Mesopotamia. One of the sources of this Greek text, according to Cullman, is associated with the name of the Lord's brother James and suggests Jewish Christian-Gnostic circles of the first half of the second century; it could be based on an even older collection of Logia. (Cf. Cullmann, Oscar article, *Thomasevengelium,* in *RGG* VI, col. 865 ff; Haenchen, Ernst: *Die Botschaft des Thomas-Evangeliums.* Berlin, 1961, p. 8) It is a matter of dispute whether the Gospel of Thomas contains a tradition independent of the synoptic Gospels, if not necessarily older than them. It is hard to come to a firm decision. (Cf. also the report on literature in Haenchen, Ernst: *Literatur zum Thomasevangelium.* (In) *Theologische Rundschau.* New Series, year 27, 1961, p. 147–178; 306–338, and Bultmann: *Synopt. Trad. Ergänzungsheft,* p. 15 ff.) Joachim Jeremias, the expert on the parables, accepts an older and independent tradition for the parables of the Gospel of Thomas. (Cf. Jeremias: *Gleichnisse,* passim, especially p. 86 ff.)

18. *Leviticus Rabba* 1 (105c). (Quoted in) Strack-Billerbeck I, p. 774
    Babylonian Talmud, Tract Sanhedrin 100b. (Quoted in) Strack-Billerbeck I, p. 441
    Midrash, Tannaim to Deuteronomy 15:9 (Quoted in) Jeremias: *Gleichnisse,* p. 205

19. Grant, Robert M. and David Noel Freedman: *Geheime Worte Jesu.* Frankfurt, 1960, p. 112

20. Jeremias: *Gleichnisse,* p. 70
    Bultmann: *Synopt. Trad.,* p. 191
    Kümmel, Werner Georg: *Verheissung und Erfüllung.* 2nd ed., Zürich, 1953, p. 76
    Conzelmann: *Grundriss,* p. 70

21. Jeremias: *Gleichnisse,* p. 181

22. Bornkamm, Günther: *Der Lohngedanke im Neuen Testament.* (In) Bornkamm: *Studien,* p. 71

23. Jeremias: *Gleichnisse,* p. 181

24. Bornkamm, Günther: *Die Verzögerung der Parusie.* (In) *In Memorium Ernst Lohmeyer.* Ed. Werner Schmauch. Stuttgart, 1951, p. 119–126

25. Ben-Chorin: *Jesus,* p. 95. "Jesus' images are not poetic but entirely realistic. They are taken from the background and the daily life of his surroundings, with the possible exception of the parable of the wise and foolish virgins, in which it is incomprehensible that *one* bridegroom should celebrate marriage with several virgins at once."

26. Jeremias: *Gleichnisse,* p. 186

27. *Babylonian Talmud, Tract Shabbath* 153a

28. Jeremias: *Gleichnisse,* p. 56

29. Jeremias: *Gleichnisse,* p. 64, 17

30. Bultmann: *Synopt. Trad.,* p. 222

31. Ben-Chorin: *Jesus,* p. 108 ff.

32. Jeremias: *Gleichnisse*, p. 200
    Braun: *Jesus*, p. 130: "It must be understood for the whole of this period that an open relationship with non-Jewish neighbors had not yet been fundamentally established; it is still within the scope of Jewish limitations; it occurs from case to case and is relative. This relative, not fundamental openness towards the non-Jewish neighbor may well be traceable back to Jesus. The exemplary tale of the good Samaritan, in which a member of the religious dissenters rejected by the Jews stands as a model of true neighborliness never since forgotten in world history, comes from Jesus himself, or, if it is an invention of the community, it is entirely in line with Jesus' thinking and not with Jewish religious ideas."
33. Josephus: *Ant.* XVIII, 2.2
34. Jeremias: *Gleichnisse*, p. 202
    Flusser: *Synagoge*, p. 35
35. Manson, Thomas Walter: *The Sayings of Jesus.* London, 1954, p. 249
36. Trilling, Wolfgang: *Das wahre Israel.* 3rd. ed., Munich, 1964, p. 88–90
37. Bultmann: *Synopt. Trad.*, p. 39
38. *Morning Prayer* (quoted from) *Sidur sefat emet*, with German translation by Rabbi Dr. S. Bamberger, Basel, n.d., p. 5
39. Braun, Herbert: *Vom Verstehen des Neuen Testaments.* (In) Braun: *Gesammelte Studien*, p. 295
40. *Babylonian Talmud, Tract Berakhoth* 34b
41. *Jesus or Christ* (debate report) p. 30
42. Blank: *Christus*, p. 227
43. Flusser: *Synagoge*, p. 34: "So the true opponent of Jesus was not the 'orthodox' Jew — he was that himself — but the fanatic obsessed with formalities, exemplified in literature by Dostoievsky's Grand Inquisitor."
44. Holl: *Jesus,* p. 133
45. Jeremias: *Theologie* I, p. 122, 118
46. Bultmann: *Synopt. Trad.*, p. 97 ff.
47. Strack-Billerbeck IV, 2, p. 698–744
48. Hansemann, David (liberal Prussian agricultural politician, finance minister of Prussia in 1848): Speech in the united Assembly on 8 June 1847 in the discussion of the loan for the building of the East Prussian railway: "Kindliness comes to an end in money matters (amusement in the assembly), that is where reason must lead us." (Quoted in) *Reden und Redner des ersten Preussischen Vereinigten Landtags.* ed. Rudolf Haym. Berlin, 1847, p. 417
49. Conzelmann: *Grundriss*, p. 270; cf. also Leviticus 18:22; 20:13
50. Cf. also Ben-Chorin: *Jesus*, p. 82: "This warning (Matthew 7:6) can be understood from Deuteronomy 23:18: 'You shall not allow a common prostitute's fee, or the pay of a male prostitute (*Authorized Version:* or the price of a dog) to be brought into the house of the Lord your God.' The 'dogs' here are the male temple prostitutes of the Canaanite heathen cults (among the Babylonians they actually wore dogs' masks). They were called 'dogs' because in the temple orgies they were used sexually 'in the manner of dogs'. That is why the price of a dog is mentioned together with the fee of a

prostitute. The prostitutes are obviously equated with this kind of 'dogs' when they are referred to in Jesus' no less rude expression as 'sows'."

51. Bultmann: *Jesus*, p. 55
52. *Jesus or Christ* (debate report) p. 31
    Jeremias: *Theologie* I, p. 164 ff
53. *Babylonian Talmud, Tract Shabbath* 13a
54. *Jerusalem Talmud, Tract Berakhoth* 9,1 (Quoted in) *Der Jerusalemische Talmud in seiner haggadischen Bestandtheilen*, trans. August Wünsche. Zürich, 1880, p. 35 ff.
55. Ben-Chorin: *Paulus*, p. 193 ff. According to an interpretation of Ben-Chorin given verbally, the bung hole test was carried out by Rabbi Gamaliel the elder. In the text of the *Babylonian Talmud, Tract Kethubboth* 10b, however, it is attributed to Rabbi Gamaliel ben Rabbi (? = Rabbi Gamaliel ben Jehuda Hanasi, who lived about 220).
56. *Babylonian Talmud, Tract Baba Bathra* 10b (Baraitha): Rabbi Jonahan ben Zakkai later changed his opinion on this. (Cf. Strack-Billerbeck I, p. 204 ff)
57. Cf. Eusebius *Hist. Eccl.* VI, 8.12 trans. Lawlor and Oulton, S.P.C.K., 1927: "At that time, while Origen was performing the work of instruction at Alexandria, he did a thing which gave abundant proof of an immature and youthful mind, yet withal of faith and self-control. For he took the saying, *There are eunuchs which made themselves eunuchs for the kingdom of heaven's sake*, in too literal and extreme a sense, and thinking both to fulfil the Savior's saying, and also that he might prevent all suspicion of shameful slander on the part of unbelievers (for, young as he was, he used to discourse on divine things with women as well as men), he hastened to put into effect the Savior's saying."
58. Ben-Chorin: *Jesus*, p. 127 ff; Ben Chorin: *Mirjam*, p. 109 ff. 198 ff.
59. Braun: *Jesus*, p. 128: " . . . Jesus, the advocate of the fourth commandment, the advocate of an active love towards parents, a love which may not be replaced by an actual, still less by the outward appearance of, dutifulness towards God and the temple."
60. (Quoted from) *Sidur sefat emet*, with German translation by Rabbi Dr. S. Bamberger. Basel, n.d. p. 5
61. Holl: *Jesus*, p. 20; cf. p. 85 ff., 94 ff.
62. Ben-Chorin: *Jesus*, p. 122
63. Braun: *Jesus*, p. 63, 131
64. Braun: *Jesus*, p. 140
65. Shaw: *Prospects*, p. 48
66. Ben-Chorin: *Jesus*, p. 123
67. Rilke, Rainer Maria: *Pieta* *

    So, Jesus, once again I am beholding
    those feet that seemed so youthful to me there
    when I unshod and washed them, greatly fearing;
    oh, how they stood entangled in my hair
    like some white wild thing from a thorn-bush peering.

*Rainer Maria Rilke: *Selected Works* Vol II trans. J.B. Leishman © The Hogarth Press Ltd 1960. By permission of New Directions, New York.

Those limbs, from every lover so withholding,
for the first time in this love-night I view.
We've never felt each other's arms enfolding,
and now I only weep and watch for you.

But, look, how torn your hands have come to be —
not from my bites, beloved, not by me.
Your heart stands open now for all to share;
I only should have had the entry there.

Now you are tired, and your tired mouth is urged
by no desire for my sad mouth, alas! —
O Jesus, Jesus, when did our time pass?
How strangely both of us are being submerged.

68. Origen: *Contra Celsum* II, 55: "While he (Jesus) was alive he did not help himself, but after death he rose again and showed the marks of his punishment and how his hands had been pierced. But who saw this? A hysterical female, as you say, and perhaps some other one of those who were deluded by the same sorcery, who either dreamt in a certain state of mind and through wishful thinking had a hallucination due to some mistaken notion (an experience which has happened to thousands), or, which is more likely, wanted to impress the others by telling this fantastic tale, and so by this cock-and-bull story to provide a chance for other beggars."

69. Stauffer: *Jesus*, p. 146

70. Holl: *Jesus*, p. 146
Stauffer: *Jesus*, p. 45

71. *Midrash, Song of Mourning* 2,2 (64a) cf. Strack-Billerbeck I, p. 1047

72. Cf. *Die Welt* of 29 Feb. 1972 (Dankwart Guratzsch: "Ist die Kirche ein Beat-Schuppen?"): "Prof. Thielicke: 'We Protestants often take the Bible too seriously. But at the wedding in Cana Jesus may have been among those who were playing jokes. Humor has some part in salvation, in the conversion of the world.' "

73. Ben-Chorin: *Jesus*, p. 126; cf. *Babylonian Talmud, Tract Taanith* 23a
Jerusalem Talmud, Tract Taanith 3,9

Jeremias: *Gleichnisse*, p. 225 ff.

Wilckens Bible, p. 341

74. *Mishna, Tract Pirqe Aboth* 2,6. Cf. *The Mishna. IV. Seder.9.Tract: Aboth.* Ed. Karl Marti and Georg Beer. Giessen, 1927, p. 45

75. Schneider, Hans G.: *Die Zukunft wartet nicht.* Stuttgart, 1971, p. 319 ff.

76. Blank: *Christus*, p. 240

77. Jourdan, Johannes: *Der umstrittene Jesus.* (In *Deutsches Pfarrerblatt.* Year 69, 1969, p. 691

Chapter 10

1. Schopenhauer, Arthur: *Neue Paralipomena: vereinzelte Gedanken über vielerlei Gegenstande.* (In) *Arthur Schopenhauer's handschriftlicher Nachlass,* ed. Eduard Grisebach. Vol. 4. Leipzig, 1892, p. 447
2. Wrede, William: *Das Messiasgeheimnis in den Evangelien.* 4th edition, Göttingen, 1969, p. 3
3. Rabbi Hillel according to *Tract. Shabbath* 31a of the *Babylonian Talmud*
4. For the "golden rule" cf. Dihle, Albrecht: *Die Goldene Regel.* Göttingen, 1962; Jeremias, *Theologie* I, p. 204—206
5. Gollwitzer, Helmut: *Die Bibel — marxistisch gelesen.* (In) *Verkündigung und Forschung.* Year 14, 1969, p. 17
6. Jeremias: *Gleichnisse*, p. 201; Jeremias: *Theologie* I, p. 206, note 44; p. 241
7. Bloch: *Atheismus*, p. 170 ff.
8. Cf. Bultmann: *Jesus*, p. 64, 74, 78: "It is thus excessively clear that there are actually no 'new' ethical demands of Jesus, that his concrete prophecies have numerous parallels in the Jewish tradition."
9. Braun: *Jesus*, p. 149
10. Blank: *Christus*, p. 240, 227
11. Kahane, Peter P.: *Kunst und Kultur der herodianischen Zeit.* (In) *Mann aus Galiläa*, p. 286
12. Freud, Sigmund: *Das Unbehagen in der Kultur.* (In) *Gesammelte Werke*, Vol. 14, London 1948, p. 473
13. Cf. Nietzsche, Friedrich: *Der Antichrist*, p. 22: "Christianity wants to be master over beasts of prey; its method is to make them ill — weakening is the Christian recipe for taming . . . "
14. Bultmann: *Synopt. Trad.*, p. 40
15. Burrows: *Mehr Klarheit*, p 54
16. The miracle stories in the Synoptics correspond in form and atmosphere with those from the Jewish and Hellenistic tradition. Cf. Bultmann: *Synopt. Trad.*, pp. 223—260, especially 236—241 and 247—253; also Petke, Gerd: *Die Traditionen über Apollonius von Tyana und das Neue Testament.* Leiden, 1970, p. 125—137, 170—182
17. Käsemann, Ernst: *Begrundet der neutestamentliche Kanon die Einheit der Kirche?* (In) *Exegetische Versuche und Besinnungen*, Vol. 1, Göttingen, 1960, p. 215
18. Haenchen: *Weg Jesu*, p. 193—195; *Wilckens Bible*, p. 146
19. Jeremias: *Theologie* I, p. 95
20. Schweitzer: *Leben-Jesu-Forschung*, p. 633
21. Daniélou: *Qumran*, p. 111: "If there . . . is one certain fact in the life of Jesus, it is this: that not only by his words but by his whole conduct he claims heavenly privileges for himself."
    Schweitzer, Albert: *Von Reimarus zu Wrede. Eine Geschichte der Leben-Jesu-Forschung.* Tübingen, 1906, p. 367
22. On this so-called Corban institution: Strack-Billerbeck I, pp. 711—717; the Qumranic Damascus script: CD VI, 15 ff.; XVI, 14 ff.; Braun: *Qumran* I, p. 68
23. Fuchs, Ernst: *Das Zeitverständnis Jesu.* (In) Fuchs: *Hist. Jesus* II, p. 356

24. Cf. Klein, Gunter: *Jesus und die Kinder.* (In) *Ärgernisse.* Munich, 1970, p. 68
25. Wellhausen, Julius: *Das Evangelium Marci.* 2nd ed., Berlin, 1909, p. 81
26. Bloch: *Atheismus*, p. 184 ff.
27. Cf. Braun, Herbert: *Die Bedeutung der Qumranfunde für das Verständnis Jesu von Nazareth.* (In) Braun: *Gesammelte Studien*, p. 91
28. Jaspers, Karl: *Der philosophische Glaub angesichts der Offenbarung.* Munich, 1963, p. 364
29. Burrows: *Mehr Klarheit*, p. 45 ff.
30. Käsemann: *Hist. Jesus*, p. 203: "We can no longer take for granted the reliability of the synoptic tradition about Jesus in general. Indeed, the tradition by itself is no longer helpful in critical correction. As a result of the form-historical work our investigations have so sharpened and broadened in scope that it is no longer the possible ungenuineness, but on the contrary, the genuineness of particular passages that we now have to test and endorse. We now have to demonstrate, not the justness of the criticism, but what are its limits."
31. Jeremias: *Theologie* I, p. 45: "Without prejudice to which, we can say quite firmly that the linguistic and stylistic finding shows such great faithfulness to, and such great reverance for, the tradition of the words of Jesus that the methodical principle seems to be justified. It is not the genuineness, but the ungenuineness, of the words of Jesus in the synoptic tradition that has to be proved."
32. (Quoted in) *Jesus or Christ* (debate report) p. 15
33. Jeremias, Joachim: *Abba,* p. 55
34. (Quoted in) Typescript of the ZDF broadcast, "Jesus — a heretic?", Karlheinz Müller, Rudolf Pesch und Klaus Schäfer, p. 20
35. Jeremias: *Theologie* I, p. 73
36. For example, Braun: *Jesus*, p. 42; Bultmann: *Jesus*, p. 15; Jeremias: *Theologie* I, pp. 14–19; against these, Stauffer: *Jesus*, p. 54, according to whom the everyday speech of Jesus was Aramaic with a Galilean accent; he certainly spoke Greek with Pilate and Latin, when he was still a little village youth, with the legionary of Sepporis. He could read the Hebrew Bible and quoted it at many decisive moments; and he also spoke Hebrew in the liturgy.
37. Cf. typescript of the broadcast: "Jesus—a heretic?", p. 20
38. Strack-Billerbeck II, p. 50
39. Jeremias, Joachim: *Abba*, p. 59
40. Cf. Strack-Billerbeck I, p. 394, 395.
41. *Wilckens Bible*, p. 35
42. Burrows: *Mehr Klarheit*, p. 43
43. Jeremias: *Theologie* I, p. 188
44. Bultmann: *Synopt. Trad.*, p. 110
45. Bultmann: *Jesus*, p. 15
46. Jeremias: *Theologie* I, p.43 ff.; Jeremias, Joachim: *Kennzeichen der ipsissima vox Jesu.* (In) Jeremias: *Abba*, p. 148 ff., 151
47. Jeremias: *Theologie* I, p.38 ff.
48. Schweizer, Eduard: Art. πνεῦμα κτλ (In) *ThWB* VI, p. 395

49. Stauffer: *Jesus*, p. 85
50. *Wilckens Bible*, p. 168
51. Julius Wellhausen (quoted in) Bultmann: *Synopt. Trad.*, p. 233
52. Bultmann: *Synopt. Trad.*, pp. 25, 66; likewise Braun: *Radikalismus* II, p. 83, note 2
53. Käsemann: *Hist. Jesus*, p. 208
    Braun: *Jesus*, p. 73 ff
    Jeremias: *Theologie* I, p. 202 ff.
54. Braun: *Jesus*, p. 73 ff.
    Flusser: *Synagoge*, p. 33
55. Zahrnt, Heinz (quoted in) *Jesus und Freud. Ein Symposium von Psychoanalytikern und Theologen.* Ed. Heinz Zahrnt. Munich, 1972, p. 188
56. Bultmann: *Synopt. Trad.*, p. 275
57. *Wilckens Bible*, p. 159
58. Schweitzer: *Leben-Jesu-Forschung*, p. 441
59. Wrong translations taken from among others Jeremias: *Theologie* I, p. 122; Jeremias: *Gleichnisse*, pp. 8–14
    A misunderstanding by the evangelist, see for example Haenchen: *Weg Jesu*, p. 173; Jeremias: *Gleichnisse*, p. 14; *Wilckens Bible*, p. 142
60. Gnilka, Joachim: *Das Verstockungsproblem nach Matthaus* 13, 13–15. (In) *Antijudaismus*, p. 123
61. Cf. the Qumranic *Gemeinderegel* 1 QS IX, ff.; X, 24 ff.; see also Braun: *Radikalismus*, II, p. 21, note 4; 40, note 1; Burrows: *Mehr Klarheit*, p. 241; Jeremias, *Theologie* I, p. 243 ff.
62. Otto: *Reich Gottes*, p. 5
63. Bultmann: *Synopt. Trad.*, p. 132
64. Jeremias: *Theologie* I, p. 140 ff.
65. Bultmann: *Synopt. Trad.*, p. 132
66. Holscher, Gustav: *Der Ursprung der Apokalypse Mrk 13.* (In) *Theologische Blatter.* Year 12, 1933, col. 200 ff.
67. Cf. Pesch, Rudolf: *Naherwartungen. Tradition und Redaktion in Mk. 13.* Düsseldorf, 1968, pp. 215–243; text of the leaflet, p. 208 ff.
68. Marxsen, Willi: *Der Evangelist Markus.* 2nd ed., Göttingen, 1959, p. 123 ff.
69. Trocmé, Etienne: *La formation de l'évangile selon Marc.* Paris, 1963, p. 164 ff.
70. O'Callaghan, Jose: *Papiros neotestamentarios en la cueva 7 de Qumran?* (In) *Biblica.* Vol. 53, 1972, p. 93; 91, notes 1 and 2; 940
    Cf. the photograph and transcription of the fragment in Baillet, Maurice, Jozef Tadeusz Milik and Roland de Vaux: *Discoveries in the Judaean Desert of Jordan.* III *Les 'Petites Grottes' de Qumrân. Plates.* Oxford, 1962, Plate XXX; Baillet, Maurice, Jozef Tadeusz Milik and Roland de Vaux: *Discoveries in the Judean Desert of Jordan.* III. *Les 'Petites Grottes' de Qumrân. Texts.* Oxford, 1962, p. 144 ff., and against that the reconstruction of O'Callaghan: *Papiros*, pp. 93–97
    Wilhelm Schubart, in his standard work on Greek palaeography, still current (*Palaographie. Part One. Griechische Paläographie.* Reprint of the 1st ed. of 1925, Munich, 1966, p. 111 ff.) dates the ornate style in the period

from the first century B.C.E. to the second (normally the first) century C.E. Benoit, Pierre (Quoted in) *Spiegel* 23/1972, p. 127

71. Cf. Hengel: *Zeloten,* pp. 296–307
72. Cf. Strack-Billerbeck I, p. 83; Hengel: *Zeloten,* pp. 299–302
73. Cf. Josephus: *Ant.* II, 17.8–10
74. Gressmann, Hugo: *Die religionsgeschichtliche Problem des Ursprungs der hellenistischen Erlösungsreligion* I. (In) *Zeitschrift für Kirchengeschichte,* Vol. 40, 1922, p. 189
75. Cf. Clemen, Carl: *Religionsgeschichtliche Erklärung des Neuen Testaments.* 2nd ed., Giessen, 1924, p. 197
76. Schmidt, Karl Ludwig: *Der Rahmen der Geschichte Jesu.* Berlin, 1919, p. VI
77. Wrede, William: *Das Messiasgeheimnis in den Evangelien.* 4th ed., Göttingen, 1969, p. 129
78. Bultmann: *Jesus,* p. 144: "He has given men no sensible explanation of suffering, not even for his own suffering."

Chapter 11

1. Luther, Martin: *Lection wider die Rottengeister und wie sich weltliche Obrigkeit halten soll.* 1525. (In) Luther: *Werke,* Vol. 51, p. 315
2. Heinemann, Gustav: *Evangelische Kirche heute.* (In) *Bekennende Kirche auf dem Weg.* Year 1, 1950, No. 1, p. 9
3. Gollwitzer: *Krummes Holz,* p. 262
4. Rabbis Hija, Akibah, Johanan: Cf. *Babylonian Talmud, Tractate Pesachim* 49b
5. *Wilckens Bible,* p. 401
6. Conzelmann, Hans: *Geschichte des Urchristentums.* 2nd ed., Gottingen, 1971, p. 24
7. Kilian, Hans: *Das enteignete Bewusstsein.* Neuweid, 1971, p. 185
8. Lemberg, Eugen: *Ideologie und Gesellschaft.* Stuttgart, 1971, p. 131
9. Bloch: *Atheismus,* p. 104
10. Kautsky, Karl: *Der Ursprung des Christentums.* 13th ed., Berlin, 1923, p. 345
11. Origen: *Contra Celsum* III, 55
12. Bornkamm, Günther: *Mensch und Gott in der griechische Antike.* (In) Bornkamm: *Studien,* p. 37
13. Kant, Immanuel: *Über das Misslingen aller philosophischen Versuche in der Theodizee.* (In) *Werke.* Ed. Wilhelm Weischedel. Vol. 6, Wiesbaden, 1964, p. 116
14. Heine, Heinrich: *Zum Lazarus.* (In) *Werke,* Insel-Ausgabe, Vol. I. Frankfurt, 1968, p. 242
15. Lichtenberg, Georg Christoph: *Werke.* Hamburg, 1967, p. 132
16. Engels, Friedrich: *Das Buch der Offenbarung.* (In) Marx, Karl and Friedrich Engels: *Werke.* Vol. 21. Berlin, 1969, p. 11
17. Seneca: *Letters to Lucullus,* 47. " . . . for you must remember that free and unfree lie equally within the power of fate. Therefore I can only smile at people who think it a disgrace to eat together with their slaves."
18. *Wilckens Bible,* p. 772

19. Luther, Martin: *Ermahnung zum Frieden auf die zwölf Artikel der Bauernschaft in Schwaben.* 1525. (In) Luther: *Werke,* Vol. 24, p. 271
20. Jeremias: *Theologie* I, p. 291
21. Conzelmann: *Grundriss,* p. 341
22. *Jesus oder Christus* (report of debate) p. 11
23. Gollwitzer: *Krummes Holz,* p. 205
24. Kracauer, Siegfried: *Geschichte—Vor den letzten Dingen.* (In) *Schriften,* Vol. 4. Frankfurt, 1971, p. 33
25. Engels, Friedrich: *Zur Geschichte des Urchristentums.* (In) *Die Neue Zeit. Revue des geistigen und öffentlichen Lebens.* Stuttgart, 1895. Year 13, Vol. 1, p. 37
26. Lenin: *Sozialismus und Religion.* (In) *Werke,* Vol. 10. Berlin, 1958, p. 70 ff. Münzer, Thomas (Quoted in) Bloch: *Atheismus,* p. 189
27. Robbe, Martin: *Der Ursprung des Christentums.* Leipzig, 1967, p. 140
28. Burckhardt, Jacob: *Die Zeit Constantin's des Grossen.* 2nd ed. Leipzig, 1880, p. 449
29. The French sociologist and publicist Albert Bayet (1880–1961): "What really triumphed in the church of the fourth century was neither the idea of a just and good God, nor the thought of redemption, nor the idea of heaven and hell, nor the thought of baptism and communion, for all these ideas were to be found in other religions; it was rather the thought of a state religion serving political ends, it was the intolerance that subjects the rights of the spirit to the rights of the sword. Those two principles have weighed heavily on the history of our western world." Bayet, Albert: *Les religions de salut et le christianisme dans l'empire romain.* (In) Alfaric, Prosper and Albert Bayet: *Le problème de Jésus et les origines du christianisme.* Paris, 1932, p. 187
30. In a message of greeting, Bloch hailed Angela Davis as a philosopher "in whose important feminine outlook we see again Rosa Luxemburg and — cum grano salis — the ancient Thinker of Light, Hypatia." (In) *Süddeutsche Zeitung* of 5 June 1972
31. Augustine: *De civitate Dei* XVIII, 51: "When now the devil saw that the temples of the demons stood empty while men hastened to the name of the redeeming mediator, he introduced heretics into his plan, who contradicted Christian teaching under the disguise of the name of Christians; as if such people were to be tolerated indiscriminately and without correction in God's state, as the state of the Babylonian confusion had listened indiscriminately to philosophers of different and opposed views."
32. Augustine: *De civitate Dei* XV
33. Heer, Friedrich: *Jugend zwischen Hass und Hoffnung.* Munich, 1971, p. 146
34. Halbfas to a meeting of the Paulus Gesellschaft. (Quoted in) Uellenberg, Gisela: "Fragwürdiges Verhältnis von Politik und Religion." (In) *Süddeutsche Zeitung* of 3/4 June 1972
35. Pulgar, Hernando del: *Crónica de los Reyes Católicos.* Vol. 5. Madrid, 1943, p. 337 (Quoted in) Kamen, Henry: *Die spanische Inquisition.* Munich, 1969, p. 46 ff.

36. Jaspers, Karl: *Der philosophische Glaube angesichts der Offenbarung.* Munich 1963, p. 468.
    See also Thomas Aquinas: *Summa Theologica* XVIII, 57.3: "Slavery among men is something ordained by nature; for many are slaves by nature, as philosophy shows. Thus the peoples' law is the law of nature . . . That this man is a slave rather than some other has, considered by itself, no natural reason, but exists by reason of an acquiescent profitability, in that it is proper for this man to be guided by a wiser man, and for that man to be helped by such a one (Aristotle). Thus slavery, which is according to international law, is enjoined by nature in the second way, not the first."
37. Fromm, Erich: *Das Christusdogma.* Munich, 1965, p. 49 ff., 62 ff.
38. Harnack, Adolf von: *Kirche und Staat bis zur Gründung der Staatskirche.* (In) *Geschichte der christliche Religion.* 2nd ed., Leipzig, 1922, p. 143
39. Holl: *Jesus,* p. 50 ff.
40. Jones: *Studie ü.d. Hl. Geist,* p. 139
41. Bultmann: *Johannesevangelium,* p. 521
42. Freud: *Mann Moses,* p. 194
43. Augustine: *Sermo CXXI, In Natali Domini:* "Deus per angelum loquebatur, et virgo auribus impraegnabatur."
44. Augustine: *De civitate Dei* XXI, 5: "In Cappadocia etiam vento equas concipere, eosdemque fetus non amplius triennio vivere."
45. Jones: *Studie ü.d. Hl. Geist,* p. 133 ff.
46. Freud: *Mann Moses,* p. 245
47. Tertullian: *De virginibus velandis* VI
    Origen: *Contra Celsum* I, 32—37
48. Thomas Aquinas: *Summa Theologica* III, 27
49. Rilke, Rainer Maria: *Nonnen-Klage.* (In) *Sämtliche Werke.* Vol. 2 Wiesbaden, 1963, p. 32
50. Freud: *Zukunft,* p. 352
51. Freud: *Mann Moses,* p. 154
52. Cf. Freud, Sigmund: *Massenpsychologie und Ich-Analyse.* (In) *Gesammelte Werke.* Vol. 13. 4th ed. Frankfurt, 1963, p. 158 ff.
53. Freud: *Mann Moses,* p. 238
54. Jones, Ernest: *Zur Psychoanalyse der christlichen Religion.* Frankfurt, 1970, p. 126
55. Freud: *Mann Moses,* p. 146, 194
56. Wyss, Dieter: *Marx und Freud.* Gottingen, 1969, p. 37
57. Blank: *Christus,* p. 239
58. Jung: *Antwort,* p. 88 ff.
59. Luther, Martin: *Vorrede zur Offenbarung St. Johannis vom Jahre* 1522 (suppressed by him in later editions of the New Testament). (In) Luther: *Werke,* Vol. 63, p. 170
60. Freud: *Mann Moses,* p. 199
61. Fromm, Erich: *Das Christusdogma.* Munich, 1965, p. 83, 91
62. Jones: *Studie ü.d. Hl. Geist,* p. 136
63. Reik: *Gott,* p. 63

64. Luther, Martin: *Predigt am Tage der Heimsuchung Mariä*, preached in 1533 on Luke 1:39—56. (In) Luther: *Werke*, Vol. 6, p. 303
65. Weber, Max: *Die protestantische Ethik und der Geist des Kapitalismus*. (In) Weber: *Aufsätze*, Vol. 1, 4th ed., p. 17 ff.
66. Weber, Max: *Die protestantische Ethik und der Geist des Kapitalismus*. (In) Weber: *Aufsätze*, Vol. 1, 4th ed., p. 205
67. Weber, Max: *Die Entfaltung der kapitalistischen Gesinnung*. (In) Max Weber, *Die protestantische Ethik* I. Ed. Johannes Winckelmann. 2nd ed., Munich, 1969, p. 352 ff.
68. Weber's "wrong idea": See the American Ephraim Fischoff: "It has become a general axiom in the writing of history and in cultural research that every generation of the past has to be freshly interpreted in the light of its own experience. Weber wrote his essay in conscious reaction to the interpretation of capitalism through Karl Marx. That explains his overevaluation of consistency and the effectiveness of ideal factors." (Fischoff, Ephraim: *Die protestantische Ethik und der Geist der Kapitalismus. Die Geschichte einer Kontroversie*. (In) Max Weber: *Die protestantische Ethik* II, ed. Johannes Winckelmann. Munich, 1968, p. 353)
69. Weber, Max: *Die protestantische Ethik und der Geist des Kapitalismus*. (In) Weber, *Aufsätze*, Vol. 1, 4th ed., p. 94 ff.
70. Uellenberg, Gisela: "Moral im Wandel." (In) *Süddeutsche Zeitung* of 13 Oct. 1971
71. Holscher, Emil Erwin: *Vom römischen zum christlichen Naturrecht*. Augsburg, 1931, p. 87
72. Gollwitzer: *Krummes Holz*, p. 299
73. Epictetus: *Dissertationes* IV, 1.89
74. Freud: *Zukunft*, p. 328
75. Kilian, Hans: *Das enteignete Bewusstsein*. Neuwied, 1971, p. 83
79. Engel, Friedrich: *Profile*. Selection of his works and letters. Wuppertal, 1970, p. 272
77. Marx—Engels: *Feuerbach*. (In) Marx—Engels, *Studienausgabe* I. Frankfurt, 1971, p. 92

Chapter 12

1. Augustine: *De civitate Dei* XXII, 30.4: "Dies enim septimus etiam nos ipsi erimus."
   Freud, Sigmund: Letter to James J. Putnam of 8 July 1915. (In) Jones, Ernest: *Das Leben und Werk von Sigmund Freud*. Vol. 2. Berne, 1962, p. 489
2. Heinemann, Gustav: *Synode und Parlement. Zum Gedenken an die Emdener Generalsynode von 1571*. (In) *Mitteilungen für die Presse*. Pub. by the Office of the Federal President, 5 Oct. 1971, p. 9
3. Sölle: Dorothee: *Stellvertretung. Ein Kapitel Theologie nach dem "Tode Gottes."* 6th ed., Stuttgart, 1970, p. 176 ff., 189, 17, 178, 190, 163 ff., 200, 150
4. Augustine: *Soliloquia* I, 2.7: "Deum et animam scire cupio. — Nihilne plus? — Nihil omnino."

5. Bonhoeffer, Dietrich: *Widerstand und Ergebung. Briefe und Aufzeichnungen aus der Haft.* Ed. Eberhard Bethge. Munich, 1964, p. 180 (letter of 18 July 1944)
6. Scholem, Gershom: *Zum Verständnis der messianischen Idee im Judentum.* (In) *Judaica.* Frankfurt, 1964, p. 227
7. Bloch, Ernst: *Geist der Utopia. Bearbeitete Neuauflage der zweiten Fassung von 1923.* Frankfurt, 1964, p. 227
   Rahner, Karl: "Was Hoffnung vermag." (In) *Süddeutsche Zeitung* of 1–3 April 1972
   Moltmann, Jürgen: *Theologie der Hoffnung.* 8th ed. Munich, 1969, p. 28 ff.
   Moltmann, Jürgen (quoted in) Auer, Alfons: "Wo steht heute die katholische Ethik?" (In) *Deutsche Zeitung/Christ und Welt* of 28 July 1972
8. Nietzsche, Friedrich: *Der Wille zur Macht,* §445. Stuttgart 1964, p. 312
   Thielicke, Helmut: *Und wenn Gott wäre . . .* 2nd ed., Stuttgart, 1971, p. 255 ff.
9. Interview with Harvey Cox: "Wir müssen uns Gott als Mann und Frau denken." (In) *Deutsches Allgemeines Sonntagsblatt* of 23 July 1972
   Halbfas, Hubertus: *Weihnachten.* (In) *Was soll verkündet werden?* Ed. Ludwig Klein. Limburg, 1972, p. 31
   Moltmann, Jürgen: *Theologie der Hoffnung.* 8th ed., Munich, 1969, p. 150
   Thielicke, Helmut: "Wo steht heute die evangelische Ethik?" (In) *Deutsche Zeitung/Christ und Welt* of 21 July 1972
10. Zahrnt, Heinz: "Der Tod des Todes Gottes." (In) *Deutsches Allgemeines Sonntagsblatt* of 2 April 1972
11. Cardonnel, Jean: *Gott in Zukunft.* 2nd ed. Munich, 1969, p. 30
12. Translated from "Der Ursprung der Dinge," *Rig-Veda* 10, 129. (In) *Die Geheimlehre des Veda*, trans. Paul Deussen. 6th ed., Leipzig, 1921, p. 4
13. Burrows: *Mehr Klarheit*, p. 38
    Zimmerli, Walther: *Das Alte Testament in der Verkündigung der christlichen Kirche.* (In) *Das Alte Testament als Anrede.* Munich, 1956, p. 81
    Noth, Martin: *Die Vergegenwärtigung des Alten Testaments in der Verkündigung.* (In) *Evangelische Theologie.* Year 12, 1952/53, p. 16
    Bornkamm, Günther: *Das Gottesgericht in der Geschichte.* (In) Bornkamm: *Studien*, p. 61
    Stauffer: *Jesus*, p. 98
    Koch, Klaus: *Krise um die Bibel?* (In) *Glauben heute.* Ed. Gert Otto. Hamburg, 1965, p. 47
14. Pannenberg, Wolfhart: *Dogmatische Thesen zur Lehre von der Offenbarung.* (In) *Offenbarung als Geschichte.* Ed. Wolfhart Pannenberg. 4th ed. Gottingen, 1970, p. 104 ff., 100
15. Bultmann, Rudolf: *Marburger Predigten.* Tubingen, 1956, p. 38
16. Gollwitzer: *Krummes Holz*, pp. 355, 309, 191, 365, 343
17. Thielicke, Helmut: *Und wenn Gott wäre.* Stuttgart, 1971, p. 207

18. Gollwitzer: *Krummes Holz*, p. 371; Cox, Harvey: *Der Christ als Rebell.* 2nd ed., Kassel, 1968, p. 85
    Moltmann, Jürgen: *Theologie in der Welt der modernen Wissenschaften.* (In) *Perspektiven der Theologie.* Munich, 1968, p. 283
    Bornkamm, Günther: *Das Gottesgericht in der Geschichte.* (In) Bornkamm: *Studien*, p. 48
19. Bultmann, Rudolf: *Welchen Sinn hat es, von Gott zu reden?* (In) Bultmann: *Glauben und Verstehen* I, p. 27 ff.
    Gollwitzer: *Krummes Holz*, p. 378, 349, 339, 312
    Mynarek, Hubertus: *Der Tod Gottes und die Zukunft des Menschen.* (In) *Hat die Religion Zukunft?* Ed. Oskar Schatz, Graz, 1971, p. 174
    Kafka, Franz: *Betrachtungen über Sünde, Leid, Hoffnung und den wahren Weg.* (In) *Hochzeitsvorbereitungen auf dem Lande und andere Prose aus dem Nachlass.* Frankfurt, 1953, p. 54
20. Gollwitzer: *Krummes Holz*, p. 170, 336
    Wilder, Thornton: *The Ides of March*
21. Wittgenstein, Ludwig: *Tagebücher 1914—1916.* (In) *Schriften.* Vol. 1, Frankfurt, 1960, pp. 165—167
22. Kant, Immanuel: *Prolegomena zu einer jeden künftigen Metaphysik, die als Wissenschaft auftreten können.* (In) *Werke.* Ed. Wilhelm Weischedel. Vol. 3. Wiesbaden, 1958, p. 245
23. Dirac, Paul: "Grundprobleme der Physik." Address given at the meeting of Nobel prize winners in Lindau, 1971. Manuscript. p. 11 ff.
    Heisenberg, Werner: *Positivismus, Metaphysik und Religion.* (In) *Der Teil und das Ganze.* Munich, 1969, p. 293
24. Cf. Heisenberg: *Erste Gespräche über das Verhältnis von Naturwissenschaft und Religion.* (In) *Der Teil und das Ganze.* Munich, 1969, p. 122
25. Monod, Jacques: *Zufall und Notwendigkeit.* Munich, 1971, p. 211, 178 ff., 144
26. "Is life older than the earth?" Report of a conference of Soviet and American astrophysicists at Byurakan. (In) *Neues Deutschland* of 20 Nov. 1971
    Professor Reinhard W. Kaplan, director of the Institute of Microbiology at the University of Frankfurt, comes up with a substantially higher figure in his book, *Der Ursprung des Lebens*, Munich 1972: "If we assume . . . just one (heavenly body not too different in character from the earth) in every tenth to hundreth system of planets, and assume further that every hundreth star has planets, then we can expect to find among the 10^{11} stars in our Milky Way between 10^7 and 10^8 bodies where life could possibly exist. Since we have good reason to assume that life can actually come into existence where the conditions are favorable, given sufficient time, we can count on an unimaginably large number of heavenly bodies where there is life." (p. 236)
27. Mezger, Manfred: *Wer ist das eigentlich — Gott?* (In) *Glauben heute.* Ed. Gert Otto. Hamburg, 1965, p. 232

28. Goethe to Eckermann on 2 May 1824. (Quoted in) Eckerman, Johann Peter: *Gespräche mit Goethe in den letzen Jahren seines Lebens.* (In) Goethe, Johann Wolfgang von: *Gedenkausgabe der Werke, Briefe und Gespräche.* Vol 24. Zürich, 1948, p. 115

29. Braun, Herbert: *Vom Verstehen des Neuen Testaments.* (In) Braun: *Gesammelte Studien,* p. 298

30. Hirsch, Maielies: *Welche Rolle spielt der christliche Glaube in der psychotherapeutischen Praxis?* (In) *Jesus und Freud.* Ed. Heinz Zahrnt. Munich, 1972, p. 123

31. Freud: *Mann Moses,* p. 157

32. Rosenberg, Alfons: (Quoted in) *Hat die Religion Zukunft?* Ed. Oskar Schatz. Graz, 1971, p. 324
    Rabut, Olivier: *In Ungewissheit glauben.* Munich, 1970, p. 27, 47
    Mezger, Manfred: (Quoted in) *Was soll verkündet werden?* Ed. Ludwig Klein. Limburg, 1972, p. 14

33. Cf. the investigations of the Canadian Peace Research Institute, Oakville, Ont.: Paul, John and Jerome Laulicht: *In Your Opinion; Leaders' and Voters' Attitudes on Defence and Disarmament.* Clarkson, Ont. 1963; and Eckhart, W. and N. Alcock: *Ideology and Personality in War and Peace Attitudes,* Oakville, Ont. 1968

34. The Pope's Christmas Message. (In) *New York Times* of 26 Dec. 1969
    Gehlen, Arnold: *Religion und Weltstabilisierung* (In) *Hat die Religion Zukunft?* Ed. Oskar Schatz. Graz, 1971, p. 90
    Adorno, Hans: *Das enteignete Bewusstsein.* Neuwied, 1971, p. 81

35. Lemberg, Eugen: *Ideologie und Gesellschaft.* Stuttgart, 1971, p. 132
    Heisenberg, Werner: *Das Naturbild der heutigen Physik.* Hamburg, 1955, p. 17
    Holl, Adolf: (Quoted in) *Jesus oder Christus* (report of debate), p. 64
    Berger, Peter L.: *Auf den Spuren der Engel.* Frankfurt, 1971, p. 108
    Schütz, Alfred: *Don Quixote and the Problem of Reality.* (In) *Collected Papers.* Vol. 2, The Hague, 1964, p. 157

36. Horkheimer, Max: *Spiegel* interview: "Was wir 'Sinn' nennen, wird verschwinden." (In) *Spiegel* 1–2/1970, p. 79 ff.

37. Dilthey, Wilhelm: *Einleitung in die Geisteswissenschaften.* (In) *Gesammelte Schriften.* Vol. 1, 2nd ed., Leipzig, 1923, p, 211

38. Marcuse, Herbert: *Versuch über die Befreiung.* Frankfurt, 1966, p. 315

39. Horkheimer, Max: "Letzte Spur von Theologie. Paul Tillichs Vermächtnis. Eine Gedenkrede." (In) *Frankfurter Allgemeine Zeitung* of 7 April 1966

40. Heidegger, Martin: *Über den Humanismus.* Frankfurt, 1968, p. 37, 47
    Heidegger, Martin: *Nietzsches Wort "Gott ist tot"* (In) *Holzwege.* 3rd ed., Frankfurt, 1957, p. 249

41. Heidegger, Martin: *Die Technik und die Kehre.* Pfullingen, 1962, p. 45

42. Heidegger, Martin: *Wozu Dichter?* (In) *Holzwege.* Frankfurt, 1957, p. 249
    Heidegger, Martin: *Über den Humanismus,* Frankfurt, 1968, p. 46

43. Heidegger, Martin: *Nietzsche.* Vol. 2. Pfullingen, 1961, p. 391
    Heidegger, Martin: *Überwindung der Metaphysik.* (In) *Vorträge und Aufsätze.* Pfullingen, 1954, p. 92

Heidegger, Martin: *Die Frage nach der Technik*. (In) *Vortrage und Aufsatze* Pfullingen, 1954, p. 44

44. Schäufele, Hermann: "Hat das Christentum noch eine Zukunft?" Address at the opening of the 13th meeting of Catholic publicists from France and Germany on Reichenau Island. (In) *Rheinischer Merkur* of 22 Oct. 1971 "A priest who says a thing like that is no longer a priest." Interview with Domenico Grasso. (In) *Quick* of 29 Sept. 1971

45. Horkheimer, Max: "Letzte Spur von Theologie." (In) *Frankfurter Allgemeine Zeitung* of 7 April 1966

46. Augustine: *Contra epistulam Manichaei quam vocant fundamenti* I, 5.6: "Ego vero Evangelio non crederem, nisi me catholicae Ecclesiae commoveret auctoritas."
    Gehlen, Arnold: *Religion und Umweltstabilisierung*. (In) *Hat die Religion Zukunft?* Ed. Oskar Schatz. Graz, 1971, p. 86

47. Hohoff, Kurt: "Neue Religionen." (In) *Rheinische Merkur* of 11 Feb. 1972

48. Letter from Helmut Thielicke to Hans Habe. (In) *Welt am Sonntag* of 14 Nov. 1971
    Thielicke, Helmut: *Und wenn Gott wäre . . .* 2nd ed., Stuttgart, 1971, p. 73

49. On 18 April 1941 there died in the Auschwitz concentration camp the Polish Franciscan Maximilian Kolbe, who, though himself consumptive, had declared himself ready to go into the starvation-bunker in place of Franciszek Gajowniczek, the father of a family. He was beatified by Pope Paul VI on 17 Oct. 1971.

50. Letter from Sigmund Freud to Oskar Pfister, 24 Feb. 1928. (In) Freud, Sigmund and Oskar Pfister: *Briefe 1909—1939*. Frankfurt, 1963 p. 132

51. Cicero: *De re publica* III, 33: "Est quidem vera lex recta ratio, naturae congruens, diffusa in omnis, constans sempiterna, quae vocet ad officium iubendo, vetando a fraude deterreat, quae tamen neque probos frustra iubet aut vetat, nec improbos iubendo aut vetando movet. Huic legi nec obrogari fas est, neque derogari aliquid ex hac licet, neque tota abrogari potest, nec vero aut per senatum aut per populum solvi hac lege possumus, neque est quaerendus explanator aut interpres Sextus Aelius, nec erit alia lex Romae alia Athenis, alia nunc alia posthac, sed et omnes gentes et omni tempore una lex et sempiterna et immutabilis continebit, unusque erit communis quasi magister et imperator omnium deus." (Sextus Aelius, consul 198 B.C.E. His book *Tripertita*, on the Laws of the Twelve Tables, was called in Rome the "cradle of justice" — cunabula iuris.)

52. Letter from Sigmund Freud to Oskar Pfister, 24 Feb. 1928. (In) Freud, Sigmund and Oskar Pfister: *Briefe 1909—1939*. Frankfurt, 1963, p. 132
    Mayakovsky, Vladimir: *Wolke in Hosen*. (In) *Frühe Gedichten*, translated into German by Alfred A. Thoss. Frankfurt, 1965, p. 46.

53. Heidegger, Martin: *Wozu Dichter?* (In) *Holzwege*. 3rd ed., Frankfurt, 1957, p. 248

54. Gollwitze: *Krummes Holz*, p. 143

55. Pascal, Blaise: *Über die Religion und über einige andere Gegenstände (Pensées)* Trans. into German and ed. Ewald Wasmuth. 7th ed., Heidelberg, 1972, p. 120 ff.

56. Merleau-Ponty, Marcel: *Lob der Philosophie*. (In) *Das Auge und der Geist*, Reinbek. 1967, p. 138

405